HISTORY OF
THE SECOND WORLD WAR

UNITED KINGDOM CIVIL SERIES

Edited by W. K. HANCOCK

The authors of the Civil Histories have been given free access to official documents. They and the editor are alone responsible for the statements made and the views expressed.

FOOD

VOLUME I
THE GROWTH OF POLICY

BY

R. J. HAMMOND, M.A.

LONDON: 1951

HIS MAJESTY'S STATIONERY OFFICE

AND

LONGMANS, GREEN AND CO

First published 1951

HIS MAJESTY'S STATIONERY OFFICE

London: York House, Kingsway, W.C.2 & 429 Oxford Street, W.1
Edinburgh: 13a Castle Street   Cardiff: 1 St. Andrew's Crescent
Manchester: 39 King Street   Bristol: Tower Lane
Birmingham: 2 Edmund Street   Belfast: 80 Chichester Street

LONGMANS, GREEN AND CO LTD
6 and 7 Clifford Street, London, W.1
also at Melbourne and Cape Town

LONGMANS, GREEN AND CO INC
55 Fifth Avenue, New York, 3

LONGMANS, GREEN AND CO
215 Victoria Street, Toronto, 1

ORIENT LONGMANS, LTD
Bombay, Calcutta, Madras

Price £1 5s. 0d. net

Printed in Great Britain under the authority of H.M. Stationery Office
by Sanders Phillips & Co. Ltd., London, S.W.9

CONTENTS

APPENDICES

TABLES

EDITOR'S NOTE

SINCE the content of a policy and its degree of success are revealed in the process of administration, something would have been gained by postponing the present volume, which deals chiefly with problems of policy, until the author had completed the studies of administration and control designed for Volume II. Indeed, this was the original idea of the author himself. He was overruled by the editor, who has been asked and has consented to work to a time-table of publication, so far as circumstances permit. The editor, indeed, sees great advantage in publishing substantial volumes as they become ready, even if their conclusions may sometimes be modified by research which is still continuing. These tactics of publication were followed at the beginning of this series and will be pursued until its conclusion.

W. K. H.

PREFACE TO VOLUME I

THIS study is not intended to be an encyclopædia of food control; it does not contain comprehensive statistics,[1] assembled for their own sake, or a catalogue of every administrative order issued by the Ministry of Food. It does not set out to describe, even superficially, each and every commodity control, or recount every change in the amount of war-time rations. Such details would hinder rather than assist what has been the writer's aim throughout, to present food policy and administration as a whole. While not neglecting its nutritional, technical, and political implications, he has regarded it primarily as a successful attempt to solve a problem in the economics of war. The solution of that problem may be conveniently treated under two heads. The first of these, which forms the main theme of the present volume, is that of the evolution of food policy in the face of circumstance; it is concerned with ends. The second, with which the next volume will deal in some detail, comprises the means by which these ends could be carried into effect. The lines of demarcation cannot, of course, be sharply drawn; there is much of tactics in Volume I, and there will be something of strategy in Volume II. But it is hoped that each will be intelligible, though not complete, without the other. The history of food production will form a separate study by another author.

The rubric facing the title-page of this book indicates the conditions under which it was written; the problems facing the contributors to the series of Civil Histories, and the spirit in which they have been tackled, have been set out in the Preface to the introductory volume.[2] The account there given, however, leaves some margin for comment by the writer on his own experience. His work has been largely shaped by the discovery that, even when one is dealing with the main issues of policy, there is no escape from the task of examining an immense mass of departmental material. It might be supposed that the civil service practice of referring problems upwards in writing according to their importance would make it possible to establish the main lines of an authentic history on the evidence of 'high level' papers alone. For the matters with which the writer has been concerned, nothing could be further from the truth. In the first place, official skill in detecting, particularly in its infancy, a major issue of policy is great but by no means infallible. Secondly, and more

---

[1] For these, reference should be made to the *Statistical Digest* in this series. Some of the more important facts will be found tabulated on pp. 391-400 of this volume.

[2] *British War Economy*, by W. K. Hancock and M. M. Gowing.

important, the statements embodied in these documents must undergo historical examination before they can be accepted in evidence.

But—it may be objected—did not the blow for blow of inter-departmental debate, together with the probing of such central planning organisations as the Economic Section of the War Cabinet Offices, enable agreed facts to be established on which decisions could be based? The answer is that valuable though such contemporary activity was, it addressed itself mainly to current, or occasionally to past, departmental arguments and could not go behind them to departmental files. Again and again the last word—at any rate on technical questions that reason and common sense alone could not decide—was with those who had a virtual monopoly of detailed knowledge; and this was true also within the Ministry of Food itself.

The historian, merely in the interests of intelligibility, thus finds himself forced to think out many problems afresh. It will not suffice to set out, however fully, the arguments used on any occasion; they must be reconciled with what was thought and said previously. Contemporaries can be inconsistent from choice or inadvertence; the historian is obliged to bring the whole of his allotted study to the test of critical analysis, without which, indeed, the story of food control at any rate would emerge with little meaning or usefulness.

Critical analysis calls for critical method. The writer's principle has been to treat food strategy and tactics broadly as if he were writing military history. In particular, he has sought to avoid judging them merely by the fact of success or failure, but has tried to indicate the reasons why success or failure might be expected. He has not, except rarely, used military terminology; but good and bad generalship or staff work, 'soldiers' battles', strokes of good or bad fortune, well and ill co-ordinated operations, will all find their civilian counterparts in his pages. No attempt has been made to conceal the element of personal judgement that must enter into any such analysis; but an effort has been made to base that judgement on evidence and on secure reasoning, and to express it without equivocation.

The writer's task would have been all but impossible had he not received ready help and co-operation from officials at all stages. A full list of those to whom he is indebted—whether for the supply of material or for help in elucidating it—would occupy several columns of type. One debt, however, demands personal acknowledgement; to C. H. Blagburn, now of the University of Reading, without whose almost daily counsel during the first years of the task the writer might never have found his feet. Thanks are also due to the Statistics and Intelligence Division, Ministry of Food, for preparing the tables and charts, and to Constance Felvus for help in seeing the volume through the press.

January 1951   R. J. HAMMOND

PART I

CHAPTER I

The Tradition of Control and the Beginning of Food Defence Plans

I

'. . . State trading in food is practicable and in times of prolonged shortage is necessary. It is within the wit of man to find an alternative to competitive private enterprise with market prices as a means of obtaining and distributing food, to replace economic by human laws, to substitute managed for automatic provisioning of the people'.

THIS, according to one of its most distinguished participants[1], was the main lesson of British food control in the War of 1914. To some of his readers, even so early as 1928, that dictum must have seemed strangely dated; it would indeed be odd (they might think) if the nineteenth-century free-enterprise solution to the problem of feeding Britain's millions should be the only possible one. To many contemporaries, however, including some of those responsible for bringing the first Ministry of Food into being, food control was a leap in the dark; not for nothing was the first full-scale account of it entitled *A State Trading Adventure*.[2] This sense of being pioneers, of conducting *Experiments in State Control*,[3] of wonder at achieving so much in so short a time, was common to all those who wrote afterwards of their war-time experience in Lord Rhondda's Ministry.

The success of the first Ministry of Food, then, had some of the challenging quality of an apparent miracle, and some of the traditional effect of miracles upon the sceptical. If, by ill-fortune, another war should come, there could be no excuse for a repetition of the doubts and hesitations that had delayed even the appointment of a Food Controller till December 1916, 'as a reluctant sacrifice on the altar of industrial unrest',[4] and that had prevented complete control, including rationing on a national scale, from being achieved until July 1918, almost on the eve of the Armistice.

A great part of the success was credited to the personality of Lord Rhondda, appointed Food Controller at a critical time (June 1917)

---

[1] Beveridge, Sir William H. (later Lord). *British Food Control*. 1928. The quotation is from pp. 337-8.
[2] Coller, F. H. (later Sir Frank). *A State Trading Adventure*. 1925.
[3] Lloyd, E. M. H. *Experiments in State Control*. 1924.
[4] Coller, *op cit.* (opening sentence).

and spared just long enough to see his creation triumphant over all obstacles. A great part too was owed to 'luck and time and determination'; the successful introduction of rationing, for instance, was 'a supreme case of muddling through by brilliant improvisations, made necessary by shifting policy and division of counsels'.[1] Accidents of fortune apart, however, it was possible to analyse in reasonably simple terms the conditions and limitations of the achievement.

First and foremost was its completeness. There was no satisfactory half-way house between 'business as usual' and complete control of supplies and distribution, including rationing where this was necessary and practicable. Control of price alone was nugatory. Interference by Government in an existing system of private trade, or resort to exhortation and sumptuary prohibition, such as had enlivened the brief career of Lord Devonport, the first Food Controller, were alike ineffective, not to say disastrous. Competitive private trade, in bulk foodstuffs at any rate, must be superseded both nationally and internationally; the Inter-Allied Food Council of September 1918, with its provisions for co-ordinated buying and allocation of food and shipping, was essential to the success of control in the United Kingdom, and, moreover, to the carrying out of the plans for bringing over the American Army to finish off the war, had it continued into 1919. For 1918–19 there was, that is to say, a reasoned *import programme* for food; and that in its turn implied complete control of shipping.

Had they had another war definitely in view, the writers on food might, perhaps, have made more of this point, underlining as it does the essential interdependence of food control and other measures of economic management in time of war. Certainly it seems to have been lost sight of in the years after 1936, at any rate so far as the Government as a whole was concerned. What they did make clear was that the very circumstance that made food control vital for the United Kingdom—dependence on imported supplies—not only made its effectiveness greater, since ships and ports provided a ready-made bottleneck at which the Government could lay hands on commodities, but also reduced it to a secondary rôle in winning the war. 'If the submarine could be kept in check, the bringing of sufficient supplies was simple; if not, then nothing availed.'[2]

The estimate of food control implied in these words was put forward in explicit contradiction of exaggerated claims in the other direction, and was perhaps too modest. By itself the most skilful management of food supply and distribution could not have secured victory or even avoided defeat. But weakness on the food front was generally held to have been an important factor in lowering the

---

[1] Beveridge, *op. cit.* p. 229.

[2] Beveridge, *op. cit.* p. 333.

resistance of the Central Powers; and mismanagement in the United Kingdom might have had no less grave consequences. In Britain, however, ingenuity of administrative contrivance was, under Lord Rhondda, informed by the best scientific advice of the day. In particular, the insistence of the Food (War) Committee of the Royal Society on the need for maintaining a supply of breadstuffs sufficient to ensure that no-one went short of essential energy requirements measured in calories, provided the rock on which a sound food policy could be built.[1]

To these basic conditions of success—adequate control in related fields of Government activity, and sufficient knowledge to determine the ends at which food control should aim—there was added another: the existence of a considerable degree of organisation in the trades it was desired to control. Imported foods, therefore, presented the least difficulty.

By contrast, the highly successful scheme for the marketing of home-produced livestock, and the chequered career of potatoes under control, illustrated the difficulties that confront the most resourceful of officials when he comes to deal with the marketing of home produce. (One might add that it is this foundation of control in an existing trade organisation that accounts for the unimportance of the sheer size of the Ministry of Food's problem. To organise the feeding of forty or fifty million people would indeed be a formidable task if undertaken *de novo*, though hardly more so in proportion than the feeding of forty thousand in identical circumstances. Given the existence of private trade machinery that is already feeding those numbers, it becomes quite manageable.)

However complete and successful, food control (it was said) had inherent limitations and disadvantages. It could not prevent all rises in price, unless it were accompanied by a wholesale recourse to subsidies. It might prevent profiteering, that is the exploitation of a seller's market in the face of unlimited demand, but could not prevent the more efficient trader from prospering exceedingly under a regime of standard prices that must allow the less efficient to survive. It meant the disappearance, or the submersion in pooling arrangements, of the better qualities of butter, meat, cheese, bacon, or tea (and also of the cheaper grades—a fact that might bear heavily on the poor). For these reasons, and on account of the intricacy and expensiveness of its machinery, and the tax it levied on limited supplies of administrative energy and ability, it was not to be lightly undertaken.

Particularly was this true of rationing, in the form in which the Ministry of Food had successfully practised it. The feature of British rationing that evoked especial pride was the absolute guarantee of

---

[1] Starling, E. H. *The Feeding of Nations.* 1919.

rationed supplies. Rationing was not a mere restriction, nor the coupon a form of currency that of itself might act as a magnet to draw supplies where they were needed. On the contrary; rationing presupposed a complete mechanism which should put each consumer's supplies in a particular shop, where he might be certain, and where he alone was entitled, to obtain it. The tie of consumer to retailer, and its implications at earlier stages in the distributive chain, presupposed not only a control organisation for distributing each rationed food, but a series of local food offices that alone could maintain an up-to-date register of consumers. For the consumer-retailer tie must be constantly in need of breakage and renewal, in accord with the multitudinous movements to and fro of individual citizens. Other powerful arguments could be drawn up in favour of the decentralised administration of food control; this one was inescapable.

Inescapable, that is, granted that the consumer-retailer tie could not be dispensed with. In retrospect, this had become almost an axiom, namely something not requiring proof; in 1917 it had not been so. Registration of consumers, together with the establishment of local Food Committees, had originally been introduced in an attempt to avoid sugar rationing by regulating distribution. It naturally, therefore, came to form part of the permissive rationing by these committees that was introduced at the end of 1917, and it was duly embodied in the national rationing scheme of July 1918. There had been much controversy about it, controversy almost inextricably mixed with other issues, such as household *v.* individual ration cards, and the need for a central index of consumers. A proposal foreshadowing in all essentials the 'points' rationing scheme of 1941 had been mooted, only to be rejected, by a Ministry of Food committee about January 1918:—

'As to the coupons themselves the Committee had before it two main alternatives

    (*a*) of coupons each representing a prescribed quantity of a prescribed food or foods . . . .

    (*b*) of interchangeable coupons valid for all rationed foods, to each of which a particular value in coupons or "rate of exchange" is assigned, the rate being varied from time to time as required so as to divert consumption from one class of food to another.

'On the whole the Committee came to the conclusion that the disadvantages of the latter plan (which has never been tried in practice) outweighed its advantages. The former plan has been adopted accordingly'.[1]

Like the central index itself, this more flexible type of rationing

---

[1] The passage quoted is from a draft *Outline of National System of Compulsory Rationing,* discovered by the Food (Defence Plans) Department among the few remaining records of the old Ministry of Food. It is undated, but from internal evidence would appear to emanate from the committee on rationing machinery mentioned by Beveridge (*op. cit.* p. 195).

must have been swept aside by the combined pressure of events and the vested local interest that had already been established. Logically speaking, registration demanded local food offices; historically speaking, local administration of food control tipped the scales in favour of registration. The ration coupon, which might have been the motive force of the whole system, became at most an additional check on its accuracy. Whether the rejected alternative would have worked as well as that adopted, or at all, must remain a matter of conjecture. Had the decisions of 1917–18 gone another way, and had they been justified in their outcome, the history of food control in the Second World War might have been very different.

So much for what one may call the written tradition of British food control, as set down in the late nineteen-twenties. It embodied a great deal of detailed experience, more especially in the realm of commodity control.[1] There was, besides, a tradition not codified, but none the less living on inside the Civil Service in the memories of those former Ministry of Food officials who might still recall a brief hour of administrative triumph in an unaccustomed field. Vaguer yet, but not altogether to be disregarded, was the widespread conviction among those not directly concerned with it that food control had been well done and could be safely revived if need arose. There was, too, within the Board of Trade, a tiny handful of survivors from the final liquidation of the Ministry who kept in being its last direct legacy, the Civil Emergency Food Organisation for use in the event of industrial disputes. Many of the traders who had helped with food control were comparatively young men, whose services might be called on again in time of emergency. In short, there was, as there had not been in 1916, an immense reserve of experienced talent at the disposal of any Government that might need it.

On the other hand, there had been little attempt to analyse in any detail the lessons of the first world conflict with specific reference to what ought to be done in another. In the times of Briand and Stresemann, when the Anglo-Japanese Alliance was still a recent memory, and Bolshevism, for good or evil, a political rather than a military force, this is understandable enough. Sir William Beveridge, bringing to an end his study of *British Food Control*, could write:

'The account that has been given here . . . long as it may seem, is no more than a surface gleaning of the archives. There forms and circulars, reports and instructions, schemes and counter-schemes and plans for another war, all so many monuments of toiling ingenuity, lie mouldering gently into dust and oblivion—lie buried, please God, for ever'.

Not five years after that book was published, its author was called in to advise a Government committee on price policy in a major war.

---

[1] Lloyd, E. M. H., *op. cit.* This experience will be referred to in the detailed commodity studies of Vol. II.

II

It was historically appropriate that the first suggestion that a
department of food defence be set up in peace-time should arise from
a desire to forestall inflation in war-time, for it was high prices and
industrial unrest, rather than actual shortage of supplies, that had
led to the appointment of the first Food Controller. The course of
Government, and particularly Treasury, opinion on the problem of
war-time price policy has been recounted in another volume of the
Civil Histories.[1] Here it will be sufficient to say that, as early as 1933,
a representative body of officials reporting to the Committee of
Imperial Defence was contemplating a high degree of control over
prices, wages, and profits, from the outset of a major war. Measures of
food control—over imports, home production, manufacture, and
distribution; over prices and margins of profit; over consumption, i.e.,
rationing—all these might, it was thought, be necessary from the
outset, not on account of shortage of supplies or shipping, but on
anti-inflationary grounds alone. In particular a decision to prepare
for 'card rationing' should not be 'unduly postponed'. It was suggested that the Government should set up a peace-time 'nucleus
organisation' to maintain touch with the food trades and secure their
co-operation, and to collect information about food supplies and
prices.

The report embodying these recommendations was dated
February 1933; it was approved by the Committee of Imperial
Defence in May 1934. In May 1935 the Board of Trade, as the
Department responsible for food, set up a departmental committee on
food supplies in war-time; a parallel committee on war-time food
production policy was set up in the Ministry of Agriculture. In 1933
also a large-scale investigation was started into the problems of shipping and transport that would arise if an enemy were able largely to
deny to the United Kingdom the use of the South and East Coast
ports.[2]

The Abyssinian crisis, and still more the remilitarisation of the
Rhineland, were evidently responsible for converting these quasi-
theoretical activities into matters of practical urgency. The appointment of a Minister for the Co-ordination of Defence, in March 1936,
meant that these questions were henceforth the daily specific care of
a member of the Cabinet. In April 1936 a new Sub-Committee of the
Committee of Imperial Defence was appointed to go into the whole
question of Food Supply in War; it included five Cabinet Ministers
and the Financial Secretary to the Treasury. The new body at once

---

[1] Hancock and Gowing, *British War Economy*, pp. 46-52.
[2] See below, Chapter IX.

initiated two specific inquiries of the first importance; by Sir Ernest Gowers into the practical problems raised by a policy of Government storage; and by Sir William Beveridge and a group of assisting officials into the administrative arrangements for rationing. The inquiry into storage, and even, perhaps, the appointment of the new committee itself at this juncture, reflected a widespread public agitation in favour of the accumulation of strategic reserves of food-stuffs.[1] For the moment, they took second place to the inquiry into rationing, chiefly because Sir William Beveridge refused to be bound by the narrow terms of reference given to him. Rationing, he pointed out, was a late, not an early, stage of food control. It required an immense administrative machine, which it was not worth while to set up except for an acute and prolonged shortage of supplies, and which it was futile to set up unless the rationing authority was in a position to guarantee the individual citizen his ration, neither more nor less. 'Rationing assumes control of supply and distribution . . . in framing proposals for rationing we are in the position of designing a top storey in the air, without knowledge of the structure on which it will rest'. This did not prevent the Committee from drawing up a pretty full and detailed specification of a scheme for general rationing, largely based on the rationing documents used in the last war. Many, though not all, of its proposals were to be adopted by the Food (Defence Plans) Department.

More important, however, was the brief, incisive, yet comprehensive review of the whole problem of food control in war-time that Sir William Beveridge put in as an Annex to the Report he had been asked for. This *Note on the Wider Aspects of Food Control*[2] stands out as a landmark among State papers on the subject. The whole subsequent history of food policy bears witness to its mastery of first principles and grasp of essential detail. Sir William Beveridge pointed out that unless a Food Controller with a policy thought out in advance was in the saddle from the outset of war, problems would be

'dealt with piecemeal and the seeds of future trouble will be sown. The dis-co-ordination which in the last war led to the imported meat supply of the civilian population being controlled in the interests of the fighting forces . . . and to the setting up of independent Sugar and Wheat Commissions never fully absorbed in the Ministry of Food, was a weakness which should not be repeated'.

He insisted that the true purpose of reserve food stocks was not to avoid starvation in the first year of war:—

'if the enemy were able . . . to deny us for any appreciable time the use of most or all of our ports, the war would be over for reasons other

---

[1] See Chapter II. Sir Ernest Gowers, though a member of the Civil Service, at this time occupied the somewhat detached post of Chairman to the Coal Mines Reorganisation Commission. His inquiry, like that of Sir William Beveridge, was essentially a personal one, although both were assisted by departmental representatives.

[2] The full text is given as Appendix A.

than starvation'—but 'to give us time to develop home production, perhaps in a protracted war,[1] as attrition and diversion of shipping, or desire to economise defensive effort, brings a gradual decline of imports'.

He argued that the Government should consider beforehand what the war-time diet ought to be; what should be done about live-stock policy and the rate of extraction of flour from wheat. He foresaw a general policy of subsidising food prices in order to prevent inflation. He drew attention to the usefulness of the recently established marketing boards and commodity commissions as a nucleus of food control, while emphasising that the very existence of these bodies made centralised food control the more necessary. The expected initial air attack on London, he said, would necessitate not merely the emergency feeding of refugees, but a comprehensive plan to ensure the internal distribution of food from ships diverted to unaccustomed ports. He summarised the 'substantial requirements for dealing with food in a future war' as four:

'1. A decision to appoint a Food Controller with full powers as from the outbreak of war.

2. A feeding policy, thought out in advance, for adequate total supply in the country at all stages of a possibly protracted war.

3. A control plan, prepared in advance, in regard to each essential food—for taking over supply, regulating prices, and directing distribution.

4. "Outbreak plans" for the probable initial emergency resulting from air attack'.

and he added—'To think out in advance *and as a whole*, the civilian side of the next war is as important as to design measures of military attack and defence'.

In so far as they clinched the case for setting up a food defence organisation immediately, Sir William Beveridge's arguments were welcome; the idea of such an organisation had, after all, been in the air for several years previously. The Sub-Committee on Food recommended, on 11th November 1936, that Sir William Beveridge should be asked to undertake the preparation of the plans for food control. What subsequently passed between him and officials appears to have left very few traces in the records. This much, however, is clear: that Sir William's ideas about the scope and authority of the task were altogether too ambitious for the Government.

The question was one, as an official minute put it, 'involving inter-Departmental matters of some delicacy'; the heads of major Ministries, with peace-time responsibilities touching the problem of food control at numerous points, were reluctant to yield authority to

---

[1] In an earlier note he had written:—'Is a short *victorious* war against Germany likely? Even if either by passive or by active defence we had kept London habitable and had no fear of immediate defeat ourselves, could we bring Germany to early peace, except by indiscriminate frightfulness against her towns'?

an outsider, however able and experienced. Indeed, the very force and range of his thinking made him that much more disturbing, particularly to those who were not yet convinced that war was inevitable. They therefore decided to go ahead without him; he disappears henceforth from the history of food control. The establishment of the Food (Defence Plans) Department was publicly announced on 29th November 1936; Mr. (later Sir) Henry Leon French, then Second Secretary of the Ministry of Agriculture and Fisheries, was appointed to be its Director.

The new Department was to be a sub-Department of the Board of Trade, reporting through the Permanent Secretary; that is to say, its status was a step below that of a full Department of State.

It was:—

'to formulate plans for the supply, control, distribution and movement of food (including feeding-stuffs for livestock) during a major war with a view to ensuring that the food supplies of the United Kingdom are maintained and distributed in all eventualities, including aerial attack'.

Its main function would be:—

'to prepare in advance plans for execution by the Board of Trade immediately on the outbreak of war and by the Ministry of Food as soon as constituted. The preparation of plans will include proposals for the Headquarters as well as the local organisations which will be required in the event of war and the preparation of the necessary legislation'.

It would also take over the existing civil emergency organisation. But, on the other hand, it would not be directly concerned with home production, nor, for the present, with storage. (It was to take over responsibility for the latter within a few months.)

The terms of reference make no mention of a 'feeding policy', the second of Sir William Beveridge's desiderata. There seems to have been a notion at the Committee of Imperial Defence (it recurs after the outbreak of war) that feeding policy could somehow be divorced from the task of planning food control.[1] At one stage there had been a suggestion that Sir Ernest Gowers should be asked to formulate it, but this appears to have been dropped. Perhaps the intention was that the Food Supply Sub-Committee of the Committee of Imperial Defence should itself undertake the task, but it never did so. *A fortiori*, no attempt was made anywhere 'to think out in advance and as a whole the civilian side of the next war'.

Concentration on practical details and the relegation of first principles to a rather dim background is so characteristic of the pre-war plans affecting food, and so far-reaching in its effects, as to demand further scrutiny. If one looks, for instance, at the factual material put before the Food Supply Sub-Committee during 1936, one is struck by

---

[1] See below, Chapter IV.

the contrast in quality between the contributions from the service departments and those from the civil: The one closely reasoned, expert; the other (with rare exceptions) pedestrian and lacking in penetration. The reason is not far to seek. Service questions— strategy, tactics, logistics—have a long tradition behind them of quasi-scientific, detached, minute study. They are the permanent concern of General Staffs, who, because wars are intermittent occurrences, are not continually in danger of distraction by day-to-day questions of administration. For civilian questions as a whole there is no comparable tradition, expertise, or organisation. The art of administration in a modern state has its own skill and finesse; but they afford little help in the task of formulating a series of strategic assumptions. Indeed, they are liable to intrude questions of day-to-day expediency into what ought, in the first instance, to be a process of pure reasoning. Even the particular contribution to planning that administrative experience can bring, its insistence on the uncertainty of human calculation and the need for flexibility and adaptability in advance arrangements, can readily become, through over-emphasis, a dangerous impatience with logic or even a sort of intellectual nihilism that denies the need to think in general terms at all.

This sort of approach to problems that, if looked at intently, are seen to have wide implications beyond their obvious range at first sight, may hinder freedom of action instead of helping it. To take but one simple example among many afforded by the history of food control: it was agreed that the food plans should be such as to enable the Government of the day, should it so desire, to introduce complete import control for the principal foods at the very outbreak of war. It was an indispensable condition of such a control's effectiveness that control of shipping should also be complete. If, therefore, those responsible for planning shipping, for whatever reason, should choose (as in fact they did choose) to make preparations on the assumption that full shipping control would not be necessary from the start, the Government of the day would not in fact enjoy its expected power to introduce complete food control. It would be a counsel of perfection to suggest that such loopholes could be altogether avoided in practice, if only because of limitations of time and staff. But the provision of adequate central planning machinery, and still more the cultivation of an outlook transcending immediate Departmental concerns, might have done much to reduce their occurrence.

CHAPTER II

The Acquisition of Security Food Stocks

I

THE setting up of the Food (Defence Plans) Department had been in line with previous official thinking on the war-time food problem; only in its timing did it owe anything to the international situation or the pressure of public opinion. But that pressure had not sought to secure this result at all; it had been directed towards another form of defence preparation, the establishment of Government food reserves.

The idea of a food storage policy was by no means new. On at least two occasions since the beginning of the century it had been propounded as a safeguard against the danger to national security represented by the country's manifest and increasing dependence on imported food supplies. The danger itself had been recognised long before even by those who rated most highly the benefits of such an international division of labour. Richard Cobden, at the time of the American Civil War, during which the cotton-producing Southern States had been blockaded by the Federal Navy, had drawn attention to it. For him, the remedy lay in the amendment of the international law so as to limit the definition of contraband to arms and ammunition. Cobden was thinking mainly of the position of the United Kingdom as a neutral; but twenty years later Henry Sidgwick was already conscious of the possibility that she might become a belligerent. Writing in 1883, he was prepared to admit the need for agricultural protection on defence grounds.[1]

With the passage of another twenty years, in 1903, the subject had become of such concern as to cause Mr. Balfour's Government to appoint a *Royal Commission on the Supply of Food and Raw Materials in Time of War*.[2] Various schemes for storing foodstuffs, especially wheat, were propounded to the Commission, but after an exhaustive examination it rejected them all. They were, it held, unnecessary—the Navy could be relied on to protect merchant shipping, a serious shortage of which was not expected. The Commission accepted the Admiralty view that there would be 'no material diminution in the

---

[1] This paragraph is based on a valuable, and, it seems, little known discussion by Sir William Ashley, appended (p. 205) to the *Final Report of the Agricultural Tribunal of Investigation*. 1924 (Cmd. 2145).

[2] Cd. 2643/44/45 contain its Report.

supplies of wheat and flour reaching the United Kingdom'. Moreover, storage schemes were inexpedient, for they would mean Government interference with private trade. (It must be added that some of them, at least, were on the same level of practicability as the schemes of the 'projectors' who so assiduously courted the Government of Queen Elizabeth.)

The Commission could scarcely be blamed for failing to foresee the development of the submarine, or its unrestricted use. In the worst period for wheat supplies during the war, the spring of 1917, sinkings of grain cargoes for the United Kingdom were running at the rate of ten per cent. or more, and stocks of wheat and flour represented less than six weeks' consumption. During only four months of the war did they attain the thirteen weeks' level prescribed by a decision of the War Cabinet in March 1917[1]. Nevertheless, the Admiralty seem to have been more impressed by the effect of the convoy system than that of the submarine campaign to which convoys were the answer. When, in 1923–24, the possibility of a wheat storage scheme was again canvassed at the Committee of Imperial Defence, it was turned down just as firmly as before. The Admiralty—it was reported—were confident that by the end of the first three months of a major war the submarine menace would be under control; normal wheat stocks were likely to amount to at least ten weeks' supplies at any time; a storage scheme would 'handicap the smooth and cheap distribution of wheat,' and be 'extremely difficult to provide and unpalatable to the public'.

In 1924 the notion of a major war was too vague, and its possibilities still too remote, for a break with precedent to be likely. In 1936 it was otherwise; one of the first tasks of the newly appointed committee on food supplies was to re-open the storage question. The desirability of storage was referred to the air and naval staffs; its practicability to an *ad hoc* inquiry by Sir Ernest Gowers.

From 1935 onwards a considerable body of informed public opinion had grown up in support of a storage policy. The most carefully reasoned case for it, and the earliest in this phase of the discussion, had been put forward by Viscount Astor and Mr. Seebohm Rowntree.[2] They urged it as an alternative to an uneconomic fostering of home production which, they argued, would actually weaken the country in war-time by reducing foreign trade and hence the merchant shipping and ship-building industries. Instead, they suggested storing a year's supply of wheat, at an estimated cost of £40 millions. In April 1936, *The Times* expressed alarm at the low stocks of wheat in public granaries at the ports—some 200,000 tons—compared with storage capacity estimated at seven times that amount. (This comparison

---

[1] Ashley, *op. cit.*, p. 209 *seq.*

[2] Astor, Viscount, and Rowntree, B. Seebohm. *The Agricultural Dilemma.* 1935.

overlooked the large stocks normally in the port millers' own silos, but went uncorrected.) *The Times* suggested that the Canadian Wheat Board might be persuaded to hold some of its surplus stocks in the United Kingdom if the British Government would bear the extra cost. In July 1936 Lord Phillimore initiated a full-dress debate on storage in the House of Lords. He urged that the millers be asked to store three months' wheat supplies. Although the Government had already set on foot fresh inquiries into storage, its spokesman, the Lord Chancellor (Lord Hailsham), appeared inclined to pour cold water on it. Wheat, he suggested, might not keep; if we lost command of the sea we should lose the war, storage or no storage.

This seeming firmness concealed, for the Government as a whole, a very real perplexity; for their expert counsellors were unable to provide firm guidance upon the need for storage. Broadly speaking, the naval and air staffs agreed that unrestricted air and sea attacks on shipping must be expected; but they disagreed about the likely effects of such attacks. The Admiralty were confident that convoys and improvements in undersea detection could deal with the submarine menace; they also thought that suitably armed convoys could meet attack from aircraft. The air staff, on the other hand, thought that the naval staff over-estimated the anti-aircraft gun and under-estimated the bomber, and that convoys, so far from protecting ships against air attack, might provide a ready-made target for the enemy. The staffs were so far agreed as to regard aircraft as more dangerous and incalculable adversaries than submarines or surface raiders; they listed the 'accumulation of reserve stocks dispersed throughout the country' as among a number of useful measures of passive defence that might be taken. Beyond that they were not, as yet, prepared to go.

Unless and until the service chiefs could provide a more positive lead, the civilians would perforce be driven back on stating arbitrary assumptions of their own. In July 1936 the Sub-Committee on Food Supplies adopted the following bases for planning, which it thought should provide a 'sufficient margin of safety':—

'(a) that we are liable to a severe temporary interruption and major dislocation of our transport and distribution arrangements for as long as three months after the outbreak of war, and that, as far as practical conditions will permit, it would be advantageous to have in the country on the outbreak of war supplies of essential foods and feeding-stuffs amounting to not less than three months' normal consumption;

(b) that an over-all decrease of imports of food of twenty-five per cent. should be assumed for the whole duration of the war;

(c) that throughout the whole period of the war the avenue of supply from the North Sea would be closed to the extent of ten per cent., from the Baltic to the extent of ninety per cent. ; and that freedom of supply could be maintained from the Mediterranean'.

The third of these postulates does not call for discussion, since there is no evidence that it played any part in moulding the control plans. The others, especially the second, need closer scrutiny. At the time they were laid down it seems fairly clear that they were intended to assess no more than the *resultant*, so to speak, of the various forces affecting war-time food imports. The effect of war, they said, would be in the short run to dislocate food imports, or to interrupt them altogether; over the long run to reduce them, as compared with normal, by one-quarter. How far these results would be due to the efforts of the enemy, and how far to the Government's own actions, was not considered. The effects, transient or permanent, on shipping of port congestion, or of such war-time precautions as convoys or evasive routing, were not mentioned, nor was the possibility that the Government might wish to divert ships from food to other cargoes or for the transport of troops.

For the limited purpose of providing some sort of measure of the size of a food reserve, if it should be decided to create one, the assumptions were as useful as any that could have been made. They made it possible to get out detailed plans and estimates of cost. But, just because they were admittedly arbitrary and without expert authority, they did not help much towards deciding whether a storage policy should be adopted, or on what scale. In fact these decisions were to be made, not on the basis of an expert assessment of strategic possibilities, but on rule-of-thumb considerations of finance and public morale. More important than the influence of the assumptions on storage, however, was their extension to the wider problem of war-time food imports generally. It was here that their want of rigour, particularly when the passage of time had eradicated the memory of their context, led to misleading and even dangerous conclusions being drawn from them.[1]

Working out the practical details of a storage scheme was bound to take some time, for the ground was entirely unfamiliar. As early as September 1936, however, Sir Ernest Gowers was able to produce a first report on the possibilities of a store of wheat.

The vital feature of any successful scheme, he realised, was provision for turning over and replacing stocks from time to time; and this led him to postulate that ordinary trade machinery should be used, in such a way as to dislocate its normal working as little as possible. Members of the trade concerned should build up and turn over the extra stocks required, 'buying, holding and selling as Government agents parcels earmarked as the Government's'; or, alternatively, they might be subsidised to maintain their stocks at the required level. The Government would have to take powers requiring participants in the scheme to make returns of their stocks.

---

[1] See below, Chapter V.

The difficulty of applying these principles to grain lay in the multifarious and conflicting interests of those handling it. The highly rationalised milling industry was dominated by three large enterprises, the privately owned firms of Ranks and Spillers, and their natural enemy, the Co-operative Movement, which was outside the millers' trade association and which on principle did not use the services of the specialist grain importers and brokers who operated on the terminal markets of London and Liverpool. These in their turn were concerned lest they be squeezed out of business by direct purchase by millers in the country of origin—the policy of the Co-operative Movement and to some extent of Ranks also. But they were not accustomed to working together, and some of them were foreign-owned—clearly a disqualification for operating a British Government security stock. Lastly, there was an important and quite separate group of traders in imported flour, mainly in London and Glasgow.

A storage plan that would command the agreement of so many conflicting interests would clearly be difficult to find. Moreover, the existing state of the wheat market was unfavourable to a large-scale Government operation; four successive short crops in the United States and Canada, a crop failure in the Argentine, and two years of large imports into the United States, normally an exporter of wheat, had reduced world wheat stocks to normal proportions, and produced a seller's market in wheat for the first time since 1927. The experts of the corn and milling trades, disagree though they might on everything else, were unanimous in declaring that for the Government to enter the wheat market, even under the cloak of some well-established trade organisation, would be liable to send prices sky-high. The only workable scheme Sir Ernest Gowers could suggest was to by-pass the market and purchase secretly and directly from the Canadian Wheat Board a large block of 'May futures', i.e., options on wheat to be delivered in May 1937; to build silos to hold this purchase on delivery; and in due course to announce to the trade that the wheat had been bought as an emergency reserve, and that no further purchases would be made so long as trade stocks remained normal. The cost of such a purchase of, say, 50 million bushels (1,300,000 tons) was put at £16 million initially, and £1 million annually thereafter.

The risk of upsetting the market might have had to be taken if the case for acquiring a wheat reserve immediately had been overwhelming. But on the evidence before the Government in October 1936 it was anything but that. The Admiralty still held that the very proposal for a wheat reserve cast aspersions on the ability of the Navy to protect shipping: 'nothing', it was said, 'could be done in the air to prevent shipping reaching our south and west coast ports'. (A recent exhaustive inquiry had led to the conclusion that these ports, and the rail network serving them, would be able to handle the extra traffic that would result from a diversion thither of three-quarters of the imports normally handled on the east coast.[1]) Nevertheless, the Admiralty would not take upon itself the responsibility of opposing the establishment of food reserves. The Sub-Committee on Food Supplies recorded approval of the policy in principle, and asked that detailed investigation be extended to other foods than wheat.

By December, when the Sub-Committee met again, Ministers had become more favourably disposed to a wheat reserve, if only on grounds of public morale. They thought it ought to be large enough, together with normal trade stocks, to last six months. Despite cries of alarm from the Treasury, and some scepticism from Sir Ernest Gowers himself, they asked him to prepare detailed plans. They also referred to the Cabinet a proposal for buying a month's supply of wheat immediately from the Canadian Wheat Board; but this was, after further discussion, turned down on the ground that the market was unfavourable. Even so, the Cabinet asked that the question of a Bill empowering the Government to buy reserves of essential commodities should be explored and a Draft Bill prepared. By February 1937 four detailed schemes for the storage of a balanced group of foodstuffs were ready, ranging from Plan I, an emergency scheme for feeding London for a month, to Plan IV which would provide, together with normal trade stocks, for six months' supply of wheat, four months' supply of oilseeds, three months' supply of sugar, a large supply of whale oil (for cooking fat and margarine) and quantities of canned meat, canned milk, and cheese, together with no less than six months' supply of feeding grains for animals.

By this time the chief question at issue had become how much ought to be spent on a storage scheme. The Treasury set its face against borrowing for such a purpose, and wanted expenditure limited to £25 millions, spread out over a number of years. This meant, in practical terms, the adoption of the 'minimum' Plan II, which included only so much wheat (188,000 tons) as could be housed in existing storage accommodation. (It was the need for building special stores that made the larger Plans III and IV so much more expensive.) The Cabinet put off a decision in principle until the ways and means had been more fully explored; meantime, in order to make the announcement of a food storage policy more palatable, the Minister of Agriculture, at his own suggestion, was authorised to prepare proposals 'for increasing the productivity of our own soil with a view to ensuring increased food production in time of war'.

In July the subject came up yet again, on the report of officials[2] who had been asked to work out the terms and provisions of a Storage

---

[1] The validity of these conclusions will be examined in Chapter IX below.

[2] The primary responsibility for storage questions had now passed to the Food (Defence Plans) Department.

Bill; and yet again the Cabinet put it off; this time because a 'conspectus' of defence expenditure was being undertaken. The most Ministers would agree to was that a food storage scheme, based on Plan II and an expenditure of £20 millions, should be brought up as part of the conspectus. Even so, approval of the scheme in principle would not mean that the sum to be spent on it would not be whittled down. There matters were to rest for another nine months.

II

Three times—in December 1936, in February 1937, and again in July 1937—the Minister for Co-ordination of Defence had tried and failed to get the Cabinet to take decisive action on food reserves. Meantime it fell to him, as the responsible Minister, to defend his colleagues' inaction against steady and weighty public criticism, headed by Sir Arthur Salter, M.P., who, by private interviews and memoranda, Commons speeches, and press articles[1] strove to impress on Ministers that food storage was not, as some thought, 'a kind of luxury addition to our main war preparations'. Sir Arthur saw it clearly as a means of reducing the demands on shipping once war had broken out; it would release tonnage for munitions and raw materials, relieve us of the need, otherwise imperative, of importing more than our current war-time consumption of food in order to build up stocks. The effect would be felt not only in lessened strain on the Navy and merchant marine, but in the wider field of general strategy. Ample food stocks

> 'would exempt those who have to take the highest decisions of policy from the panic atmosphere that must result if only a few weeks' supply separates the country from starvation. Repeatedly during the last war the gravest recommendations were made as to the need of closing down some of the military expeditions and even the main conduct of the war in consequence of the shipping shortage and the danger of starvation; and the character of this danger several times led to the actual gravity of the transport and supply situation being greatly exaggerated'.

For this purpose, however, small additions to existing port stocks, on the lines Sir Arthur rightly suspected the Government to be contemplating, were inadequate. What was wanted was dispersed inland storage of foodstuffs equivalent, say, to a year's supply of wheat; but there was no need to have the stocks as wheat, or ingeniously balanced between one commodity and another. Sugar, which was cheap and stored better than wheat, would be especially suitable for security stocks, and since ships were completely interchangeable between

---

[1] Most notably in the *Economist*, 10th October 1937. The proposals in this article had been sent to Sir Thomas Inskip in July.

wheat and sugar, having the one was equivalent to having the other. Besides these technical arguments for a security stock, there was one strong political argument, namely that they could not provoke a competitive armaments race.

The Minister for Co-ordination of Defence and his advisers, so far from accepting the need for ambitious schemes of this kind, had in fact agreed to scale down the proposed capital expenditure from £20 millions to £10–12 millions before putting it up to the Cabinet again. For this purpose the original Plan II (described at the time as a 'minimum') was reduced to a simple proposal to buy 400,000 tons of wheat, 150,000 tons of sugar, and 100,000 tons of whale oil[1]. The chief economy was at the expense of oilseeds; reduced from 375,000 tons to 75,000, they were to disappear altogether when the Treasury reversed its views of the previous year, decided to cover the expenditure by borrowing, and decreed that it should be reduced by the amount of the annual interest charge. There could be no pretence that the revised plan constituted an adequate insurance; officials supporting storage in principle regarded it rather as a lever to secure Ministerial agreement to the establishment of any Government reserve at all. If that could be done without upsetting the market and the trade concerned, it would be relatively easy to increase the stocks later on.

The new proposals, while differing not at all in principle from those of Sir Ernest Gowers, were almost ostentatiously based on consultations with the trade; the elaborate arrangements for an *ad hoc* Statutory Commission that had been discussed the previous July were allowed to fall into the background. The first breach in the opposition front—opposition, that is, to storage in practice rather than in theory —was made on 2nd February 1938, when the Cabinet agreed to a stopgap arrangement Sir Thomas Inskip proposed to make with Lever Bros. and Unilever,[2] by which they would undertake to maintain their stocks of whale oil in England for the next year at not less than 60,000 tons by regular shipments from Holland, if the Government would pay the extra cost.

The crucial commodity, for which a convincing and successful scheme must be produced, was of course wheat; and the Food (Defence Plans) Department therefore advised Sir Thomas Inskip to call upon the leading millers for assistance. In March, directors of Spillers, Ranks, and the English and Scottish Co-operative Societies'

---

[1] Financial provision was also proposed for emergency 'iron rations' for air raid refugees; but nothing was done about this till after Munich.

[2] This plan was first mooted at an interview between the Minister and the Chairman of Lever Brothers and Unilever, on 10th December 1937, of which the most significant feature was an *obiter dictum* of which Sir Thomas Inskip left note. '[He] told me that there is not more than three weeks' stocks of fats in Germany at any given time, and from conversations which he has had in Germany, he regards any possibility of war in these circumstances as wholly remote.'

milling departments agreed to co-operate in purchasing and maintaining a stock of 400,000 tons of wheat, to be held on Government
account in addition to their normal stocks, and turned over and
replaced in the course of trade. A Committee, representing the
participating millers, with an independent 'small' miller as Chairman, would be responsible for managing the stock, which was to be
acquired in a single secret purchasing operation, if possible within
twenty-four hours of the word 'go'. This plan, together with similarly
'trade-sponsored' arrangements for sugar and whale oil, passed the
Cabinet on 6th April.

In anticipation of the Cabinet decision the Department had
summoned the millers' committee to meet next day; and there it was
agreed that, in order to preserve absolute secrecy, the decision to
begin actual buying should rest with Sir Henry French alone, and
that the operation should be undertaken jointly by Mr. J. V. Rank on
the Baltic and a Co-operative Wholesale Society buyer working under
his instructions in Winnipeg. No-one at the meeting, except Sir
Henry himself, knew that Cabinet approval had already been given.
That very night he telephoned from his home to Mr. Rank to ask how
markets had closed, and was told that conditions were not unfavourable for a large purchase. Next morning the Government agents were
told to go ahead, and within twenty-four hours had secured seven-
eighths of the desired amount, only ceasing operations when the
market showed signs of rising more than the shilling above opening
prices fixed by Mr. Rank as his limit. The remainder of the 400,000
tons—half 'spot' Australian, half Winnipeg 'futures' for October
delivery—was secured by 11th April.

The surprise tactics had been a complete success; but so large a
purchase on a single day, even by a firm of the size of Mr. Rank's, was
bound to arouse suspicion that the Government was behind it. If the
market were not to remain disturbed and uneasy, the trade must be
reassured; and for this purpose the bald statement in the Chancellor
of the Exchequer's budget speech[1] that the Government had acquired
reserves of wheat, whale oil, and sugar was hardly sufficient. Early in
May, therefore, meetings of grain trade and milling representatives
were held at which the way in which the scheme would work was
confidentially explained. The milling concerns, who would do the
work without remuneration, had been chosen because they alone
could turn over the wheat without a second market transaction. It
would be stored in existing granaries; but every effort would be made
to avoid incommoding the trade's normal operations. While the
amount of the reserve could not be disclosed, no further additions to
it were contemplated. These statements served to calm grain traders,

---

[1] It was at Sir Thomas Inskip's own request that the announcement was so made,
instead of separately by himself.

C

if not to allay their disappointment at not having been employed, or even consulted, in advance.

In purchasing a store of whale oil the Department, for temporary tactical reasons, went back on its general principle of working with the trade. At the time the Cabinet decision was taken it had still not completed a formal agreement with Unilevers for the maintenance of a minimum stock at Bromborough. Meanwhile, the German Government had bought some 100,000 tons of the current catch, leaving some 160,000 unsold; clearly a bulk purchase of 100,000 tons by the British Government might raise the market against any other buyers, of whom the chief was likely to be Unilevers themselves. The Department, rather than take them into its confidence, preferred to work secretly through a leading broker;[1] but his initial purchase of 40,000 tons immediately became known to the trade through the whale oil sellers' pool, of whose existence the Department appears to have been unaware; the price was immediately put up from £12 15s. to £14 a ton. There followed protests from Unilevers that the Government had treated them shabbily. After all, it was they who had suggested the creation of a reserve in the first place; they were even then arranging to assist the Government in a stopgap scheme without profit to themselves; surely the least it could do in return was not to force the market up against them. As a result, the stopgap scheme was abandoned, and Unilevers were offered and accepted a share in the Government's remaining purchases, made at an average price of £13 4s. The feeling engendered by this episode on both sides had so far died down by July 1938 that Unilevers were prepared to join with the other principal consumers of whale oil, Thomas Hedley & Co. Ltd., and the Southern Oil Co. Ltd., in arranging for the safe keeping of the Government reserve on their premises. These arrangements were well in train by the time of the Munich crisis, which, however, saw nearly half of the Government reserve still stored on the Continent.

The purchases of wheat and whale oil were complete though not delivered by the time they were announced; but only an interim stopgap purchase of sugar had been made. The two main trade interests, namely the State-sponsored British Sugar Corporation controlling the manufacture of home-grown beet sugar, and the refiners, Tate & Lyle Ltd., were agreed that the best way for the Government to obtain a dispersed sugar reserve would be for the greater part of it to consist of home-grown raw sugar that would otherwise be sold by the Corporation to the refiners;[2] the amount thus withdrawn from

---

[1] The broker employed stipulated for commission from the Government as a buyer, contrary to the custom of the trade. This leaked out when a rival firm of brokers claimed that he had deprived them of commission that they would have otherwise have enjoyed as the seller's agent.

[2] i.e., sugar surplus to the Corporation's own refining quota, under the industrial agreement with the refiners.

consumption would, of course, be made up by further imports. This arrangement could not be put into force before the autumn, when the sugar 'campaign' began, and then only gradually. It was in the summer, however, that sugar stocks were at their seasonal lowest; to tide over the next few months it was agreed that the Corporation, on behalf of the Government, should purchase from and subsequently resell to Tate & Lyle 50,000 tons of Empire sugar then in stock in Liverpool. This would, in effect, immobilise sugar that would otherwise have gone for refining, and oblige the refiners to import an equivalent amount for immediate use. In addition, Tate & Lyle were asked, and agreed, to maintain their minimum seasonal stock at 50,000 tons more than the normal. The effect of these measures would be that bulk stocks of sugar would be increased by 100,000 tons that summer and a further 100,000 when the complete Government reserve of 150,000 tons had been bought.

Meantime it remained to legalise what had been done. The Essential Commodities (Reserves) Bill was introduced into the Commons on 26th May, passed its second reading without a division on 2nd June, and finally received the Royal Assent on 2nd August. It empowered the Board of Trade (in effect the Food (Defence Plans) Department) to acquire, by direct or indirect means (e.g., through subsidies to traders), stocks of essential commodities, and provided funds for the purpose. It further gave powers to the Department to require the disclosure of trade stocks. The policy of food storage had at long last been translated into accomplished fact.

III

The smoothness with which the storage operations (apart from the whale oil incident) had begun was not to be maintained for very long. The first difficulties arose from the decision to use existing stores, largely in Liverpool, for the storage of 'security' wheat and of the 50,000 tons of sugar to be bought by Tate & Lyle in replacement of that immobilised in their own warehouses. Within a few days of the decision to buy there were complaints from the Mersey Docks and Harbour Board that to put these foodstuffs into dockside warehouses would be completely contrary to the policy of keeping ports clear, laid down by the Port and Transit Committee of the Ministry of Transport[1]—complaints to which the Food (Defence Plans) Department could only reply that that aspect of the matter had not occurred to it. The Liverpool authorities refused to allocate more than half the

---

[1] See Chapters IX and X below.

available dockside space to Government wheat; but even so there was at one time in the autumn of 1938 no less than 160,000 tons of it there; and the grain trade complained that this would leave insufficient elbow room for the forward purchases of Australian and Plate wheat that would be arriving in March and April 1939. The trade asked that 90,000 tons should be moved to up-town warehouses; the Department counter-proposed that trade wheat should be put into these, which were not certainly suitable for long term storage, the Government to make a contribution to the extra cost.

Arguments continued throughout the winter, and late in February the millers advising the Department at last agreed to reduce the stock on Merseyside to 100,000 tons. Before anything was done about this, a telephone call came through from Liverpool one day in mid-March, to say that two-and-a-half cargoes were due and there was no room for them in the stores. Space was cleared for one cargo, but the second ship had to be kept on demurrage because she could not unload; the Department undertook, with Treasury consent, to pay part of the demurrage charges. The Liverpool grain storage authorities now came forward with an offer to contribute towards the cost of moving 20,000 tons of wheat up-town, and this was at last agreed to. Even so, the crisis seems only to have been satisfactorily surmounted because less wheat came forward than was expected—or in other words, because trade stocks were reduced below expectation.

A more general trade grievance, not confined to Liverpool, arose only incidentally from the Department's activities. The early meetings of the wheat storage advisory committee had been notable for sharp conflicts between the Co-operative and 'capitalist' millers; but better acquaintance, and the tact of officials, had so far removed this antagonism that in the autumn of 1938 the rivals joined in a big purchase of wheat direct from the United States Government, so that the grain trade was deprived of the commission. More provoking still was the Government's decision, on political grounds, to buy 200,000 tons of wheat from Roumania. This proposal was first mooted in July 1938, and was backed strongly by the Foreign Office and the Government's Chief Economic Adviser. The millers did not want Roumanian wheat; they had already covered their requirements of soft wheat months ahead at lower prices than the Roumanians were asking. The wheat was not suitable for the security stock, since it had indifferent keeping qualities, and anyway (the Department pointed out) there was insufficient money to buy more wheat and nowhere to put it except on the east coast, which was considered vulnerable.

Nevertheless, Ministers decided that the purchase must be made if a reasonable price could be fixed; and in fact the Roumanians, who had been asking 74s. a metric ton f.o.b. Braila, were forced down, thanks to the Department's opposition, to 62s. 6d., or no more than the market price—a saving to the Exchequer of £100,000. The millers urged that the new purchase should be milled on arrival, but the Essential Commodities Act did not empower the Government to buy except for storage; the Roumanian wheat was, therefore, used to replace existing security wheat, and within a few months was in its turn taken out for milling. The millers—notwithstanding their dislike of the whole proposal—co-operated in making this arrangement work smoothly; but it aroused the greatest indignation in the grain trade. In November a deputation from the trade alleged that if these direct purchases (in which it included, of course, the millers' own American deal) were to continue, the trade would be unable to carry on; and their protests were so far heeded that an assurance was given that there would be no more such purchases during the current cereal year. Moreover, the trade was invited to confer with the Department and the millers on ways and means of associating it more closely with the storage scheme. But the very first meeting in March 1939 served only to disclose the acrimonious gulf that lay between millers and grain traders.

Meantime, the sponsors of the Roumanian purchase were hatching plans for an Economic Mission to Roumania and a further purchase of wheat. The Food (Defence Plans) Department did its best to discourage them; it pointed out that the Co-operative Wholesale Society, and probably the other millers, would refuse to work the storage scheme if the Government gave way to the grain trade's demand that future purchases on Government account should be made on the open market through the trade; on the other hand, the trade could not be expected to bring forward wheat for the country's normal needs if it were completely uncertain whether the Government would not at any time enter into competition with it. In the end the Economic Mission was sent, and did agree in principle to a further purchase of 200,000 tons from the 1939 harvest, if available at world prices. When the time came, however, German bidding forced up the price so high that the British representatives were shut out; only on the 27th August did the Roumanian Legation in London come forward with an offer of 200,000 tons of wheat and a proposal to store a further 150,000 tons in this country on behalf of the Roumanian Government—the one impracticable for want of storage accommodation, the other too late. War came, in fact, before any solution of the problem of political purchases and the grain trade's relation to the storage scheme could be found. Departments had by then agreed on a compromise that would have given the trade assurances that only 250,000 tons of wheat was likely to be purchased in the cereal year 1939–40, and that it should be possible to give two months' notice of any arrivals of wheat directly purchased. Even this concession had only been wrung from the Foreign Office by 'straight and forcible talking' from the Food (Defence Plans) Department, and it seems very unlikely that it would have satisfied the trade.

The diplomatic merits of the Roumanian purchase cannot be discussed here. But it not only risked the goodwill of the millers by dictating the composition of their grist; it roused all the antagonisms latent among the private interests handling grain. Apart, however, from this last straw, the resentment of grain traders at being shut out of the scheme was natural. It was difficult for them to believe that the participating millers were not making something out of it, if only from their knowledge of the size and composition of the Government stock. To them it seemed that the Government was aiding and abetting a millers' buying ring, at a time when the enormous world wheat surplus was causing markets to tumble. It was, therefore, only politic for the Department to attempt to allay these suspicions, if only by adding a grain trader to the advisory committee. The millers opposed this on the ground that it would lead to prices being forced up against the Government; and since the millers' co-operation was essential if the Government were not to be constantly buying and selling wheat, they were in a strong position to make their views felt; all the more so since they were doing the work without profit to themselves.

A scheme, however convenient and inexpensive, under which the State was beholden to one particular section of a trade while the remainder was out in the cold could scarcely endure, assuming as it did in effect that the organised grain market was nothing more than a speculators' racket. If the grain trade were not good enough to be the suppliers of the Government's food stores, the sooner they were deprived of the much more important task of handling the nation's wheat supply, the better. The Department was not so naive as to swallow arguments of this kind when they were put forward explicitly. But its whole practice had been based on the unspoken assumption that tactics had more influence on prices than had underlying economic trends; it did believe that the original highly dramatic and secret purchase of wheat was the only way of doing the job without raising prices. On the contrary; as a leading grain trader pointed out to the Department in 1939, the futures market offered the ideal means of acquiring a reserve quietly and with the minimum of disturbance. All that a buyer need do was to accumulate futures to the desired amount over a period of months, and take them all up in a body when they matured. Indeed, it is at least arguable that to proceed by a sudden *coup de main* was to invite the maximum of speculative dislocation. On that view, the success of the operations of 1938 must be attributed mainly to the world glut of wheat.

That this must have been largely true is confirmed by what happened over sugar, where an equally ample world supply was controlled by an international restriction scheme that strove to adjust export quotas very closely to consumption. Since the total regulated world supply of sugar was of the order of 3 million tons, the amount to go into the Government store—150,000 tons—was such as to call for a very watchful eye on the market, so that application could be made for an increase in quotas directly the price looked like getting out of hand. It so happened that 1938 was the worst season for the British sugar crop for years; the sugar content of the beets was so low that the Sugar Corporation could only spare 60,000 tons for store instead of the 100,000 promised. In mid-December, therefore, recourse was had to Empire sugars to make up the balance; but by that time the market had so hardened that these could only be obtained at a reasonable price through the good offices of Tate & Lyle, who agreed to exchange Empire sugar in transit to themselves for foreign sugar purchased by the Corporation.[1]

Nevertheless, the Food (Defence Plans) Department appears to have disinterested itself in the question of export quotas, and the British delegation to the January 1939 meeting of the International Sugar Council not only made no attempt to get them increased—an attempt that might well have been blocked by the producer countries —but took no steps to make sure that any deficiency was in fact remediable at short notice under the terms of the Agreement. In this attitude officials appear to have had the support of the refiners, notwithstanding that in November these had hinted at a shortage. Late in April, Tate & Lyle raised the alarm afresh, declaring that their stocks would fall to vanishing point in July unless they could get further supplies; and as a result, the Board of Trade did secure from the Council in April, May and June, releases of sugar that stayed the upward rise of prices. Much of this sugar was, however, either refined sugar and, therefore, of no use to the refiners, or was from sources too far away for it to arrive in this country till after the seasonal low of stocks had passed.

Moreover, since the increased demand for security hoards was by its nature temporary (and likely to be at its highest in the summer, the war season) forward sugar for September-October delivery was standing at 1s. 6d. to 2s. per cent. below spot prices for July and August. This was an invitation to all sugar users to cut their stocks to a working minimum during those months[2]—how strong an invitation may be judged from the fact that Tate & Lyle stood to lose £100,000 if they carried out their undertaking to maintain an extra 50,000 tons in stock; indeed, they would have preferred to let their stocks fall *below* normal by that amount, thus saving £200,000. They put

---

[1] Empire sugar was preferred for storage purposes as being sufficiently pure to be usable without refining in case of emergency.

[2] The British Sugar Corporation, in July 1939, asked unsuccessfully if it might borrow 30,000 tons of Government sugar till October, when sugar would be cheaper.

their case to the Department and it was agreed that they could not be asked to carry out their full undertaking; at the specific request of the Minister[1] they did undertake to keep their stocks at the normal seasonal low of 100,000 tons.

That the leaders of the trade should so miscalculate the position does no more than palliate the failure of those officially responsible for looking after United Kingdom interests. It needed no very great penetration to see, at any time after September 1938, that the combined effects of security hoarding and crop failure might do more than wipe out any excess of quotas over consumption; and that if this occurred, there would be a temporary hump in the price curve and a consequent reduction of trade stocks. The conviction of most officials (and traders) that no general shortage of sugar was likely was beside the point, which was one of position and timing. The Food (Defence Plans) Department, though certainly at fault in not raising the question on its own responsibility, had at least the excuse that it was not consulted until the refiners had raised the alarm.

IV

The Department was at its resourceful best in the second whale oil purchase in the spring of 1939. The whale oil catch was disappointing that year; and when news reached London that the German buyers, who by arrangement with Unilevers had a prior claim on supplies of Norwegian oil, had failed to agree with the Norwegians on price, the Department saw an opportunity to corner the world supply, and thus not only add a valuable asset to our own food reserves, but deprive Germany of it at one and the same time. Unilevers and the other users of whale oil agreed to share in the purchases which were made anonymously through a leading broker,[2] and after some anxious moments—chiefly because the Department's Treasury Authority to purchase ran out before negotiations could be brought to a head[3]— they were completely successful. Besides 80,000 tons from the Norwegians, the Department had already acquired a further 60,000 from British and South African sources; and the trade some 90,000 tons, including nearly 50,000 tons from Japanese catchers. Only leavings of not much more than 10,000 tons remained to the Germans,

---

[1] Mr. W. S. Morrison, Chancellor of the Duchy of Lancaster, had been made responsible for food defence in March 1939.

[2] Not the broker who had made the 1938 purchases.

[3] It ran out at the week-end—just when the Norwegians showed signs of coming to terms—and had to be renewed after hasty consultations with the Treasury and the Foreign Secretary himself on the following Monday morning. As with the 1938 wheat deal, all the preliminary negotiations were carried out, on the Government side, by Sir Henry French, single-handed and in secret.

who had clearly counted too much on their knowledge that all the existing commercial storage space in this country was full; and supposed that the Norwegian whalers would have had no alternative but to sell to them. Storage for the new purchases was indeed a serious problem; pending the construction of further tanks, some of it had to be left on the Continent, and the rest put either into laid-up oil tankers or into fuel oil storage at Thameshaven. The latter was admittedly vulnerable to air attack, and the Admiralty in September 1938 had actually recommended that whale oil reserves should rather be kept in Holland or Belgium, despite the chance that these countries might, under enemy pressure, put an embargo on its export after war had broken out. By May 1939, however, the Admiralty had discovered by experiment that whale oil was not as dangerous as petrol or fuel oil; moreover, the air defences of the region had been much improved in the interim.

The Treasury, whose insistence on financial economy had half-strangled the original storage schemes, co-operated readily in this and other proposals for increasing food reserves that the Department put up during 1939; indeed, it went further and actually invited them. This change of front was due to its increasing concern about war-time foreign exchange difficulties; its interest in judicious advance purchases of essential raw materials appears to have been aroused by Mr. J. M. Keynes' scheme, propounded at a British Association meeting in August 1938, for free or cheap storage facilities to be offered in this country to Empire primary producers. In January 1939 an Interdepartmental Committee on Exchange Requirements and Essential Materials in Time of War was set up, and at the end of that month the Food (Defence Plans) Department secured sanction for the purchase of 20,000 tons of South American canned meat, to be used as a reserve iron ration for the evacuation scheme. (In practice it proved impossible to buy so much, and the deficiency of about 2,000 tons was made up with British-canned herrings.) In March, proposals were approved for building silos to hold 250,000 tons of wheat, for a further purchase of 200,000 tons to be put in them when built, and for a subsidy scheme to encourage bakers to hold an extra week's supply of flour on their premises. Early in April the Department secured assent in principle for a reserve of 400,000 tons of oil-seeds—included in the original proposals but dropped for reasons of finance; and for no less than 1,500,000 tons of fodder grains, to tide over the animal population until the first war harvest should become available.

Such schemes as these were obviously for the long term; but by this time it was more and more evident that the sands were running out. Sir Arthur Salter and his friends, who had never ceased to criticise the inadequacy of the existing programme, now redoubled their efforts; 'I do entreat you' (wrote Sir Arthur to Mr. W. S. Morrison in April) 'to give your personal attention to the question of bringing in large supplies at once. A great deal could be done by urgent action in even a few weeks'. In July the outside agitation was reinforced from within Whitehall by the unanimous report of the Interdepartmental Committee that 'no effort should be spared to reduce foreign exchange requirements in war-time by pre-war purchases'; on the 26th the Cabinet approved the immediate purchase of £5 millions worth of food and £15 millions worth of raw materials. So much food was not, however, immediately available; and the purchases actually approved by the Treasury amounted to considerably less than this. They included 100,000 tons each of wheat and of 'forward' sugar for September delivery; frozen meat to the value of £900,000 and a further 10,000 tons of canned meat. War broke out before any of them, except the wheat, could be delivered. The bulk reserves of foodstuffs held by the Government on 3rd September 1939, amounted to just under 500,000 tons of wheat, 150,000 tons of raw sugar, and 240,000 tons of whale oil.

Except for whale oil, the influence of these stocks on war-time food supplies was not very great. Their importance lay rather in that they had been acquired without bringing about the disasters that many, including some Ministers who favoured the policy in principle, expected from an entry by Government into the commodity markets. The Department believed that the original purchases of 1938 were decisive in raising its prestige with the food trades and making smooth the path of control preparations in general. Certainly it was to show a gift for timing and tactics that need not shame the ablest market operator; in the main it chose its trade advisers wisely and used them well. Its troubles with wheat and sugar stocks in 1939 indicate, however, a weakness—an inability to take a broad and long view of economic strategy—that was to recur more than once in the later history of food control. The management of pre-war reserve stocks already showed the strength and limitations of that collaboration between trader and civil servant on which the Ministry of Food was based. Officials were to have little difficulty in picking up the tricks of the trade, or traders in learning the conventions and customs of the Civil Service. Neither accomplishment, though indispensable, was sufficient for a world in which, even before the war had broken out, the trend towards national and international interference in economic matters had more and more displaced or distorted the measuring rod of market price. It was not enough to rely on a combination of official secrecy, trading acumen, and untrained common sense to bring success to a Government economic enterprise. The majority of traders and civil servants, though they might consider themselves very different sorts of person, were alike in having a long-standing, often consciously cultivated, tendency to improvise policy, even where they would not dream of improvising machinery; a quality that though it would get them out of many a tight corner, seldom prevented them from getting into one. It is this improvised quality that gives the commodity dealings of 1938 and 1939, for all their operational skill, an anachronistic air not proper to the age of 'sophisters, economists, and calculators' that had already come upon us.

CHAPTER III

Planning the Machinery of Food Control

I

THE Food (Defence Plans) Department began its work in a strategic vacuum. A few notions about what the next war would be like were generally current, in Government circles as elsewhere. The principal enemy, and his main weapon, the bombing aircraft, were identified; it was expected that war would be ushered in by devastating air-raids on British cities, particularly London; the prospect of blockade was implicit in the decision to begin food planning at all. But no comprehensive and coherent hypotheses of war, and its implications for civilians, had been or were to be attempted. This may be credited, in the last resort, to the certainty that it would be a defensive war; no Government bent on aggression, meditating time and place for a *coup*, could have left so unexplored the non-military aspects of its conduct. The political climate of Britain, in the years before 1939, was not propitious for the type of ruthless calculation that the prospect of modern war demands; the governing view of the time hated war and distrusted collectivist planning such as war must entail. It would be surprising if this attitude of mind had not spilled over into the way in which war plans were tackled.

Such general reflections must be tested by historians of wider themes than the present—food control. Whatever be the explanation, the fact remains that the food planners were thrown back almost entirely on their own intellectual initiative.[1] It was not merely that, apart from the Air Raid Precautions Department of the Home Office, they constituted the only civilian body specifically charged with defence planning, and defence planning alone. Other Departments of State may well have been employing comparable resources, without the publicity that was given to food, on these tasks; the war-time aspects of shipping, transport, military and industrial conscription, to say nothing of agriculture, were by no means being neglected from 1937 onwards. What was lacking, at any rate until after Munich, was any continuous, informed, central pressure that should keep these departmental activities in step, either in the sense of being mutually

---

[1] One reason seems to have been that Ministers regarded the Department's work as purely administrative, and therefore took little or no interest in it.

consistent or the more practical sense of moving towards completion at a uniform pace.

But (it may be objected) did not the Committee of Imperial Defence, with its sub-committees, provide such guidance? In the economic field, the answer can only be no; the Committee did not, could not, give a lead, and the Departments seldom sought it. The Food Sub-Committee, for instance, met in all but three times between March 1937 and the outbreak of war. On those occasions it certainly took important decisions, such as authorising the printing of ration books in peace-time. But it never developed the corporate existence or the nucleus of expert, extra-departmental advice that would have enabled it to keep even the limited range of its responsibilities under continuous oversight. The image of the pre-war plans, in their civilian sector, is not that of an army, moving towards its objective in accordance with a flexible, adaptable strategy. Rather is it that of a number of intelligent individuals making each his own way towards a common destination, and finding mutual interests *en route*.

Hence the conception of the plans, as well as their execution, could not but become almost exclusively departmental. Agreed common hypotheses, or even formulated disagreement, scarcely existed; assumptions separately made might never be confronted with one another, let alone reconciled; indeed, they might never reach the point of overt statement. The possibilities of latent conflict that should only be resolved in the event are obvious. So too is the likelihood that Departments' peace-time policies would be allowed to get in the light of their war preparations.

From this latter pitfall the Food (Defence Plans) Department was safeguarded by its terms of reference. In its case, the absence of external criteria by which its plans could be tested had the effect of strengthening the Ministry of Food tradition. Individuals might have their doubts about that tradition's applicability:

'I have never been quite satisfied'—wrote one who had been a member of the Beveridge committee on rationing—'that we did the whole of our job, which was to provide a scheme suitable for the *next* war'. But there could be no conclusive, authoritative reason against taking it as the main guide to conduct; and the arguments for so doing were strong and obvious. It embodied methods that had been tried and found successful; that were familiar to the trades who would have to work it; that needed little advance explanation or defence to Ministers, Parliament, or public. To a Department so small in relation to the task put before it,[1] the revival of Lord Rhondda's

---

[1] As founded, it had, under the Director, only six officials of administrative or quasi-administrative status; two assistant directors and four heads of branch. When the storage scheme was adopted in the spring of 1938, a third assistant director and two more heads of branch were added. There was a great expansion after Munich (p. 43 below).

Ministry, with such improvements as experience suggested, might well seem the only practical course.

In effect, one might say, the Department took as its point of departure the impossibility of forecasting what the war would be like. 'Since the precise nature of the emergency to be faced cannot be determined beforehand, the plans must be flexible and adaptable to varying circumstances'. Forced by its inadequate resources to economise effort, it chose to concentrate on the problems that must be faced. Rather than speculate on matters of policy that would in the end have to be settled by the Government in office at the time of an emergency, it set itself to provide the essential machinery without which no Government could act.

This does not mean, of course, that its members were unaware of those aspects of its work that might be comprehended under Sir William Beveridge's heading of 'feeding policy'. Such questions as the need to reduce livestock numbers in war-time, and its corollary, the rate of flour extraction, or the implications of price stabilisation and shipping diversion (to take two widely separated aspects of the war economy); these and many others were ventilated from time to time both internally and in discussion with other Departments. But they were not systematically explored or brought deliberately into relation with one another, so as to make up a coherent whole. For instance, no attempt was made to build up a picture of the war-time food requirements of the population that might serve as basis for an import programme.[1] The question of rations for young children, adolescents, and heavy workers was raised, not as part of such a general inquiry, but in the purely practical context of the printing of ration books.[2] There was, in short, no pattern to the Department's thinking other than that imposed by the process of working out the practical plans themselves.

Work thus began, almost without argument, on the assumption that the methods and devices of 1918, if they were introduced sufficiently promptly, would at any rate serve to tide over the first six months of war, and that sufficient time would then be granted for their revision and adaptation. The Department noted that the 'maintenance of imported supplies in war-time is . . . the key to food defence', and it set itself the task of devising machinery to ensure that they continued uninterrupted, and that in so far as they fell short, 'equality of sacrifice'[3] was ensured. Its task was mobilisation of the food trades of the country to serve the national need; and it paid more attention to the changes that had certainly taken place in them, than

---

[1] For the attempt to estimate food supplies on another basis, see Chapter V.

[2] See below p. 40.

[3] Quotations from *Report of the Food (Defence Plans) Department for 1937*, pp. 11, 12.

to those that might conceivably affect the conditions under which they would serve.

Changes since 1918 in the pattern of the United Kingdom's food supplies and distribution had not been very remarkable, from the point of view of planning food control, with perhaps two exceptions. The first was that Southern Ireland no longer formed part of the United Kingdom; the second, and more calculable, was the change in the sources of supply of a major commodity—sugar. One of the major problems of the earlier war had been presented by the cutting off, overnight in August 1914, of imports of refined sugar from the Central Powers. That pattern of trade had been broken for good; in 1937[1] the recently established, heavily subsidised sugar beet industry accounted for about one-quarter of the total sugar consumed; the remainder was almost all raw cane sugar, imported from tropical producing countries for refining in Great Britain. The haul was longer, but at any rate there was no prospect of an immediate and sudden total interruption in supplies.

So far as home food supplies were concerned, one development, as yet in its infancy, had important implications for planning; the setting up since 1931 of marketing boards and control commissions for the majority of farm products. While the amount of home production had not as yet been increased by these measures, the existence of organised marketing suggested a greater ease in establishing war-time control, while the staffs working the schemes provided cadres of informed persons on whom a future Food Controller could draw.

The pattern of food manufacture and distribution seems to have changed but little. In flour milling, oilseed crushing and sugar refining there had been a tendency to combination, but this had in all cases stopped short of monopoly; and concentration of ownership had not done away with dispersal of plant. Other trades, and retailing generally, remained the province of the small man; multiples and chain stores, though they often grew to impressive individual size, were far from dominating the picture.

Broadly speaking, there was nothing in the 1936 pattern of food supplies and distribution, intricate though it was, that would make the controls of 1918 obsolete. Plans for a future war, assuming it to be of a similar character to the last, could reasonably be based on them, with only such modifications as previous experience, and the opportunity of planning the structure as a whole, would obviously suggest. The Food (Defence Plans) Department could not have seen itself as embarking on a second 'state trading adventure'; it was arranging to revive, in an improved and up-to-date form, an organisation of proven worth, in the confidence that it would justify itself yet again.

---

[1] *op. cit.* p. 17.

II

From the very beginning, the two-fold nature of the British system of food control was apparent in the way the new Department split up its planning duties. On the one hand, the future Ministry of Food would have to trade in, or at any rate exercise some control over, individual foods or groups of foods; this would be the function of commodity controls based on the trades concerned, which together would form the mechanism of procurement and supply. On the other hand, the Ministry would have to organise and control demand, whether by rationing the ultimate consumer, or some form of quasi-rationing or allocation on a predetermined basis of entitlement; catering establishments provide an obvious example. This side of its work entailed the preparation and issue of documents—ration books, permits, and so on—and the setting up of divisional and local food offices.

In outline the machinery of commodity control, and the procedure for its introduction on the outbreak of war, were simple. Existing trade stocks and incoming cargoes would be requisitioned, and future purchases, whether overseas or on the farm, be made directly or indirectly on Government account. A system of bulk purchase and/ or long-term contracts would replace hand-to-mouth buying on the existing produce exchanges, whose members would become Government agents; by this means it was hoped to stabilise prices and eliminate speculation. Co-ordinated buying on behalf of allies and even neutrals was envisaged. Processors, such as flour millers, sugar refiners, and oilseed crushers, would operate as directed on allocated raw materials, at margins of profit to be negotiated with the Ministry of Food. So, too, wholesale distribution would be subject to Ministry orders. 'The final stage is reached when the retailer, registered with his local Food Control Committee, has delivered to him at a fixed price the regular weekly supplies required to meet the needs of his registered customers', to whom he in turn would sell at a fixed price.[1]

The embodiment of these simple principles in mechanism suited to the idiosyncrasies of each food and each section of the trade was, however, a task for patient labour and negotiation. If food control were to come into being without a hitch, the planners must carry the traders with them, even at the risk of undue concessions to practices not really suited to a war economy. Directly it passed from the stage of elaborating principles to translating them into terms of men and forms, the Department found itself hampered first by lack of staff and secondly by the requirements of official secrecy which forbade it to

---

[1] In fact the Ministry of Food control Orders were to prescribe maximum, not fixed prices. The Ministry made much of this distinction, but in practice it was of little importance for foods subject to rationing by a tie to the retailer.

associate large outside staffs, such as those of the Marketing Boards and Control Commissions, with the preparation of commodity schemes. Before the Munich crisis, through no fault of its own, this side of its work had become immersed in a mass of seemingly interminable discussions.[1]

The preparation of the rationing machinery, while throwing up more knotty problems for immediate resolution than that of the commodity controls, nevertheless made rather better progress, partly because there was not the same need for outside consultation, partly because it leant even more heavily on previous experience, as summarised in the work of Sir William Beveridge's Sub-Committee on rationing. That experience prescribed a national rationing system based on a consumer-retailer tie and hence the establishment of a network of divisional and local food offices.

A shadow divisional organisation was ready to hand in the civil emergency food organisation that had been maintained, as a legacy from the old Ministry of Food, on account of its proven utility in the great Railway Strike of 1919. The Divisional Officers, persons of local standing who received a small retaining fee for their readiness to serve in emergency, were brought into consultation with the Department, and a few of the older ones were persuaded to make way for younger men.

The local organisation, too, was taken from the last war not merely in essential principle—namely the setting up of local food control committees, nominated by the local authority, as well as food executive officers to control the day-to-day work of local offices—but in details that were the result of historical accident. The decision to make the local unit in England and Wales the sanitary authority— the borough or district council—and in Scotland the county or large burgh, was supported by practical arguments. But it ultimately went back to 1917, when the English county councils had declined, and the Scottish county councils accepted, the task of forming food control committees. It was indeed proposed that some of the smaller authorities should combine to form joint committees—a recommendation that proved difficult to enforce in practice. The food control committees themselves, which in the last war had often intervened actively in distribution and even pioneered local rationing schemes ahead of general rationing, were now to be more circumscribed. It was granted that the Minister might delegate to them certain administrative functions,[2] but their chief purpose was clearly

---

[1] An account of these negotiations, as they concerned particular foods, will appear in Vol. II.

[2] These were listed in the Department's *Report* for 1937 (*loc. cit.* § 70) as follows: Registration of consumers: licensing of retailers and 'adjustment' of supplies to them and to catering establishments; consideration of applications for change of retailer; issue of ration documents; collection of returns and information; inspection of records; enforcement. Only the last of these could be described as other than a routine function.

D

thought of as being a safety-valve for discontent and a shield against accusations of bureaucracy. The local Food Executive Officer was this time to be the servant, not of the Committee but of the Food Controller.

The Food (Defence Plans) Department was not long in deciding that local authorities ought to be asked at once to designate 'shadow' Food Executive Officers and Chairmen of Food Control Committees. A minor delay occurred over finance, since it was proposed that in war-time the Ministry of Food should bear the whole cost of local food administration, whereas the Treasury was even then bargaining with the local authorities about the proportion of the cost of air raid precautions that should be borne by the Exchequer, and did not want to weaken its bargaining position by offering to pay the whole cost of another part of civil defence. By November 1937, this obstacle had been overcome, and the President of the Board of Trade announced in the House the decision to set up a shadow divisional and local organisation. By 31st May 1938, nine in every ten local authorities had agreed to come into the scheme.

More difficult than securing their consent to nominate a Committee was to determine its composition and numbers—another problem that had troubled the earlier Ministry of Food. It was first suggested that there should be twelve members, four representing local retailers and eight the general public. The non-trade seats presented little difficulty, though the Co-operative movement did put forward a claim that it should be represented as 'the only body of organised consumers in the country'. For the trade seats, however, there was a regular scramble. The retail co-operative societies wanted one seat for their officials (their members, of course, were entitled to sit as consumers); the butchers' and grocers' organisations wanted to be empowered to nominate representatives. Officials of the Grocers' Federation and the Co-operative Union agreed to support each other's claims for a trade seat.

The Department, fearing that nominated members might be able to use the Committee as a means of putting trade pressure on the Ministry of Food, sought allies by calling upon the bakers and dairymen, who, since they did not deal in foods expected to be rationed, had not hitherto been consulted, to give their views on the filling of trade seats; and as it had expected and hoped, these strongly opposed giving grocers and butchers preferential treatment. The controversy dragged on for months; it was eventually settled by increasing the membership to fifteen seats, of which five should be traders; one a co-operative official, one a private butcher, one a private grocer, and the remaining two, other retailers. Traders were not to be eligible for non-trade seats; and all appointments were to be made by the local authority, subject to the approval of the Food Controller.

So far as ration documents were concerned, the Beveridge Sub-Committee had been content to begin where the last Ministry of Food had left off. 'So far as we can judge, the form of leaves [of the ration book] and instructions used in July 1918 are as good a basis to start from as anything we could devise now'. It had pointed out, however, that provided the customer was tied to the retailer, detachable coupons could, and at any rate at the beginning of war should, be dispensed with in order to save time in the shops. They were only necessary if, for instance, meat meals in restaurants required the surrender of a coupon, or two foods, for instance meat and bacon, that are habitually bought at different shops, were subjected to a joint ration. Otherwise the counterfoils lodged with the retailer and making up his register of customers provided a sufficient basis for supplies.

So far as the major foods to be rationed were concerned, the Food (Defence Plans) Department rejected this contention out of hand. Some people might not want to take up their rations, and the retailer's right to buy must be adjusted not to his nominal roll of customers but to his actual requirements. 'The disciplinary control of the retailer is a matter of the first importance', it wrote in 1937; and it proposed to discipline him, not merely by requiring him to collect and account for coupons, but also by insisting on returns of stock, sales and purchases of rationed food at frequent intervals. In this attitude it was, paradoxically enough, reinforced by the attitude of the traders themselves to a suggestion that for commodities not expected to be very scarce—sugar,[1] tea and cheese—there should be 'registration' without rationing. Representatives of retail butchers, grocers, and co-operative stores rejected almost unanimously, in January 1938, any half-way house between complete freedom and coupon rationing, as placing too much responsibility on the trader and favouring the dishonest at the expense of the honest. It was this alone that led to the inclusion of sugar coupons in the first war-time ration book.

Another departure from previous suggestions was the decision to print ration documents in advance of hostilities. Sir William Beveridge's advice, both in 1933 to the Sub-Committee on Prices, and in 1936, had, on the basis of experience in 1918, been that two or three months would be sufficient time in which to get the rationing machine into operation and that, therefore, documents need not be printed in advance. The Department felt that rationing might be required not more than a month after war broke out, and was prepared to make do with an interim, simplified scheme for three months while the documents for the full scheme were being printed. The Stationery Office, facing an avalanche of printing orders to be executed urgently

---

[1] The principal reason adduced for rationing sugar was to reassure the public that the queues of the last war would not recur.

on the outbreak, could not guarantee to deliver interim ration cards under a month or full ration books under six months. There was nothing for it but to abandon the interim scheme and print sufficient ration documents for the permanent scheme before war broke out. [1]

This decision, though made on grounds of administrative convenience, implied some attempt to anticipate food policy, i.e. to decide what was likely to be rationed. In the absence of an expert appraisal of shipping, foreign exchange and the other relevant prospects, the Department had to fall back on rule of thumb; a desire to make provision against all likely contingencies warred with the need to keep down the bulk and cost of the ration book. In the end, named coupons were provided in the draft book for six commodities: meat, bacon, butter, margarine, cooking fat, and sugar. Three spare sets of coupons and four further spare counterfoils were added for insurance purposes. [2] The provision for ration books for special classes of consumer—children, adolescents, heavy workers—also rested on previous practice. The decision to make six, rather than eight, the age at which a child should qualify for a full meat ration was indeed verified by expert advice; not knowing what the general supply position would be, the experts could not be positive whether supplies of extra meat should be given to adolescents or heavy workers; and the Department's decision to print special ration books for these classes was its own. [3]

Yet another point on which the Department parted company with the Beveridge Sub-Committee was in insisting that there should be no irrevocable link, overt or covert, between the rationing machinery and the proposals for a National Register that were being worked out by the Registrar-General. The Registrar-General had not only been a member of the Beveridge Sub-Committee; he was also the author of the central clearing house for sugar 'ration papers' that had been scrapped in mid-passage in 1918[4] in favour of a purely local system of issuing ration documents and registering consumers. He was still convinced that the latter would have broken down in the long run for want of a central index that could keep pace with births, deaths and migrations; and he held that a National Register, compiled by the

---

[1] Approval for advance printing was given in July 1937, but for technical reasons it was not until after the Munich crisis that printing actually began.

[2] Other candidates for inclusion were cheese, tea, bread, milk, jam, fish, potatoes, green vegetables, fruit, and eggs.

[3] Only enough books were printed for *boys* between 13 and 18. The outcry from women's organisations that this would provoke (and did provoke in 1939, when news of the proposal got abroad) seems to have been entirely unforeseen.

[4] See Chapter I. The accounts of this episode in Beveridge (*British Food Control*, p. 188 *sq.*) and in the secret history of the first Ministry of Food are in some respects incomplete. The reasons for which the central index was discontinued were transient and partly political ones which had nothing to do with its merits in principle. This was not clearly understood by the Food (Defence Plans) Department; hence, in part, its unwillingness to be closely associated with the reincarnation of the index in the National Register.

simultaneous enumeration of the whole population, as at a census, would be indispensable to the Food Controller as a check on fraud and duplication. He persuaded the Beveridge Sub-Committee to recommend that a detachable portion of the national registration certificate, or identity card, might be used as a voucher for the initial issue of ration books. It might be sent to the Food Office along with a household application form, such as had been used in the last war. The primary purpose of National Registration, that of enforcing military conscription, would thus be at once cloaked and reinforced by its rationing functions.

The Department was prepared to agree that an up-to-date National Register at the point when rationing was decided on would be useful, but found both political and administrative objections to proclaiming that it was indispensable. A National Register compiled (as was at one time proposed) in peace-time, would lack the rationing sanction on which the Registrar-General relied to make it continuously effective, and therefore could not be relied on to form the basis for a ration book issue; people could not be denied rations because they had lost their identity cards in the interval. Conversely, the Department dared not run the risk that a Cabinet decision against an immediate National Register, whether on political grounds or on account of population movements at the outbreak of war, should leave it without the means of introducing rationing. It did not want a future Food Controller to find himself tied, on purely administrative grounds, to an unpopular policy of conscription.

Even Sir John Anderson's announcement, in December 1938, that a National Register would be compiled immediately war broke out did not cause it to abandon its desire for independence or its own household application forms.[1] It did now agree that the enumeration schedules for the National Register should be so drafted as to be capable of use for the issue of ration books; but insisted that nothing should be said or done that might conceivably hint that the schemes were mutually dependent. It would not allow the enumeration schedule or identity card to contain any rationing reference, even the code letters 'R.B.1', 'R.B.2', etc., designating the different kinds of ration book; it would not hear of the identity card being printed with a detachable half that could be used as a ration book voucher, since its purpose would have to be disclosed in confidence to future National Registration Officers and might lead to confusion and outcry. The numerous local officials who doubled the shadow posts of Food Executive Officer and National Registration Officer must have wondered at the resulting contortions of the two Departments, as they scrupulously kept to the terms of the agreement between January

---

[1] They were the only ration documents whose printing had been completed at the time of the Munich crisis.

and August 1939; and rubbed their eyes when the B.B.C. announced flatly, off its own bat, that the proposed National Register would be used for food rationing.[1]

III

The crisis of September 1938 at once illustrated the need for the Department and the inadequate *tempo* at which its preparations had —through no fault of its own—been moving. Its main preoccupation during the days of crisis was inevitably with the air raid danger and evacuation, official and unofficial. For two days and nights the main flour mills were run continuously so that there might be adequate stocks in the 'safe' areas, to which large quantities of refined sugar were also moved. Last touches were hurriedly put to schemes for removing tea and butter stocks from London, supplying London with milk, decentralising Smithfield and Billingsgate Markets, and increasing to a maximum the output of the Hull oilseed crushers. Flour millers, sugar refiners, and wholesale provision merchants were asked to speed up deliveries to retailers as a measure of dispersion and to prevent local shortages owing to panic buying. This had begun in many districts; in Newcastle-on-Tyne the leading retail grocer's had to close its doors for a time; in Birmingham the Lord Mayor issued an appeal against hoarding. On 28th September the Department itself had to broadcast a similar appeal. Serious shortages would almost certainly have arisen had the Government evacuation scheme been put into operation. Reports of unofficial migration were alarming; the South Wales Divisional Food Officer reported that an estimated 130,000 people had fled into his Division within the first two or three days of the crisis.

An attempt was made to get together the emergency iron ration that it had been intended to provide for the 'official' refugees, estimated at two millions. 'By great good fortune'—says the official report on crisis measures—'there were sufficient stocks of canned beef, canned milk, and slab chocolate available', and thanks to the cooperation of the firms concerned, a satisfactory ration of these was provided at the scheduled railheads round London; or rather would have been, had not the Home Office revised the original evacuation train schedules twice within four days. The Department was less lucky with the fourth item in the iron ration, biscuits: 'it was found possible to scrape together a miscellaneous collection sufficient to provide one half-pound packet of biscuits per head for rather more than twenty-five per cent. of the estimated evacuees from London'; arrangements were, therefore, made for baking bread and rushing it

---

[1] 9 p.m. News, 16th August 1939.

to the railheads at thirty-six hours' notice. 'It is probable that the bread would have arrived, but the accumulation of thirty or forty thousand loaves at some stations and their distribution, possibly in heavy rain, would have been an appalling business'.

No amount of improvisation or good fortune could have quickly overcome the unreadiness of the commodity controls and rationing arrangements. The numerous traders who, during August and September 1938, had agreed to serve either at headquarters or as port or area officers for the various imported foodstuffs, found themselves without the tools for the job. The documents and records for requisitioning stocks and cargoes had not been prepared, nor the arrangements for allocating them when requisitioned; there was no means, for example, by which freights and dues on incoming cargoes could be paid. For meat and livestock alone had any detailed price arrangements been worked out. Not one of the numerous control Orders that would have been immediately necessary to give legal effect to the control schemes was ready in draft; nor were there legal powers to prevent panic hoarding, or to compel the dispersal of food from vulnerable areas. For minor foodstuffs, such as coffee and cocoa, fruit and vegetables, hops and alcoholic liquor, there was not even a paper plan of control. There were household application forms for ration books, but no ration books or permits to supply had yet been printed. The Department candidly admitted that there would 'have been a very real danger of a breakdown' if an attempt had been made to put the schemes into operation; it was still far too sanguine when it supposed that the dislocation could have been overcome within three or four weeks. Actually it was to take the Department's legal experts, when at last they were appointed at the end of March 1939, five *months'* incessant work to get the main schemes ready for instant operation. The printing of the principal ration books was completed only in August 1939; that of the permits and other traders' forms not until after the outbreak of war.[1]

Early in November 1938 a secret official inquest on the crisis accepted its clear lesson for food planning, namely that the task of preparing detailed control schemes for immediate operation was beyond even an enlarged and strengthened Food (Defence Plans) Department, and that the requirements of official secrecy must be so relaxed as to enable those who would staff the controls to be earmarked and brought into consultation forthwith. Bodies like the Wheat Commission and the Milk Marketing Board made suitable nuclei for the control of most important foodstuffs; the only exception was oils and fats, for which, after some hesitation, an offer from Lever

---

[1] When it found that the books, for technical reasons, would take so long to print the Department revived the scheme for temporary ration cards; these were ready by March 1939.

Brothers and Unilever Ltd., to provide the staff of a 'shadow' control was accepted.

During the early months of 1939 work went on apace; in April the Department at last became free of the leading-strings of the Board of Trade, when the Chancellor of the Duchy of Lancaster became the Minister responsible for food defence plans. The Department now turned to elaborating a constitution for the future Ministry as a whole. At the end of May this was sent forward to the Treasury, but owing to some accident did not reach its destination and had to be re-submitted in July. This hindered the earmarking of civil servants from other Departments for service in the Ministry of Food, but fortunately did not hinder the recruitment of trade staff. It became possible to visualise the overnight expansion of the existing Department, now enlarged to six Divisions from the original two, into a full-blown war-time Ministry.

From the very first discussion on organisation in 1936, there had been general agreement that the last-war Ministry had been insufficiently integrated, because it came into existence only when a great part of the field of food control was occupied by strong *ad hoc* organisations, particularly for wheat and sugar. Nevertheless, in these last few months before war broke out, those centrifugal tendencies, against which Sir William Beveridge had uttered a warning, showed themselves, particularly for those foods where a strong and expert marketing board or control commission existed. Thus it was proposed to establish a Cereals Control Board, staffed largely from the Wheat Commission; a similar proposal for sugar was dropped only at the eleventh hour; and the organisations for potatoes and milk looked as though they too might be difficult to keep in line with a general Ministry policy, acknowledge though they might the authority of the Minister.

To some extent these trends may have been unconscious; to some extent they were due to the expectation of heavy air raids and the proposals for removing Government departments from London. The Director of the Department, addressing trade advisers in April 1939, referred to this:—

> 'Trade Directors and Civil Servants associated with them will frequently have to act on their own judgement. The obtaining of covering authority from the Food Controller or the heads of the Ministry may often be impracticable'.

Nevertheless, the Department was confident that there would be no difficulty in subordinating trade interests to general policy; particularly as it had taken the greatest care in the selection of the persons to serve as commodity directors.

In the sphere of imports, provision had already been made to secure co-ordination, both in buying policy and the procurement of freight. Those responsible for planning shipping control had been quite prepared to allow the Cereals Control Board to do its own chartering; it was on the Food (Defence Plans) Department's own initiative that arrangements were made, in conjunction with the Baltic Exchange, for a central chartering office to be set up there on behalf of the Ministry of Food directly war should break out. Similar plans were made to take over all refrigerated liner space.

For import policy generally it was decided to set up a central Overseas Purchases Board, that should give general directions to the purchasing divisions, not merely after war broke out but at once. The need for such a 'shadow' board was cogently asserted:

'Each buying division, prior to the commencement of its activities, must know the aims of general policy as applied to this particular sphere and . . . the limits within which it can exercise discretion'.

To frame such a policy, having regard to nutritional, economic, and political circumstances, and to translate it into operational orders for each commodity or country involved, would be the duty of the Overseas Purchases Board. However, time was now too short, and the whole subject too unexplored, for the shadow Board to do very much. It had not got beyond a rather desultory discussion of individual commodities when war broke out.

IV

The enlargement of its staff made it possible for the Department to give renewed attention to the likely consequences of heavy air attacks on London immediately war should break out. Early in 1937 a good deal of preliminary work had been done on this, particularly on the dispersal of the largest stocks (tea, meat, butter, and cheese) and plans were reported to have been ready at the time of the Munich crisis. Further investigation, in which an outside transport expert took part, suggested that existing schemes were inadequate and over-sanguine about transport possibilities. Of the numerous reforms and new plans proposed, there was only time for one—the revision of dispersal arrangements for 10,000 tons each of meat and butter, and 60,000 tons of tea. Thanks to the Port of London Authority and the railways, it proved possible to arrange for the simultaneous, instead of the successive, removal of the meat and butter upon a given signal. The original proposal to move tea by rail was abandoned in favour of a dispersal, partly to the provinces by canal and coaster, partly along the whole length of London river by Thames lighters. The transport problem was thus settled; but another question arose for decision almost at the last moment. The control schemes provided, of course, for requisition of tea, meat, and butter stocks once war had broken out; the dispersal arrangements were timed for the 'precautionary' stage. Ought the Department to requisition stocks earmarked for dispersal, or all stocks, directly a decision to disperse was taken? The point arose most acutely in the case of tea, because blenders are accustomed to make daily withdrawals of tea from bond, and if some only of these withdrawals were stopped by requisitioning, some blenders would gain an advantage over others through being able to continue producing their standard blends. The tea trade, therefore, pressed for complete requisition at once and the immediate introduction of the proposed National Control Tea. The Department for its part could not take any decision at all until it knew whether it would have the legal power to requisition in the precautionary period—knowledge which did not reach it until 28th August. On 30th August the decision was taken to requisition only the stocks actually moved; and the next day instructions were given for the dispersal to begin.

The legal uncertainty overhanging requisition extended to every aspect of the Department's preparations. Not until the end of March 1939 had it acquired a legal staff of its own. Hitherto it had relied on the Board of Trade Solicitor; but he and his staff could not, if only because they were housed some distance away, give the food plans the constant attention required if they were to be ready by 1st August —the deadline set for the Department after the inquest on Munich. Commodity schemes required Orders for taking over plant and requisitioning stocks. Constitutions, memoranda and articles of association must be drawn up for the companies it was proposed to set up under the meat and bacon schemes. In short, the proposals of the planners, as they took detailed shape, had to be clothed in, and often trimmed to fit, an appropriate legal garb; and this task, involving months of patient and strenuous labour, had to be undertaken without certain knowledge of the legal framework into which they must fit. An Emergency Powers (Defence) Bill and a full code of Defence Regulations had been in draft ever since 1937, and their main provisions—including the Regulation for control of industry[1] under which the Food Controller would act—had not been substantially changed thereafter. The form these powers would take, therefore, was well known. What remained necessarily uncertain was whether the Government of the day would take any or all of them at the very outset of a war crisis. It might prefer, on political grounds especially, to take preliminary defence measures under Regulations not backed by a specific Act of Parliament, that is to rely solely on the Royal Prerogative in the first instance. Promptness being of the essence of the food control orders, the Food (Defence Plans) Department's legal advisers were constrained to draw them up in two forms

---

[1] Defence Regulation 55.

accordingly. Despite the extra labour involved, every Order deemed to be essential was ready when the time came.

Thus painfully but surely the food defence plans advanced towards completion. 'Rehearsals' of the main commodity schemes were undertaken in late July, and the Director of the Department, in evidence before the Prime Minister's advisory panel of industrialists who were looking into emergency preparations, felt able to say that the working out of the schemes was going extremely well.

> 'The aspect of our preparations'—he said—'which still gives a good deal of anxiety is not really at the centre of affairs at all. The great difficulty is to get one's ideas and plans down into the minds of the persons who are going to work them, shall we say in Pembroke, Inverness and Cornwall . . . the problem is largely one of time . . . if we are given another three or four months that is the thing that we shall have to concentrate on most'.

Then again, the all-important task of selecting trade directors and advisers had been a lengthy business. There were still gaps in the plans to fill in, and others, such as the problem of the remuneration of controlled firms, that could not be filled in until the war actually came. Nevertheless he was confident that 'if an emergency occurred next week all these schemes would function'—a statement that could scarcely have been made three months earlier.

Broadly speaking it was true to say that the tasks the Department had set itself in 1936 had been, by August 1939, completed; the divisional and local organisation was ready to function, the emergency supplies for the four million persons expected to leave London and the large towns under the official evacuation schemes were delivered to the destination stations; the main ration books (though not the equally important permits) were printed and distributed throughout the country. A scheme for the emergency marketing of fresh fish was ready; plans were afoot to increase the country's capacity for hydrogenating whale oil, to build reserve warehouses inland, to promote a Bill that would oblige owners of food factories to take A.R.P. measures. The Department's storage division, having acquired bulk stocks of wheat, sugar, and whale oil, and emergency iron rations for the evacuation scheme, had now got down to useful refinements, like subsidising an increase in bakers' flour stocks and creating a reserve of plum pulp for jam.

One important piece of preparation must be mentioned at this stage, though its details fall without the scope of the civil histories, the arrangement whereby the Ministry of Food would undertake responsibility for bulk supplies of food to the Services. In 1914–18 the existence of separate procurement agencies for the armed forces, even after the establishment of the Ministry of Food which was in some degree modelled on them, had been a constant source of friction, difficulty, and expense. Co-ordinated buying, under the Inter-Allied Food Council, had been established only in August 1918. In November 1936, almost at the same time as the decision to set up the Food (Defence Plans) Department was being taken, representatives of the three Services were reporting in favour of co-ordinating service and civilian food procurement. Thereafter close liaison between civilian and military and naval plans was maintained through a special inter-departmental committee; and at the outbreak of war a Services Supplies Branch was duly set up within the Ministry of Food.

The adequacy of these preparations—and some others that can be more conveniently analysed in relation to the problems as they arose in war-time—will have to be assessed in the light of events. But the work of the Department can also be referred back to the criteria laid down by Sir William Beveridge in 1936. Three of these four had been satisfied by September 1939, except in so far as their satisfaction was conditional upon the fourth. The Food Controller was to be appointed with full powers as from the first day of war; the machinery of control for each essential food was ready; certain precautions against an initial air attack had been taken. But behind all these measures there lay no clearly defined, generally agreed 'feeding policy,' whether this be looked at from the nutritional or the economic point of view, nor any consistent conception of the situation and needs of the civilian population in time of war.

The contradictions, open or latent, that resulted from the want of such a conception may be exemplified on every side of the preparations affecting food; the mild and gradual controls proposed for shipping and inland transport were in sharp contrast with the drastic immediacy of the food controls. So too the Ministry of Health had taken over from the Air Staff a grim picture of air-raid victims being buried *en masse*, of hospital beds being wanted by the hundred thousand within a matter of weeks.[1] But the food planners had devised a rationing scheme of infinite precision and complication, of manifold internal checks and balances, that might well have broken down under the conditions of social dislocation that other officials were envisaging. Much of the story of war-time food control is the story of how, and how far, these contradictions were ironed out by the pressure of events.

---

[1] For the origin of this assumption see Titmuss, R. M., *Problems of Social Policy*, Chapter II (in this series).

PART II

CHAPTER IV

The Structure of Food Control, 1939-40

I

THE second Ministry of Food was formally established by Order in Council[1] on 8th September 1939. Mr. W. S. Morrison, K.C., M.P., who as Chancellor of the Duchy of Lancaster had been the Minister responsible for the last few months of food defence planning, became the first Minister of Food; at his personal request the title Food Controller was not revived. The powers relating to food hitherto exercised by the Board of Trade were thereupon transferred to the new Ministry; the Defence Regulations by virtue of which it must operate were already in force.

Though legally and politically the Ministry was brought into existence overnight, the growth of its administrative machine was less, though still very, rapid. The staff at headquarters, numbering about 350 at the outbreak of war, had multiplied by ten by March 1940. So great an expansion could not but be accompanied by many detailed changes in organisation; nevertheless, the Ministry, in the comparatively settled form it had achieved by the summer of 1940, bore the main features that had been implicit in the Food (Defence Plans) Department of 1936, and that were to survive well beyond the actual war period. It will be convenient to sketch those features as they appeared then, because this was the only occasion on which a complete recasting of the organisation was ever proposed—partly as the result of an investigation by an 'organisation and methods' expert serving in the Treasury, partly because Lord Woolton, who had succeeded Mr. Morrison in April 1940, asked that the Department should overhaul its organisation in preparation for the trials ahead.

On the trading side, or *Supply Department*, of the Ministry, the unit was the *Commodity Division or Branch*.[2] For each controlled food there was a Trade Director or Directors, having general responsibility for

---

[1] The Ministers of the Crown (Minister of Food) Order, 1939. S.R. & O. No. 1119.

[2] Throughout this volume the word *division* will be used in this context. *Branch* was used in the early stages, when several commodities might be grouped in one division under an Assistant Secretary. The distinction is one of presumed importance rather than of function.

N.B.—The use of *division* in the headquarters organisation must be distinguished from its territorial sense, *i.e.* denoting a unit of *regional* organisation. The word *region* is now (1950) employed.

the Ministry's dealings in that particular food up to the point at which it passed out of Ministry ownership. The subdivision of responsibility as between, say, importing, manufacture, and distribution, varied from commodity to commodity in accordance with circumstances; the Director of one major food might have subordinates charged with these matters, the Director of another be acknowledged as *primus inter pares*.

Besides the headquarters commodity organisation, which was often exceedingly small in numbers, most Divisions had area commodity officers, charged with a general oversight of supply and distribution in that area. Some (for instance Meat and Bacon) had *agents* in the principal ports. Even so, the Divisions did not generally concern themselves with the actual handling of foodstuffs; in accordance with the principle of using the trade as far as possible, this work was usually given over to groups of traders either already in existence or formed *ad hoc*. (Meat was exceptional in that slaughtering of home-fed animals was undertaken by men employed directly by the Ministry.) The arrangements for this had formed one of the more arduous tasks of the Food (Defence Plans) Department.[1] In effect, traders were to become the Ministry's agents on a fee basis; the assessment of the fees was a complicated matter, but fortunately the traders agreed to act first and leave till later the precise form and amount of their remuneration.

Complementing the Supply Department was all that part of the Ministry concerned with providing a yardstick by which Commodity Divisions could gauge their allocations, where it was not thought sufficient to base these on a datum level of past performance. This, comprising what was called at its zenith the *Divisional and Local Services Department*, was charged, basically, with issuing, renewing, and maintaining *documents of entitlement* to controlled food—consumers' ration books, retailers', caterers' and other permits. As such it came into continual contact with the public and those traders who directly served it, and its unit was the local Food Office—some 1,500 in England and Wales, about fifty in Scotland.[2]

Between the local Food Offices and Headquarters there were interposed the Divisional Food Offices—thirteen in England and Wales, five in Scotland.[3] Their purpose was, under normal war-time conditions, to oversee the work of the local offices and the functioning of control generally; in the divisional offices were officers responsible for supply, rationing, enforcement, transport, and so forth. But the Divisional Food Officer had also another latent function. He formed part of the Regional System for Civil Defence, and should a break-

---

[1] They will be discussed in detail in Vol. II.

[2] See Chapter III.

[3] There was also a Chief Divisional Food Officer for the whole of Scotland.

down of communications occur and responsibility for government in the region be assumed by the Regional Commissioner, the Divisional Food Officer would become his Food Controller.

This dual function affected food control in two ways. In the first place it meant that the Divisional areas were determined, not by the lines of flow of food distribution, but by extraneous considerations; they were identical, in fact, with the regions established for civil emergencies under the Emergency Powers Act of 1920. Some Food Divisions, for example those based on Glasgow, Manchester and Newcastle, might be considered viable if cut off from the rest of the country; others, such as those based on Caernarvon and Chelmsford, were almost certainly not. In the second place, it sharpened the conflict of jurisdiction between the Divisional Food Office and the Area Offices of the Commodity Divisions. It was clear, for instance, that in emergency the Area Meat and Livestock Officer would come under the Divisional Food Officer's orders; and it was natural that the latter should want to establish his authority over the former ahead of the emergency. It was no less natural that the Trade Director at headquarters should insist that *his* authority should not be invaded.

Nor was it open to the Ministry to resolve these differences by fiat from above, on officers who had no career to consider and who often were giving their services. Some of the difficulties might have been forestalled in the pre-war stage—one Area Meat and Livestock Office was in a locality many miles from a Divisional Food Office, for no better reason than that the individual selected for the post lived there. Once the organisation was established, the Ministry had to content itself with making changes that would, at any rate, secure closer geographical contact. But it seldom got as near perfection as at Glasgow, where from the beginning all the Area Commodity Officers were housed in the same building as the Divisional Office.

As things turned out, this particular conflict of jurisdiction had no serious results. But it was only one among several. Besides the Area Commodity Officers, there were other officials whose allegiance and authority were not rigidly defined. The Transport Division had Port Food Movement Officers who might or might not have the right to overrule the port officers of other Divisions. How did they, and how did the Assistant Divisional Food Officers (Transport) stand in relation to the Divisional Food Officer, particularly where he too was located in a port?[1] An over-assertion of personality in these cases might gravely affect the Ministry's efficiency.

Moreover, until 1941, when the Trade Directors were explicitly granted overlordship within their headquarters divisions, their own authority remained undefined and partial. For each had set along-

[1] See below, Chapter IX.

E

side him an administrator—sometimes a career civil servant, sometimes not—whose voice was the voice of general Ministry policy and who, unlike the Trade Director, was integrated into the civil service hierarchy. For each division also there was a Finance Director, a professional accountant responsible to the Financial Secretary and thence to the Permanent Secretary as Accounting Officer—to say nothing of a statistician responsible to the Director of Statistics.

Such a Ministry—whose apparent want of cohesion was rubbed home by the dispersion of its headquarter offices, particularly after the move to Colwyn Bay in June 1940—was a sight to appal the tidy-minded. No wonder it both evoked and defied an attempt at root-and-branch reconstruction. Yet one may say that if the Ministry of Food's main problem of organisation—that of integrating innumerable pieces of administration—was never wholly solved, it never got completely out of hand. The Ministry did contrive something more than the appearance of wholeness; it was never a mere aggregation of separate controls.

II

The chief weakness of the organisation of food control, as seen by the would-be reformers, was its subdivision vertically by commodities rather than horizontally in terms of the stages through which food must pass from producer to consumer. They proposed the breaking-up of commodity divisions into functional parts and their reintegration into separate pyramids of responsibility. Instead of a Director of Sugar, taking charge of sugar from oversea purchase to the point where it left Ministry control, there would be separate Directorates of, say, Sugar Supply, Sugar Refining, and Sugar Distribution, each forming part, together with similar divisions for other commodities, of a separate Department of the Ministry.

This functional arrangement, it was claimed, would get rid of much overlapping between different parts of the organisation. It would help to solve the problem of Trade Director *vis-à-vis* Civil Servant by removing the need for a trade man of sufficient stature to cover the whole field. It would dispose of the very real difficulty that foods change their identity in the course of moving from producer to ultimate consumer, and that a division of responsibility based on the earliest form in which they happened to come under control might be inappropriate at the later stages. It would ensure that proper weight was given to problems of distribution as contrasted with those of supply.

Had it been propounded before the war, this scheme might have got further than the drawing-board stage. One cannot but feel that, even so, its application might have proved more difficult than its sponsors appear to have imagined. The functional approach, invaluable though it is in the understanding of an administrative problem, regrettably neglected though it was in much of the pre-war planning, is a limited guide when it comes to setting up detailed machinery for dealing with individual trades. The Food (Defence Plans) Department had not made the mistake of imposing an *a priori* pattern of control; the need for working through the trade and of securing a smooth transition from peace to war had saved it from that. Its Commodity Divisions might seem untidy, but their untidiness was rooted in the soil of history; the pre-war organisation of the food trades, offend though it did against orderly notions, at any rate kept the country fed.

These arguments applied with even greater force once the war had started and the pattern of food control had been established. Even were it true that the dividing line between functions could readily be drawn—and there was a hint to the contrary in the reformers' own uncertainty whether home supplies should be grouped with overseas supplies or wholesale distribution—to introduce it after a year of war might have created fresh confusion at a critical moment. Moreover, there were obvious personal difficulties in the way of suddenly depriving the Ministry's Directors, chosen for their very pre-eminence in their trades, of a great part of their authority.

It was not as if the existing arrangements, for all their want of clear definition, had led to unresolvable difficulties in working any Commodity Division. Those arising from personal want of *rapport* could not be cured by reorganisation; for the rest, traders, civil servants, and the many others, such as accountants and dons, who made up the Ministry, worked together amicably—more so, perhaps, after the move of most of them to Colwyn Bay compelled them to spend much even of their leisure in one another's company. In the later years of the Ministry, conflict of view tended to be between, rather than within, different Divisions; on broad matters of outlook rather than in day-to-day administration.

Moreover, the Minister had ordered the review of organisation in August 1940; by the time it was complete, the Ministry was in the midst of the critical winter of 1940–41. The conclusion that changes should be in the line of past developments, that instead of tearing down the edifice it should be furnished with buttresses and cross-ties, was inescapable.

There had already come into existence, during 1939–40, two elements making for better co-ordination of policy and administration than was provided for by the repository of ultimate authority in the Minister and the Permanent Secretary.[1] The first was the establishment of a number of internal committees to deal with problems common to a number of Divisions. One of these—the Overseas Purchases Board—had begun before the war, and, together with a series of sub-committees, had from the first effectively dealt with import policy. Equally important was the Orders Committee, set up in December 1939, by which all proposals initiated by Divisions for the issue or amendment of Statutory Rules and Orders had to be approved before being put into force. The Margins Committee, whose purpose was to harmonise the principles on which prices and margins of profit were allowed to traders in controlled foods, was only less so because, for special reasons, certain important foods like milk and bread were excluded from its operations. The virtue of these Committees was that they enabled views to be exchanged at a sufficiently early stage of action, preventing those at the very top of the Ministry from being overburdened with a flow of inconsistent proposals, or projects that had already been tried and found wanting by other Divisions.

The second element consisted in the growth of a staff whose task it was to think ahead, and which ideally should be free from day-to-day administrative preoccupation. From September 1939 onwards there had been an Economics Division, which had promoted coherent thought and action on diverse matters such as price and import policy. The Statistics and Intelligence Division had conceived of itself as a creative, policy-making force, and indeed had not been spared the accusation that it was trespassing on the territory of the administrators. Last but not least, the Ministry in March 1940 had appointed as Chief Scientific Adviser a distinguished biochemist who had originally come on to its staff as Adviser on the protection of food against poison gas. But this machinery of forethought was as yet imperfectly co-ordinated; and the Economics Division in particular had been distracted from its real task—formulating principles—by a mixture of administrative jobs that, like the allocation of raw materials to food manufacturers, had come to it because they were no one else's business, together with detailed and controversial negotiations over agricultural prices.

It was for these reasons, rather than any want of talent, that the Minister could write in August 1940:

> 'I find the administration of the Ministry vague in the matter of economic policy. . . . This [the Economics] Division does not get its opinions into the machine early enough for them to be useful. . . . I do not think we have gone as far in the direction of co-operation between the Commodity and Economic Divisions as is possible. . . .'

---

[1] A force making in the opposite direction was removed when the Cereals Control Board was abolished, and replaced by a Division of the Ministry, in June 1940.

and again, referring to such problems as that of cheap food for poor consumers:

'I know that this problem has been in the mind of the Economics Division: that its views have not got into the machinery of the Ministry is demonstrated by the fact that the pressure to consider the problem of communal feeding, factory feeding, etc., had to come from outside of the administrative organisation.[1]

I find in practice that the Minister is lacking in the stimulative service that such a department is able to render to him on the political economic field'.

It was in response to these comments that officials conceived the idea of a *General Department* within the Ministry. While in no sense the superior of the other two Departments, it should be

'the focus, under the Secretary, for the consideration and presentation of all questions of general policy, whether emanating from the Minister or the Secretary, from outside the Ministry, from the Departments at Colwyn Bay, or arising within the General Department itself. . . .'

'The General Department should so conduct itself as to avoid being thought of by the other Departments, and particularly by the Trade Directors, as a body of theorists, or critics, or superior persons interfering with and hampering people who know their own job and want to get on with it. . . . The business of the General Department . . . is to help and relieve the other Departments, by exploring, in consultation with them, problems affecting more than one Department; by collating the views of different Departments on common problems; by foreseeing, so far as they can, the emergence of new problems before their solution becomes urgent; and generally providing the machinery through which the thought processes of the Ministry as a conscious entity, as distinct from the separate elements which compose it, may function with the greatest possible measure of success'.

These words of the Secretary to the Ministry, written in November 1940 just before the General Department was brought into existence, mark the very great advance that had been made in little more than a year, not so much in the Ministry's outward and visible organisation as in its ideas about itself. It was indeed a far cry from the semi-independent commodity controls of 1939, from the notion, expressed by one official on the day after war started, that 'the Ministry should have available some general advisers, e.g. economic. . . . A main object is to get public confidence; but I think we should do well to have such people watching developments, e.g. prices generally', to the conception of a whole Department charged with planning on a wide front. The degree in which this conception was realised in practice forms a major, if largely implicit, theme of this history. Here one need only emphasise its existence, as revealing the

---

[1] i.e. from the Deputy Prime Minister (Mr. Attlee). Communal feeding will be fully discussed in Vol. II.

extent to which, by the autumn of 1940, the Ministry had taken the measure of its task.

One other point is worth mentioning about the review of the Ministry's functions; the Minister's own insistence on the importance of good public relations. 'It is not enough', he wrote in August 1940

'to have the food in the country and to be an efficient organisation for distributing it. We have to give the public a sense of confidence that they are being cared for. It is the business of the public relations department not only to maintain public confidence in the Ministry, but to reflect back to the Ministry public opinion and the trends of public opinion'.

Lord Rhondda was said to have 'set up a "press barrage" of favourable opinion behind which his department could work without disturbance'.[1] So too the second Ministry of Food, under Lord Woolton, employed all the resources of modern publicity to explain what it was doing and why. This public relations work deserves a specialist monograph to itself; in the critical years of the war its importance would be difficult to overrate. But the Ministry's sense of being responsible, not only to Parliament and informed public opinion, but to each and every individual citizen with whose feeding it felt itself to be charged, went beyond the confines of the Public Relations Division. It was present, acknowledged or unacknowledged, at almost every decision that might affect the consumer. The principle that the ration, be it meagre or generous, must at all costs be honoured was an overriding consideration that turned the scales at many a departmental conference. It would be tedious to cite it in discussing every occasion where it was relevant; but it may be taken for granted as a constant undertone of policy.

III

The emergence of the Ministry of Food as a single organism, conscious of direction and purpose, had another aspect than that of its relation to its component parts. It was reflected in the Ministry's relationship to other Departments and to the network of Cabinet committees responsible for the central direction of the war. The image of the Ministry, as it appears in these internal discussions of 1940, as the prime mover in all matters concerning food, had not been so clearly defined a year earlier.

The Permanent Secretary to the Treasury, transmitting to the Lord Privy Seal (Sir Samuel Hoare) the Prime Minister's suggestion that the Home Policy Committee of the War Cabinet should set up a

---

[1] *D. A. Thomas, Viscount Rhondda*, by his daughter and others, pp. 246–47; Beveridge, *op. cit.* pp. 74–77.

Sub-Committee on Food Policy, could write, on 23rd November 1939:

> '. . . it does not seem to have been very clearly laid down in the C.I.D. papers which led to the establishment of the Ministry of Food that that Ministry was to be regarded as responsible for food policy in general, over and above their responsibility for the purchase and distribution of food. But there can be scarcely any doubt that the Ministry will in fact and in practice be expected to shoulder the general responsibility'.

The difference of emphasis between 1939 and 1940 was a great deal more than verbal. The discussions on rationing[1] in the autumn of 1939 indicate a feeling among Ministers that food *policy*, as distinct from food *administration*, was a Cabinet matter, not merely in the sense that the Minister of Food should take counsel with his colleagues, but that the initiative ought to rest with them rather than with him. The concept of the Food Policy Sub-Committee as a creative force rather than a clearing house seems to show itself also in the parallel appointment of a sub-committee of senior officials.[2] Throughout Mr. Chamberlain's administration, the voices of other Departments made themselves heard on food policy quite as loudly as that of the Ministry of Food. The food production campaign for the first year of war was mainly framed, not only as to means but as to ends, by the Agricultural Departments; and it was the Minister of Health who expounded, in accordance with his Department's long-standing responsibilities, the basic principles of nutrition which food policy would ignore at the nation's peril; whether in pointing out that sugar rationing must lead to a higher consumption of other energy foods, or insisting on the paramount importance of maintaining milk production and stimulating milk consumption.

It is conceivable that, given the leadership and organisation of the Lord President's Committee of 1941, the Food Policy Committee might have taken firm control in its allotted sphere, and have evolved and enforced a coherent food policy of which the Ministries of Food and Agriculture were but the agents. The debates of the Committee were fruitful in general principles; but it never assumed a directing role. Like its predecessor before the war, the Food Sub-Committee of the Committee of Imperial Defence, it did not gather round it that body of expert knowledge without which a central planning machine cannot function.

So, too, the other committees of 1939–40, whether ministerial, like the Economic Policy Committee, or official, like the Inter-depart-

---

[1] Chapter VIII, below.

[2] This did not survive the Chamberlain Government. At the same time as it was abolished, in May 1940, the Ministerial Committee was reconstituted without change of departmental representation, as a full Committee of the War Cabinet. It will be referred to throughout this history simply as the 'Food Policy Committee'.

mental Committee on Food Prices, can scarcely be said to have transcended, except perhaps on occasion, the day-to-day issues that required urgent settlement. Here again a principal reason can be found in the rudimentary development of an economic general staff,[1] such as served the Lord President's Committee at its zenith. The resulting inter-departmental conflict cannot but have hastened the development of such staffs within individual Ministries; the Ministry of Food's General Department, that is to say, was designed to strengthen the Ministry both within and without.

It was not that the General Department was narrowly departmental in outlook. On the contrary; it would be truer to say that at times it ranged over areas whose connection with the business of food control in war-time was perhaps a little esoteric. Certainly there was to be a tendency to move, if only in the realm of speculation, into territory that in a strict sense belonged to other Ministries. Certainly also some of its fact-finding—in the realm of minimum stock-levels for instance—was tinged with normative considerations of a kind that might not have been present in an inquiry undertaken, say, by the Central Statistical Office. In short, there were elements of overlap and of departmental bias present that might have been avoided, or more readily discounted, had the governmental planning intelligence developed on more centralised lines. On the other hand, there was merit, even from the sheer point of view of vulnerability, in dispersing thought as well as action; and it was certainly vital to maintain close contact between the two. Hence the decision first, that the General Department, though centred on London, should be represented alongside the other Departments evacuated to Colwyn Bay; and secondly, that certain parts of those Departments should themselves remain in London.

Criticism of the working of the whole Ministry must be tempered by recognition of these geographical factors. It was not merely a matter of London and Colwyn Bay: the Potato Division and at various times the Fish Division and those dealing with jam, pickles and sauces, were at Oxford; the Imported Cereals Division was run throughout the war from Mr. J. V. Rank's house at Godstone; Liquid Milk was at Thames Ditton, also in Surrey, but Condensed and Dried Milk were in Colwyn Bay; Canned Fish was for a time in Liverpool. Senior officials of the Ministry spent much of their lives in railway trains, and the filing and transit of documents became exceedingly complicated.

Had the dispersal taken place at the outbreak of war, the handicaps of distance might, one feels, have been fatal to the development of a

---

[1] See Hancock and Gowing, *op. cit.* pp. 92–95, 220–223. The treatment in that volume perhaps exaggerates the extent to which even the Lord President's Committee exercised positive direction over, as distinct from effective adjudication in, general economic questions. Later chapters in the present study will offer some evidence on this point.

sufficient unity of purpose and direction. The nine months during which the greater part of the Ministry remained in London were just—but only just—sufficient for its staff to become used to working together, and to get the feel of the problems they must jointly tackle. Control was still confined to a few major foodstuffs; the supply situation did not as yet call for heroic measures such as might have overtaxed it before it had been properly run in. On the other hand, the experience had been testing enough to suggest that, so far as it went, the organisation was free from fatal weakness. Except for one food—fresh fish, whose circumstances were altogether exceptional[1]— nothing had happened to shake either the Ministry's self-confidence or public confidence in the administration of food control.

When Mr. Neville Chamberlain reconstructed his Government in April 1940 he brought in from outside politics to be Minister of Food a well-known Liverpool business man, Lord Woolton, whose name was to become identified in the public mind with food control during the back-to-the-wall period of Mr. Churchill's national coalition Government. This official history does not set out to discuss the contribution of individuals to the war effort, nor do the sources on which it relies afford the kind of personal evidence on which such a discussion must mainly rest. But it seems right to record here that the new Minister took over from his predecessor a Department already formed as to most of its essentials, already set upon the paths it was to tread, and embodying a tradition that went back not a few months, but twenty-odd years.

---

[1] It will be discussed in Vol. II.

CHAPTER V

Import Problems in the First Year of War

I

THE problem of imports, as it would face the Ministry of Food at the outbreak of war, was two-fold. It was, immediately and continuously, *operational*; that of taking over in working order, and without interruption, the machine of private enterprise. The requisitioning of cargoes on arrival, their unloading, sorting and transport under Ministry control to designated stores or controlled processing plant; this, the first stage in the assumption of authority, must simultaneously be accompanied by the substitution of direct Ministry or Ministry-licensed procurement for open market operations. Henceforth the Government would undertake continuous responsibility for procuring, shipping, and allocating to the distributor or processor all the major food supplies of the country. It would become, overnight, the greatest world trader in imported food-stuffs.

That operational task would be, in any circumstances, an exacting one, though eased by the fact that all the experience of the food trades would be at the Government's disposal. But it represented only half what had to be done. The other half would concern *policy*; the determination of a programme to govern the multitudinous separate jobs that would make up the day-to-day work of the importing divisions. A programme would be necessary, not only because the substitution of a directed for a free economy prescribes the formulation of known rules by which operations must be guided, but also because the fact of war itself might be expected to create shortages of one or more of the elements that made unrestricted food imports possible—shipping, foreign exchange, port capacity, perhaps even food itself.

In the last months of peace, the Food (Defence Plans) Department had begun to attend to this question of an import programme. For lack of time it had not gone very far; only far enough, in fact, to disclose the rudimentary stage at which thinking on the most important of the determinants affecting food imports—the amount of shipping that would be available—had left off. There had, in fact, not merely been no advance in this field since 1936; the rough assumptions laid down at that time by the Sub-Committee on Food Supply in War[1] had undergone curious and contradictory trans-

---

[1] See Chapter II.

formation at the hands of different departments within one Ministry —the Board of Trade. In order to understand these changes, and their effect on the advance planning of food imports, it is necessary to set out some general principles affecting merchant shipping in time of war, and particularly at its outbreak—principles that can be established without recourse to any statistical estimates.

The carrying capacity of a merchant fleet, in war as in peace, will depend on two variables: the number of ships; and the efficiency with which they can be employed. The first variable—the pool, so to speak, of ships—will tend to diminish in war by reason of losses from enemy action, the hazards of the sea, or requisition for military purposes; it may be increased by purchases, captures, transfers from other flags or other trades, and by new building. The second variable, which may be usefully expressed in terms of the number of round voyages the average ship can make in a given time, will be reduced, compared with peace-time, by the need to sail in convoy, *i.e.*, at the speed of the slowest ship, and with delays consequent on assembly and dispersal; by evasive routing; by diversion to unaccustomed ports; by delays in turn-round arising from port congestion, itself arising from many causes, such as internal transport difficulties, or working in 'black-out' conditions. It may be increased, on the other hand, by advance planning of cargoes, shortening of hauls, and other control measures, not the least of which is the very existence of import programmes themselves.

It must further be emphasised that sinkings and other marine losses are mainly important in relation not to cargoes, but to the total supply of ships. Suppose, for example, that the rate of loss be ten per cent. of all voyages, distributed equally between inward- and outward-bound vessels; and that the average round-voyage time is three months. In that case a five per cent. deficiency on arrivals in port, compared with overseas loadings, would correspond to a loss, over a year, of forty per cent. of the average tonnage at risk. Turning the argument round the other way, and expressing it more generally, a tolerable rate of cumulative loss of ships, such as could be made good to a sufficient extent by acquisitions or new building, implies a very low rate of *current* loss.

A long-continued reduction in food imports, of the order of twenty-five per cent., such as took place in 1917–18 and was postulated as a basis of planning in 1936, must therefore be attributed very largely not to current marine losses but to (*a*) a fall in the importing capacity of a given amount of tonnage, (*b*) a reduction in the number of ships available for food imports, due either to the cumulative effect of losses already incurred or the deliberate decision to divert ships to other employments. If, that is to say, one is devising an import programme for food, one must assume that loadings will fall by almost as much as the twenty-five per cent. prescribed for arrivals.

It will be noted, however, that one of the factors affecting the supply of ships—marine losses—will, *ex hypothesi*, only begin to be of importance after the war has continued for some time. If, as was the case in the years before 1939, there is a considerable surplus of world shipping, the pool of ships may remain adequate, other things being equal, for months or years of war. It was, in fact, the existence of this surplus that accounted for the confidence of those responsible for the shipping plans. So, too, in the first months of war, the deliberate diversion of ships away from food imports is not likely to achieve large proportions, if only because it cannot be undertaken until the pattern of war-time demand is known and the machinery of shipping control established.

On the other hand, the loss in importing efficiency will make itself felt immediately war breaks out; indeed, it may well be at its severest. Naval precautions such as evasive routing and diversion to 'safe' ports will be applied to ships on the high seas; the 'black out' will at once affect port and railway working. These are likely to result in delays in the turn-round of vessels in port. The organisation of convoys will entail initial dislocation and a lasting decline in importing capacity. Moreover, mitigating factors, such as shipping and import controls, however efficient and resolute, must take time to become fully effective. Even if preparations are complete, even should enemy submarines and aircraft be inactive or ineffective, there is bound to be an initial period when seaborne trade will fall not only below peace-time levels, but reasonable war-time expectations.[1]

The hypothesis of 1936, on the basis of no more evidence than was available at that time, could thus have been re-stated in terms that would not only have provided a useful basis for planning, but would have precluded the contradictory inferences that were in fact drawn from it. A twenty-five per cent. reduction in food imports might have appeared as a relatively late war development; on the other hand, full weight might have been given to the initial dislocation that was indeed mentioned, but never closely analysed. This would have underlined the case for prompt shipping control, advance programming, and precautionary measures of storage. The question of shipping allocations, not only between the food and other programmes, but within the food programme itself might have been raised. The problem of advance planning might have been seen from the first as how to make the best use of a mercantile marine whose effectiveness had been reduced by the mere fact of war.

---

[1] Mr. Churchill himself illustrated this principle in the most vivid way when he wrote in November 1939: 'We shall have failed in our task if we merely substitute delays for sinkings'. (Minute by Mr. Churchill as First Lord of the Admiralty, 9th November 1939: printed in Churchill: *The Second World War*. Vol. 1.)

What actually happened was very different. Early in 1938 the Food (Defence Plans) Department set about making an estimate of the food supplies that would be available overseas during the first year of a war between the British Commonwealth, France and Czecho-Slovakia on the one hand, and Germany (with or without Italy) on the other. Setting off the loss of supplies from European neutrals against the gain from diversion of Empire supplies normally going to the Axis, and making various other assumptions about, for instance, food from the Western Hemisphere, it concluded that overseas purchases of the principal foods (excluding animal feeding-stuffs) would amount, for the year, to just under 15 million tons. To work out how much would arrive in the United Kingdom, it reduced each and every separate figure making up the total by twenty-five per cent. 'for sinkings and delays'. From the result, together with an estimate of home production, it computed the food value of the probable total supplies in terms of calories and found it to compare favourably with the situation in 1918.

The labour and time employed in the preparation of this estimate must have been very considerable, for it went into great detail.[1] Its cardinal error consisted in using the twenty-five per cent. cut out of its context and without regard to its implications. To say that arrivals would be down one-quarter compared with pre-war was emphatically not the same thing as to say that they would be down one-quarter compared with current loadings. On the latter hypothesis, there would be no merchant fleet left to carry on the second year of war. But, besides some weaknesses in detail—the estimate of home-grown sugar supplies, at 571,000 tons, was impossibly high, and that of home-grown flour supplies assumed a harvest above the normal, the securing of eighty per cent. of the harvest off the farms (only possible if the war began in the early autumn), and the raising of the flour extraction rate at once to eighty-five per cent.—the whole procedure was also questionable, in that it assumed that a food programme totalling 11 million tons would be in the same proportions as one totalling 15 million tons. Clearly, however, this would not be so; the latter would have to contain relatively more necessities and less luxuries. (The Food (Defence Plans) Department had previously criticised a Ministry of Agriculture calculation of feeding-stuffs supplies in the first year of war, on the very ground that it assumed that all imports would be cut in the same ratio.)

---

[1] For instance, prospective wheat loadings were put at 6,918 thousand, i.e., 6·918 million tons. One may frequently observe in official calculations estimates which, if expressed in terms of a large unit and its fractions, would instantly be exposed as impossibly fine-drawn, passing muster because the decimal point has been shifted so far to the right as to disappear. This habit of attending to the notation rather than the meaning of a set of numerals has the curious effect that figures become apparently more accurate in proportion to their magnitude.

Nevertheless, the estimate passed without comment, either from the Food Supply Sub-Committee or from the Mercantile Marine Department of the Board of Trade. It was to the latter that the next development of the original assumption was due. In September 1938 there was submitted to the Committee of Imperial Defence an esti-mate of the adequacy of the British Mercantile Marine in the first year of war. Its conclusion, namely that British shipping alone, without the aid of neutrals, would be adequate, with a margin of one million tons, to meet estimated requirements, was based on a number of assumptions that will not be examined here—with one exception.[1] This was an especially helpful assumption—that require-ments of food and feeding-stuffs could be reduced, in accordance with the 1936 decision of the Food Supply Sub-Committee, by one-quarter, or five million tons.

Later official critics were perhaps going beyond the evidence when they accused the Mercantile Marine Department of arguing in a circle, of using a 'hypothesis intended as a measure of the severity with which our imports would be affected by war' to support an optimistic view of shipping prospects. Had the 1936 assumption been as unequivocal as that, and had not the view that a cut of that magnitude was feasible been supported, in a sense, by the Food (Defence Plans) Department's calculation of total calories a few months earlier, it would scarcely have been possible for the most inattentive to arrive at such a conclusion. The very erroneous and sanguine result which the Mercantile Marine Department reached must not, that is to say, be imputed to an isolated piece of reasoning, but to a widespread want of rigour in dealing with matters of this sort. The importance of the result can scarcely be overrated. It pro-vided reinforcement for the view, based no doubt originally on simple observation of the world glut of shipping, that freight rates would not rise on the outbreak of war, and that there would be no objection to competitive chartering by Departments and even by separate com-modity controls. Fortunately for itself, the Food (Defence Plans) Department did not act on these beliefs, but took every step open to it to ensure an uninterrupted supply of ships for controlled foods should war break out.[2] Its ability to insure itself, however, was limited by the Mercantile Marine Department's plan to introduce only partial control of shipping at the start.

Moreover, when in the summer of 1939 the Food (Defence Plans) Department set up its shadow 'Overseas Purchases Board', and began to prepare tentative buying programmes for individual commodities, it made no attempt, except for Argentine meat, to relate them to available tonnage. So far from restricting the demands of food on

---

[1] This examination belongs to the history of shipping.

[2] See Chapter III.

shipping, the Department envisaged a considerable shift from nearer foreign to farther Empire sources of supply, whether because the former might be cut off (e.g., Danish bacon) or in order to save foreign exchange (e.g., sugar and wheat). For sugar alone was any deliberate cut in imports planned in advance, and even here any saving to shipping would be offset by the longer haul.

But the Department did not stop there. Trade Directors were told, having established their requirements, to write up their purchases by one-third, the equivalent of a twenty-five per cent. short-fall of arrivals compared with loadings, to take care of sinkings and delays. No incongruity was seen between the assumption that there would be plenty of ships and the proviso that one-quarter of all cargoes would fail to arrive.

Not till August 1939 did anyone raise the question of the initial dislocation that would result from the introduction of convoys and other naval precautions. Then, from information obtained from the Admiralty, the Food (Defence Plans) Department concluded that supplies might be held up on the high seas for as much as $1\frac{1}{2}$ to 2 weeks on the outbreak. This conclusion came too late to be generally useful, though it may have contributed towards a last-minute, and very important, decision to buy wheat futures in Canada before war broke out. In any case, it did not go to the root of the matter.

Thus it was that Whitehall as a whole—though individual officials had their doubts—never envisaged an immediate and continued shortage of shipping, severe enough in itself to demand the limitation of imports beyond the point dictated by lack of foreign exchange and the loss of sources of supply. In consequence, the outbreak of war found the Government without the complete machinery of shipping and import control that the situation demanded.

II

The establishment of control for the principal imported foods was accomplished swiftly and according to plan. Stocks in store and afloat were requisitioned; the commodity markets closed; and price restrictions put into operation. Trade Directors for the controlled foods began at once to elaborate their buying programmes; and the task of welding these into a single food import programme was begun. The groups of traders, such as the Port Area Grain Committees, whose duty it would be to supervise the landing and disposal of cargoes on the Ministry's behalf, entered on their executive duties. The Port Food Movement Officers, responsible to the Ministry's Transport Division, took up their stations. Within a week or two of 3rd September it could fairly be said that the whole machine of State trading in food was in working order; and it may be added at once that it never showed any signs, throughout the whole duration of the war, of breaking down.

But—if one may pursue the image a little further—the most admirably designed motor-car, though it enable a man to travel easily, fast, and for a long distance from his starting-point, possesses of itself no sense of direction. Food control would in any case have had difficulty at first in finding its way, for the ground, though not untrodden, was certainly unfamiliar from having been long deserted. Planning the imports of individual commodities was a complicated task. Account had to be taken of the quantity, quality, and price of the supplies from a given source, the season at which they were available, and the distribution of shipping between different routes. Due weight had to be given to the shortage of hard currency, especially dollars; the demands of economic warfare; the terms of existing international agreements for wheat, sugar, tea, and beef, and of treaty commitments to Empire and foreign suppliers; to the needs of Allies; to the mutual reaction of imports and exports. An attempt must be made to foresee the long-run effect of the war on sources of supply; how far it was prudent to insure future supplies of, say, bacon by contracting for amounts beyond present needs. The Ministry's Trade Directors were often vexed at first to find that what appeared to them a straightforward business deal had not merely to be approved by the Ministry's own Overseas Purchases Board, but must run the gauntlet certainly of the Treasury and the Ministry of Shipping, possibly of the Board of Trade and the Foreign, Dominions and Colonial Offices. Any sizeable transaction was almost bound to become a political and diplomatic question.

In these matters of negotiation and procurement the Ministry's Supply Department displayed a high level of acumen which rose in many instances to mastery.[1] But for many months of the war it had to operate, not in accordance with a firm programme, based on reliable estimates of food requirements on the one hand and shipping prospects on the other, but against a background of continual uncertainties. To the unforeseeable hazards of the military situation there were added incomplete control of shipping and inland transport, want of knowledge about a considerable number of foodstuffs not subject to Ministry control from the outset, and the absence, for some considerable time, of any established criteria for food policy as a whole. The vicissitudes of the import programme were attended by sudden crises in the supply of particular commodities, more especially wheat, sugar, and frozen meat.

The first of these crises occurred within a few weeks of the outbreak of war. Not merely did arrivals of foodstuffs fall, despite the absence

---

[1] Some examples will be given in the second volume of this history.

of air raids and the loss of relatively few cargoes, to about half normal; it proved unexpectedly difficult to hire ships. Cereals were the worst affected; at the end of September the tonnage actually chartered for them to arrive during the next two months was put at nearly a million tons short of requirements. Ships were hurriedly diverted to the St. Lawrence to load Canadian wheat before the close of navigation, but this did not help the coarse grain situation which was exacerbated by the sinking of several maize ships from the Plate. On 19th October the Minister of Food told the War Cabinet that the maize and barley situation was 'really desperate'. He criticised the slowness of the methods by which British shipping was secured; and pointed out that a too-rigid fixing of the maximum freight rates that the Ministry of Food might pay for neutral tonnage was preventing it from securing Moroccan barley and Plate wheat at f.o.b. prices so low that even with the higher freight they were still cheaper than Canadian grains. Meantime there was, he said, danger that stock would be slaughtered for lack of feeding-stuffs and the starch and glucose factories closed down for lack of raw material. 'The safety of the country is at stake unless . . . a great volume of additional tonnage is made available for cereals without depleting the amount of tonnage required for other foodstuffs'. Negotiations with Greek and Norwegian shipowners were hanging fire; in the blunt words of the First Lord, 'we have not obtained any neutral tonnage worth mentioning'. Three weeks later, notwithstanding that Ministers had agreed that negotiations must be pressed with the neutrals even at the expense of higher prices, there was no substantial improvement in the immediate prospect for cereal shipments. The German magnetic mine was a fresh deterrent to neutral shipowners.

By mid-November stocks of wheat in flour mills and port granaries had fallen to 630,000 tons, or less than six weeks' supply: and this was worse than it sounded because, owing to the uncertainty of arrivals, the diversion of ships, and the fact that the Government wheat reserve had been held on the less vulnerable West Coast, East Coast mills were living from hand to mouth. One or two of them had actually been stopped for a few days for lack of grist. The possibility of relieving the situation by recourse to the home crop was limited, for the rate of threshing was limited by shortages of machinery and more particularly labour. Authority was indeed secured from the War Cabinet for making an Order that two-thirds of the home-grown wheat actually marketed should be sent for milling, but this was little more than a gesture.[1] The possibilities of raising the extraction rate of flour, of diluting bread with coarse grains, and even of bread rationing, were mooted. The crisis was to pass as the emergency measures to rush wheat from Canada bore fruit; but even with the assistance

---

[1] See Chapter VI below.

F

of loans of wheat from France, it was not until April 1940 that stocks of wheat and flour reached the minimum safety level of thirteen weeks' supply that had been laid down by the Government in 1917,[1] and that the Ministry of Food had persuaded the War Cabinet to reaffirm on 6th December 1939, in the middle of the supply crisis.

This formula was henceforth to be the touchstone of the Ministry's wheat policy; and it is important to note the form in which it was first put up to Ministers. Thirteen weeks' supply of wheat and flour, it was said, was 'the minimum with which we, could safely face the spring and summer months when there will be no home crop left.' In other words, the Ministry needed this supply so as to have something to fall back on if imports fell short of consumption; and it was implied that, in so far as the home crop could be brought under control, and a minimum flow of supplies from it secured, a proportionate reduction in the safety level could be secured. It is indeed self-evident that, for purposes of insurance against a shortfall of imports, the significant ratio is that of stocks to net consumption of imported wheat, not of all wheat. In its passage through Ministerial Committees to the War Cabinet this qualification fell by the way unnoticed, and thirteen weeks' supply in terms of total consumption was thus fixed as the minimum. No-one suggested, however, that supplies to the consumer would at once be jeopardised if stocks fell below that level. In other words, the thirteen weeks' rule embodied what, at a later stage in the war, the Ministry of Food was to call a *minimum prudent level*. The failure to define this clearly at the time was to have far-reaching effects.

The shipping situation not only called for special measures to get essential foods in, but made it imperative to keep inessentials out. The pre-war assumption seems to have been that this would be the job, not of the Ministry of Food, which had to procure and control the essentials, but of the Board of Trade and the Treasury. When war began a number of more or less luxury foods became subject to the import licensing machinery of the Board of Trade and were either, as with caviare and crystallised fruits, prohibited altogether, or subjected to degrees of restriction varying with the country of origin and the nature of the food. At first the chief reason for restriction was shortage of foreign exchange—it was not until mid-November that a representative of the Ministry of Shipping appeared on the inter-departmental Import Licensing Committee—and foods were on the whole treated more leniently than other things. Any tightening of the screw could only be made gradually, because of the strain on the staff of the Import Licensing Department; at the end of October its food section was already 'in serious difficulties', though it was handling trade valued at a mere £10 millions a year; trade worth ten times

---

[1] See Chapter I.

that sum was free of all effective control. Even so, the pressure of work was so great that restrictions on a number of minor foods had to be temporarily lifted. The Treasury pressed for a closing of the gap between import licensing and the operations of the Ministry of Food, but the latter was not willing, even supposing it had been able, to extend its controls purely for exchange or shipping reasons at a time when they were supposed to be unpopular.

As a result, the very thoroughness of the control of essentials diverted the energies of individual exporters and importers alike to such things as coffee, canned fruit, canned fish, and sago and tapioca, which flooded in at rates far exceeding the normal. Moreover, there was nothing to prevent controlled foods being sent 'on consignment' to this country, obliging the Ministry first to requisition them and then to find them a market; bacon, lard, dried fruits, and tea, all caused embarrassment in this way until January 1940, when their import on private account was prohibited except under licence. Desultory discussions continued about the fate of, for example, agar-agar and cereal breakfast foods; towards the end of February a general import prohibition for all foodstuffs was mooted. Not until 28th March was this actually brought into effect[1].

So drastic a measure had political as well as administrative reper-cussions; for any departure from pre-war buying policy was naturally unwelcome to exporting countries. It was not possible for the United Kingdom to exclude completely all the luxuries produced by her French Ally; it was by no means easy to persuade the United States and Canada that she must do without many of their goods. Only after much argument did the Canadians agree to restrict exports of apples to the United Kingdom to one half the normal quantity; and though at the same time Britain excluded all United States apples and pears, it was some months before the Government felt strong enough —or hard-pressed enough—to go further. However sympathetically the American administration might view British difficulties, however well it might realise that the United Kingdom was placing heavy armament orders whose value much exceeded that of the goods it was excluding, the fact remained that orders for aircraft did not help American fruit growers. United States irritation reached its height when canned and bottled fruits were at long last subjected to import licensing; and it was partly to appease American feelings that the Ministry of Food made a large-scale purchase of maize—which it none the less badly needed—from the United States in the spring of 1940. Such a shift from luxuries to necessities was inherent in being at war at all, but the expectation of an easy shipping position to begin

---

[1] It put an end to such anomalies as the exclusion of concentrated canned soups, which ranked as canned vegetables, while more watery soups were admitted without restriction, and that Empire sago should require separate licences for each shipment, while foreign tapioca came in under open general licence.

with, together with the illusory appearance of normality that character-
ised the first six months of war, had left Governments, if not peoples,
psychologically unready for it.

The exclusion of luxury or semi-luxury foods made only an indirect and gradual contribution towards releasing shipping for
essentials, since the tonnage of luxuries was not large and they came
not in tramps that could readily be diverted to other trades, but in
liners that had for the most part to continue on their existing routes.
The saving of foreign exchange it effected was not merely important
in itself but in its repercussions on shipping. For as it became clear
that tonnage was so short as to compel concentration on the shorter
hauls—that, for instance, it would take several years to lift the
1,500,000 tons of Australian wheat the Ministry of Food had contracted for, in the hope that more ships would become available, as
late as January 1940—it was vitally necessary to spend dollars only on
necessities. Even apart from this, there was something repugnant to
common sense about a situation in which imports of sugar might be
restricted, but not those of sago and tapioca; where cuts could only be
applied to essentials which alone were under Ministry control and for
which alone any criterion of need existed. For reasons which need no
further emphasis, the pre-war planners had not realised early enough
that a Ministry of Food would need to be an authority *on*, if not *over*
all imported foods, even though it might directly control only the
essentials; they had not thought in terms of an all-inclusive food programme or considered the effect—whether from the point of view of
shipping or consumption—that changes in the amount of one food
imported would have on the rest. Until the leaks in the control were
stopped, talk of import programmes could not be carried into effect.

III

Discussions about import programmes were almost incessant during the winter of 1939–40. Towards the end of October the Ministry
of Shipping gave warning that importing capacity in the first year of
war was likely to be about one-fifth less than the total imports for
1938. In mid-November Ministers agreed to an import programme of
47 million tons, of which 19·8 millions was to be allotted to food and
feeding-stuffs. This figure was about 1 ½ million tons below the average
pre-war total imports on which the Ministry of Food had been basing
its initial attempt at a programme; and though the Ministry accepted
it, it refused to admit that a 21 million ton programme was too high,
or ought to be reduced except on account of the shipping shortage.
It claimed that the pig and poultry population would be reduced by
at least one-quarter as a result of the cut of some 600,000 tons in

feeding-stuffs imports that conformity to the new figure would impose.

By the time the 47 million ton programme had been agreed on, however, the German magnetic mine campaign had started; besides doing direct damage, it made neutral shipowners even less willing to hire their ships to the British. The Minister of Shipping pressed, therefore, for further reductions in consumption, and just before Christmas the War Cabinet asked the Lord Privy Seal (Sir Samuel Hoare), a Minister without Departmental responsibility in the matter, to have prepared a report on the implications of the shipping shortage. This report, which went into the position in considerable detail, was not ready till the third week of February; its conclusions—not unnaturally since they could only be based on the expert analysis of the Ministry of Shipping statisticians—supported the view of the Minister of Shipping that the level of consumption was higher than could be justified by the import prospects. Imports in the first year of war—it pointed out—would not only probably fall short of 47 million tons in quantity but would include many inessentials. In the second year of war the country might have to face difficulties it had hitherto been spared, for example, extra military demands and increased diversion to West Coast ports. An immediate review of the whole current import programme was recommended; provisional tonnage allocations between the Ministry of Food and the Ministry of Supply should be drawn up at once on alternative hypotheses, the more favourable of which should assume that importing capacity would be seriously curtailed. Without such a reallocation of tonnage, the War Cabinet would find it difficult to impose a simple reduction of consumption levels of, say, ten per cent, as proposed by the Minister of Shipping.

The Ministry of Food expressed alarm at these suggestions. A ten per cent cut in the food import programme would amount to two million tons. There would be no point in reducing meat imports, because refrigerated tonnage was not at present scarce; to cut wheat would mean bread rationing—'clearly the last resort of a starving nation'. Even if the sugar ration were brought down to half-a-pound, and margarine and cooking fats rationed at 3 oz. and 2 oz. respectively, there would still have to be a direct reduction in supplies of animal feed of a million tons a year, plus a consequential reduction in oilcake supplies of 320,000 tons. The Minister of Agriculture agreed that a ten per cent. cut must fall mainly on feeding-stuffs, and he declared that this would 'extinguish' the pig and poultry industries. He went on to argue, with remorseless but defective logic, that the loss in human food could only be made up by imports at the expense of a further cut in feeding-stuffs 'many times greater than two million tons', which would bring 'disaster' to domestic agriculture. (Actually, of course, the weight of feeding-stuffs far exceeds that of the meat they produce, and a substitution of imported meat for imported feeding-stuffs constitutes a major economy in shipping.) The Ministry of Food further pointed out that in framing its programme it had to take into account considerations of economic warfare, the need to provide a market for Empire produce, and the need to economise hard currency, all of which might be wasteful of shipping; it suggested that hauls might be shortened. The Chancellor of the Exchequer declared, however, that too many dollars had already gone on foodstuffs, many of them imported on private account free of control. In January alone nearly £4 millions worth had been spent, as against a little over double that amount originally estimated for twelve months.

The War Cabinet, on 1st March, accepted the Lord Privy Seal's proposal for a review of programmes; but in the ensuing discussions the Ministry of Food was able to make its case good against any serious immediate reduction in its programme. It merely undertook to explore the possibilities of rationing margarine, and to reduce imports of canned salmon, fresh fruit, and liquid eggs (for the baking trade), changes of no consequence. Virtually the whole of the proposed import economies were debited to the Supply and Miscellaneous programmes; the *ad hoc* committee of officials, to whom the task of reporting on the problem had been delegated, accepted the argument that the only alternative would be such a cut in feeding-stuffs imports as to mean embarking on a deliberate, large-scale slaughter of pigs and poultry immediately. There was indeed a strong case for postponing so drastic a step, so long as the shipping position remained merely threatening, until the first harvest of war-time was in; for this had been planned to increase very considerably the supply of home-grown feeding-stuffs. Stocks of the major foods needed building up rather than running down; even an extension of rationing, carrying with it as it did a Government guarantee of supply, could not be undertaken, it was argued, on a hand-to-mouth basis. Thus feeding-stuffs could not be rationed immediately. In short, the Ministry of Food had no sufficient margin of safety, and it had to be allowed to create that margin, and to complete its organisation, before major economies in food consumption were possible.

IV

These conclusions were not shaken by the conquest of Denmark and Norway; but the German successes on the Western Front caused the subject to be abruptly reopened. On 5th June, the morrow of the Dunkirk evacuation, the Economic Policy Committee asked the Ministry of Food to prepare a programme totalling 15 million tons, one-quarter less than that to which it was then working. Those advising Mr. Arthur Greenwood, the Minister without Portfolio who at this time was responsible for a general surveillance of economic problems, were especially impressed by the danger that port congestion, from large-scale shipping diversion together with air attack, would seriously limit imports. Together with the extra demands from France to compensate for the supplies and industrial capacity she had already lost, this might reduce total imports to 35 million tons a year.

The Ministry of Food was given only forty-eight hours to get the new programme ready, and naturally safeguarded itself by calling it 'hypothetical'. Ministers were told that it would have 'very grave consequences'; a large-scale slaughter of livestock, a cut in the meat ration from 1s. 10d. to 1s. 4d. worth and serious difficulties with Empire countries who depended on the United Kingdom market for their fruit. After some discussion, the 15 million ton programme was adopted not as a maximum, but as a minimum, and the Ministry was invited to prepare a supplementary programme showing various degrees of priority. Before it had got any distance with this, the fall of France once again changed the short-term outlook. Whatever the future might hold, there was for the moment ample shipping; and the Minister of Food at once urged—and his colleagues agreed—that long-term programmes be disregarded in an effort to bring in as much non-perishable food as possible before the German besiegers closed in.

During July and August the 15 million ton programme was gradually abandoned. On 19th July the Economic Policy Committee, which had not met at all for six weeks, accepted as satisfactory an undertaking by the Minister of Food 'that we should aim at reducing consumption towards the level which will be necessary whenever circumstances render an import of 15 million tons of food and feeding-stuffs a year the most we can achieve'. It also agreed that it would be 'reasonable, so far as surplus shipping was available', to import extra feeding-stuffs in order to ease the transition from peace-time to war-time animal husbandry, and 'moderate quantities of Dominion and colonial produce such as fruit'—practical conclusions that nullified the assertion of principle; for clearly feeding-stuffs and fruit would not be stored, but eaten. Indeed, it was on the strength of this decision that the Ministry postponed cuts it had proposed in the releases of cereals for animal feeding.

At the beginning of August Mr. Churchill called two meetings of Ministers to discuss the shipping and food situations at which the 15 million ton programme was unequivocally buried. The Minister of Food urged that the possibility of restriction in food consumption was strictly limited, and that rationing should be employed only when absolutely necessary; he wished to increase rations of sugar, margarine, and meat for the winter, and would have liked to deration tea altogether. He hoped that the Government would set its face firmly against the restriction of food imports. The Ministry of Shipping thought it might be possible to get in 42 million tons of imports during the second year of war; though this figure might be reduced as much as ten per cent by port congestion or delays,[1] on the other hand it might be increased by further concentration on the North Atlantic route. The Prime Minister, supported by his statistical adviser Professor Lindemann, declared that the country should not inflict upon itself present injury through fear of future dangers; that the Minister of Food should restrict consumption to the smallest extent compatible with the building up of adequate reserves; and the Minister of Agriculture should aim at a large but not excessive expansion in home food production. So far from reducing its programme, the Ministry of Food was encouraged to increase it; for its original plans for the second year of war had assumed that imports totalling 17·4 million tons would provide enough for humans and animals. The total second year of war programme now presented to the Exchange Requirements Committee was nearly $1\frac{1}{2}$ million tons higher than this. It was indeed divided into *minimum* and *supplementary* programmes, the former adding up to 15 million tons; but the Ministry stated quite clearly that this was a purely hypothetical statement indicating how imports would be divided up

'if at any time we were forced by enemy action to reduce our imports to this low figure . . . [It] does not represent a programme which is put forward by the Ministry of Food as working proposition. Our programme is the total programme . . . which amounts to 18,867 thousand tons.'

At the end of the first year of war the Ministry of Food viewed its import prospects comfortably and its import record with fair satisfaction, for it had beaten off all internal attacks on its programme and had more than fulfilled it; though it had been helped by a very big windfall—a million tons—of cargoes diverted from the Continent. (Sinkings had been half this amount, or about $2\frac{1}{2}$ per cent. of arrivals.) In the light of later years it was to look back on 1939–40 as a halcyon time when ships were to be had for the asking and the only restrictions were supply and foreign exchange. A good summer, and the completion of control of the major commodities, including rationing where necessary, had enabled it to more than recover from a shaky start. The stock position for the major commodities, which had been much worse in March than at the outbreak of war, had by now fully recovered. Wheat stocks were some 600,000 tons, or fifty

---

[1] The Ministry of Transport believed that the West Coast ports and their railway network could cope with 43 million tons of imports a year—see Chapter IX below.

per cent. higher than they had been a year earlier; sugar and oilseeds stocks were now protected by rationing, which had also halted the heavy drop in stocks of tea. The Ministry was now capable, as it had not been a year previously, of dealing with a crisis should it come.

It is no derogation of the Ministry of Food's accomplishment during the first year of war to emphasise what an exceedingly slender margin of safety there had been in food stocks at the end of 1939. Except for whale oil, the reserves acquired before the war had not sufficed to stave off a crisis. The sugar reserve had been largely dissipated in the period of unrestricted consumption and though that of wheat had remained all but intact, its location had prevented it from being brought into play when East Coast mills were running short of grist. As the Minister of Shipping had pointed out in November 1939, 'the whole shipping problem has been aggravated by the fact that we did not start the war with larger reserves of vital commodities'. The reasons for this do not need to be enlarged on further. But one cannot escape the conclusion that, had there been air or submarine attack on anything approaching the expected scale—or even on the scale of 1940–41—the country might have looked defeat in the face before the first Christmas of the war.

CHAPTER VI

Home Production and Producers' Prices,

1939-40

I

As in the war of 1914, the Ministry of Food was to have no direct part in the food production campaign. Food control, by common consent, must be a United Kingdom affair if it were to be effective. But there were already in existence, alongside the Ministry of Agriculture and Fisheries, established Departments of Agriculture for Scotland and Northern Ireland; and this fact alone would have made the union of food and agriculture in a single Ministry a revolutionary and unpopular step, even supposing that the arguments in its favour were otherwise conclusive. During the period of pre-war planning, from 1935 onwards, there is no evidence that it was ever seriously considered. So, in the series of civil histories of which the present study forms part, agriculture is dealt with in a separate book.

The responsibilities of the Ministry of Food, so far as home production was concerned, would, therefore, begin 'at the farm gate'. The marketing and distribution of the principal foods, all of which, with the very important exceptions of liquid milk and main-crop potatoes, are imported as well as home-produced, would have to be integrated with the general system of control that it was proposed to introduce as soon as war broke out. The regulative functions, and the staffs, of the various marketing bodies that had been set up since 1930, would be taken over wholly or partly by the Ministry of Food, which would fix guaranteed prices and provide a guaranteed market for all essential farm products. In doing so, it would (the pre-war plans presumed) take into account the effect the level of those prices would have upon the farmers' readiness to increase production—a subject on which the agricultural departments as well as farmers themselves would naturally have views.

If, however, those directly responsible for production would expect a voice in the Ministry of Food's price-fixing activities and in the details of its marketing arrangements, the Ministry itself would be no less concerned with the results of the food production campaign. It would wish to prescribe, so far as possible, the types and amounts of food which the farmers should be asked to produce; and it would be anxious to secure the maximum amount of what was produced for the common pool of supplies. Moreover, the United Kingdom live-stock industry largely depended on imported feeding-stuffs, to the amount of seven or eight million tons a year, or above one-third of the total pre-war imports under the heading of food. Although any increased contribution from home agriculture to food supplies could only come to fruition when the first harvest planned under war con-ditions was gathered, the import position would, from the very beginning of the war, react upon home production prospects.

In the long run, and provided the shortage of shipping became sufficiently pressing, the ends of food production policy stood clearly defined; namely, to secure the utmost supplies possible of foods for direct human consumption, such as bread-grains, potatoes, and sugar-beet. This could only be done at the expense of livestock, whose numbers would have to be reduced as their food either ceased to be imported or was diverted to man. *In extremis*, even dairy cows, whose milk was regarded by experts on nutrition as the most valuable of all livestock products, as well as the most economical from the point of view of 'converting' animal to human food, would have to be sacrificed. Pigs, poultry, beef cattle, and sheep, in that order, were held to be expendable at an earlier stage. Particular importance was attached to maintaining, at any time, only so many livestock as could be adequately fed on the feeding-stuffs expected to be available.[1]

In 1918 this process had been arrested by the Armistice just at the time when a substantial sacrifice of livestock was thought to be inevitable, and by scientists, overdue; farmers, they said, tended to preserve their animals at all costs. In Germany such resistance to a rational policy of livestock reduction had been carried to suicidal limits.

> Large quantities of vegetable food and of food which might have been utilised by man were wasted in the mere maintenance of cattle and pigs without any production of meat or fat. The ill-fed cattle deteriorated in quality, their working powers diminished, the milk supply became less and less, and there was a fat famine throughout the land with the final result of the physical and moral collapse of the population of Germany, which rendered further carrying on of the war impossible.[2]

---

[1] 'It has never been proposed that in times of scarcity all livestock should be destroyed, but that it should be reduced to the minimum necessary: (*a*) for working the land, (*b*) for the production of milk; (*c*) for preserving the breed. For these purposes feeding-stuffs must be provided, even if man has to go short. Only after man's calorie needs (not his desires or necessarily his habits) have been satisfied, is it justifiable to use cereals for fattening animals for food. The number of animals fattened must then be limited by the amount of feeding-stuffs available; no useful object is served by keeping a number of animals on a bare sustenance ration, so that they produce no fat, and by their numbers prevent the rearing of a more limited number of fat animals'.—Starling, E. H. *The Feeding of Nations* (1919, *loc. cit.*, pp. 110–11).

[2] Starling, *op. cit.* p. 100.

To the experts, a powerful weapon in overcoming the reluctance of farmers to sacrifice their animals for the national good was a price policy carefully devised to make that reluctance unprofitable. They were prepared to construct a calculus of farm prices that should infallibly achieve the direction of cereals for human consumption. (They were also prepared to enforce it by requisition.) 'This', remarked Sir Frank Coller,[1] 'is a most fascinating theory, but was it ever politics'? Certainly it was not during the first World War, given agricultural departments whose 'efforts', according to the same witness, 'were mainly directed to placing producers' prices on a pinnacle which became an eyesore to the industrial consuming public'.

These reminiscences of the earlier war indicate the main issues on which inter-departmental divergence was likely next time. So far as production policy was concerned, the question was one of extent and *tempo*; would it be necessary to make major adjustments to the pattern of British agriculture, or could one be content, at any rate at first, with a general increase in output, not directed very forcibly towards any particular crop? More specifically, would it be possible to encourage farmers to grow feeding-stuffs to replace those that could no longer be imported, or would there at once be import reductions on a scale that would enforce wholesale slaughter of animals and a changeover to the production of human food? During 1936-39 opinion veered from the latter alternative to the former; the clue was clearly shipping, about which no even moderately convincing hypothesis had been framed.

By the same token, the need for a comprehensive price policy had been recognised, and machinery intended to secure one had been agreed upon, in the form of an interdepartmental committee to be set up when war came. But no sort of priority schedule for farm products had been drawn up. Nor had the more active attitude on the part of Government towards agriculture, compared with that of the years before 1914, done very much, if anything, to promote the cause of a unified, rational, 'scientific' policy towards farm prices, or indeed towards the planning of agricultural output. Policy in the nineteen-thirties had been a policy of *assistance*, financial or other, to specific, sometimes competing, parts of the agricultural industry that could convince the Government that they were in difficulties; and although this assistance had, by 1939, extended to most branches of agriculture, it cannot properly be said to have comprehended agriculture as a whole.

Moreover, at the time war broke out, the instruments of a comprehensive control of marketing and prices were not completely ready;[2] nor, as it turned out, was the Government of the day in-

---

[1] Coller, *op. cit.* pp. 107, 180.

[2] It had been agreed before the war that an Interdepartmental Committee on Food Prices should be set up; but in the event this was not done until late in November.

doctrinated completely with the need for prompt and simultaneous action over the whole field. There followed a confused period recalling Sir William Beveridge's description of the Devonport regime at the Ministry of Food in 1917:

'a period of food control without principle on practical lines; a scurrying hither and thither in chase of the unapprehended consequences of ill-considered actions'.[1]

Gradually, a pattern of policy was to emerge. After the first few months there appears a conflict of opposites; on the one hand the economists and scientists, uppermost in the Ministries of Health and Food, pressing for a policy based on nutritional needs and reinforced by strong marketing controls, deliberate livestock reductions directly the need should become apparent, and a price structure that should sharply distinguish between products more and less desirable under war-time conditions: on the other, the agricultural departments, insisting that neither nature nor the farmer could be driven, judging cropping programmes as much by their feasibility as by their theoretical merits, aware from long experience of the political factor, and sceptical about the value of differential price inducements. What was wanted, argued the latter, was an increase in prices generally sufficient not only to cover ponderable increases in cost, but also to provide the incentive, and the wherewithal, for the capital outlay that expansion of production must entail. 'A general improvement in the price level coupled with a fear of a shortage of imported feeding-stuffs', wrote the Ministry of Agriculture in December 1939, 'is likely to promote a greater expansion of total production than any special inducement to expand production of particular crops'. However, compulsory cropping directions might be issued should this prove necessary.

Production and price policy for agriculture had to be seen, moreover, against the wider background of anti-inflation measures in general. A prime purpose of the Ministry of Food was to check a runaway rise of prices; it would be frustrated if, in the name of higher food production, the Government should be forced into a policy of controlled inflation. Whereas in 1917–18 home producers' prices, even at their most generous, were below the world market level, there was good reason to expect, this time, that world prices would continue to be lower than those on the home market. The Ministry of Food and the Treasury thus had the strongest of motives for fighting to keep the guaranteed prices to farmers within bounds.

The debate was to be prolonged, detailed to the point of aridity, and at times heated. In retrospect it may seem to have decided very little; if after, say, mid-1941 a production policy, sufficiently rigorous to please the most severe of critics, and based on the substantial agree-

---

[1] Beveridge, *op. cit.* p. 342.

ment of all parties, was adopted, that reflects the pressure of events rather than the triumph of one view over another. It would be historically wrong, however, to slur over its details, or to allow the passage of time to obscure the enthusiasm that contemporaries brought to their discussions. If at times these seem remote from the harsh realities of Dunkirk, the great air raids, and the Battle of the Atlantic, that itself is no insignificant contribution to the history of the war.

II

The first few weeks of war exposed two serious gaps in the food control front, gaps through which the forces of inflation made haste to push their way. The first, and more avoidable, lay in the fact that while the Food (Defence Plans) Department had intended that the Food Controller should become the sole purchaser 'off farms' of the three principal cereals—wheat, barley, and oats—it had ready in September 1939 control orders for wheat alone. Pressure of work was undoubtedly the main reason for this; and it was natural that wheat, on account of its supreme importance as human food, should get first priority when it came to drafting control measures.

It would have accorded better with the prospective supply situation, however, had priority in control been allotted to barley and oats. The very fact that wheat imports would be the last to be restricted made it less necessary to impose controls on it at once. Conversely, grains used mainly for animal feeding would be the residual item in any import programme; the proposal to create a reserve of them—for this very reason—had not been put into effect. It is true that an immediate shortage of freight was not generally expected, but even so, any temporary dislocation there might be would fall on barley and oats rather than on wheat, and control was, therefore, indicated as a precaution. Contrariwise, to peg prices and control usage of home-grown wheat, without controlling barley and oats, was the shortest way to send prices of the latter sky-high should any shortage of any grain occur.

And so it proved in practice. In peace-time substantial amounts of home-grown wheat, marketed as 'millable' and ranking for deficiency payments under the Wheat Act, were eventually used for feeding animals, particularly poultry. The first reaction of the Cereals Control Board[1] to the shortage of freight and the shrinkage of port stocks was to ask that an Order be made compelling all approved buyers of home-grown wheat to send it to the mills. The Ministry, lest this should cause public alarm and an excessive slaughter of

---

[1] See Chapter IV.

poultry, directed that two-thirds of the wheat be sent for milling. Ministers were led to understand in November that this would produce on the average 130,000 tons of home-grown wheat a month for milling between 1st December and 31st March; equivalent to a diversion of wheat from animals to humans at the rate of 650,000 tons a year.

These claims were misconceived, for they assumed both that all the marketable wheat (instead of about four-fifths) leaves farms by the end of March, and that the effect of the Order would be felt immediately. They thus exaggerated the amount of wheat that would come on to the market, and the speed with which relief would come to millers' stocks. Thus while 180,000 tons were bought by approved buyers during December, only 76,000 reached the millers that month; and during the whole four months December-March they received 365,000 tons, a little less than two-thirds of the amount marketed. In March the position had eased sufficiently for the two-thirds rule to be relaxed to one-half; but even so, in April the millers received an amount of wheat equal to three-quarters of that marketed, and even in May nearly three-fifths. If one looks at the disposal of the 1939 wheat crop as a whole, the proportions milled, fed to animals, and used for seed closely approximated to the pre-war average. It looks as if the Order was largely ineffective, though it may have caused local dislocation and shortages in the feeding-stuffs market. The most hardship was felt, however, on account of the shortage of imported feeding wheat in areas like South-West England and Lancashire; and this was only alleviated by the release of foreign wheat, in the early months of 1940, to the amount of some 40,000 tons.

Insofar as the wheat restriction Order was effective, it must have exacerbated the shortage of other cereal feeding-stuffs. Had the control orders for barley and oats been ready, they would almost certainly have gone into effect automatically on the outbreak of war; as it was, the whole policy of full control lay open to challenge. The Cereals Control Board argued at the outset that barley should not be controlled at all. Its members, mostly traders, thought that with imports cut off or restricted, the price would rise sufficiently to stimulate production and obviate an Exchequer subsidy, but would be kept in check by the proposed restrictions on the output of beer and whisky; and that to impose a price ceiling would do no more than prevent brewers from competing for the comparatively small supplies of high-grade barley suitable for pale-ale brewing.

The Ministry of Agriculture began by favouring a *minimum* price for malting barley (to prevent brewers of stout and vinegar, who use low-grade barley, from 'squeezing' the grower) together with a fixed price for feeding barley. These would be in addition to the existing levy-subsidy scheme for barley, introduced in August 1939 under the

Agricultural Development Act,[1] by which an acreage subsidy was financed by a levy on brewers and distillers. By the end of October, however, the rise in barley prices caused both scheme and proposals to be abandoned.

Within weeks, however, barley control was to be mooted again on account of the shortage of imported feeding-stuffs. The Ministry of Agriculture raised the alarm of a shortage of barley for seed, and an Interdepartmental Committee was hurriedly set up to consider whether to restrict the supply of barley to brewers and distillers. (An effort to persuade distillers to close down voluntarily had been unsuccessful.) Although the Ministry of Food discovered, after the Committee had reported, that brewers and maltsters still had on hand nearly a quarter of a million tons of old crop barley, more than double what had been supposed, the War Cabinet on 14th December accepted a recommendation that the supply of grain to distillers should be limited to one-third of their last season's purchases, authorised the Ministry of Food to bring home-grown barley under control as soon as possible, and instructed it to obtain a lien on brewers' and maltsters' stocks.

This proposal coincided with an independent decision, arising out of sugar rationing, to reduce the allocation of sugar by thirty per cent. for brewing. This would, if beer output was to be maintained, increase the brewers' usage of barley.[2] The brewers were not slow to point out the contradiction and as a result both proposals were shelved while their technical implications were gone into. The Ministry now appointed an independent expert Adviser on Brewing and Distilling, who declared that any attempt to obtain a lien on these barley stocks was (*a*) unnecessary, since there was no shortage (*b*) futile inasmuch as they would already be mixed and blended in such a way as to make them useless for seed. Eventually the Ministry of Agriculture was persuaded to be content with an undertaking from the trade to release barley if it should be necessary; and its fears of a shortage were in fact not fulfilled.

Nor did the War Cabinet decision lead to a revival of plans for full control of barley; the malting and distilling seasons were over before any action was taken to limit supplies to these trades. In consultation with them, plans were prepared in time to come into operation next season, i.e. in 1940–41. Brewers and maltsters were to be licensed to purchase only so much barley (or its equivalent in malt or other cereals) from the 1940 crop as would, together with their stocks at the beginning of October 1940, suffice to meet their requirements to the end of the next malting season; the number of 'standard barrels'

---

[1] 2 & 3 Geo. 6, cap. 48; S.R. & O. (1939), No. 926, (8th August 1939).

[2] The amounts at stake were relatively small; 15,000 tons of raw sugar would be balanced by 40,000 tons of barley.

of beer brewed over the whole country was not to exceed that in 1938–39. Distillers were to be dealt with in the same way, except that their quota was limited to one-third of pre-war. The price of barley for malting, however, was still left uncontrolled; evidently the restriction on purchases coupled with a reduction in beer consumption that was expected as a result of the increased excise duty, was relied on to steady the market. In fact the price of home-grown malting barley, though high, did remain fairly steady throughout 1940, and it cannot be said that, given the decision to maintain beer output, the production of barley was overstimulated.

Oats policy was equally hesitant. The first thoughts of the Ministry of Agriculture favoured an acreage subsidy coupled with a fixed buying price of 6s. a cwt. for all oats; the Cereals Control Board at first favoured a free market, but then veered round to support price control for feed oats only, oats sold for milling to be free of price control. The Ministry of Agriculture agreed to this, but debate continued about the level of the prescribed price—whether or not it should contain an element of subsidy. Technical difficulties and pressure of work held up the drafting of a control Order, and led the Cereals Control Board to propose once again that the market should be free.

Mid-November was reached, and still nothing was decided; the shortage of imported feeding-stuffs became more and more acute, the price of oats rose sharply and threatened to rise still further in face of the restrictions on the sale of wheat for animal feeding. Complaints flooded in, particularly from Scotland, of the shortage and high price of oats for milling into oatmeal. Meantime imported feeding oats, to say nothing of maize, were still being offered under control at about half the market price. Even so, it was not till 18th December that instructions were given to prepare a control Order; at the end of December a Press Notice was issued forecasting control, but the Order itself was not ready until the last week in January. It canalised the trade through 'approved buyers' and fixed a ceiling price for all feeding oats (imported as well as home-produced) of 11s. a cwt.; oats for milling were to be 13s. a cwt., until 29th February, thereafter 12s., while seed oats were to remain uncontrolled. Even these high prices were still below those asked by the farmers; and there was some doubt whether they might attract enough oats off farms to meet the requirements of oatmeal millers and working horses. A certain amount of oats was, therefore, imported and held in reserve for these purposes.

Control had only caught up with the prices of feeding oats and barley when they were about double the pre-war price. This put an end to any hope of devising, at leisure, an orderly structure of prices for home-produced food; the high price of feeding grains was bound

G

to lead to demand for higher prices for livestock and milk from those farmers who were accustomed to buy food for their animals. The initial schedule for livestock prices under the scheme for full control had been published in November 1939; but the scheme itself had been delayed by Ministers' objections both to rationing and to the reduction in the number of slaughterhouses. The interim standstill price orders, issued on the outbreak of war pending the introduction of control, were being widely criticised and evaded, so that they too were completely abandoned over the Christmas period.[1] A new schedule had, therefore, to be negotiated before the old one could come into operation.

Meantime general approval had been given to the Agricultural Departments' plans for increased home production. When the ploughing-up campaign had been launched in September, the Government announcement had laid stress on the importance of sowing wheat and potatoes, i.e. crops for human consumption, rather than animal feeding-stuffs—a hangover, so to speak, from the original plans of 1936–37, based on the hypothesis of the twenty-five per cent. cut in food imports. But the Agricultural Departments, with the assent of the Ministry of Food, had now come to conclusions on production policy which were at once less drastic and, it was argued, more realistic. Some increase in wheat and potatoes was still looked for. But—on the assumption that essential imports of human food would not, but that bulky cereal feeding-stuffs would, have to be restricted; that the existing pattern of the nation's diet, and more particularly its home-grown meat and milk, should be maintained so far as possible; that agriculture should be kept on 'a properly balanced system which will not collapse at the end of the war', as had the system of guaranteed prices embodied in the Corn Production Act of 1917—it was thought wise to look for a general all-round increase of production, and in fact to allow farmers the utmost latitude in the use to which they put the newly ploughed-up land.

In the light of later events it is perhaps necessary to emphasise the commonsense appeal of this programme, at a time when the future course of the war could scarcely be foreseen. But it made price policy a very arbitrary and haphazard affair. In peace-time farmers had at any rate market prices, determined however imperfectly by consumer preference, to guide them. Now there was a controlled and guaranteed void, left vacant by the controllers' reticence in expressing their preferences. A discriminatory price structure, that might set off the enhanced prices of one set of products against the discouragement of others, was ruled out in favour of a general rise afforded to all.

Translated into practice this meant that in December 1939 live-

---

[1] Chapter VIII below.

stock producers were awarded a new scale of prices that, despite the protests of the Ministry of Food and the Treasury, embodied an allowance for rising costs *plus* something for 'incentive'. When, in February 1940, milk prices for the summer were discussed, they too were enhanced in the same way by an incentive element, since it was argued that otherwise milk producers might switch over to beef production. (The Agricultural Departments supported this, though they had denied when discussing livestock prices that there was any danger of such a switch, and were to deny in July that farmers were affected by differential prices.)[1] Thus to the effect of uncontrolled prices for coarse grains was added a piecemeal approach to individual prices under control by which, in effect, the price of one acted as a lever forcing up that of another—the negation of the 'fully co-ordinated system of comprehensive price control' foreshadowed by one official committee[2] before the war.

III

Not much could be done by administrative means to mitigate the shortage of feeding-stuffs during the winter of 1939-40. Rationing, the only solution if the shortage were to be permanent, was ruled out because the Ministry of Food had not at hand a stock that could be used to even out supplies so as to guarantee a ration for each animal. From January 1940 onwards the Ministry was able to release imported supplies to the trade at two-thirds of the average pre-war annual rate, i.e. considerably less than two-thirds of the seasonal demand. Merchants were called upon to distribute these supplies as fairly as possible, giving preference to the owners of dairy cows. An attempt was made to meet complaints that the trade was attempting to maintain its pre-war output of compound feeding-stuffs at the expense of 'straights' by extending price control to a standardised range of compounds and issuing instructions that the pre-war ratio of compounds to straights was to be maintained. The shortage of imported milling offals on which certain districts had relied was mitigated by a redistribution of the home-milled product. Nevertheless, if there was no major crisis in feeding-stuffs supplies this must have been due partly to economies and improvisation on the farm itself. To some extent the shortage was reflected in falling milk yields and a slowing up of the rate of fattening in beef animals.

---

[1] An earlier example of an 'incentive' bonus had been an increase of 2d. a lb. in fat sheep prices, urged by the Agricultural Departments on the ground that sheep did not consume imported feeding-stuffs and might therefore be increased in numbers even under war conditions. This thesis was contrary to last-war experience and was not borne out in practice. The technical reasons fall for discussion in the history of the food production campaign.

[2] The Committee on War Emergency Legislation, presided over by Sir Claud Schuster.

During the early months of 1940 hopes still lingered that the shortage might be temporary and that the harvest might put an end to it. So, too, it still seemed possible that producers' prices for the season 1939–40 might be held stable. Early in May the Food Policy Committee sanctioned a further small rise in the price of imported feeding-stuffs (to balance the Ministry of Food trading account), without granting compensation to livestock and milk producers. But the very next day after this decision, the Germans invaded the Low Countries, and agricultural prices, along with so much else, went into the melting-pot again.

Two important changes in production policy followed almost immediately. In the first place, plans already under discussion for the second year's ploughing campaign, i.e. for the harvest of 1941, were made more ambitious. As late as the end of March there had seemed to be a choice between a moderate programme, within the industry's existing capacity, of bringing 500,000–1,000,000 more acres under the plough for the harvests of 1941–42, and an effort on a more heroic scale, which would mean supplying agriculture with more labour, fertilisers, and capital than were then available or in prospect. The German advance turned the scales in favour of the latter; and though specifications for the new campaign were left for decision in August, it was decided to raise agricultural wages at once, in order to enable farmers to keep their men from drifting away from the land. It followed that they must be given higher prices, not merely for the produce of subsequent years, but immediately.

Secondly, the hope of maintaining feeding-stuffs supplies at a level that would obviate any livestock reductions had to be abandoned, and with it the policy of non-discrimination between different types of livestock. On 24th May the Food Policy Committee, with general assent, laid down a scale of priorities:—

'(i) Our first aim should be to avoid any appreciable diminution in the output of milk.

(ii) The production of fat cattle and sheep should be maintained so far as was consistent with (i) above.

(iii) Any necessary economies in imports of feeding-stuffs should be made at the expense of the cereals required for pigs and poultry. Steps should, however, be taken to mitigate as far as possible the very serious hardships involved to large numbers of specialist producers, particularly of poultry, if the reduction in cereal imports required was of a substantial character. In any event every effort should be made to maintain an adequate nucleus of pig and poultry breeding stock.

(iv) The prices of livestock should be so adjusted as to give to production, by varying the incentive in different branches, the general direction indicated in (i) to (iii) above.

(v) A system of rationing of feeding-stuffs should as soon as possible
be made ready to be put into operation at short notice.'

The task of calculating a new price scale that should at once compensate farmers for the rise in wages and any other costs, and
establish 'the proper relationship between the prices of different
products' was remitted to the Interdepartmental Committee on
Food Prices. The Committee found, after an exhaustive examination,
that the increased returns *per annum* already obtained by farmers
(some £62 millions) would more than cover their increased costs to
date (£35 millions) together with the £14·8 millions they would now
have to find on account of higher wages. Nevertheless, the Government was morally bound to make this latter sum good to them.
Theoretically it would be possible so to rearrange prices as to limit
farmers' returns to the amount of the wage increase and at the same
time provide a rational set of incentives in place of the existing
haphazard ones. But it would be scarcely politic to reduce any individual price, or to refrain from giving livestock producers, who had
done exceptionally well out of previous awards, something to compensate the rise in wages. Officials proposed to get over these
difficulties by a grant of £20 millions, instead of £14·8 millions, to
farmers; but on the distribution of this amount between the various
products they were unable to reach complete agreement.

However, the Committee had no sooner reported than the Agricultural Departments came forward with a more generous scale of
prices, which they justified on the ground that farmers must not only
have justice done to them, but feel that it had been done: 'we cannot
afford under present conditions', they said, 'to run any risk at all of
recrimination, uneasiness and discontent on the home food front'.
Farmers were having to readjust their whole scale of values to the
new wages bill, and were consequently in a state of 'nervous apprehension'. If the new prices were felt by farmers to be insufficient, the
whole production policy might be endangered. After sounding the
farmers' leaders, the Agricultural Departments had drawn up a scale
of prices which they thought would be acceptable. This scale meant
an increase in farmers' returns estimated at £34½ millions,[1] and the
maintenance of the existing price ratios between individual crops
and livestock.

To the Ministry of Food these arguments, reminiscent as they were
of those from the same source six months earlier, seemed special
pleading. There was no guarantee that this 'cumulative provision of
incentives' would produce a commensurate amount of food; indeed,
the Ministry doubted whether home food output could possibly be
increased by more than a few per cent. The previous proposals

---

[1] In the documents, £34·54 millions.

amounted to giving farmers replacement prices instead of cost prices; the system of guaranteed markets was itself an almost certain source of abnormal profits. But the worst feature of the new scales, said the Ministry, was that they perpetuated an order of priority—oats, eggs, pigs, fat cattle, wheat, sheep, milk, sugar beet, and potatoes—that was directly opposed to the war-time requirements and to the policy laid down only a few weeks previously, that prices should so be adjusted as to encourage milk production and discourage pigs and poultry.

The Food Policy Committee were unable to reach agreement, and the case went 'on appeal' to the newly-established Lord President's Committee, which accepted the Agricultural Ministers' figures, but stipulated that they should only apply to the current season (1939–40), and reiterated that the price schedules for 1940–41 ought to conform with the priorities laid down by the Food Policy Committee. In announcing the new interim prices on 29th June, the Government explicitly reserved to itself the right to vary prices up or down as occasion demanded. Moreover, farmers whose profits exceeded a certain amount (to be agreed between the Agricultural Departments and the Treasury) were no longer to have the option of being assessed for income tax under Schedule B, i.e. on rent instead of profits.

When, however, the prices for 1940–41 came under discussion in August, the Agricultural Departments attempted to stereotype the existing interim pattern of prices, on the grounds that any departure from it would have a disturbing effect upon the confidence of farmers. In particular, it was argued, the Government was in danger of sacrificing other branches of agricultural production to the fetish of milk. The dispute was taken from committee to committee; the Ministry of Food at length put forward compromise proposals which included some reduction of the current prices for pigs and fat cattle; the Minister of Agriculture was only willing to accept these if feeding-stuffs prices were stabilised at their July levels and an announcement made to that effect—a request which the Minister of Food, though sympathetic to it in principle, could not definitely accept on the spot. Consequently the War Cabinet itself had to decide the point; and in the event the Minister of Agriculture had to be content with a public undertaking to 'consider the possibility' of stabilising prices of feeding-stuffs and fertilisers. It was finally decided to do this on 23rd September; the new price schedule had been announced on 30th August. It went a little way towards vindicating the principle of differential price inducement; though it was far from rearranging the price incentives wholesale, in the way desired by all save the Agricultural Departments, it did tilt the balance slightly less in favour of oats, feeding barley, and fat stock, and slightly more in favour of milk and potatoes. Moreover, it did assert in practice the Government's power to adjust downwards as well as upwards; and it did save the Treasury, on paper at any rate, some £2 millions.

IV

During the summer of 1940, therefore, there was no means other than exhortation available to put into effect the reduction of pig and poultry numbers that it had been agreed was inevitable. The animal rationing scheme was not yet ready; and price discrimination was ruled out. Price control of home-produced eggs was nugatory without control of distribution, which was not to come for another year. Pig prices were not immediately reduced, in order to discourage production; on the contrary, the price of baconers was temporarily put up by 2s. a score to enable the specialist producer, who had been warned that his feeding-stuffs were going to be shorter than ever, to reduce the number of his animals without incurring loss. Even this small measure got into difficulties, for farmers had either to be told that the rise was temporary—which might result in flooding the bacon factories with pigs, or diverting them to the presently unrationed pork market—or they had not to be told, which would counteract the effect of any exhortation to reduce production. Faced with this choice of evils, the Government opted for both; the latter in June, the former in September, when an announcement that pig prices would be reduced in October provoked a marketing rush all the more embarrassing because it coincided with an unprecedented autumn glut of cattle and sheep for slaughter, which all but overwhelmed the collecting centres of the Ministry of Food's meat and livestock division.

An *ad hoc* committee of experts and practical farmers advising the Ministry of Agriculture on future livestock policy in July 1940 forecast this glut from the abnormally high figures, revealed by sample returns from the June census of livestock on farms,[1] of older cattle and sheep; coupled with the reduced rate of spring slaughterings compared with the previous year, this was held to indicate that the rate of fattening had been slowed down the previous winter by the shortage of feeding-stuffs. Beasts that would normally have been marketed earlier would be 'finished' on the summer grass and sent to market in the autumn. The Committee feared that the numbers marketed would also rise above normal because farmers, apprehensive of a worse shortage of feeding-stuffs next winter, would tend to carry

---

[1] So far as cattle were concerned, the sample was misleading; the full returns showed no significant change in the numbers of cattle (other than milch cattle) over one year old, compared with 1939.

over as few stock as possible till the spring. It was estimated, however, that even if supplies of feeding-stuffs fell to the level prescribed by the Ministry of Food's hypothetical 15 million ton import programme, they would, together with the 1940 harvest, suffice to carry over the usual numbers of sheep and cattle into 1941. Abnormally heavy marketings, which would be at the expense of future meat supplies, were therefore undesirable; on the other hand, there was no point in encouraging farmers to hold over the winter stock that was already ripe for slaughter. These arguments were reflected in recommendations about seasonal cattle prices. A complete schedule of variations, fortnight by fortnight, for the season 1940–41 was set out, with a maximum—in June—that should be 10s. a live cwt. above the minimum, which itself should be 'an adequate price' for October. This schedule was adopted; but it is difficult to see why anyone should have believed it would have the desired effect on marketings, since the seasonal range was actually less than the pre-war variation of approximately 15s. in relation to a lower basic price. The logic of the Committee's findings had given way before its conviction that to offer a deliberately unremunerative price at any time would 'cause severe hardship to the producer'. In any event, the forces making for a glut were so strong as to outweigh the influence of price announcements and Government exhortation.[1]

The Committee, while noting that on its chosen assumptions there would only be one-third of normal feeding-stuffs supplies for pigs and poultry, made no comment on the fact that the June agricultural returns showed no very marked change in pig and poultry numbers. This undermined the basis of its calculations. If imports did fall to 15 million tons before a rationing scheme was ready, these pigs and poultry must, to a greater or less extent, be fed at the expense of higher priority stock; and the adjustment of the animal population to the supplies of food available would be made, not on the principles laid down by the Food Policy Committee, but on each individual farmer's judgement. Thus the cardinal problem of livestock policy was left aside while the Committee occupied itself first with minor details of sheep and cattle marketing and later with the extreme case of a state of siege where slaughtering on a heavy scale would be necessary. Whatever it had done, however, would have made little difference; for by August 1940 the 15 million-ton programme had been abandoned as a basis for planning; the Ministry of Food was talking of bringing in two million tons of Argentine maize alone, had postponed until October any further cuts in releases of cereals for animal feeding, and was congratulating itself that the livestock population had been maintained.

---

[1] A full discussion of the technical agricultural factors belongs to the separate history of food production.

This attitude is paralleled by the resistance of the Ministry of Agriculture, not only to the idea that the Ministry of Food might have to requisition feeding grains on farms, an admittedly drastic measure that would 'very seriously undermine the confidence of the whole farming industry', but to such an obvious precaution as the extension of control over home-grown wheat. In August 1940 the Ministry of Food argued that, now that it had been decided that the maximum price of wheat for all purposes should be the same as the 'standard price' under the Wheat Act, the incentive to marketing hitherto provided by the deficiency payment on millable wheat would disappear. Recent sinkings of imported wheat had been heavy; stocks, though very high, had actually fallen in July; and it seemed only prudent to secure for human consumption at least that part of the crop which was marketed through approved buyers. The Ministry of Agriculture, however, even now wanted one-quarter of it left free for animals; only under persuasion would it agree that this proportion should be reduced to one-tenth after 1st October, when the reduction in the poultry population, to which farmers had been exhorted, was expected to be complete. It scouted the notion that wheat would be retained on farms; there was a 'general tendency to sell wheat and retain oats' which would only cease to operate if imports of feeding-stuffs fell well below those provided in the 15 million-ton programme. It instantly demurred to the mere suggestion that wheat might have to be requisitioned from the farmer.

Such a temper among officials generally was not likely to favour the *basal diet* proposals put forward by the committee of distinguished scientists, headed by the President of the Royal Society, who had been appointed that summer to advise the War Cabinet on food policy. Shortly after the French collapse, they set out a plan for organising home production and import policy so as to provide, as soon as possible, the following items per head per day, sufficient by themselves to maintain health and the basic metabolic processes:

Bread	.	.	12 oz.
Milk	.	.	·6 pint
Oatmeal	.	.	2 oz.
Fats	.	.	1 oz.
Potatoes	.	.	16 oz.
Other vegetables		6 oz.

This basal diet or 'maintenance ration' (to apply to human beings the terminology of the experts on animal nutrition) would need to be added to by foods drawn from a 'supplementary list'—cheese, pulses, meat and fish, bacon, sugar, eggs, dried fruit—or if these were not available in sufficient quantities, by more of the elements of the basal diet itself, in order to provide the energy necessary for the

population to do its work, i.e. a 'production ration'. Such a programme was not, and could not, be intended to provide a solution to
any immediate emergency; it was meant by its sponsors to be of
assistance during a war of attrition, or if, after such a war, this
country should be forced by world food shortage or lack of foreign
exchange to rely to an unprecedented extent on home-produced food.
The opportunity should be taken, the scientists thought, to move
towards a permanent improvement in the national diet:

> 'while it may be expected that the actual consumption of the popula-
> tion will always have a wider range, the basal diet will serve as a
> guide to the essential elements and the minimum quantities which
> must be assured to the population under any conditions if health is
> to be maintained.'

Departmental representatives who were asked to report on the
practical measures that would be required to give effect to this programme found ready objections not merely to this and that detail,
but to the whole idea of committing the Government then and there
to a long-term policy of drastic changes in the national diet and in the
pattern of agriculture. So far as imports were concerned, the Ministry
of Food must, with shrinking resources, move in the directions laid
down by the scientists; and indeed it was already planning its import
programme on a basis that experts in nutrition would approve. As
for home production, the scientists had (said the officials) under-
estimated the difficulties of producing the home-grown elements in
the basal diet. It was doubtful whether milk production could be
maintained at the pre-war level, let alone increased by one-fifth;
people would not eat so many potatoes, and to grow them in the
amounts desired, allowing for waste, would be impracticable except
at the expense of sugar beet or fodder crops, i.e. at the possible
expense of the milk supply. If oatmeal consumption were to rise to
two ounces per head per day, that is be multiplied ten times, over a
million tons more oats, forty per cent. more than in 1940, would be
required. (They might have added that the plant for husking and
milling oats could not have coped with a tithe of this amount—but
this was only realised later.) Green vegetables were unsuited, by
reason of their perishability and their dependence on the weather, to
a system of guaranteed prices and markets by which alone the grower
could be induced to plant them. It was quite impossible to foresee
what was going to happen in 1941–42; let us then pursue a 'flexible'
policy of growing crops that would serve for both human or animal
consumption as occasion demands; sow more wheat and beans this
autumn, but allow farmers as much latitude as possible; when the
spring sowings came we should know better where we stood. 'The
broad general result' of these findings, the Minister of Food was
officially advised, 'is to put the basal diet to sleep for the duration of

the war. It would, of course, be rude to say this but it is a fact all the same'.

This comment is eloquent of the official attitude, not merely to the particular proposals under discussion, but to any suggestion that the Government should plan ahead for what later came to be called 'austerity'. The scientists were indignant; they felt that the officials had usurped their functions in pronouncing on the ends, as well as the means, of food policy. They protested against the implication that 'consumption . . . should be adjusted to the results of the existing system of guarantees and subsidies rather than the latter adjusted to ensure the quantities which scientific research shows to be desirable'; and they read into the arguments of the officials a wish to superimpose the food production campaign on the pre-war pattern of British agriculture, rather than change that pattern radically.

To impugn departmental detachment is not necessarily to endorse the scientists' proposals. The basal diet, as set out, had an appearance of exactness and simplicity which was delusive. It was not stated whether the amounts specified represented the supposed requirements of, say, a normal male individual, or an average amount got by first calculating the total requirements of the population and then dividing by its numbers. The basal diet, even in principle, might thus be rejected as 'void for uncertainty'. Again, it is of the essence of such a nicely balanced collection of ingredients that failure to provide the right amount of one element will seriously upset the whole. Thus so large a consumption of oatmeal, with its high content of phytic acid, might lead to serious calcium deficiency if not offset by a sufficiency of milk; the adequacy of supplies of the anti-scorbutic Vitamin C appeared to rest hazardously on the yield of that 'puckish vegetable',[1] the potato. Indeed, the very reliance of the basal diet on home production made it impracticable to specify guaranteed quantities of anything in advance. The inherent uncertainty of harvest yields meant that imports must be relied on to provide a balancing factor in the food-supply budget; of the two—imports and home production—the former were more predictable and controllable under any condition compatible with victory in the war.

In rejecting the basal diet, officials were not sinning against the light or refusing to work to a blue-print set out by expert nutritional engineers. More sophisticated, if no wiser, than the scientists, they were rather taking advantage of the impractical nature of the proposals as they stood, in order to indulge their own preference for empirical action. It was a pity that the case for planning ahead should have been so unrealistically presented as to go by default; for if the basal diet policy failed by being too dogmatically positive, the official policy was, as yet, an equally unrealistic negation. To grow dual-

[1] Sir William Beveridge's phrase: *op. cit.* p. 54.

purpose crops was only a 'flexible' policy if they could be diverted to human consumption at a moment's notice. There could be no flexibility without control of all cereal sales off farms, and rationing of all farm livestock; and that control was needed, not merely for the harvest of 1941, but for that of 1940. On such details as these the Scientific Food Committee was well ahead of the officials, but was ignored. The weakness of the Committee lay in its remoteness from the day-to-day experience of the Departments in which the essentials of policy are forged; it was only possible for scientists to influence food policy if they were behind the scenes and privy to the innermost counsels of the Ministries of Food and Agriculture. *Ex cathedra* pronouncements from outside at once provoked opposition and were more vulnerable to it than would have been a steady pressure from within. It was this that led, towards the end of 1941, to the substitution for the Scientific Food Committee of a body no less expert, but closer in touch—the Ministry of Health's Standing Committee on Medical and Nutritional Problems. By that time, moreover, there could be no dispute at all about the need for scientific advice in the framing of food policy.

CHAPTER VII

Consumers' Prices and the Cost-of-Living Index, 1939-40

I

PREPARATIONS for food control in war had first been suggested as an anti-inflation measure.[1] The Treasury memorandum of 1929 on the *Course of Prices in a Major War* had seen the control of food prices, together with consumer rationing, as a means of keeping down the cost of living, a *sine qua non* of a policy of wage restriction, a way of forestalling the vicious spiral. It recognised that wider measures of control, particularly in the field of taxation and monetary policy would be needed; it also admitted that some increase in prices, under war-time conditions, was to be expected: 'It could only be avoided by a complete system of financial expropriation, labour conscription and rationing of consumption. As this is unlikely to be practicable, some measure of inflation is almost inevitable'.

The particular emphasis on food prices appears to have been due to the heavy weighting they had in the compilation of the official cost-of-living index, in which roughly three-fifths of working-class expenditure was attributed to food. 'If the problem of food can be met', the Committee of Imperial Defence was told in 1933, 'the objects set out in our reference are in a fair way to attainment'. The role of the Food Controller, in relation to prices, was two-fold. As the sole purchaser of the principal foodstuffs he would be able to prevent the forcing up of producers' prices and of other charges, such as freights, by the pressure of competition. As the sole seller, he would institute distribution through controlled channels, at controlled margins of profit, to consumers whose demand was restricted where necessary by rationing.

However, as the Food (Defence Plans) Department pointed out as early as May 1937, the possibility of controlling the price of food would depend not only on limiting the demand for it but on factors affecting its cost; and the Food Controller would need assistance in checking increases in costs that were outside his control.

---

[1] See Chapter I.

'For example, the cost of imported foodstuffs will depend largely on the sterling rate of exchange. Will this be pegged and not allowed to fall? Will freight rates be prevented from rising by controlling the costs of operating ships? Will costs of road and rail transport remain stable? This will depend partly on the extent to which petrol and coal prices are controlled . . . it will be difficult, if not impossible, to hold the level of food prices unless the materials and services entering into the cost of food can be prevented from rising.'

Neither at the time this passage was written nor at any later stage in the pre-war plans was any considered answer to its questions forthcoming. Eighteen months later, in January 1939, it was put, unaltered, before a meeting at which the Food (Defence Plans) Department and the Agricultural Departments were ventilating problems of war-time price control. Freights were not expected to rise on the outbreak of war, for reasons that have already been examined.[1] The Treasury, though expressing concern about the prospective shortage of hard currency, appears to have been silent about rates of exchange. The financial terms under which the railways were to be controlled had not been settled, nor in consequence the trend of railway rates and charges. Above all, the 'fixation' of wages, the object for which control of food prices had been originally urged in the Treasury memorandum of 1929, had 'slipped quietly away'. The passage of ten years, so far from clearing the 'misty landscape of war economy', had replaced it by a patchy fog, whose sunlit places throw up in more vigorous relief the murky areas adjoining.[2]

This did not make the proposals for the control of food prices any less important. But it did mean that the Food (Defence Plans) Department, right to the very eve of war, was working in the dark; and it posed an administrative, as well as an economic, problem. The task of price-fixing was bound to occasion complex negotiations with the trades concerned, in which the Food Controller would need to fortify himself with the evidence of cost accountants. Orders would have to be drafted, embodying in minute detail and precise legal form the maximum prices and margins allowed on every type of transaction in controlled foods, from Ministry to ultimate consumer. This process was bound to take time, and it was desirable that it should not be hurried, because the first set of controlled prices would tend to set precedents for the remainder of the war.

If, that is to say, the machinery of price-fixing were to operate smoothly and satisfactorily, there should be an interval after the outset of war of at least several months, during which prices of controlled foods could be frozen at or near their pre-war levels: and thereafter price-changes must not be so frequent as to involve the

---

[1] See Chapter V.

[2] Hancock and Gowing, *op. cit.* pp. 46-52. The passages quoted are on pp. 47 and 50.

frequent reopening of negotiations with the trade. Fluctuations of daily or weekly occurrence, which are readily absorbed in a free market, would be out of the question.

In the last months of peace, this point was strongly urged by the Agricultural Departments in relation to the price of animal feeding-stuffs. They pointed out that feeding-stuffs were a special case, in that their prices had immediate repercussions on a whole range of other farm products, particularly those derived from livestock. A system of controlled prices for home-produced food would, that is to say, be seriously dislocated by a rise in the price of imported feeding-stuffs; and it might be worth while to subsidise them, at least for a period of time, in order to insure against this happening. It would be possible, they urged, for the Treasury to recoup itself when, after say six months, feeding-stuffs prices, and with them all other farm prices, were revised. This proposal was on the point of being submitted to the Treasury when war broke out. It came to nothing at the time, because what would have been its essential corollary —Ministry of Food purchase and price control of *home-grown* feeding grains—lapsed through administrative unreadiness and subsequent division of counsels.[1] Within a few months all hope of avoiding substantial increases in the prices paid to the home producer was swept away.

Even so, it was import prices that rose the more sharply when war broke out. The Ministry of Food was not to blame; it had at once gone into action according to plan, making bulk contracts—for the supply of Empire sugar, for instance—where this was possible and convenient, avoiding them—as with Canadian wheat—where more advantageous terms could be obtained on the open market. (The speculative rise that occurred on the Winnipeg grain market had been successfully forestalled by a last-minute secret purchase of 10 million bushels of wheat from the Canadian Wheat Board at the end of August.) Some rise in f.o.b. prices could scarcely be avoided, particularly as world price levels, particularly of wheat, were almost spectacularly low in 1938–39. But the rise of about one-quarter in landed prices that occurred between September and December 1939 must largely be attributed to causes outside the Ministry's control; depreciation of sterling (by about one-sixth in terms of dollars); rises in freight charges; and the cost of insurance against war risks.

Nor had the Ministry been dilatory in imposing maximum price orders. The initial price-freezing orders, however, had very shortly to be replaced by others embodying higher prices. By the end of October, the food items in the Ministry of Labour Index had risen by sixteen points over two months. A greater rise than this had only been prevented because the Ministry of Food was incurring heavy

---

[1] See Chapter VI.

losses on its trading account—losses that by the middle of December were running at the rate of £1 million a week. If these were stopped, the food index would have to go up another twelve points. Bread, in particular, assuming only pre-war rates of profit to the controlled millers, whose rate of remuneration had not yet been settled, would have to go up from 8d. to 9d. a quartern loaf—the figure at which it had been pegged in the last war.

Changes of this magnitude and suddenness threatened to undermine the policy of voluntary restraint on wage claims, which the Government was even then urging on the trade unions. It would be difficult for the leaders of organised labour to keep their membership in check if, at the very moment when they were being exhorted to moderation, there was an abrupt jump in food prices. For the moment, therefore, the concealed subsidy was allowed to continue, though the Treasury still hoped that it might be possible to abandon it after a few weeks. By January 1940, however, Treasury and Ministerial opinion had come round to the view that it might be well not merely to continue to peg food prices for the present but perhaps to extend stabilisation to the whole of the commodities entering into the cost-of-living index. This, it was thought, might stave off, or at any rate mitigate, pressure for an increase in money wages that might, in the long run, be more costly to the Exchequer than a direct subsidy.

Even so, the Treasury was loath to contemplate a policy of cost-of-living subsidies 'for the duration', though experience suggested that once started they would have to go on. Fear of the financial burden partly accounted for the Treasury attitude; but there is not wanting evidence that it had not yet made up its mind whether food subsidies or food taxes were the right way to stop inflation. After all, part of the price rise that had already taken place was due to an extra tax on sugar, imposed in the emergency budget of September 1939. This ambiguous attitude towards the price of items in the cost-of-living index was to persist for some time; witness the imposition of purchase tax on clothing in the budget of April 1940.[1]

II

Part of the Treasury objection to food subsidies appears to have been that they would stimulate consumption, which on grounds of national economy ought to be restricted. The ghost of the ill-advised and ill-fated voluntary rationing scheme of 1917, that was broken 'remorselessly on the wheel of science'[2] at the time, had still to be

---

[1] Although a scheme for 'standard' clothing was already under discussion. (Hancock and Gowing, *op. cit.* p. 167.)

[2] Beveridge, *op. cit.* p. 38.

laid by the physiologists. The Minister of Health had, he told some of them in December 1939,

'found it difficult to convince some of his colleagues of the truth of the law of conservation of energy as applied to man. They seemed to imagine that the reductions in energy intake, which rationing would involve, need not necessarily be met from other sources. They seemed to have the idea that sugar, for instance, was really a luxury.'

As late as April 1940 Mr. Elliot thought it necessary to remind his colleagues in the Food Policy Committee

'that the consumption of food in this country cannot be materially reduced, but can only be diverted from one foodstuff to another.'

Indeed, experts on nutrition, so far from envisaging any deterioration in the national diet, were urging that the war presented an opportunity to bring about some reform of dietary habits, by pegging the prices of a few of the essential foods, particularly bread, potatoes, and milk. The price of milk, they thought, should be specially reduced to encourage its consumption by children and expectant and nursing mothers.

When it became clear, therefore, in December 1939, that the public would shortly have to pay more for milk unless it were subsidised, the Ministry of Health expressed alarm lest this should lead to a fall in milk consumption, especially by mothers and children; and in announcing the new prices the Ministry of Food was constrained to add that the existing welfare schemes for the supply of cheap milk should be stimulated. Early in 1940 these schemes were reviewed by departmental representatives convened by the Ministry of Health. They concluded that the only way of making sure that the 'priority classes'—mothers, and children under five—got enough milk was to supplement or even to supersede the existing schemes by a national scheme, that would provide milk at 2d. a pint to all of them without regard to means. Machinery of administration lay ready to hand in the local food offices; moreover, to have such a scheme in being would make it easier to secure priority in supply to mothers and children should a shortage of milk develop, as it was expected to do later in the war.

To the Treasury, however, such a proposal was no less unwelcome because there were already food subsidies in existence. It was inflationary, obviously; it was calculated to increase demand, at a time when supplies were expected to diminish, for a food that could not be rationed equitably; it was likely to be costly to the Exchequer. The very idea of starting a new social service in war-time was objectionable; if (the Treasury argued) political considerations precluded a means test, the scheme ought to be dropped. Official supporters of the scheme found this attitude unreasonable:

H

'The real question', a Ministry of Health official remarked in April 1940, 'seems to be how far the considerations which moved the Treasury and the Government in December last to take immediate steps to peg the price of milk . . . are likely to hold good when on the 1st July the price, if unpegged, is almost certain to increase by 4d. a gallon. . . . If those considerations do hold good, it seems curious to jib at a much more scientific "pegging" which, at perhaps a third of the cost, will keep the price down for the section of the population to whom milk is an essential, and for that section alone. I have never been able to discover from the Treasury whether, if the considerations which were thought to have weight in December last have now lost weight, it is because the aim of avoiding a vicious spiral by keeping down prices and wages has been achieved, or because the hope of achieving it has been abandoned. There seems to be a mixture of both elements in their present attitude'.

As late as April, it looked as if a long battle over the scheme was in prospect. But retail milk prices were now threatening to rise farther and faster than had been counted on when the scheme was first discussed. Apart from the award to producers, there was a claim from distributors for higher margins to meet increased costs. Early in May, therefore, the new Minister of Food (Lord Woolton) proposed to his colleagues that, in announcing the new prices, he should temper the blow by reminding people that their effect would be greatly mitigated by the existence of the pre-war cheap milk schemes. But —as the Minister of Health pointed out—this was not so. On the contrary, the milk-in-schools scheme had lost ground through population movements; and local authorities covering more than half the population of England and Wales had refused to work the permissive scheme for supplying cheap milk through maternity and child welfare centres.

At this point in the negotiations Mr. Churchill's coalition Government took office; and for whatever reason, the obstacles to the scheme seemed thenceforth to fade. Towards the end of May the Minister of Food secured from the Chancellor of the Exchequer a temporary subsidy on all milk prices till the end of July, in order to get elbow-room for introducing the national scheme; he also got the distributors to work the scheme for a reduced margin of 10d. a gallon. Moreover, he proposed a very important addition to it, namely that very poor mothers and children should be entitled to free milk. On 7th June 1940 the Food Policy Committee approved the scheme and authorised the Minister of Food to work out the details without further reference to it. A social reform of the first magnitude, that at one time looked like languishing for months, if not years, was put into effect almost within days. The morrow of Dunkirk was a fitting time for so generous a gesture.

The insertion of free milk into the scheme was in accordance with a principle with which the Ministry of Food was much preoccupied at the time, namely, special provision for the poor consumer. When control had been first introduced the previous autumn there had been some criticism of the way in which, by pooling the cheaper qualities of, for instance, butter and bacon with the dearer, it caused especial hardship to the poor, who had to foot an increase in their food bills that was higher than the average increase in food prices. When, in January 1940, the War Cabinet had approved the continuance of the subsidy policy, its application was left somewhat vague. It obviously implied a considerable extension of food control, for subsidies could not be given on foods whose price and distribution were unregulated. But were they, for example, to be applied to all qualities of a given food, or only to those standard qualities presumed to be eaten by the poor, leaving luxury qualities to find their own level? Were they to aim at stabilising the cost of purchasing a minimum diet (as some experts on nutrition urged) or merely the cost-of-living *index?*

For some months officials were to wrestle with the problem of reconciling, if it were possible, these objectives—maximum discouragement of inflation and maximum assistance to the needy. A plan was mooted for providing the poor with vouchers to enable them to obtain certain foods at reduced prices, on the lines of the American 'blue stamp' plan by which surplus foods were distributed to persons on public relief, and the famous experiment in Bishop Auckland, Co. Durham, before the war when potatoes were sold below cost to the unemployed. Members of the Food Manufacturers' Federation were approached with a view to the production of specially cheap lines of canned goods.

These inquiries, however, bore little fruit,[1] because differential subsidies of this kind could not be used to stabilise the cost-of-living index. The index was compiled from the actual prices paid for a list of commodities, not from an ideal diet that it was open to people to buy. This difficulty could have been got over by constructing a new war-time index of basic necessities, and a proposal to do this had been put forward to Ministers as early as January, only to be turned down largely on the tactical ground that the existing index, on account of its out-of-date weighting, under-estimated the extent to which the cost of living had actually risen. It was this fact—offering the possibility of shrinking real wages, as would undoubtedly be

---

[1] One important outcome of the original objection to pooling had been the production of two grades of margarine of which the dearer should subsidise the cheaper. The subsequent history of these grades forms an instructive comment on the whole policy of cheap food for the poor under war-time conditions. As the war went on the so-called 'Special' margarine, selling at ninepence a pound, almost completely supplanted in public favour the 'Standard', selling at fivepence, although the difference in quality was by no means commensurate with the difference in price, and the food value of the grades, once it had been decided to add vitamins to all margarine, identical.

necessary in war-time, without appearing to do so—that was in the end to dominate price policy.

A step towards closer definition of the Government's attitude towards subsidies was taken in mid-August, when the War Cabinet resolved, on the Minister of Food's proposal, 'that the prices of essential foods should be kept down by subsidy in order to secure cheap food, to restrain a rise in the cost-of-living index figure, and to prevent wages rising . . . luxury foods shall be allowed to find their own price level'. Reservation was indeed made that the 'relative pressure on the Treasury from expenditure on food subsidies and from the demands of increased charges and allowances shall be the subject of constant review'. But this was no more than a sop to those who persisted in looking at the narrow financial rather than the wider economic aspect of the subsidy policy; who talked of a time when the Exchequer 'could no longer afford' to subsidise food prices and would have to let them go up, as if by that means the Government could somehow evade bearing the brunt of price increases. As the share of national production that was directly for Government account was all the time increasing, this was becoming less and less the case; unless circumstances so changed as to make a tight control of wages easier to achieve than it had been in December 1939.

August 1940 is thus a landmark in the history of war-time price policy. No problem had been more thoroughly and thoughtfully discussed in all its aspects from December 1939 onwards. The Government's eyes were fully open to the pros and cons of the path it was to take. But one cannot but feel that it had really no choice, and that the official discussions were no more than a vain attempt to find an emergency exit. The Treasury hope of avoiding large-scale food subsidies really foundered on the abrupt rise of prices when war broke out. Had that been foreseen, it might also have been forestalled; the subsidy policy might have been undertaken from deliberate choice, and the controversies of the first year of war mitigated, if not avoided altogether. Moreover, the Treasury would probably have saved money; for prompt price control and subsidy of those imports, such as wheat and feeding-stuffs, whose c.i.f. cost is closely related to that of the finished product, would have made it easier to keep down margins of profit, which tend to rise at least in proportion to costs and thereby enhance the price paid by the final consumer.

It was a Treasury official who, in November 1939, described the way in which food price problems were then being tackled as 'haphazard and largely irrational', and had urged that the 'part which food prices should play in the general mechanism' of price control 'ought to be played consciously and effectively at once'.

There could be no better epitaph on the nature of the pre-war plans for price control, or on the fate of the principles that the

Treasury had asserted in 1929. The thought that, in those days, had been devoted to general problems of war economy, instead of being elaborated and subtilised as the prospect of war itself became more concrete and immediate, had been superseded by concentration on the details of administrative action. Instead of a marriage of theory and practice, there had been a breach of promise. Even in August 1940, moreover, the Government stopped short of an unequivocal avowal of the subsidy policy.

III

Any conscious direction of food prices was dependent, of course, on the Ministry of Food's ability to devise effective means of price control. In so far as it controlled supplies, there was no difficulty about this in principle; but the fixing of prices and margins of profit for controlled foods proved to be a complicated and lengthy business. Such were the idiosyncrasies of different commodities that it was impossible to reduce price-fixing to a simple formula, and it was only over a period of time that the Ministry was able to evolve reasonably consistent principles on which to work.

The Ministry's problem, stated in its simplest terms, was to arrive at a maximum retail price that should incorporate margins providing for the remuneration of all the links in the chain of distribution at its longest—an important qualification because the number of middle-men intervening between dealers at first hand and the retailer varied considerably. A single retail price had to cover, for example, the operations of a small village general store, receiving its goods in small quantities through primary and secondary wholesalers, and the multiple shop buying direct at first hand, perhaps owning its own farm or bacon factory. It must cover the costs of distributing imported produce in remote rural districts or home-grown food in large cities.

This sort of uniform price-fixing is, of course, common in peace-time for all kinds of branded goods. But the manufacturers of such goods neither enjoy a statutory monopoly nor are directly accessible to public criticism. The Ministry of Food was uniquely vulnerable, particularly at the beginning of the war when controls were a favourite object of Press attack. It was in no position, therefore, to dispose readily of trade agitation about 'double margins' to multiples, which began almost immediately control was introduced.

Double margins were really only an extreme and well-defined case of the general problem presented by the need to fix prices to cover the marginal cost of distribution; namely that firms whose costs were less than those on which the margin was calculated made extra profits. It was, of course, extremely difficult, even with the aid of elaborate costings investigations, to discover what the appropriate margin of gross profit for each class of trader on each type of food ought to be, or even to classify traders at all. First-hand distributors or wholesalers pure and simple were rarely found in practice; the slogan 'one firm, one function, one profit', said to have been employed during the previous period of food control, could seldom be applied. In seeking a representative firm whose accounts might serve as a guide in negotiating margins, the Ministry's Costings Division was often confronted with the problem of securing a representative specimen of an abstraction. Nevertheless, the effort had to be made if the Ministry were to have any independent check on traders' claims.

When all was said and done, however, the most scientific and accurate assessment of margins could not prevent abnormal profits being made by the fortunate, any more than it could compensate for changes in the turnover of individual enterprises. (The Treasury had laid down that there should be no compensation to a trade as a whole for loss of turnover through war conditions, but that is a different point.) One class of trader—the multiple firms who bought at first hand, did their own wholesaling, and hence might lay claim to a *double margin*—was identifiable and therefore susceptible of special treatment.

At the outbreak of war, the task of negotiating the remuneration of controlled firms was left very largely in the hands of the commodity branches. Within a matter of weeks—in mid-October 1939—the question of the multiples' margin had come to a head, mainly perhaps because different branches were treating it in such different ways as to cause protests both from multiples and from independent retailers. The Butter Branch was arousing resentment by allowing a leading multiple to buy at the first-hand price of £7.5s. a cwt., whereas other retailers had to pay £7.12s. On the other hand, for condensed milk, dried fruits, and bacon, it was proposed to classify the same multiple as a retailer, and grant it only a part of the full wholesale margin. The position was further complicated by the claim of the Co-operative Wholesale Society to be a *bona-fide* wholesale organisation and therefore entitled to the full wholesale margin.

High-level opinion within the Ministry was sharply divided on the question. It was agreed that the multiples' costs were lower and that in normal times they charged lower prices. But under rationing with a tie to the retailer, there would be no incentive for them to do this, and it was agreed that they would therefore make excessive profits unless they were deprived of, at any rate, a proportion of the double margin. (The independent retailers, on the other hand, were opposed to granting multiples double margins because they feared that price cutting would continue.) Most of the Ministry's Trade Directors were of this opinion. The Financial Secretary of the Ministry (Sir Harry

Peat, the distinguished accountant) and others felt that the claim for the double margin could not be resisted 'on a logical basis', and that there was no strong case for making a 'substantial variation in the normal methods of trade'. Lord Stamp's committee of economists[1] were asked to advise; though they agreed with double margins in principle, they did not object to a compromise being negotiated whereby the multiples were allowed only a proportion of the wholesale margin.

An attempt was made to reach a solution by applying the principle that the remuneration of controlled firms should bear no necessary relationship to pre-war circumstances, but should be on the basis of the services actually rendered under war-time conditions. This meant that if a firm performed the functions of a wholesaler it should receive the wholesale margin, but should not be allowed to do so (i.e., to buy at the first-hand price) merely because it had done so before the war. The multiples were prepared to admit that they did not perform all the services of the independent wholesaler, since, for instance, they neither employed travellers nor incurred any risk of bad debts owed by retailers. They were therefore willing to forgo a part of the wholesale margin. The independent retailers, for their part, were prepared to waive any rights that individual retailers or retailers' buying groups had enjoyed of buying at the first-hand price.

This compromise solution, however, broke down directly an attempt was made to apply it to butter and bacon, two commodities for which, because they were shortly to be rationed, some solution was urgent. Part of the difficulty arose because the multiples objected to the Co-operative Wholesale Society receiving the full wholesale margin—on the ground that it was the property of the retail societies; whereas (as the C.W.S. pointed out, and the Ministry was inclined to agree) its wholesale functions were not confined to its member societies, nor did they buy all their supplies from it. But the conditions of the butter and bacon trade were so different that it was possible to reach agreement by applying completely divergent principles.

The solution favoured by the Butter Branch was to fix the price at which the Ministry would sell to the trade, to specify maximum wholesale and retail prices, and to allow any firm which had bought at first-hand before the war to continue to do so, i.e., to get the double margin. The Bacon Branch, on the other hand, proposed to fix first-hand and wholesale prices (with a maximum retail price) and deal with deviations from this pattern of distribution by a system of surcharge and rebate to multiples and secondary wholesalers respectively. In effect, the most roundabout chain of distribution would be financed out of a levy on the most direct. Treasury sanction was sought and obtained for both procedures.

---

[1] Hancock and Gowing, *op. cit.* p. 47.

The arguments used in favour of this inconsistent treatment—apart from the practical one that the multiples and the C.W.S. were prepared to accept it—are instructive. The butter wholesaler, it was urged, was little more than a forwarding agent for a standardised, pooled product. The bacon wholesaler, on the other hand, undertook a certain amount of processing and cutting, bore a risk of loss through evaporation and shrinkage, and in war-time might have to do some 're-conditioning' of the bacon passing through his hands. The implication was that the extra duties performed by the wholesaler compared with the multiple in respect of bacon were so much greater as to justify a difference in remuneration; but that this was not so in the case of butter. Certainly the wholesale margin for bacon was much greater, in relation to the total cost of distribution, than for butter, and the saving to be derived from denying it to multiples worth while.

Nevertheless, the inconsistency was difficult to defend in public, all the more so since during the first months of rationing some multiples continued to sell butter below the maximum price. (Margarine was still unrationed at less than half the price of butter; and it was to be expected that traders would do all they could to increase their butter sales at a time when the maximum ration was so high —8 oz. per head per week—as not to be taken up.) Independent retailers naturally compared the bacon and butter schemes to the latter's disadvantage, and complaints to the Ministry were numerous. It was therefore decided to set up a standing committee—the Margins Committee—which should review existing schemes for margins and before which all future proposals involving margins should go.[1]

The Margins Committee first met in April 1940, and its findings on the subject of double margins were confirmed, broadly speaking, by the Minister, though not without considerable further discussion. The butter scheme—i.e., the grant of double margins to multiples— was accepted as the norm for future guidance, though for bacon it was decided to let sleeping dogs lie. The butter scheme was preferred, despite the fact that it appeared to contravene the principle of 'payment only for services rendered', because it preserved the pre-war practice and avoided the administrative difficulties of separate treatment for different types of firm, as well as the political ones presented by the C.W.S.

For a time the double-margins controversy was to remain dormant, mainly because, with the growing stringency of supplies and the extension of rationing, the price-cutting that had caused the independent retailers to complain ceased. It was revived towards the end

---

[1] The Committee was originally constituted as a Sub-Committee of the Interdepartmental Committee on Food Prices, but in practice it appears to have functioned as a purely internal Ministry committee, and was later formally constituted as such.

of 1941, but although various means of reducing the margin allowed to multiples on controlled commodities were explored, no satisfactory solution could be found, and early in 1943 the matter was allowed to drop.

It will be noted that on the only occasion when professional economists were consulted (in October 1939) they could see no reason for denying multiples the double margin. An outside observer, free from trade preoccupations, could scarcely not agree with that view. There was, after all, no distinction in principle between allowing the full wholesale margin to multiples and allotting all wholesalers, irrespective of their costs, an identical margin. The Ministry did not set out to secure to each individual food trader the same net profit; why then should it seek to discriminate against a particular class of traders merely because its methods of operation appeared to be readily distinguishable at sight? Surely the interception of individual excess profits was not for the Ministry but for the Inland Revenue? Was it right for the Ministry even to appear to be a stalking-horse for the operations of a trade association against price-cutting? In short, it would seem that the double margins issue was without economic significance—nothing more than a piece of retail-trade politics.

It has been discussed at some length here, therefore, less because of its intrinsic importance than because of its effect on the Ministry's whole treatment of the margins problem. By sharply focusing attention on the kinds and types of work actually done by different classes of trader, rather than on broad concepts of economic function (by which, for instance, multiples on the one hand and wholesaler *plus* retailer on the other would be deemed identical), it eschewed broad general distinctions, such as an economist might draw, in favour of the more detailed, more specific analyses of the cost-accountant. Principles, such as that of payment for services rendered, broke up, in process of application, into innumerable small facets of detail, different for each trade, and each offering prospects of long negotiation. Those laid down in the spring of 1940 are quoted therefore only by way of illustration:

> 'The governing principle is that remuneration must be related to the services rendered in war-time and no compensation can be paid in respect of claims for loss of profit. . . .
>
> The pre-war rate of margin . . . is to be regarded as forming the basis of war-time remuneration subject to the qualifications referred to below:
>
> (a) . . . only if the Ministry is satisfied that the profit accruing from it in war-time will not be more than a reasonable one having regard to the capital employed and the risk involved.
>
> (b) Consideration will be given to any difference between the functions of traders in peace-time and war-time. . . .

(*c*) The pre-war margin will be expressed in relation to a unit of quantity and not as a percentage of value. . . .

(*d*) Consideration will be given to increases in operating expenses . . . which are substantiated by costings investigation.

The fact that a reduction in turnover results in the incidence of overhead expenses becoming heavier will not in all circumstances be regarded as justifying an increase in the war-time margin. The Ministry will endeavour to fix the margin at such a figure that the gross earnings derived by the trader from his reduced turnover are adequate to enable him to carry out his services as a distributor of foodstuffs. The Ministry will not, however, undertake to increase margins in respect of reduced turnover to the extent necessary to maintain gross earnings or net profits at their pre-war level.'

How far the Ministry was successful in applying these principles can only be usefully discussed in terms of specific foods.[1] But two points need emphasis here. The first is that the principles were laid down for guidance in negotiation; they might be overridden by special circumstances or by the general principle, which the Ministry invariably observed, that in cases of doubt it is best to be generous, since food control is only possible if the traders are satisfied. The second is that action on these lines could not easily be hurried. It is not, therefore, a matter for surprise that the extension of price control in the first year of war was gradual. As late as the autumn of 1940 it covered less than twenty commodities, and such staples as fish (other than herrings, canned salmon, and frozen cod fillets), oatmeal, cocoa, and jam, were still excluded. Even supposing, therefore, that the Treasury had wholeheartedly embraced price stabilisation at an early date, it is doubtful whether the means could have been found to put it into effect. As things turned out, the evolution of policy and that of price control machinery were to go hand-in-hand.

---

[1] It is hoped to attempt this in Vol. II.

CHAPTER VIII

The Beginning of Rationing

I

LONG before the war it had been presumed that certain staple foods—meat, fats, bacon, and sugar—would need to be rationed as early as possible after war broke out.[1] Of the tentative buying programmes that had been discussed with the Trade Directors-designate in the summer of 1939, one at least—that for sugar—was only feasible if consumption were reduced. On several occasions public reference had been made to these plans. Though Cabinet sanction would, of course, be necessary before they could be brought into effect, no one doubted that it would be immediately forthcoming. True, the decision whether or not national registration should be linked to rationing from the outset was reserved, by official agreement, to Ministers; but in the eyes of the Food (Defence Plans) Department at any rate it was the former, not the latter, which might run into last-minute political jeopardy. The Department was confident that it would be able to ration the individual consumer within three or four weeks of the outbreak; and even this delay was only expected because people must be given time to settle down after the mass migrations that would follow the outbreak of war.

Advance preparations had been made in great detail. The ration books had been printed and stored in dumps all over the country; arrangements had been made whereby the local food offices, to be opened on the outbreak of hostilities, should address and post one of them to each individual citizen.[2] The source from which the names and addresses would be obtained was to be decided at the time; it would be either an application form, delivered by the postman to every household and returned thereafter to the food office, or alternatively, the enumeration schedules of the National Register, handed over by the local national registration office. On receipt of the ration book, each member of the public would have to register with a retailer, who in his turn would have to apply to the local food office for a permit to obtain rationed food. This in its turn would have to be

---

[1] Chapter III.

[2] With certain exceptions, e.g., residents in institutions.

lodged with a supplier, and the information in it passed up the chain of distribution to the appropriate commodity division of the Ministry of Food, which would authorise the release of food at first hand. At that point, the whole machinery of guaranteed supply, from Ministry to rationed customer, would be in complete working order.

The Food (Defence Plans) Department had not quite completed these arrangements when war broke out; there were certain forms that still remained to be printed. But the procedure was well under-stood, and in particular the local officers had made all ready for the writing up and posting of the ration books. It was now to appear, however, that no one had drawn up a clear time-table, stage by stage, of the rationing preliminaries. More especially, no account at all had been taken of the time the Post Office would need for the sorting and delivery of 45 million ration books superimposed upon its normal routine, or the cumulative small delays implied in the posting of a succession of forms between food offices, retailers, and suppliers. Nor had it been realised that a great part of the pre-rationing opera-tions of Commodity Divisions must wait upon the receipt of ration books by the public. On the contrary; it was tacitly assumed that rationing could begin in a matter of days from the completion of ration book delivery.

The initial decisions about rationing, that is to say, were taken with imperfect apprehension of their administrative consequences. On 4th September 1939, the War Cabinet was asked to agree that, to avoid delaying rationing too long, it should be based, not on the National Register but on the Department's own household application forms. National Registration Day was fixed for 6th October; and Monday 2nd October was the provisional date set for rationing to begin. Two days later, however, officials discovered that it could not begin so soon, because the commodity controls would not be ready to allocate supplies in accordance with rationed demand. The ninth of October was now thought to be the earliest date; and this would admit of using the national registration schedules after all, if National Regis-tration Day could be advanced by a week to 29th September. The Registrar-General at once agreed; and on 7th September the War Cabinet authorised the change; but insisted, as it had on the previous occasion, that rationing must not actually be introduced without its specific sanction. Nevertheless, the next day the newly-appointed Minister of Food publicly forecast rationing four weeks hence. On National Registration Day itself the Minister made a broadcast in which it was implied that rationing was imminent, and had only been postponed that far so as to use the national register.

By this time the Ministry was in process of discovering further flaws in its time-table. Assuming that it would take a week from 29th September to get the national registration schedules into the food offices, the writing up of ration books could not begin until 6th October; even if only ten days were allowed for this process, and a further week in which the public could choose its retailer, rationing could not begin before 23rd October. But the commodity divisions responsible for butter and meat had already pointed out that they could not begin distributing on a rationed basis until the information in retailers' permits had been received. If this argument were accepted, the earliest date for rationing would be 6th November; and it was this date which was put up to the Home Policy Committee meeting on 8th October as that on which bacon, meat, fats, and sugar, should be rationed.

To the administrative stumbling-blocks was now added one of policy; the Minister of Food's colleagues demurred to rationing at all. The argument turned, not on the economic case for rationing as a precautionary measure, but on the actual and prospective supply situation. Oddly enough, the chief opposition to rationing was based on the view that the rations were too small—as if the Ministry of Food could vary the supplies of food at its immediate will. The Home Policy Committee questioned whether the proposed scales were not needlessly drastic, referred them back to the Minister, and when he was unable to modify them to its satisfaction, set up an *ad hoc* sub-committee, which reported a fortnight later in favour of rationing 'some commodities', but against rationing margarine and cooking fats 'for the present'. Discussion on the report revealed a sharp division of opinion, particularly on sugar and meat, between those who supported the Minister of Food in wanting immediate rationing and those who followed the First Lord[1] in opposing it; and the whole question was referred to the War Cabinet that same evening (25th October). The War Cabinet postponed decision for three days, while the Minister of Labour made soundings on its behalf among various bodies 'representative of public opinion' to see how rationing would be received. His report was reassuring; of nineteen 'contacts' only two were actively hostile, while enquiries in Fleet Street had elicited the 'significant fact' that rationing was not foremost in the public mind. On 28th October, therefore, the War Cabinet agreed to ration butter and bacon; but despite a further plea from the Minister of Food, sugar and meat rationing were turned down.

The Ministry's Sugar Division claimed to be ready for rationing[2] at the outbreak of war and had been pressing for it ever since. Its policy of buying only within the Empire stood or fell by the restriction of consumption; but so far from falling, sugar sales had increased

---

[1] Mr. Churchill has published one of his minutes, addressed to the Home Secretary, referring to rationing: '. . . then look at all these rations, devised by the Ministry of Food to win the war. . .' Churchill, *op. cit.* Vol. I. p. 458.

[2] This claim must have been mistaken. The Division, like any other, must wait upon the machinery to be set in motion at the retail end.

by roughly twenty per cent. even before war broke out. Arrivals from overseas were unexpectedly down, and future prospects were rendered worse by the diversion of ships to cereals; the refineries were only kept going by drawing on the home-grown crop at an abnormal rate. The Division's arguments to this effect, however, seem to have been compromised with Ministers, first by its announcement that it had purchased the whole Empire crop and therefore had ten months' supplies on hand or 'in sight', and secondly, by a completely wrong estimate of sugar stocks, giving them as over 500,000 tons instead of less than 300,000, that had been put about in early September.[1] Indeed, the gravity of the position appears to have been not altogether clear to the Minister of Food and his senior advisers; for the documents before the War Cabinet on 25th October relegated the Sugar Division's gloomy calculations of future prospects to an Appendix, while describing the sugar situation as 'at present favourable'.

On the day the War Cabinet was deciding not to ration sugar, the Division was forecasting a ration of no more than 8 oz. per head per week unless more shipping was forthcoming; it was not, the Director of Sugar Supplies told the Colonial Secretary, 'a question of whether to ration or not, but what the amount of the ration could be'. In mid-November the Division rubbed its argument in by asking not only for more tonnage, but for authority to buy 300,000 tons of 'dollar sugar' between January and May 1940, at an estimated cost of £3 millions. On the 22nd, the Treasury's Exchange Requirements Committee declined to sanction dollar expenditure for more than 50,000 tons, unless the case for immediate rationing were at once submitted to the War Cabinet; declaring that if it had been introduced earlier, consumption might have been balanced by supplies on the basis of a 1 lb. ration, without the expenditure of dollar exchange. This was an over-simplified view; speaking roughly, the excess consumption of sugar over normal from September to December was of the order of 100,000 tons, and the remaining 200,000 for which the Division asked was due half to short shipments and half to the desire to build stocks to a safe war-time level.

Where the elaborate statistical calculations of the Division had failed, the argument of the purse succeeded; on 28th November the newly formed Food Policy Sub-Committee recommended, and on 6th December the Home Policy Committee and War Cabinet endorsed, that sugar rationing should begin on 8th January, on the basis of 12 oz. per head. Ministers would not hear, however, of an announcement being made till after Christmas. In the meantime the

---

[1] There is no written evidence as to how this wrong figure was reached. Verbal evidence is to the effect that it was obtained by asking all the refiners by telephone on 3rd September how much they had in stock; but no immediate check appears to have been made against the pre-war stock figures in the Department's possession.

Ministry of Food was to remain in a false position. Early in November it had sought to make the best of a bad job by asking consumers to restrict themselves to 1 lb. per head per week and to assist distribution by registering with a retailer. On second thoughts registration was made to seem obligatory in press announcements—it could not really be made so without an Order—and this carried with it the implication that the sugar would be forthcoming to guarantee the voluntary ration. There were widespread protests from traders when, on Sugar Division instructions, refiners and wholesalers declined to furnish extra sugar pending the examination of the registration returns. It was not, indeed, till after the Cabinet had made up its mind to full rationing that the 'voluntary' system was really got going; as late as 9th December the Ministry was quoted[1] as saying that sugar would not be rationed and that there were adequate supplies.

While Ministers were debating the pros and cons of rationing, the actual machinery was falling more behindhand. Even before the decision to ration butter and bacon was taken, 6th November had become 27th November, on account of the delay in handing over the national registration schedules; not till the last week in October was the task of writing up the ration books completed in local food offices. Then the Ministry discovered that their delivery by the Post Office might take up to a fortnight, i.e., till mid-November. Even then there would be thousands of people to be traced who had moved house since National Registration Day; so that to fix November 23rd as the last date for registration with retailers was to cut things very fine. In any event, the Ministry of Food could not refuse rations to latecomers. Early in November, it concluded that rationing of butter and bacon must be postponed till well after Christmas, and it was fixed for 8th January. Since consumers had registered for sugar along with butter and bacon, sugar rationing was enabled to begin at the same time.

The preoccupation of Ministers with the public reception of rationing, though important evidence of their general state of mind, had in the end little influence on the time when these three foods could be rationed. A possible exception is the delay in handing over the national registration schedules, which held up the preparation of ration books in some areas by as much as a fortnight. The Registrar-General claimed that if he had been given an urgent rationing time-table to work to, he could have arranged to fulfil his original pre-war undertaking to hand over all schedules to the Food Offices one week after National Registration Day.[2] It was this undertaking on which he

---

[1] *The Times*, 9th December 1939. On the same day *The Daily Telegraph* wrote: 'There is no shortage of imported or home-grown sugar'.

[2] These transactions will be more fully examined in Vol. II.

had based his claim that the issue of ration books via national registration was almost as swift as using a separate household application form; without it the change of plans at the outbreak of war would never have been made. No doubt instructions to local offices from Somerset House would have been different, had the Cabinet decided on 7th September that rationing must begin, say, on 23rd October. But it remains unlikely that the national registration officers could have got the schedules and transcript books (into which the contents of the schedules had to be copied) back from enumerators in time to hand the former over within the week allowed.

Even supposing that this part of the operation had gone according to plan, the recourse to national registration at all was bound to mean a delay that need not have occurred if the original decision to use household application forms had been adhered to. (It does not follow, of course, that national registration did not have countervailing advantages from other points of view, e.g., the prevention of fraud and duplication.)

Leaving aside the question of national registration, however, it is clear that nothing serious went wrong with the administrative arrangements. Where the planners had been mistaken was in supposing that these could by any conceivable possibility have been put into force within the three or four weeks that had been postulated; ten weeks would have been nearer the mark. It is pertinent to consider whether this period could have been reduced by alternative measures. On any assumption it must have taken three to four weeks from the outbreak of war to get the ration books out, for a beginning could not be made with their issue until the initial population movements had settled down. Some saving might have been possible by dispensing with postal issue and substituting, say, personal issue against identity cards. But the greater part of the delay was due to the last-minute tacit assumption that because rationing in full operation depended on a process of allocation beginning at first hand and going right down to the retailer, it could not begin until an initial allocation had put the food in the shops.[1]

This was to make the best the enemy of the good. No doubt if rationing had been ordered before the commodity divisions' arrangements were complete, there would have been some difficulties, maladjustments and evasions; there might even have been complaints

---

[1] The first explicit acknowledgment of this appears to have been in late February 1941, when cheese rationing was under discussion. 'The rationing of cheese or of any other commodity'—wrote the senior official who had been most concerned with the rationing plans before the war—'must, I think, inevitably take eight or nine weeks because such a system presupposes that supplies will be directed on the way down the chain of distribution in accordance with consumers' registrations which must first, in the form of permits issued by the Food Office, have trickled all the way up'. The point was especially clear in the case of cheese because it had always been considered to be 'unrationable', and rationing was not therefore proposed until trade stocks had given out.

that the ration was not being honoured. But any restriction, however rough and ready, on the ability of favoured or wealthy customers to buy what they would, must have been better than nothing. Particularly was this true of hoardable goods like sugar; the mere fact of making replacement of stocks depend on the surrender of coupons by the trader would have imposed a measure of discipline that would have held the position while the allocation machinery got under way. To restrict demand was in itself to assist the mechanism of supply. Moreover, rationing based on the consumer-retailer tie could not otherwise be introduced with swiftness and secrecy enough to prevent a pre-rationing rush.

II

Delay in rationing sugar might make it impossible for the commodity control to function fully, but it did not affect its structure, since that had taken shape automatically with the outbreak of war. It was otherwise with meat; for while the Ministry already controlled imported supplies, had decentralised the Smithfield meat market, and set up its retail butchers' buying groups, the remainder of the meat and livestock scheme was in abeyance. Pending the introduction of rationing, control of home-produced meat had been limited to orders in effect freezing pre-war price levels at each stage and prohibiting the sale of livestock except through recognised markets. Refusal to ration left these interim measures in the air, and it was not long before their inadequacy gave rise to what were called 'grave anomalies, abuses, and evasions'. In some places, it was said, the buying groups established by the Ministry for its own purposes were forcing down livestock prices; the retail price restrictions were being disregarded, notably in Manchester and Liverpool, and pigs were being slaughtered young for pork instead of being kept on to bacon weights. Farmers, said the Agricultural Departments, had inferred that no meat rationing meant the indefinite postponement of Ministry purchase at guaranteed prices; and symptoms of their disquiet were to be found in the abnormally heavy marketings now taking place. (In fact, these seem to have been due to nothing more sinister than the weather.) The Ministry of Food, pressed and itself anxious to introduce Government purchase, felt that nothing short of complete control right down to the retail butchers' counter, but without rationing, would meet the situation.

The salient points of the scheme were two. First, livestock auctions would be superseded; the auctioneers, acting for the Ministry, would supervise sale at fixed prices at some 800 collecting centres throughout the country. Secondly, slaughtering would be concentrated in some 600 selected abattoirs, and the small private slaughterhouses, some 15,000 in number, would be closed; only thus could illicit slaughter be prevented and the valuable by-products be put to the best use. All this had been worked out in the greatest detail before the war, with the agreement of the trade; nevertheless the Home Policy Committee feared that its drastic suddenness might cause political outcry. The Committee, and thereafter the War Cabinet, tempered a reluctant approval of the scheme in principle with a request that if possible the reduction in slaughterhouse numbers should be 'modified or alleviated'. Nevertheless a published assurance was given that control was coming shortly; even the prices to be paid for livestock were announced.[1]

In point of fact, control was farther off than ever. On 22nd November an *ad hoc* meeting of Ministers was told that the scheme as recast (in which the number of slaughterhouses was raised to some 800) could not come into effect before mid-January, while to revert now to the original scheme would only enable control to be introduced in the middle of the Christmas trade—obviously an impossibility. Some means of bridging the gap had to be found; various interim plans had been discussed within the Ministry of Food, only to be rejected as unworkable. The Minister could only suggest that the market for home-produced supplies be freed entirely, pending the introduction of full control; and though the Minister of Agriculture protested that this would be breaking faith with farmers, it was nevertheless adopted as a *pis aller*.[2] While, however, the control orders were revoked, the Ministry of Food secretly arranged to check any undue rise in prices by releasing imported meat from day to day as occasion required—a course which irregular arrivals from overseas had hitherto prevented.

Neither the Ministry nor the retail trade liked the prospect of control without rationing, and the forward supply position now looked less favourable than when the War Cabinet had rejected rationing a month earlier. Shipping delays had increased; the magnetic mine had appeared; the French had asked for 10,000 tons a month of British-controlled refrigerated space; the shortage of feeding-stuffs was held to point to a reduction of home supplies. For all these reasons, officials were now prepared to recommend to Ministers that consumer registrations for meat should begin on 1st January, the control scheme on 15th January, and meat rationing on 5th February; and on 6th December the War Cabinet accepted meat rationing along with sugar rationing. There were those within the Ministry who doubted whether livestock control could in fact come into operation on the appointed day, owing to the difficulty of organising the

---

[1] Ministry of Agriculture and Fisheries Press Notice 92 (11th November 1939).

[2] 'The meeting finally came to the conclusion that there was no satisfactory way out of the difficulty and discussion then turned as to the best way of putting it to the farmers.'

necessary transport. Such hitches as there were, however, were readily overcome; more serious was a fall in slaughterings at the outset owing to exceptionally severe weather and the holding back of fat sheep for a seasonal rise in price at the end of January.

Until the control scheme settled down the initial amount of the ration could scarcely be decided on, and until this was fixed the preliminaries of rationing on the commodity side, themselves taking several weeks, could not be set afoot. The original date approved by the War Cabinet was postponed first to 26th February, then 4th March, and finally to 11th March; the delay was in part due to the need to submit the amount of the ration to the War Cabinet and to announce the proposals in the House of Commons, in accordance with the Prime Minister's pledge that changes in rations would not be made without consulting it. The actual amount fixed was largely guesswork; the calculations of Meat and Livestock Division suggested 1s. 6d. worth a head a week (half rations for children under seven); but this did not allow for those consumers who, from poverty or other reasons, would not take up the full ration, which was therefore set at 1s. 10d. As introduced, meat rationing was much simpler than the pre-war plans had envisaged, for the special rations (and hence the books) for adolescent boys and heavy workers had been dropped after due but secret consultation with the medical experts and the Trade Union Congress.

More important still, it had been decided not to enforce the surrender of coupons for meat meals in restaurants, as had been the rule for a time in the last war. Considerations of strict equity gave way before the desire to avoid administrative complications, at any rate for the moment, and to spare the public extra annoyance. Mr. Ernest Bevin, for organised labour, had pleaded that factory canteen meals should be free of coupon; the Board of Education urged the same for school meals. On balance the Ministry felt that it would suffice to restrict supplies to caterers without rationing their customers; a view with which Ministers readily concurred, as also with the decision not to impose a meatless day, which it was thought would have a 'depressing effect'. Thus almost casually, without controversy, a capital and in the end permanent decision of policy was taken.[1] From time to time coupons for meals were to appear on the horizon, most notably in 1942–43; but they never again got so near being imposed. As time went on, the absence of meal coupons became a cornerstone the disturbing of which would have meant a tremendous upheaval.

Ministerial assent to meat and sugar rationing went far towards abandoning an attitude that may well have taken officials by surprise. On 4th November, at the express instructions of the War Cabinet, the Lord Privy Seal had asked the Minister of Food (and the other

---

[1] There was no written submission to the War Cabinet on this point.

Ministers responsible for controls) to have prepared a 'short memorandum explaining the nature of the present system, how it works,
and the reasons for which it is required'—a request which the Ministry
answered in the main by sending the Lord Privy Seal a copy of the
report of the Food (Defence Plans) Department, issued in 1938.
Years of discussions with the interests concerned had paved the way
for the smooth introduction of these controls; the public had been
warned what to expect if war should come; yet an Administration,
most of whose members were collectively responsible for these preparations,[1] seemed apprehensive now that the time had come to put
them into practice.

The immediate cause of Ministerial anxiety was without doubt a
debate on the Defence Regulations in the House of Commons on 31st
October, in which the Government had come under heavy fire.[2] The
economic controls as such were scarcely mentioned by the critics, who
were mainly concerned with restrictions on personal liberty. The
journalist, quoted by Mr. Kingsley Griffith in the House, who compared the Regulations as a whole to the various devices collected by
the White Knight in *Through the Looking-Glass*, was nevertheless
making a comment of wider application. Many of the White Knight's
contrivances were, no doubt, efficient of their kind. But even for the
Knight himself they bore no relationship to one another: he had not
thought out what they were *all* for. So, when Ministers were attacked
on this detail or that, their response was to inquire into the validity
of all controls *de novo*. It was as if rationing, so far from being an
integral part of the war economy, were an overcoat that could be put
off if the political climate became too warm.

In a democracy, the planner cannot free himself from the contingent difficulty this episode reveals. The civil servants who worked
out the war-time controls were bound to add saving clauses in order
to avoid binding the 'Government of the day', if only because a
change of Government might occur before the controls were put into
operation. But they might have been in a better position to 'educate
their masters', to ensure that Ministers took decisions in full knowledge of what they implied, if their own thinking over the whole field
of war economics had been less empirical and opportunist in spirit.[3]

---

[1] The most vigorous opponent of rationing had not, of course, been a member of the
Government before the war.

[2] It was on the same day that one official witness wrote that the Lord Privy Seal 'takes
the view that unless the Government lets up on some of its controls, or gives some indication of its willingness to consider complaints and, if necessary, to alter existing arrangements, the Government may get blown out of office'.

[3] Cf. Sir William Beveridge's comment (*op. cit.* p. 230) on the introduction of rationing
in 1917: 'In this matter the Government of 1917 appears almost incredibly hesitant and
slow, obviously far behind public opinion, led by events and not leading, afraid where no
fear was. Rationing was in effect demanded by the public long before the Government
could be got to decide that it was necessary and that the public would stand it; when it
did come it was accepted without question by acclamation'.

III

Hardly had the rationing of butter and bacon started when the supply conditions that had imposed it changed. The Ministry had insured itself against the failure of Danish supplies by concluding bulk supply contracts for Canadian bacon and Southern Dominions butter. Danish supplies, however, continued to arrive; and shortage of cold stores obliged the Ministry to seek means, not of restricting, but of stimulating consumption.[1] At the end of January the 4-oz. ration of bacon was doubled, and a week later the price was reduced by 2d. a lb. With margarine unrationed (and 'unpooled'), the demand for butter, whose average price had gone up nearly twenty per cent. since the war, was only four-fifths of that permitted by a 4-oz. ration; and even after that ration, too, was doubled, on 25th March, stocks in cold store continued to increase. Negotiations were actually afoot to reduce imports from Denmark when the German occupation supervened; and even so, it was not till June that stocks were so far reduced as to call for a lowering of rations to their former levels.

Sugar was in very different case; as early as January the Ministry of Shipping was asking for the loading programmes to be amended so as to spread Empire shipments over a longer period, and the Sugar Division was driven to seek dollars for a further 100,000 tons, in order to conserve stocks. The Treasury would sanction the purchase of only 50,000 tons; it suggested cuts in allowances to the Services, for which the Ministry was willing, and to sugar-using manufacturers, for which it was not. Discussions were still going on when the news came through that the British West Indies crop was short by 70,000 tons. This would mean either buying yet more dollar sugar or reducing the domestic ration; on 8th May the War Cabinet upheld the Chancellor of the Exchequer's view, and decreed that the sugar ration should now be 8 oz. The invasion of Northern France, and the consequent loss to the French of the sugar beet crop there, together with the threat to home-grown supplies of air attack or even invasion led to a swift reversal of policy, so far as dollar purchases were concerned; but there could be no question of restoring the 12-oz. ration for the present, though it continued to be the basis of the Ministry's import programme for the second year of war.

The collapse of the Netherlands, important both for butter supplies and for facilities for hardening whale oil, at once raised the question of recontrol and rationing of margarine and cooking fats, contemplated before the war but abandoned in November 1939 as a sop

---

[1] The War Cabinet was told that bacon stocks had reached a 'dangerously' high level.

to the 'anti-controllers'.[1] The case for rationing was reinforced by the vulnerability of much of the plant, situated as it was on or near the East Coast. So long as the butter ration could be kept at 4 oz., supplies of margarine and cooking fat could be left unrestricted by juggling with their ingredients, so as to use only so much whale oil as could be hardened in this country. A certain margin of safety against destruction of plant could also be provided by importing lard from the United States to be substituted for compound cooking fat in case of emergency until a rationing scheme could be brought in. These devices, however, could only hold the position for a few months, for in the autumn butter supplies were expected to fall below the 4-oz. ration level, which would make margarine and cooking fat rationing inevitable; and they would have scarcely been put forward at all but for the Minister's objection to rationing margarine 'at a time when the inhabitants of the country are being called upon to make all possible physical efforts to win the War'. Officials had, indeed, advised him that the initial level of the combined ration of butter and margarine—combined in order that the poor might take it all in margarine if they could not afford butter—would have to be not more than 6 oz., as against an estimated average consumption of more than 9 oz. with margarine unrationed. This view was based on the belief that with a combined ration of 8 oz. margarine consumption might rise above its present unrationed level to a point at which demand could not be met. Why the rationing of margarine should have been expected to lead people to eat *less* butter, on the average, than before, is not clear.

At any rate, the Minister gave instructions, on 28th May, that no steps (not even the registration of consumers with retailers)[2] should be taken to impose margarine rationing, but that the whole machinery of control (including rationing) should be ready to operate simultaneously at short notice; and that Treasury sanction should be sought for a lard purchase in the United States. To this officials objected that they could not ration at short notice unless the machinery of control was already in existence; whereupon they were told to go ahead preparing the control scheme and to report back as soon as it was ready; the Minister would then decide whether or not to introduce it at once. The trade was approached, and with the exception of the largest firm in it, agreed readily that the scheme should be introduced forthwith; and Unilevers withdrew their objection a few days later, after the collapse of France. On 24th June

---

[1] 'We departed from our plans [to control margarine] because of a newspaper clamour based largely on the loss of advertisement revenue. I am very doubtful whether we did not sacrifice public interests to clamour'. (Permanent Secretary to Minister, 25th May 1940.)

[2] Those who had registered for butter would automatically be covered for margarine; but there might be some who had not done so.

Lord Woolton agreed that the new pooling scheme for margarine and cooking fats (with two qualities of margarine, instead of the single one that had evoked so much criticism in the autumn) should come into operation on 15th July. On 8th July War Cabinet sanction was secured for the new joint rations to begin on 22nd July.

The consumer enjoyed several options under the new system. He could take 6 oz. all in butter, all in margarine, or combined in any proportions he pleased; similarly, margarine could be taken in lieu of the 2-oz. ration of cooking fat. These provisions created very serious difficulties for rationing administration, for they undermined the already complicated basis on which the retailer was allotted his supplies of rationed foods. The task of issuing permits to obtain rationed supplies devolved on local food offices. Theoretically the amounts were based on the number of a retailer's registered customers, together with suitable adjustments for other sales, e.g., to travellers, members of the forces holding leave or duty ration documents, and establishments buying at retail. The figure so obtained was a maximum, but it was open to the retailer to apply for less; moreover, the Food Office might, at its discretion, scale down his permit if it judged that his stocks were excessive. Some Commodity Divisions tended, contrary to the theory of Rationing Division, to treat permits as if they were definite orders, and honour them in full without more ado; others were stricter, and Meat Division definitely worked on the principle of not meeting permit quantities in full, i.e., of allowing for non-take-up of rations. Furthermore, there was always a considerable time-lag between the return of stock, sales, and purchases by a retailer and any adjustments of permits to it. In short, there could be no ready or exact correspondence between the supplies flowing to a retailer and the amount of his permitted sales.

The combined butter-margarine and margarine-cooking fats rations added a new element of complication. The Ministry had seen at the outset that it could not guarantee to any customer margarine and butter in the exact proportions desired, and that it would have to rely on the retailer to adjust his orders of each in the light of experience. It might have dealt with the problem of how much to issue in the first few weeks by setting an arbitrary proportion, say, of 4 oz. butter to 2 oz. margarine. Instead, it told retailers to order margarine as required during the initial eight weeks of rationing, but took a return from them after a fortnight to serve as a basis for future permits. In addition, it wrote up the existing permits for butter, relating to a 4-oz. ration, by fifty per cent., in order to make sure of covering the needs of those whose customers would want to take all butter.

The result was a run on butter within the rationing system; supplies released rose from 4,800 to 6,600 tons a week, or nearly forty per cent. Alarmed for its stocks, the Butter Division asked that the Rationing Order be amended so as to allow not more than 4 oz. of the combined ration to be taken as butter. This in turn alarmed those responsible for margarine; for there had been a run on *their* stocks between the date margarine rationing was announced and the time it was imposed, and they had no means of limiting demand until permits came into operation. Nor was that all; the apparent superfluity of butter during the first fortnight of the combined ration, or carelessness, or dishonesty, had led retailers to take a sanguine view of their chances of obtaining supplies. In Manchester, for example, the Food Office found that eighty per cent. of retailers had applied for margarine, butter and cooking fats to a total of more than 8 oz. per head of their registered customers; it was said to have a staff of fifty clerks solely engaged in checking these discrepancies. Head-quarters was at once horrified at the work involved and dubious whether the majority of food offices could undertake it.

In any event, the restriction of butter to 4 oz. destroyed the assumptions on which retailers had based their returns; and rather than make an entirely arbitrary adjustment in the initial margarine permits, it was decided to postpone their introduction till 28th September, which would allow of a fresh set of applications being collected from retailers. Butter permits were issued meantime on the basis of the existing returns, but with a ceiling of 4 oz. per registered customer. Before 28th September, however, butter supplies had so fallen as to demand that not more than 2 oz. should be issued on the ration; and yet again Food Offices had to be instructed to vary the permit quantities accordingly. Thus by October the Ministry was at last on the way to achieving the balance between supply and demand it had planned to arrange in July.

The mistake over butter permits could be readily put right; the pitfall into which the combined ration had led officials over margarine was more serious. They had been willing to accept a position in which the only control over margarine consumption for two months would be the rationing Order itself; and thus had denied the argument they had accepted the previous autumn, namely that rationing could not begin until the machinery of allocation was ready. But they had not taken warning from the example of sugar of the need to prevent over-purchases in advance of rationing, nor drawn the conclusion that if margarine rationing was to be imposed ahead of allocation, it might just as well be introduced without notice.

For tea, which was rationed on 9th July, this point had been considered, presumably because tea lends itself so obviously to hoarding. As early as May the Tea Branch had asked for some form of rationing to be introduced, in order to prevent a further fall in stocks; but they were anxious to avoid registration and buying permits, because these would mean (they held) the introduction of a pooled 'National' tea.

For Rationing Division, however, registration was the *sine qua non* of a proper rationing system; if tea was unsuited to registration, it ought not to be rationed at all. Buying permits, it was thought, might possibly be dispensed with; at any rate, they could not be introduced simultaneously with rationing, because, after four or five weeks of discussions on technique, rationing was now urgent. On the other hand, everyone still hoped that it might last only a few weeks. The misgivings of Rationing Division could not be pressed against a temporary device; the first breach with the tradition of 1918, that rationing must embody a consumer-retailer tie, came in the end quite easily. It was no more than official caution that led to the deletion of the word 'temporary' from the final form of the public announcements; not until January 1941 did the Ministry finally give up hope of freeing tea from the ration, by which time the 'loose' and 'anomalous' system was firmly entrenched. The Minister himself had rationed tea with reluctance, and he was even more strongly opposed, on psychological grounds, to depriving people of the blend of tea they preferred.

Tea rationing procedure might not appeal to those officials who were wedded to traditional methods. But it had one merit which makes tea unique among all the foods that were rationed in the first year of war, namely that it was introduced secretly and at once. Other schemes, once their teething troubles were over, settled down to a sure and well-nigh infallible *modus operandi* that the tea scheme could not achieve without heavy amendment. The history of straight rationing by registration was henceforth to be—so far as the delivery of food to the customer was concerned—the most uneventful of administrative successes.[1] But the time it took—on every occasion—to bring into operation might have been a serious handicap if the war had begun as it was expected to begin.

The Ministry was still anything but anxious to extend rationing further than it need. Setting out for War Cabinet approval, at the end of July 1940, a general statement of what food policy should be, the Ministry argued that rationing should only be imposed 'under the strictest compulsion', when scarcity was such that the rich might corner the supply. 'Rationing is', it said, 'essentially inequitable, it provides the same quantity of an article for each person without any consideration of their needs or habits or of their capacity to secure alternatives. It is a restriction of personal liberty, and it tends to undermine the morale of the nation by making people think of the dangers of shortage.'[2] These arguments were, of course, directed towards securing a generous allocation of shipping, at a time when it

---

[1] A detailed study of rationing administration will appear in Vol. II.

[2] 'I really don't want to add anything else to our rationing'. (Lord Woolton to his Parliamentary Secretary (Mr. Boothby), 3rd August 1940.)

still seemed likely that arguments could by themselves achieve it. The Ministry had relied on its own administrative weaknesses before to avoid a reduction in its import programme. They were a double-edged weapon, for the Ministry could not go on insisting on the limitations of straight rationing without incurring the obligation to devise new ways, at once more drastic and less inflexible, of meeting any further setbacks on the supply front.

CHAPTER IX

Food and Inland Transport : the Prospect of Shipping Diversion and its Consequences

I

AMONG the duties included in the Food (Defence Plans) Department's terms of reference was that of making plans for the 'movement' of food and feeding-stuffs in a major war.[1] Its inclusion was more than a formality or a recognition of the obvious fact that food control would have to make provision for the transport of supplies to wherever they might be needed; it reflected a belief that the bombing aircraft especially might make the physical distribution of food a matter of great difficulty. The aspect of the likely effects of bombing that received most attention in the early nineteen-thirties was the possible closure of London and the East Coast ports and the need to divert the greater part of merchant shipping to the West.

The experience of the previous war, notwithstanding the negligible scale of air attacks and the absence of anything like a general policy of diversion, had not been encouraging. After the adoption of the convoy system in 1917 there had been a tendency for shipping to concentrate on Liverpool; despite a sharp fall in total imports into the United Kingdom, port congestion had become so serious as to cause a serious loss of importing capacity. The lesson drawn at the time was that anything like a complete closure of the port of London, for more than a matter of days, would result in such confusion that it should at all costs be avoided. Defences must, it was thought, be provided to protect the movement of the majority of seaborne cargoes to their accustomed ports of discharge.

As memories of the previous war dimmed, however, this judgement began to seem too sweeping. On the one hand, the development of bombing aircraft suggested that diversion would be unavoidable; on the other, it began to be thought that the great growth of road transport might make it possible to solve the problems of cross-country supply that diversion would present. In 1933, at the instance of the Admiralty, a full-scale investigation of the question was begun by a sub-committee of the Committee of Imperial Defence.[2]

---

[1] See Chapter I.

[2] This committee will be referred to as the Distribution of Imports Committee. Its work will be described more fully in other volumes of the Civil Histories.

Although the assembly of data for this inquiry was undertaken in such detail as to be spread over three years, i.e., till 1936, the principles on which it worked were simple. Two assumptions were made: the first, that the United Kingdom would be able, and would need to import roughly the same tonnage as in peace-time; the second, that the East Coast ports—Tyne to Southampton inclusive—would be capable of handling only one-quarter of their normal traffics. The authorities of the ports—large and small—outside this 'danger zone' were asked to estimate the maximum tonnage each could handle, and whether their transit sheds, railways, and other facilities would be sufficient. To this they replied, in general, that each could handle, and indeed in the past had handled, from 80 to 100 per cent. more than at present. A check on these replies was furnished by a measurement of quayage in those ports, which gave a surplus over the estimated requirements.

Port capacity was, therefore, taken to be sufficient. What of the means of transport inland from the 'safe' ports? The railway companies were asked to estimate the maximum tonnage of imports that could be carried away by rail from each, and these estimates were all added together, giving a total of 75 million tons a year, nearly five times the average peace-time imports through the same ports. As for road transport, it was pointed out that the number of heavy goods lorries was four-and-a-half times as great in 1935 as it had been in 1919. The Committee thereupon concluded that a diversion from East to West of seventy-five per cent. of imports normally handled in the East was feasible. There might, it realised, be specific difficulties with commodities such as bulk grain or frozen meat needing special discharge or storage facilities, or from the dislocation of the 'normal merchanting machinery' as a result of diversion, and these would need further investigation.

There were, however, fatal flaws in the reasoning that had led to this reversal of previous opinion. Even taking the port authorities' replies at their face value, there was no warrant for adding them together, thus assuming that all the West Coast ports could be worked simultaneously at full pressure without encountering stringencies of, say, labour or internal transport. Even if in fact the railway facilities at any given port were capable of carrying four or five times the traffic normally passing through it, this did not mean that, for example, all the ports served by lines branching from a single junction could be worked 'all out' without causing a congestion of that junction that would infallibly spread beyond it. The problem of railways needed assessment in terms, not of individual ports alone, but of such things as the handling capacity of junctions and marshalling yards in the hinterland of the Mersey and Bristol Channel ports. So, too, the use to be made of road transport could only be estimated if it were known what proportion of total goods traffic was carried by road under normal conditions.

So far as the ports themselves were concerned, the provision for particular commodities was not ancillary to the main problem, but part and parcel with it; nothing useful could be concluded about port capacity in general until more was known about such questions as the supply of port equipment and the specialisation of facilities as between different ports. It was useless to swell the total of port capacity by including a great number of small ports which were not merely (as was recognised) unable to take large ships, but had no adequate means of loading, discharging, or sorting cargo. Many ports, including some described as 'first-class', like Aberdeen and Barrow-in-Furness, were either remote from or ill-connected by road or rail with the large centres of population that must be the destination of most imports. In fact, if the Thames and Humber could not be used, the only areas to which the bulk of the traffic diverted thence could go would be the Mersey, the Bristol Channel, and the Clyde; and the last-named would be undesirably remote from much of England and Wales.

The conclusion, set down in March 1939, that the findings of the Distribution of Imports Committee were 'complete nonsense',[1] was therefore strictly correct. During 1937 and 1938, however, they were accepted official doctrine, carrying the hall-mark of the Committee of Imperial Defence. In particular, the belief that the railways could deal with the extra burden without severe delays and dislocations appears to have been responsible, before Munich, for a concentration on one aspect of the problem of diversion—the control of ports in war-time—and a comparative neglect of transport inland from the ports. There appears to have been no notion at this time that war might bring with it a general shortage of inland transport facilities, such as could not readily be overcome by restricting inessential or luxury traffics. The fear of inflationary pressure, which had been so powerful a motive in setting food control preparations afoot, does not seem to have made itself felt in this no less important field. While, therefore, from 1936 onwards the food trades were being drawn into consultation, it was not, for example, until a few months before the outbreak of war that the Ministry of Transport was empowered to open talks with the road hauliers.

There were at least two occasions before March 1939 on which officials came within sight of questioning the assumption that transport facilities would be ample in emergency. In June 1937 the Food (Defence Plans) Department prepared a rough estimate of the maximum extra ton-miles *per annum* that inland transport would be required to run in respect of the principal foods, on the extreme

---

[1] Quoted in Hancock and Gowing, *op. cit.* pp. 124–25.

assumptions (*a*) that there would be no reduction in total food imports, (*b*) that there would be no imports at all into ports in the danger area. The sum amounted to about 1,000 million ton-miles. Discussions on this estimate with the Ministry of Transport were inconclusive, but threw up some suggestive pointers. It was stated, for instance, that there was 'no information at all about the haulage of commodities by road vehicles'; that railway facilities to the Bristol Channel ports might impose limitations on their use; and that the extra burden on the railways on account of diversion would amount to at least twenty per cent.[1] of their total traffic in foodstuffs.

A year later, the problem was approached again from another angle. The hypothesis of a seventy-five per cent. diversion from East to West, on which the Distribution of Imports Committee had worked, was changed. Staff opinion now tended to the view that no port area in the United Kingdom could be held immune from air attacks; if so, plans would be needed not for a deliberate long-term diversion to West Coast ports, but for a series of shifts from port to port as occasion might demand—'dispersion' rather than 'diversion.' So far as the Food (Defence Plans) Department was concerned this meant 'a comprehensive plan for feeding the country from any combination, say, of the five largest ports'. The Department went on to indicate the relevant data for such a plan, namely:—

'(1) The berthing capacity of the ports and their discharging capacity for particular kinds of cargo. . . .

(2) The storage capacity of various kinds at those ports.

(3) The processing capacity in the ports and the hinterland.

(4) The transport facilities inland, taking account of the types of conveyance needed (e.g., insulated vans, bulk grain wagons, etc.) and any bridges, tunnels or other bottle-necks which might limit inland distribution. All of these,' it pointed out, 'are required for essential raw materials and for important articles of export, as well as for foodstuffs which cannot be separated if the problem is to be considered properly . . . either the Committee of Imperial Defence or the Port and Transit Standing Committee should appoint someone to consider this problem as a whole.'

It took the opportunity to stress once more the importance of internal transport and storage for the proper distribution of foodstuffs under war conditions, and complained that there was no general picture of storage accommodation in the country. But presumably because of the Munich crisis, the matter was not followed up.

---

[1] The Ministry of Transport wrote in August 1937: 'The total ton-mileage of revenue-earning traffic classified as "Merchandise (excluding Classes 1 to 6)" . . . conveyed by rail in 1936 exceeded 5,000 millions. We are not in a position to say what proportion of this relates to food'. If, therefore, food supplies amounted to considerably less than the total figure, the relative burden on the railways resulting from diversion would be correspondingly greater.

In the spring of 1939, the officials in the Ministry of Transport who were responsible for port and transit matters re-examined the record of 1914–18 experience in diversion, and came to the conclusion that the current doctrine on the subject was gravely mistaken. They took up the estimates, made in the summer of 1937, of the extra ton-mileage that food would have to be carried as a result of diversion. They pointed out that the bulk of this extra traffic would have to go by rail; that in so far as it did not consist of whole cargoes, it would be accompanied by quantities of general goods which also would have to be handled and transported at the West Coast ports. It was obviously impossible to make an exact estimate of the burden; but the burden was obviously sizeable. Moreover, it would 'be concentrated in overwhelming volume on the connections radiating from Plymouth, Bristol, the South Wales ports, Liverpool, Manchester, and Glasgow'. 'Grave doubts must be entertained of the practicability of adding a heavy burden of this character and at short notice to the railways' capacity'. This was particularly so, it was argued, at the outbreak of war, when transport, and particularly the railways, would be bearing the strain of civil evacuation and heavy movements of men and materials for the Services. Precautionary diversion of shipping on a large scale at the outbreak of war would almost certainly create serious congestion at and behind the ports, and cause great confusion to trade.

Of the general validity of these arguments there can be no doubt. But other Departments[1] would not accept so flat a contradiction of previous beliefs; and the agreed report that went to the Committee of Imperial Defence was not only more cautiously phrased than the original draft quoted above, but included the former estimate that the railways could carry 75 million tons inland from the safe ports. However, this was now described as 'optimistic', having regard to the prospective rationing of motor fuel and the heavy demands that would be made on transport at the outbreak of war.

The effect was to set a large question mark against the policy of large-scale diversion without seriously undermining the main pillar on which it rested, namely the belief that railway capacity would be generally ample. Like the estimates of import prospects, those of inland transport facilities had reached, after years of intermittent discussion, a position that was inherently contradictory. The transport authorities, having made the point—about the riskiness of general diversion—that was of practical importance to them, appear to have decided that further speculations would be a waste of precious

---

[1] Including the Food (Defence Plans) Department, who set down the Ministry of Transport, as 'unduly pessimistic'.

In doing so they were in the company of a leading railway manager, who dismissed the fears of the Ministry of Transport as being without foundation. He adduced no solid evidence in support of his views, and no one, at that time, asked for any.

time. Henceforward they were to adopt an attitude of extreme scepticism about the possibilities of forecasting the future. All that could be done, they argued, was to set up as flexible a control machinery as could be devised, and for the rest to rely on improvisation.

This belief in flexibility, together with shortage of time, and the idiosyncrasies of the transport industries, was reflected in the plans for controlling road and rail in war-time. The control proposed for railways, though in form complete enough,[1] was in practice very loose, and the discretion allowed to the railways very wide. The financial arrangements for railway control not being complete when war broke out, no provision could be made in advance for the quotation of special rates for Government traffic, whether in order to secure special discounts for it or to simplify the system of charges. The general trend of the Government's railway policy was very aptly brought out in the financial agreement announced in February 1940, by which in effect it allowed the railways to earn as large a revenue as they could in return for a share in the proceeds.

So far as road transport was concerned, the mere number of operators—some 200,000 in all—rendered the task of control extremely difficult; and it is scarcely surprising that the Ministry of Transport should have been content to begin by organising them into local groups, which should themselves work out pooling schemes for economising vehicles and motor fuel—which was to be issued through group organisers. Although this system of control enabled the Ministry of Transport to keep a close check on the number and whereabouts of goods vehicles in the country, it was not, as it stood, capable of mobilising road transport on a large scale to meet other than local emergencies.

II

During the first year of war, therefore, the provision of inland transport in the United Kingdom, apart from the restrictive effects of motor-fuel rationing and such measures as the black-out, underwent little change from peace-time, so far as the consumer of transport was concerned. As the Ministry of Food's Director of Transport put it[2] in February 1940:

'All forms of transport operate as in normal times; they offer their services for hire or reward to the public—including Government Departments—and the contracts are common commercial contracts arranged directly between the carrying services and their customers.'

---

[1] Control of the railways was exercised by the Ministry of Transport through a Railway Executive Committee. This was composed of the General Managers of the railway companies, and was responsible to the Minister for the operation of the railways as a unified whole. In practice, this arrangement did not produce complete unity of effort by the railways in the early part of the war.

[2] In evidence before the House of Commons Select Committee on National Expenditure.

The Transport Division of the Ministry of Food had been formed in the expectation that it would, along with corresponding organs in other Departments, present its requirements to a centralised transport control; but, at any rate in 1939–40, the conditions that would have made such a control possible did not exist. Transport Division therefore took on the rôle of a defensive, almost one might say predatory, organisation, designed to make sure that food did not go short of transport whatever happened to other claimants.

This purely defensive quality was most obviously, and necessarily, displayed at the outbreak of war. It had been arranged with the Ministry of Transport that:

'vehicles normally engaged wholly or mainly for the conveyance of raw materials for food manufacture, for the bulk or wholesale distribution of essential foods,'

might not be taken for any military or civil defence purpose except by prior agreement. War Office instructions were issued accordingly; nevertheless in September 1939 numerous food vehicles were seized both by the Army and Civil Defence authorities. These were promptly reported by the divisional officers for food transport and taken up by Headquarters, and within a few days the seizures were stopped and the vehicles returned or replaced.

It was several months at least before the status and authority of the Transport Division within the Ministry of Food itself was sufficiently clarified. The separate commodity divisions at headquarters retained the right to procure their own transport; and neither the Director of Food Transport, nor his officers in the regions and in the principal ports, enjoyed unquestioned authority over the movement of individual foodstuffs. The control of Port Food Movement Officers over, for instance, Port Area Grain Committees and Port Meat or Bacon Agents tended to be rather shadowy, for all that the Movement Officer was a member of the Port Emergency Committee. As for the Assistant Divisional Food Officers (Transport), there was something in the remark of one of them at a pre-war conference to the effect that they were 'Transport Officers without transport'. Too much should not be made, however, even at the outset, of such uncertainties of duty and jurisdiction; the importance of these officers was that they provided the Ministry of Food with eyes and ears that were especially expert in the transport problems of their localities.

During the first year of war, there was no visible strengthening of Government control over inland transport. The Transport Division of the Ministry of Food appears to have been alone both in advocating that all transport could and should be planned and in attempting to treat food transport problems as a single whole. Indeed, its convictions were so strong that it tended at first to brush aside or underrate the practical difficulties in the way. Some of these were inherent in

K

food control itself, for example, the operational autonomy of commodity divisions and the limitation of effective control to the major bulk foodstuffs in the early stages of distribution. (Meat alone was in Ministry ownership down to the retail stage, and meat was to set an example in the rational use of transport.) The Ministry's knowledge of the movement of groceries and provisions at the wholesale stage was insufficient to make reform simple and free from hazards. Moreover, the whole of food control was based on the minimum of interference with normal trade practices. Any attempt to rationalise food distribution beyond the first-hand stage would mean drastically limiting the trader's right to choose his own supplier under control; it would, for instance, raise the problem of the Co-operative Movement in an acute form. However strong the *a priori* case for a revolution in distributive methods might seem to be, it was too weak in facts and figures to be able to win an easy victory.[1]

The first months of war brought with them the experience of shipping diversion in practice; the precautionary measures taken at the end of August 1939 had been relaxed in mid-September, only to be introduced in mid-October, when the first inward convoys were expected to suffer heavy attacks from the air. Although total arrivals of shipping were much below normal and the proportion of ships diverted to the West was not high, complaints were so numerous as to constrain the War Cabinet to allow ships to use East Coast ports 'where this was necessary to avoid substantially increased expense or delay that would have serious effects on production'—a proviso that may be presumed to cover the majority of cargoes normally landed on the East Coast.

However, the Port and Transit Standing Committee of the Ministry of Transport was asked to inquire urgently into the steps necessary to secure and prolong the maximum amount of diversion. But the inquiry was naturally limited to matters within the Committee's competence, such as the facilities for discharge of ships overside into barges and coasters, the capacity of the smaller ports, and the despatch of meat by rail from the West to London cold stores. Its report could do no more than hint at such measures as the more effective use of canals or the compulsory diversion of traffic from rail to coast-wise shipping. On the matters specifically remitted to it the Committee was vague but on the whole discouraging, and moved the Minister of Transport to decide that precautionary diversion had better be abandoned.

But what if diversion were to become a necessity? How far was it possible or desirable to make detailed preparations beforehand to meet it? The Ministry of Transport's attitude combined faith in the

---

[1] Cf. the fate of the 'consumer depot' scheme, Chapter X below.

ability of the 'flexible machine of transport', particularly the railways, to meet any emergency with doubt about the usefulness of making 'precise plans for transport in a series of assumed circumstances'. As to the latter, the Ministry of Food's transport experts were more sanguine. They maintained, on the basis of their experience in dealing with controlled foodstuffs, that it was quite practicable to make detailed plans for the movement of goods from the West Coast ports to prearranged destinations. In December 1939 they had set up at Ministry of Food headquarters what they called a 'Central Commodity Movement Control', which kept records of all incoming controlled food cargoes by ship and by port. It was the Port Food Movement Officer's duty to make arrangements, in conjunction with the local officer of the Commodity Division, for the clearance of foodstuffs from ships and quays to local warehouses or for their dispatch further afield. He was to see that goods were cleared away from 'the ordinary channels of movement' so that quays and transit sheds were kept clear; and he was given overriding authority to remove both uncontrolled and controlled foodstuffs from the dock side if instructions for their disposal could not be obtained. He was at all times to report his activities to Headquarters, which would also instruct him in case of difficulty.

Transport Division had, moreover, drawn up, in consultation with the railways, a special scheme for dealing with the problem of supplying East Coast flour mills with grain from the West Coast ports. This scheme involved the running of up to fourteen special grain trains a day, composed of converted coal hopper wagons, and the provision of a special conveyor at Sheffield for transferring the grain to water transport. Similar schemes were in view for meat and oil-seeds. But, as the Ministry pointed out, they must be considered in conjunction with other Departments 'in order that by advance planning conflicting demands upon the transport facilities may be reduced to the minimum'. The grain scheme was a case in point, inasmuch as in its full form it would require the services of 800 wagons normally used for coal.

When, in March 1940, the War Cabinet asked the Minister for Co-ordination of Defence to look into diversion plans afresh, the Ministry of Food explained these proposals to him; and it seems that they made some impression on Ministers. At any rate a more active approach to the problem followed. A 'Transport Planning Sub-Committee' of the Port and Transit Organisation was set up; a definite estimate (43 million tons) of the tonnage to be diverted to West Coast ports was made, and the opinion of the railway and port authorities sought upon its distribution between ports and the possibility of handling it. By the time the replies were received, France had fallen and the assumptions on which the inquiry was based had been undermined. Nevertheless, the railway reply deserves mention, not so much for its own sake as for the interpretation that was put upon it.

The railways were now rather more cautious than they had been in the days of the Committee on the Distribution of Imports. No satisfactory answer, they said, could be given 'except by the artificial elimination of a variety of disturbing elements which would in actual practice very materially affect the validity of the answer'. These disturbing elements were listed as:

(a) heavy rushes of other business, troop movements, evacuations, etc.;

(b) abnormal interruptions caused by air raids;

(c) abnormal weather.

The railways postulated further that traffic must come forward from the ports with 'reasonable regularity'; this proviso, they said, was quite compatible with the irregular arrival of shipping . . . since this irregularity will be to a large extent smoothed out by the limitations of the discharging capacity of the port itself'. Given all these conditions they thought, but for certain reservations about particular routes, that they would be able to handle the diverted traffic.

In the summer of 1940, and on a broad view of the inter-relation of different kinds of transport, the railway reply might have been taken as the reverse of encouraging. It could scarcely be expected that, in a situation calling for large-scale diversion of shipping, all else affecting railway capacity would be normal. Moreover, the reference to the limitations on discharge of ships had sinister implications; if exceptional measures were taken to speed up port working, they might be nullified by the consequent congestion of the railways. These implications escaped notice. Ministers were told, on the contrary, that the position regarding ports and railways was 'relatively satisfactory'. The absence of sufficient deep-water berths on the West was, it was suggested, far graver.

The railways' faith in themselves, and the Ministry of Transport's faith in them, were exemplified also in discussion of what should be done about imported meat if refrigerated ships had all to go to the West Coast. The Ministry of Food had been far from satisfied with the way in which rail transport for meat had operated during the winter of 1939–40; there had been numerous occasions on which, for want of specialised rolling-stock, road transport had had to be called on at the last moment. The Ministry was not convinced that the railways had in practice effected a complete pooling of individual companies' insulated vans. Insulated road vehicles, on the other hand, had been pooled under a plan sponsored by the Food (Defence Plans) Department and operated by the trade even before full control of meat and livestock had come into force.

Plans for transporting meat under diversion, therefore, were based on the full use of this road transport pool. But when they were made known to the Ministry of Transport and the railway companies, the latter protested that even under emergency conditions they would be able to cope with the bulk of this traffic. Against its will, therefore, the Ministry of Food was persuaded to amend the scheme so as to give rail the lion's share of the work. It continued to press, however, for a more effective pooling of the specialised rolling-stock; a point which was emphasised by further incidents during July and August 1940.

So far as meat was concerned, the risk that the railways might be overburdened was mitigated by the Ministry of Food's ability to ensure that road transport was maintained in readiness for an emergency. For commodities that might be dependent on general road haulage no such insurance could be effected. From the very first, therefore, the Ministry of Food had misgivings about the policy, based primarily of course on a desire to economise motor-fuel, of encouraging traffic to go by rail in preference to other forms of transport. In particular, it had decided, in choosing the means by which controlled foodstuffs should travel, to leave out of account the financial benefits that the Treasury stood to obtain from increased rail traffic by reason of its profit-sharing agreement with the companies. The reasons for this decision were financial as well as strategic, since to send food by rail instead of road would tend to increase transport costs and hence the price of food to the consumer. At a time when a policy of food subsidies was not yet firmly established over the whole field, this was a point which the Ministry might not overlook.

Nevertheless it was conscious that it must rely on the railways to transport the great bulk of foodstuffs. Transport Division was prompt to take advantage of the 'exceptional rates' to be had for individual large-scale consignments—a display of business acumen that was to serve it well when the subject of a flat rate for all Government traffic was reopened. It also established, during the early months of 1940, machinery for regular discussion of common problems with the Goods Managers of the four railway groups. Initially there was a certain amount of friction between the Ministry and the railwaymen, but this soon gave way to a sustained good relationship, based on tact and the mutual acknowledgment of expertise. Transport Division, just because its members understood the day-to-day problems confronting the railway operator, was able to get the best out of him and to persuade him to adopt new methods of operation to meet critical conditions.

During the first year of war, the Ministry of Food's transport organisation attained maturity, though not completeness. Although the Ministry was able to put its finger on the movement of bulk foods to their destination, the multitudinous movements of privately-owned foods in the later stages of distribution were as yet wholly uncharted. Even so, there existed nothing comparable at the Ministry of Supply, which was responsible for the greater part of imports not controlled by the Ministry of Food. While the picture of war-time demands on transport, even for the bulk commodities, was still incomplete, there was—partly for that very reason—incomplete mastery of the resources to meet those demands, and a lack of integrated machinery for mobilising them. These weaknesses were to be emphasised by the transport crisis that lay ahead.

CHAPTER X

Food Warehousing and Port Clearance

I

THE warehousing of foodstuffs, as of other commodities, forms part of their movement from producer to ultimate consumer. Stocks of food, and stores to hold them, perform the same function as reservoirs and storage tanks do for water supply; they smooth out irregularities in the flow in order that the consumer may draw his supplies as and when required. Again, just as water may require filtration or other treatment before it is distributed to households, so foods may require processing of some kind—the milling of wheat into flour, the refining of raw sugar, for example; or treatment that is functionally analogous to this, whether it be the mere splitting of large consignments into smaller ('breaking bulk') or the sorting of them into grades. Food coming from overseas must be transferred from one sort of transport to another. All these operations necessitate the accumulation of greater or smaller stocks. One may express the principle generally by saying that stocks will be necessary at any point in the line of distribution where the rate of movement changes; and a condition of continuous movement must be the existence of stocks sufficient to accommodate the maximum variation in this rate. That means that the warehouse or reservoir must never be so empty that no more can be drawn out of it, or so full that no more can go into it. If either of these conditions is reached, distribution will be interrupted.

If these elementary principles be applied to the problem of warehousing requirements under war conditions, it will at once become apparent that war must tend to increase the demands on storage space in terms of a given flow of supplies to the consumer. Sinkings, delays, and diversions will cause irregularity in overseas arrivals—the inward flow into the reservoir. Inland transport delays, shortages of labour, the black-out, air raid damage to processing plant—all these will upset the outward flow. At every stage, therefore, it will be necessary to hold higher stocks than are normally held, unless the consumer is to risk going short.

No less important than the increased size of war-time stocks is the problem of their location. Since the United Kingdom depends so much on imports, it is natural that both warehouses and processing plant should gravitate to the ports and indeed to the dock areas themselves. The operation of transfer from seaborne to inland transport acts, that is to say, as a magnet for other operations such as flour milling, sugar refining, and the cold storage of meat. The dockside flour mill, receiving bulk wheat by suction direct from the ship's hold and delivering bagged flour into road or rail wagons, illustrates in its most obvious form the economic advantage of location.

If bulk foodstuffs like grain, sugar, and oilseeds are to be subject to shipping diversion, i.e. landed at unaccustomed ports, stocks at those ports are bound to be increased. In so far as greater use can be made of processing plant there, the transport problem may be relatively simple; even so, minimum stock requirements for maintaining distribution may be expected to increase more than proportionately to the increased tonnage being handled. In practice, however, the problem is likely to be more complicated. Suppose the Port of London to be wholly or partly closed to shipping, but the population to remain and to require to be fed through processing plant in the London area: not only will special overland movements of bulk foods have to be devised, but minimum stocks will need to be higher than usual both at the mill or refinery and at the port of entry. In general, any departure from the normal routes of supply will entail an increase of *working stocks*. Diversion of shipping will mean increased stocks on the west, without a commensurate diminution on the east.

For other commodities, such as tea, dried fruit, and canned fish, the location of processing plant in the port areas does not present quite the same difficulty. (The concentration of tea-packing plant in London and Manchester is analogous to flour milling and cold storage; but determination can overcome it.) This type of commodity, however, is very apt to produce port congestion. It comes in as part of general, i.e. mixed cargo, and is normally sorted to marks, that is grades or varieties, and into consignments, in *transit sheds* on the quay. Now it is a maxim of port operation that 'the ship can always beat the quay'; discharging takes less time than sorting and despatch. The prospect of shipping diversion, therefore, drew attention to the need for preventing transit sheds from being choked with unsorted or unclaimed goods, lest one ship be prevented from discharging promptly by the accumulation of previous cargoes on the quayside. Before the war, however, and indeed after it had begun, this problem was seen in the narrow context of port administration rather than in the wider one of transport as a whole.

So far the problem of vulnerability of port stocks has not been touched upon. Obviously, any large concentration of stocks presents a target which would be better dispersed. But it is evident that the task of dispersal is a heavy, if not impossible, undertaking, even for those commodities not tied to their processing plant. The mere holding of additional stocks inland by way of insurance raises transport problems; and one might almost go so far as to say that such stocks tend to breed additional stocks in the ports. The greatest care will be required in choosing sites and controlling transport facilities, if the ports are not to be further congested by the very measures taken to relieve them.

One may sum up the analysis as follows. First, that the optimum level of port stocks will be the lowest that is consistent with free movement, not only through the port but at all stages of distribution. Secondly, that under war conditions this optimum can only be attained by a deliberate and sustained effort to reverse the natural tendency for stocks to pile up in port areas. Thirdly, that in so far as port stocks are kept down, there will be pressure on warehousing facilities inland. Fourthly, that an effective warehousing policy can be evolved only in the light of an understanding of transport resources and prospects.

The pre-war planners were conscious of much of the above. They saw, for instance, that it would be an intolerable waste of transport to try and move the stocks serving London's flour mills, sugar refineries, and crushing mills away from the dockside, so long as those plants continued to work. They realised also that the only London stocks that could usefully be dispersed in advance of an emergency were those of tea, butter, and frozen meat, and then only to the extent of their excess over the minimum working requirements of the London area. (Even so, the dispersal of tea caused great confusion in the trade and had hurriedly to be abandoned when the attack did not materialise.)

On the other hand, the function of port warehouses in relation to the movement of commodities was far from being clearly understood; there was a persistent tendency to suppose that the clearance of ports could and should be carried to an extent that was quite impracticable, even supposing that accommodation could have been found inland. The Food (Defence Plans) Department, discussing the effect of shipping diversion on grain imports, could write, early in 1938, that transport inland from the port was a 'limiting factor' about whose capacity nothing was known, and at the same time assert that 'under emergency conditions all grain stores [i.e., in the ports] would become transit stores.'

For grain stores attached to mills this could never be possible; the mills would have to have a working stock of grain, which, for uninterrupted operation, might need to be higher than in peace-time. Apart from this, it would seem unlikely that, in a war that was to cause ships to be diverted to unaccustomed ports, and ports themselves to be attacked from the air (to name only two of its inconveniences), transport was likely to be organised so as to render port storage all but unnecessary.

The Food (Defence Plans) Department was not alone in these views; they appear to have been widely held among those responsible for port operation, not merely at the Ministry of Transport but in the ports themselves. It was suggested that not only transit sheds but port warehouses on the West ought to be kept empty; a proposal contemptuously described later by a transport expert, who became the Ministry of Food's Director of Food Transport in September 1939, as having been propagated by those who did not know the difference between the two. He pointed out, what was certainly true, that not merely did the use of port warehouses not hinder port clearance, it actually assisted the process. Apart from anything else, the interference with normal movement that the non-use of port warehouses would entail could not but dislocate transport and thus increase the congestion it was supposed to remedy.

However mistaken the belief may have been, it served to underline the need for extra storage accommodation inland. This did not necessarily mean that new warehouses would have to be built. It might be possible, so it was thought, to improvise them for general goods. After Munich the Office of Works began a survey of premises in the Midlands, and a central register was set up on which premises could be earmarked by Departments for requisition in time of war. Specialised storage, such as was required for bulk grain, could not be improvised, as the Food (Defence Plans) Department was to learn from practical experience. Financial considerations had decreed that the Government security stock of wheat should be housed in existing warehouses. In March 1939 grain ships had to be held on demurrage in the port of Liverpool because the dockside silos were full of Government wheat.[1] Some of the demurrage charge fell on the Treasury—a useful object-lesson in the functions of port storage, which may have smoothed the way for the Department's silo construction scheme, approved about the same time but not begun until after war had broken out.

II

Cold storage, another special problem, had won special attention from the Distribution of Imports Committee, which had reported in 1936 that there was a shortage of space outside the East and South Coast 'danger zone' amounting to about seven million cubic feet. The Food (Defence Plans) Department was specifically asked to look into this by the Committee of Imperial Defence. It did not take long to discover that the estimate was framed on doubtful assumptions, chief of which was that the whole of the London cold stores were kept

---
[1] See Chapter II above.

completely full under normal conditions. The amount of traffic to be diverted to stores in the 'safe' area was therefore exaggerated, perhaps by as much as 100 per cent.

As against this, however, the estimate had not taken into account either the fact that larger reserves of refrigerated produce would normally be held in war-time, or that chilled beef, which normally goes straight into consumption ex ship, would be replaced by frozen beef, which requires cold storage. Further, experience in the last war had shown that extra cold stores were needed, and in fact had to be built by the Government. The Department therefore resolved to make a complete survey of cold storage accommodation, not merely by inviting proprietors to make returns, but also arranging for one of Lloyds' surveyors to make a complete inspection of every sizeable undertaking. This was a lengthy process—lengthier than the Department had expected—and though the questionnaire to owners was sent out early in 1938, the inspection was not complete until August 1939.

As early as April of that year, however, the Department had come to the conclusion that there would be a grave deficiency of cold storage outside the danger zone, when regard was had to the stocks of frozen meat, butter, and bacon, that it proposed to hold in war-time. Moreover, there was evidence of an increasing tendency among provincial owners of cold stores to close down their plant owing to lack of business. This was alarming, but difficult to stop; proposals for subsidising cold-store owners for keeping their empty space in working order were considered, only to be rejected as putting a premium on inefficiency. Instead it was proposed (*a*) to accumulate security reserves of butter, etc., which could be put into cold stores to provide an incentive to keep them open, (*b*) to acquire a reserve of equipment to be used in erecting Government stores after the outbreak of war, (*c*) to erect some five million cubic feet of space near the 'secondary ports' on the West Coast, such as Plymouth, which were expected to be used for meat imports in case of diversion, (*d*) to purchase a number of old refrigerated ships for use as emergency cold stores.

These proposals had not got beyond semi-official discussion with the Treasury when war broke out and rendered most of them otiose. Nevertheless, the estimates of requirements on which they were based continued to form the ground for a revised plan submitted at the end of October. This proposed to build 12 million cubic feet of 'simple standardised' cold storage accommodation at an estimated cost of £2,300,000 either near the West Coast ports or in the 'less vulnerable inland areas'. The Treasury refused sanction, however, for more than five million cubic feet, partly on the grounds that schemes for buying old refrigerated ships and getting existing stores reconditioned would cover five out of the estimated total deficiency of 13 millions, partly in the belief that the Ministry had over-stated both its probable stocks of refrigerated produce and the extent to which East Coast cold stores would prove to be unusable. No obsolete vessels were in fact available, and the Ministry had few hopes of getting much old storage reconditioned; but since it was clear that the Office of Works could not deal with a larger order, owing to competing demands on labour and materials, the position was accepted for the time being.[1]

Meantime the 'port warehouse into transit shed' theory had been carried a stage further. In April 1939, in response to a request from the Committee of Imperial Defence for an inquiry into the general storage problem, the Ministry of Transport propounded a scheme for building inland warehouses for general goods at Government expense. This was taken over and elaborated by the Food (Defence Plans) Department into a three-fold plan for providing (*a*) 'primary' warehouses capable of holding in total some 750,000 tons of food (other than grain or frozen meat), (*b*) 'secondary' warehouses, near the consuming areas, for a further 150,000 tons, (*c*) a special series of warehouses in the environs of London to hold the 100,000 tons of foodstuffs it was proposed to disperse from London stocks. This plan, first propounded in August 1939, was urged on the Treasury during that autumn. The Treasury, however, resisted, pending proof that existing accommodation was in fact insufficient, and they found an unexpected ally in the Ministry of Food's own Director of Food Transport, who claimed that he had never been properly consulted on the proposals and dismissed them with scorn.

Certainly as yet neither the Ministry nor anyone else had the detailed information or the grasp of essential principle on which a coherent warehousing policy, properly wedded to transport considerations, could be based. During the first winter of war the Ministry's premises section continued the pre-war practice of registering and earmarking premises that might be suitable for food storage. But the

---

[1] The figures given to the Treasury are open to criticism on the grounds that they exaggerated the allowance for working (i.e. empty) space, and made provision for too large a reserve of frozen meat; on the other hand they included nothing for fish, frozen eggs, or poultry. Thus, while the requirements figure actually given was rather over 34 million cubic feet, there would be no difficulty in making out a convincing case for 25 millions on the one hand or 40 on the other. On the supply side, everything depended on the use that could be made of the 27 million cubic feet in the 'danger zone'. The assumption that only thirty per cent. of it would remain in operation was clearly quite arbitrary.

The Ministry later discovered that cold store proprietors had seriously exaggerated the capacity of their stores, which it estimated in May 1940 as totalling 37 instead of 43·4 million cubic feet. As against this deficiency, however, it was able to set off the discovery that ten per cent. instead of twenty per cent. was a sufficient allowance of free space. This gave an 'effective storage capacity' of 33 million cubic feet. (The Ministry's statement, that there was then a 'small deficiency' of cold storage space as against requirements, was a mistake, due to comparing this net figure with the original requirements figure which included an allowance for working space of seven million cubic feet. A just comparison would have shown a surplus of five million not a deficit of one million.) The case for new building rested, in fact, solely on the need to provide against loss of stores by enemy action.

register so compiled omitted or garbled such essential points as rail access or intake capacity;[1] many earmarked premises were later found, on inspection, to be entirely useless for the purpose.

Even more important, the Ministry had given little thought to the problem of management and the effect of any storage scheme on the normal channels of distribution. Warehouse management was a specialised job, requiring particular skills; the movement of foodstuffs through wholesale channels was complex in the extreme, and closely wedded to the existing geographical distribution of storage space. Any plan for storing large quantities of food inland must fulfil a series of difficult conditions. It must be capable of operation alongside, or in conjunction with, the normal methods which the Ministry was committed to maintain. It must be adaptable to the varying conditions within each Food Division. It must appear convincing to the traders and warehousekeepers who would have to operate it. It must take into account war-time transport difficulties, and shortages of materials and labour. Finally, it must be capable of being brought into operation at short notice. These requirements alone, apart from Treasury objections, meant that though the principle of building stores was probably sound, the plan of August 1939 was too simple in conception.

The 'depot scheme' that Transport Division now put forward instead, though it proposed to make use of existing premises, was equally guilty of over-simplification. It proposed in principle that the whole of Great Britain should be divided into 800 areas, with a minimum population of 25,000, each area to be served by a single 'consumer' depot. Some eighty 'buffer depots' were to form an intermediate stage in the distributive chain. These depots, and the transport serving them, were to be 'neutral'; they were to supersede the usual trade methods of physical distribution, but the existing financial and accounting relationships between traders were to be preserved. The drastic simplicity of these proposals arose, no doubt, from the impatience of a transport expert with the apparent disorder of existing methods; but translating the scheme into practice was not just simply a question of putting pins into small-scale maps. One could not abstract the mere movement of commodities from the whole economic process of which it was a part; the outbreak of war had not given the Ministry a clean slate on which to work.

Moreover, Transport Division was far from carrying the whole Ministry with it. News of the proposals reached Divisional Food Officers, several of whom protested that the scheme was clean contrary to the arrangements for grouping wholesalers, and earmarking alternative premises for use in emergency, that had been agreed upon before the war. In October, therefore, the scheme was ostensibly

---

[1] Premises a mile or more from a railway station were often listed as having 'rail access'.

shelved; but it continued to be the ideal on which the Transport Division was set, and which, in the early confused months of the Ministry's existence, it could elaborate undisturbed. In March 1940 the scheme was expounded, with a somewhat greater wealth of circumstantial detail, to the House of Commons Select Committee on National Expenditure. Finally, the new Minister, Lord Woolton, was persuaded to announce it, as an all but accomplished fact, to a Press Conference on 27th May. Only after it was too late to cancel the talk to the Press did the Minister and his chief advisers discover that the whole scheme did not exist—except on paper. There can seldom have been another occasion when a Government Department was constrained to discourage discussion of its own announcement almost before the words of the Minister had died away.

III

Fortunately, the low level of food stocks during that winter had prevented any shortage of accommodation from becoming apparent; and there was still time for resolute action to be effective. The Ministry now appointed a leading London wharfinger to be Director of Warehousing, with the sole task of establishing, in the shortest possible time, those eighty or so large 'buffer depots' that had formed the least controversial part of the scheme to which the Ministry had been publicly committed. These depots could be set up without disrupting the existing channels of distribution, if they were used for goods in the ownership of the Ministry or of first-hand suppliers acting on its behalf.[1] Their use would of course complicate the physical movement of goods, though this might on the other hand be eased by the relief given to the ports; and numerous problems arose when they came into operation. But in principle, they were not subversive of existing arrangements; the only major obstacle in the way of their establishment was the sheer difficulty of finding suitable buildings. The Ministry's existing register was both incomplete and inaccurate; the only course open was virtually a fresh search 'in the field'. With the aid of Divisional Office staffs and local warehousemen, an astonishing variety of premises was pressed into service in the space of a few weeks.[2]

A buffer depot constituted a unit for management purposes, and some few did consist in fact of a single set of premises. But the majority were simply agglomerations of miscellaneous buildings, in the more rural districts often scattered in small towns or villages some

---

[1] The attempt to persuade wholesalers to use the depots was not, however, given up immediately.

[2] Among the first hundred depots were chapels, cinemas, ice-rinks, and racing stables —to say nothing of the more usual factories and mills.

distance apart. There could be no question here of parcelling up the country into neat sections, each with its own depot; nor could there be any real consideration of the relation of the network as a whole, as distinct from individual depots, to transport facilities—no nice calculation of the changing load on the railways that the establishment of buffer depots would impose. This problem might have become a serious one had the total tonnage of food moving to the depots been larger; in practice the chief problem of food movement which they presented was on account of the restricted rate at which food could go in and out of them. In the early days there were many complaints of the immobilisation of lorries and railway wagons for this cause—a serious difficulty because it could so readily infect the whole transport system, and produce precisely that strain on the ports, which the depots were designed to avoid. It was mitigated, if not avoided altogether, by a stringent central control. Foodstuffs might not move into buffer depots from the ports except after allocation by the Warehousing Division at headquarters and at a rate determined by the Commodity Movement Control after considering individual depots' handling capacity.

The progress of the scheme in the first few months is difficult to assess with any great accuracy, owing to the lag between the selection of depots, their requisitioning, the provision of gear, and the final stocking of them. By January 1941, however, the Ministry could claim that 1,000 premises were under requisition, with a total capacity of half a million tons, ninety per cent. of which was occupied. By the summer of 1941 total 'buffer and sub-depot space', virtually all of it occupied, was running at a little under one million tons. Practically all of this consisted of existing buildings; it was not until January 1941 that the Ministry had found it necessary to embark on a programme of new buildings for food storage, and by the summer of that year only the first few thousand tons of space so provided was in operation. The buffer depot scheme was first and foremost a triumph of improvisatory resource.

As such, it bore marks of its hasty origin. The charges for housing merchandise were hastily drawn up on the basis of the high London rates, and had to be scaled down after protests from Divisional Food Officers and others that the Director of Warehousing was provoking a general rise in provincial warehouse rates. The task of finding suitable sites was complicated by a fiat from the defence authorities that food stocks surplus to local needs must be withdrawn from the ten-mile coastal belt—an instruction which, literally interpreted, would have made food distribution impossible. Were, for instance, the shores of the Scottish firths to be included, it would have forbidden the use not only of Edinburgh, Dundee, and Aberdeen, but Glasgow itself. Again, Commodity Divisions were apt to apply peace-time standards to the choice of warehouses for their products, whether on account of preserving them in good condition or of the possibility of sorting to marks.

The worst difficulty of all, however, was the fact that every other Department was also on the hunt for space, whether for storage or production purposes. There was as yet no central authority to co-ordinate these demands or to determine priorities.[1] Moreover, the Ministry found itself at a disadvantage, compared with other Departments, because it had no direct powers of requisition, but must act through the Ministry of Works and Buildings—whose local regions coincided hardly at all with the Food and Civil Defence regions—a point that led to great difficulty and delay. Merely earmarking a building on the Office of Works' register was no longer enough to protect it from seizure.

The Ministry of Aircraft Production, particularly after heavy bombing started, acquired particular odium with other Departments. Letters of altogether exceptional vigour passed between the Permanent Secretaries of Food and Aircraft Production: 'we are anxious to co-operate with you', wrote the former on 23rd October 1940, '. . . but if you want us to continue you must stop your people from behaving like pirates'. In mid-October the problem of co-ordinating demands for warehouse space was taken up by the Lord President's Committee and referred to an *ad hoc* Committee on Warehousing, whose report recommended the appointment of a Controller of Warehouse Premises, responsible to a 'neutral' Minister such as the President of the Board of Trade. But before the Lord President's Committee could come to any decision, the Minister of Aircraft Production secured from the War Cabinet the right to take over all premises earmarked but not actually in occupation by another Department.[2] Not until February 1941 was Lord Beaverbrook's opposition overcome, and not until 15th May did the Board of Trade Factory and Storage Control come formally into being, and the scramble for accommodation end. In that scramble the Ministry of Food had evidently been pretty successful, as close on a million tons of storage space in under a year bore witness.

The original paper plans had contemplated the establishment of some 800 'consumer depots' to supersede existing channels of distribution. In July 1940, however, Divisional Food Officers were sounded on the possibility of setting up 'consumer depots', alongside existing

---

[1] The Food Defence Plans Department had suggested as early as 1st September 1939 that a unified control of storage space should be set up, but had won no response from other Departments.

[2] The Ministry gave secret telephonic instructions to D.F.O.s to forestall Lord Beaverbrook by putting some foodstuffs into as many earmarked premises as possible. It appears that in this Lord Woolton's officials were more zealous than the Minister himself might have approved.

channels, under the management of wholesalers or other traders. The response varied according to the area concerned. Those divisions, like the Midland and West Scotland, which were amply supplied with wholesalers, tended to regard consumer depots as superfluous; others failed to see any vital distinction between a consumer depot and a small buffer depot; others again, whose needs were largely supplied from outside their own boundaries (Eastern II, Southern, North of Scotland), seized on the consumer depots as a means of securing food reserves in time of emergency. Indeed, the North Wales Divisional Food Officer went so far as to say that in normal times the depots would be useless to the wholesale trade inasmuch as they would not be able to handle a sufficient range of groceries, not all of them foodstuffs. Again, it was urged that wholesalers in many districts would be able to carry larger stocks if the Ministry would grant them credit and release more of its own stocks to them.

In the end the discussion crystallised into a fairly clear choice for the Ministry; either the consumer depots must be 'dumps', in which the Divisional Officer could store a mixed bag of non-perishable food-stuffs against emergency, or they must be nothing more than extensions of the buffer depots, in which goods were stored at the first-hand stage of distribution. The adoption of the name 'buffer sub-depot' for them indicates the decision that was taken; in the realisation that emergency provisions must not be allowed to interfere with the smooth working of the ordinary distributive machine. Such a conclusion was really implicit in the whole divisional organisation of the Ministry, bearing as it did only a casual and accidental relationship to the channels through which food flowed to the consumer. The Divisional Food Officer could watch and warn; but his full activity would only be called for and was only possible when communications were cut.[1]

The achievement of the buffer depot scheme in its first year of operation was substantial, if regard be had only to the amount of additional storage space it provided. But the effect it had on the actual amount of food held in port areas was negligible; the Ministry's stocks survey showed that between July 1940 and May 1941 bulk stocks of food in 'inland centres' and total stocks each increased by roughly the same amount, 400,000 tons. Nearly a year's effort had only sufficed to prevent port stocks from increasing. (An attempt to put a better face on this by limiting more strictly the definition of a port area made the figures before and after May 1941 incompletely comparable without altering the picture in substance.) For reasons already explained, it was inevitable that this should be so for those commodities forming by far the greater part of food stocks: wheat,

---

[1] See Chapter IV above. 'Emergency' food stores were to be provided later, as a separate scheme.

L

raw sugar, oilseeds, and frozen meat, and for those dependent on
cold stores, namely, meat, butter, and bacon. Margarine stocks, too,
though small in amount (two to three weeks' supply), were concentrated around the two great factories at Bromborough and Purfleet.
Tea could only be dispersed when blended and packeted, and its
store life in this form is short. There remained for the buffer depots
only such things as flour, refined sugar, canned milk, canned meat,
and jam; and even of these a considerable part must be left in port
areas to feed the population. Nevertheless, it seems clear that many
actual buffer depots must have been in port areas, though not of
course on the dockside; and that some commodity divisions, notably
those controlling canned meat and jam, had been for one reason or
another backward in dispersal.

Though improvements could still be made in this commodity or
that, it was broadly true to say that by the summer of 1941 foodstuffs
were so far dispersed as to ensure that none of the 104 zones into
which the Ministry divided the country for the purpose of its stock
survey had less than three weeks' supply of the principal types of
food. Certain apparent concentrations of particular foods—butchers'
meat, canned meat, canned salmon, and cheese—were explicable in
terms of a deliberate decision to regard these as nutritional alternatives for emergency purposes.

The later years of the war were to see an immense increase in the
amount of inland storage space occupied by foodstuffs. But that increase would be no more than commensurate with the rise in food
stocks themselves as the Ministry strove to widen more and more its
margin of safety, and as the amount of home-produced grain, for
instance, rose year by year. It was only made possible by a comprehensive building programme. The proportion of port stocks was thus
to be diminished; but their actual size and their vital importance to
the maintenance of food supplies over any time above two or three
weeks were to remain almost unchanged during the whole of the war.

PART III

CHAPTER XI

Food and the Great Air Raids, 1940-41

I

IN September 1940 the enemy bombers, expected a year earlier at length appeared in force over London. Sustained air attack mainly by night, on the capital continued until mid-May 1941; in addition there were a series of heavy night raids on other towns, usually isolated or intermittent, but on occasion—as with Plymouth and Merseyside—lasting for as much as a week. With the German attack on Russia heavy raiding ceased until February and March 1944, when there were renewed attacks on London by piloted air-craft. These in turn were followed in June 1944 by the long-expected flying-bomb and rocket attacks on 'Southern England', which per-sisted until the Allied armies overran the missiles' launching sites.

These later attacks provided, for food as for other aspects of civil defence, some test of the extent to which the lessons of the earlier raids had been learnt. Whether because the attack itself was lighter, or whether the defence was organised, resilient, and adaptable, flying-bombs and rockets scarcely touched the smooth working of the food control machine. It was otherwise with the attacks of 1940–41; but even they revealed local weakness or incomplete preparation of detail, not fundamental defect. One must bear in mind, however, that even at their height they affected but a part of the total area of the United Kingdom, and that they were only incidentally directed against food supplies. Food control, that is to say, never encountered a deliberate attempt by the enemy to put it out of action by a concentrated onslaught.

Because food supplies and food undertakings suffered only, so to speak, casual effects of air bombardment, never on an overwhelming scale or sustained over years instead of months, time was given to build up an emergency food organisation that in the event was never fully tested. Moreover, it proved possible to maintain a distinction between 'normal war conditions' and 'emergency conditions' that in less favourable circumstances might have proved untenable.

One might, that is to say, sum up the whole history of food control in terms of the attack that did not happen; the attack that was expected to cause, within sixty days of its beginning, 600,000 dead and 1,200,000 seriously injured among civilians and, *a fortiori*, three or four million cases of panic and hysteria; that might bring about a 'disorderly general flight' from bombed cities, to be forestalled by a planned civilian evacuation; the attack, against which plans were made for mass burials in lime and the ejection of some 100,000 hospital patients to make room for expected air-raid casualties. These were the consequences of war apprehended in Whitehall—and not only in Whitehall—in the years before 1939.[1]

The Food (Defence Plans) Department, like others concerned with civilian planning, had to take current Service assumptions as it found them. But so far as the air menace was concerned, one cannot but detect a certain reluctance on its part to admit the full logic of expected catastrophe. An imaginative attempt by one of its members to translate the prospect into food terms evoked in his colleagues admiration rather than acceptance. He pointed out that food control, as it was being planned, would strengthen[2] the existing system of distribution, which itself was capable of withstanding considerable shocks:

'The importers, wholesalers and retailers who, after all, constitute the vital operational element in the system will, I feel sure, continue to trade even though much of their personnel, premises, running plant and transport facilities is forced out of action, provided always that they still have supplies to deal in and that there are still consumers able to buy'.

But sooner or later, as a result of concentrated or continued air attack on the vulnerable centre of London, the normal system of distribution would break down; and the people remaining there would have to be fed by direct Government action, under conditions of considerable physical difficulty.

'*Ex hypothesi* the bombardment has been very intense and very great material destruction has been caused. The remaining population is living in islands of damaged dwellings and houses, mostly vacated, in a chaotic sea of ruined structures and broken streets.

Gas, water and electricity mains will be shattered and it will be hard and risky to cook such food as may be obtainable'.

This meant creating an emergency organisation that 'is robust, direct in purpose and uncomplicated in operation', without the vulnerable features of the normal system.

'Its supply organisation, instead of being inside the damaged area, must be located outside London and so far as possible away from danger. Its stocks must have been reserved ready to draw upon at once and also ready in the sense that they are easy to handle and consume in the exceptional conditions. . . .'

The writer foresaw a system of feeding centres, supplied by State-run transport, in which 'the complications of trading can be avoided

---

[1] Titmuss, R. M. *Problems of Social Policy* (*op. cit.*) Chapter II.

[2] He used the word 'stiffen', which might be taken in another sense, namely rendering more rigid.

and free issues made to consumers'. In the damaged area, rationing and local food offices would cease to function. A separate organisation would be required for feeding air-raid refugees.

This analysis was prepared in August 1937, at a time when the Government's policy for the civilian side of war was largely unformed; and this to some extent explains the neglect into which it almost immediately fell. Such questions as the ordered evacuation by civilians of vulnerable cities, and the relief of those made homeless by enemy action, had scarcely been more than canvassed; it was not until after Munich that Departments were designated to take practical action about them. The Food (Defence Plans) Department, its hands already full, might well think twice before opening up with other Departments projects for which they were manifestly not ready. There is at least a hint, however, that its members preferred not to look too long on what might be the face of things to come.

Be that as it may, the remainder of the Department's preparations and the measures taken by the Ministry of Food during the first year of the war all had this characteristic—they might be said to contemplate air raids but not in any very concrete fashion. Virtually no plans were made for 'clearing up' after a raid. On the other hand the removal of stocks from London in advance was actively investigated and to a limited extent undertaken.[1] Smithfield Meat Market was successfully, Billingsgate Fish Market unsuccessfully, decentralised on the outbreak of war. Effective plans were made to provide 'iron rations' for those included in the official evacuation schemes. In more general ways—by setting up the Divisional Food Organisation, and by the effective work of its Transport Division, for example—food control devised machinery which was of great value in the disorganisation, not only within the bombed area, that might result from air attack.

It was the specific provision against the bomber—the 'first-aid' services of food—that received little attention. In particular, the food authorities were reluctant to take responsibility for feeding the bombed-out. Feeding in rest centres had been entrusted to the public assistance authorities answerable to the Ministry of Health; but they were expected to obtain food supplies through the normal trade channels and only in emergency to indent upon the Divisional Food Officer.

II

The fact that the first heavy raid on London, on 7th September 1940, almost coincided with the Ministry of Food's first approach to the London County Council about communal feeding centres, and

---

[1] Chapter X.

also revealed the inadequacy of emergency feeding arrangements, may have been decisive in placing responsibility for the latter (outside the rest centres under the public assistance authorities) upon the Ministry of Food. The *Londoners' Meals Service*, which was set up by the London County Council as a result, was in its beginnings an air raid service rather than the 'community kitchen' provision that the Ministry had in mind, and that, as it now appeared, local authorities had no legal powers to set up. Its rapid growth may indeed be attributed partly at least to its manifest usefulness in emergency—a point of which the Ministry was later to make much use in urging provincial local authorities to follow London's example.

London, bearing as it did the burden of enemy attack for months on end, did not need prodding to make adequate provision; possessing, in its County Council, a governing authority whose resources and staff were comparable with those of a minor sovereign state, it found little difficulty in doing so. Its sheer size enabled it to absorb punishment from the air on a scale that would, and did, temporarily paralyse smaller, yet still sizeable cities like Coventry and Southampton. It was cities and towns like these that were in fact to provide the most valuable lessons in the art of emergency feeding.

The notorious raid on Coventry—a city of over 200,000 people—on the night of 14/15th November 1940, was the first of a series that, while they never produced a breakdown of food supplies, caused officials to reflect upon the narrow margin of safety they possessed, not indeed in food stocks, but in the help that was available to a community temporarily reeling under a blow. In Coventry, gas, electricity, and water supplies were all interrupted in whole or in part; all bakeries, except one, that relied on oil fuel, were therefore out of action, as were milk-pasteurising and bottling plants. Bread, to the extent of 100,000 loaves in a single day, had to be brought from Birmingham and Stoke-on-Trent; milk from other towns. So many people had lost both ration book and retailer that rationing had to be suspended. (It had to be restored ten days later because of the influx of visitors.) Many local tradespeople, including the chairman and vice-chairman of the Ministry of Food area provisions and groceries committee, were killed or missing; of those that survived nearly all, reported the Divisional Food Officer, were 'stunned for a couple of days and dazed for some days afterwards'.

This pattern was repeated elsewhere with minor variations. At Sheffield, raided on 12/13th December, and again three nights later, nearly all the arrangements for feeding made in rest centres by the Public Assistance Committee were put out of action by bombs, or by the breakdown of public utilities, and the situation was saved by using the discarded but still usable coke ovens in the Public Assistance Institution on the outskirts of the city. The Master of this Institution had prevented the old ovens from being taken away when new gas cookers were installed; the latter were rendered useless, but the former provided no less than 80,000 hot meals in the first thirty-six hours after the raid. At Bootle, raided for a week at the beginning of May 1941, mobile canteens, belonging to the Ministry of Food's new *Queen's Messenger Convoys*, served 400,000 portions of food over a period of thirteen days; apart from four canteens set up in marquees with the assistance of the Military, they were the only means of feeding people until gas, water, and electricity were restored.

Throughout the winter of 1940–41 and thereafter, the Ministry of Food strove to provide an organisation that should as far as possible be ready for action in 'incidents' great or small. So far as emergency feeding was concerned, there sprang up a variety of arrangements in which voluntary societies, local authorities, and the new War-time Meals Division of the Ministry all collaborated. By the end of that winter, the post-raid food services became identified as three; a shelter feeding service for localities, such as Central London, where people were accustomed to spend long periods in the shelters; a 'front line' service of mobile units to provide hot drinks and snacks immediately after a raid; and feeding stations that could supply full meals for as long as might be necessary.

The numerous problems that the Ministry of Food encountered in arriving at this programme and in carrying it into effect will be discussed in the second volume of this study. The transformation in preparedness that was brought about within months parallels that in other post-raid services; it might have been even more rapid but for the unwillingness of local authorities to learn from another's experience. If the Ministry of Food found many of them sluggish[1] until stirred by attack, they often found the departmental distinction between rest centre feeding and other emergency feeding, resting as it did on purely historical reasons, difficult to comprehend. Emergency provision in its turn was perhaps biased in favour of 'static', rather than mobile, canteens, because the former could be held to serve the ambitious plans for community feeding to which the Ministry was wedded. At any rate, officials looking back on experience in the flying-bomb attacks stressed the importance of mobility.

Post-raid feeding services had become the responsibility of the Ministry of Food as a result of decisions reached while the battle was on; they were, so to speak, an additional burden. The maintenance or restoration of normal distribution were its responsibility from the beginning; and the Divisional Food Offices, on which the brunt of this task fell, rose to the occasion admirably. The extent, however, to which Divisional help might be needed in conditions like those at

---

[1] The Ministry's experience was shared by other central Departments. Cf. Titmuss *op. cit.* Chapter XV, especially p. 306.

Coventry, or still more perhaps at Bootle and Portsmouth, where the local food offices and all their records were destroyed,[1] had at first been underrated. So, too, the mutual assistance arrangements for wholesalers proved to have been conceived too narrowly; a 'saturation raid' on a single locality might destroy them all. The geographical separation of area commodity officers from the Divisional Office, and their reluctance on occasion to co-operate with the Divisional Food Officer, was also a source of weakness, and one, it must be added, that the Ministry never wholly overcame.[2]

III

One especially important task that confronted the Ministry after the first heavy raid on London was that of the salvage of food from bombed warehouses and cold stores. Some instructions had been issued to Divisional Food Officers during July and August 1940 from which it appears that the Ministry expected the owners of damaged stocks, or in the case of Ministry-owned stocks the warehouse-keeper or cold-store proprietor, to initiate action, though Divisional Food Officers and Area Commodity Officers were empowered to step in if necessary.

For isolated 'incidents' these arrangements might have been enough; for devastation and confusion such as prevailed in London's Dockland in September 1940 they were not. The Metropolitan Boroughs, whose task it was to clear air-raid debris, were overwhelmed and a Special Commissioner (Sir Warren Fisher) was appointed by the Government to deal with it. But the writ of the Special Commissioner did not run in the actual dock area, controlled by the Port of London Authority; so that there were still two organisations competing with one another for labour and materials. The Ministry of Food rapidly became alarmed at the deterioration of stocks that could not be got at, because no authority had power to put in motion the essential preliminaries to salvage. As early as 27th September the Ministry was urging on the Ministry of Home Security the need for a strong regional organisation for salvage. But —mainly it seems because the Ministry of Home Security was uninformed about the functions and possible usefulness in war of the existing salvage organisations run by the Fire Insurance Offices—

---

[1] There was at this time no duplication of Food Office records. Later this was ordered, and proved its worth on one occasion when, in 1944, the Gravesend Office was destroyed by a long-range rocket.

[2] See Chapter IV. In 1941, in the Southern Division, centred on Reading, the Area Meat Officer was stationed in High Wycombe, the Condensed Milk Officer at Guildford, the Tea Officer at Southampton, the Bread Officer at Oxford, and the Sugar Officer in London. At the time of the Bootle raid, the Port Food Movement Officer in Liverpool declined to assist the Deputy Divisional Food Officer, although their offices were in the same building. These were extreme rather than exceptional cases.

progress was slow. 'The wheels seem to be moving in the most stately manner' (wrote the Secretary of the Ministry of Food to a colleague on 7th November). 'Meanwhile the Minister is undoubtedly worried as to whether we are not laying ourselves open to a great deal of public criticism for allowing food to be wasted'.

It could certainly not be said that the Ministry did not do all that it could, within the limits set by the want of complete organisation. In Liverpool, it authorised its deputy Divisional Food Officer to spend what might be necessary on salvage operations. In London, the Divisional Food Officer received similar authority to have a damaged cold store shored up to permit the meat inside to be salvaged. This cold store, on Nelson's Wharf, presented a typical example of the kind of problem the Ministry had to tackle, and tackle quickly. When all the meat that could be got out of it had been got out, there remained about one-quarter—some 2,500 tons. Chloride of lime was poured on it, but even so it was bound to become a public nuisance in a few months' time. The owners of the cold store refused to do anything; they said, truly enough, that the meat was the Ministry's:[1]

'By leaving us with the responsibility for removing the meat they are saved the cost of demolition and clearing away of the building . . . .If we leave 2,500 tons of meat to become bad and a public nuisance . . . we shall be required by the Public Authority to remove the meat in any case and shall also incur much public odium in the neighbourhood if we do not. We, therefore, agreed that you [the Divisional Food Officer] should go ahead with the clearance and destruction of the meat.'

So, too, the Ministry had to dispose of 5,000 tons of damaged oil-seeds that were becoming overheated, lest it be exposed to a claim for damages by the owner of a wine cellar that lay beneath them.

It was the multiplication of such questions that led the Ministry, at the beginning of November, to authorise the London Divisional Food Officer to set up a special salvage organisation. Shortly afterwards, it was decided to create a similar organisation in every Food Division, with a permanent headquarters in Colwyn Bay. The latter included a Dehydration Branch whose task was to arrange facilities for the drying of food, particularly grain, that had been soaked by the firefighters' water. (Later, it was to deal also with preparation of 'dehydrated' foods, particularly vegetables.)

These measures were very effective, although lapse of time and shortage of labour prevented the organisation from overtaking all the arrears of damage. Most food proved to be astonishingly indestruc-

---

[1] Private owners of bombed stocks were no less unwilling to act, cushioned as they felt themselves to be by war risk insurance. The London Divisional Food Officer reported on 9th November that slow progress with the food trades over salvage operations was 'chiefly due to the belief that no action is to be taken by the owner . . . since all he has to do is to sit back and collect the insurance money'.

tible; nearly three-quarters of that affected by air-raids was recover-
able. It is this that accounts for the sharp fall in the tonnage of food
recorded as having been lost by air attack during the remainder of
the winter.[1] Thereafter, as it turned out, the effect of air attack on
food stocks was negligible. Even at the peak of the raids, destruction
or damage of processing plant was perhaps more serious than that of
stocks. Flour and provender mills, oilseed crushing mills, sugar
refineries, all suffered heavily. The loss of flour milling capacity was
such that, had the heavy raids not ceased after May 1941, the rate of
extraction might have had to be raised in order to get sufficient flour
supplies from a given quantity of wheat.[2]

Apart from their direct effects, the air raids made themselves felt
in almost every field of the Ministry's activities. They dislocated the
movement of goods by rail and road: they held up port working, not
only in ports under attack but elsewhere, through inland transport
congestion and shipping diversion. They caused movements of population that upset the distribution pattern for unrationed foods and
for tea, which though rationed was distributed on a datum-line
system. They added to the strain on those Ministry officials who remained in London, even while they provided them with a fresh set of
urgent problems over and above those created by the shortage of
imported supplies. (Colwyn Bay enjoyed almost complete immunity
from bombing; but matters of high policy could not be decided there.)
In short, any discussion of food problems during that winter might
have the bomber—to say nothing of the prospect of invasion[3]—as a
background. If at times that background is not obvious to one who
reads the record, that may be no more than a tribute to the adaptability of man.

The air raids may have influenced food policy in more ways than
one can count; their sudden and unexpected cessation, however, was
even more important. For it is scarcely conceivable that the developments of 1941–42—the extension of control and rationing to a multitude of lesser foods, the introduction of the points rationing scheme,
the food standards and labelling reforms, and a hundred and one
others—could even have been embarked upon, let alone accomplished,
under continual bombardment. The characteristic features of food
control at its zenith—minute and scrupulous regulation of everything everywhere, the supremacy of the account, the form, the price
control order, in short the printed word in all its manifestations—
must have given way to methods more obviously warlike.

---

[1] See Table IX p. 397.

[2] See Chapter XII. The influence of air raid damage on the principal commodities will
be dealt with in Vol. II.

[3] The Ministry of Food's anti-invasion measures, together with its preparations against
flying-bombs and rockets, will be discussed in Vol. II.

CHAPTER XII

Imports: Crisis and Recovery, 1940-41

I

IN August 1940 the Ministry of Food had declined to put forward a 15 million-ton import programme as a working proposition.[1] In September, food imports fell to that level, partly through an increase in sinkings; partly, it seems, through undue priority in loadings being given to the Supply programme; mainly, perhaps, through the diversion of tonnage to military purposes. Early in October the Minister warned the War Cabinet that he would have to ask for more ships if the situation did not improve. It did not improve; and the Ministry began to prepare a case for a tonnage allocation admittedly higher than its minimum requirements, in order to be sure of getting those. It was still at work on this when, on 8th November, the War Cabinet[2] ordered a review of programmes on the assumption that not more than 35 million tons could be imported in the second year of war. If the existing ratio between Departmental programmes were to be preserved, the share of food would be 15·42 million tons.

The Ministry responded with a programme that differed from its 'minimum' programme of August in but one major detail; cereals for human food were some 600,000 tons down, feeding-stuffs 700,000 tons up. This was because releases of feeding-stuffs since July had exceeded those appropriate to a 15 million-ton programme; the rationing scheme for them would not be ready till February, and any cuts in the meantime might, it was held, endanger the milk supply; moreover, it was thought necessary to 'taper off' supplies for pigs during the first three months of 1941, in order to avoid disorderly and wasteful slaughterings. The other consequences of the programme were those the Ministry had promised in June; no fresh fruit other than oranges (and not many of those), no nuts, no imported canned and bottled fruit, less meat, and no increase in the tea and sugar rations.

The Ministry maintained that the yield of imports on this scale, together with that from home production, would fail to supply the minimum nutritional needs of the population, as calculated by the

---

[1] Chapter V above.

[2] The Minister of Food was not present or represented at this meeting or at a subsequent meeting of the Economic Policy Committee, on the 12th November. The War Cabinet decision did not become known in the Ministry until the late afternoon of the 14th November.

Scientific Adviser. These calculations were not initiated *ad hoc*, for the procedure for drafting import programmes laid down as far back as April 1940 provided for the nutritional verification, so to speak, of the programme figures. Prospective supplies of calcium, vitamin A, and vitamin B_1, were thought to be deficient even on the basis of the original 19 million ton programme; where this was more satisfactory than that now proposed was from the calorie point of view, since it provided for greater imports of wheat and a 12-oz. sugar ration. The new programme, it was claimed, would give an average calorie intake perilously near the margin beyond which some people might begin to suffer actual hunger. The force of this argument lay not in its figures, which could readily be disputed in detail,[1] but in the practical implications of so narrow a margin of safety in current supplies. If rations were reduced too far, a strain might be thrown on unrationed bread and flour stocks which within weeks might threaten a breakdown in distribution. Unless and until (*a*) a greater supply of food was available from home agriculture, (*b*) Government and public were willing to accept high-extraction flour, with all its consequences, any further cuts in food imports would be unsafe.

Even while this programme was being discussed, food arrivals continued to decline; in November they were for the first time below a million tons. The Ministry of Food felt that this could not be allowed to go on. It roundly asserted, in presenting a revised version of the programme to the Economic Policy Committee, that the total of 35 million tons for imports was

> 'hypothetical, the proportion of it allotted to food is arbitrary . . . these programmes . . . are purely paper programmes . . . They bear no close relation to the realities of the shipping situation, either actual or prospective . . . the previously approved programme of Food Imports has not been getting anything like its approved share of the actual tonnage available.'[2]

---

[1] The difficulties attending such computations, both on the side of supply and on that of requirement, are such that the figures adduced at this time—3,018 calories per head per day for the first, 2,900, 3,000, or 3,100, according to the individual expert, for the second—must be interpreted with a good deal of latitude. It was clear, however, that supplies were falling to a level which gave no very comfortable margin over requirements.

[2] 'It occurs to me', a senior official of the Ministry had written on 11th December, 'that somebody may think that the rather persistent enquiry in our Memorandum . . . about the intention of "these programmes" is purposeless or merely petulant. The point is, of course, that we are in practice entirely at the mercy of the Ministry of Shipping, which often means a more or less obscure official of the Ministry of Shipping, in regard to priorities; and it may well happen that a food cargo is delayed on merely shipping convenience grounds in favour of a cargo of steel or timber. It would seem that this has been happening fairly frequently in recent months. ..
I think it unwise in the memorandum to bring out this point too clearly. I do not want to appear to be criticising the Ministry of Shipping. They do their best, no doubt, and anyhow we have got to work with them, and without their goodwill we shall undoubtedly suffer. My own feeling is that we are approaching the time when it will be necessary to have some independent arbitration between conflicting interests on priority questions as regards shipping. This has not been of substantial importance until recent months, but the further we decline the more important it becomes'.

It questioned whether the raw material programmes did not exceed Services requirements and productive capacity; it declared that further cuts in human food imports were impossible, and that further cuts in feeding-stuffs would mean recourse to a deliberate policy of immediate livestock reduction.

On 19th December Lord Woolton told the Committee that the present rate of food imports allowed no margin for feeding-stuffs, and the Committee agreed that until further notice essential human food should have priority over all other imports. On the strength of this, and in default of a general decision on programmes, the Ministry of Food proceeded to arrange its February loadings with the Ministry of Shipping as if the 15 million-ton programme was already in operation—as it had already done for December and January. On Boxing Day Lord Woolton saw the Prime Minister, at Chequers, and on 30th December Mr. Churchill[1] formally set up a new Ministerial Committee, the Import Executive, to determine short-term shipping priorities as well as review import programmes. The need for such a body was pressing. That very day the Minister of Food's personal intervention had been required to secure an increase in food loadings during January and February of 190,000 tons, sufficient to give food its agreed proportion of the reduced imports. Nevertheless its establishment, providing as it did for the multiplication of high-level decisions rather than the resolution of detailed problems lower down, was a palliative of bad planning rather than a contribution to good.

Yet a third variant of the 15 million-ton programme was now submitted to the Food Policy Committee and the Import Executive. This for the first time admitted that 15·42 million tons was not in fact an absolute minimum. On the contrary, it acknowledged three orders of priority, to be observed in the short run as well as the long; the first, minimum requirements for human beings and the dairy herd, the second, industrial starches and fats, together with a little extra for the dairy cows, and the third, all other feeding-stuffs. Moreover, although it made no specific provision for sinkings, it included no less than 600,000 tons unallocated to any commodity, but in theory set aside for air-raid damage; a purely academic gesture since advance loadings could only be planned in relation to actual commodities. Nevertheless, the Import Executive accepted

---

[1] Opportunity had already been taken, in reply to an enquiry from Mr. Churchill why the import of bananas had been stopped, to acquaint him with the gravity of the food import situation.

The writer cannot say whether there was any direct connection between Lord Woolton's visit to Chequers and the decision to set up the Import Executive. Mr. Churchill has printed (*The Second World War*, Vol. II. p. 632) a message, dated 26th December, to the Secretary of the Cabinet and Professor Lindemann, summoning three meetings of Ministers to discuss the import programme. This message was apparently dictated over the telephone from Chequers; but there appear to be no minutes or other evidence on official files to indicate that the meetings were ever held.

15·42 million tons as the Ministry of Food share of a total of 35 millions, agreed that the same ratio of food imports should be maintained if the total import was less, and instructed the shipping authorities to ensure that food got its full share in the short as well as the long run.

This decision was hailed in the Ministry of Food as a 'complete victory at all points'; but it soon appeared to be barren, as prospective imports for the second year of war shrank, first to 32–33, then 31, and finally 30 million tons; the last figure giving food a share well below the 13·5 millions it had included in its first priority programme. Moreover, not till mid-March did the Ministry of Shipping actually adjust its forward loadings so as to give food its due proportion of imports.

The most serious immediate shortage that resulted was of meat, the ration of which fell abruptly as a result of sinkings, diversion of refrigerated ships to military purposes, and previous improvidence.[1] By the end of January it was estimated that even by switching refrigerated ships, so far as was practicable, from the Southern Dominions to the River Plate, only enough frozen meat could be imported to make up a 1s. 2d. ration for the rest of the second year of war. To supplement the ration with canned meat would mean eating into reserves. A suggestion from the Admiralty that troopships homeward bound from the Middle East be diverted to the Plate for meat cargoes was promptly acted upon, but could, of course, bring no immediate or dependable relief. At a meeting of Ministers on 12th March, called especially to discuss the food situation, Mr. Churchill expressed alarm at the 'apparent tendency in our food policy . . . towards a basal diet of bread, oatmeal, fats, milk, and potatoes', and exhorted the Minister of Food to bear in mind the need for a varied diet and the importance of meat. On 21st March Lord Woolton again visited Chequers and formally asked the Prime Minister (*a*) that absolute priority be given to food shipments up to 15 million tons over the second year of war, (*b*) that enough meat ships be taken away from the Services to maintain the meat ration at 1s. 2d. On 25th March he informed Mr. Churchill that the meat ration must come down to 1s. the following week.

The next day Mr. Churchill made a fresh allocation of tonnage between the importing departments: assuming an import in the calendar year 1941 of 31 million tons, Food and Supply should each have 15 million; any surplus or (what then seemed more probable) deficit should be shared in the ratio Food : Supply : : 1 : 2. An *ad hoc* Committee, with a leading shipowner as chairman, was to inquire into the possibility of releasing four million cubic feet of refrigerated

---

[1] See Chapter XIII

shipping. In the event, this committee proposed instead that fourteen troopships should regularly be released at Durban to carry meat on the homeward voyage. The net gain to meat imports was not as much as the carrying capacity of the ships (some 118,000 tons a year) since some troopships were already being so used, but it was nevertheless 'very substantial'.

As for the programme generally, the new ruling represented a paper gain of nearly 800,000 tons a year, though as the calendar year was now taken instead of the second year of war, some 100,000 tons of arrears at 1st January had to be written off. Moreover, food still had no absolute priority, only an increased proportion of what seemed to be a still shrinking total. Even allowing for the revised formula, the estimate of food imports for the whole of 1941, as late as May, was but 14·3 million tons; it looked as though, like the Red Queen, the Ministry of Food must run faster and faster in order to keep in the same place. Nevertheless, the situation was brighter because the prospect of Lend/Lease supplies in the near future not merely enabled the United Kingdom to continue to concentrate tonnage on the North Atlantic, without which food shipments could not have been maintained even at their existing levels, but promised to fill just those gaps in the food front—lack of meat, milk, and eggs—that were causing most disquiet.

From May onwards, moreover, imports more than achieved the seasonal improvement that the shipping authorities had foreseen; the achievement seems to have taken both them and the Ministry of Food by surprise, to judge by the recriminations that ensued. War Transport complained of the 'inflexibility' of the food programme, which led to the extra tonnage being largely filled with cereals, while Food rejoined that better placing of ships would have avoided an insufficiency of freight for Lend-Lease goods. The Ministry of Food had little difficulty in showing that criticism of the sugar loading programme was based on a consumption figure that ignored the special demands on sugar in the jam-making season. Again, whether meat or butter should be shipped from New Zealand was no business of the Ministry of War Transport. The question of cereals, however, was both more important and more complicated.

Cereals and steel compete for the same tonnage. Steel is a difficult cargo to stow and handle at any time; in bad weather it is downright dangerous, and large shipments of it across the North Atlantic during the winter of 1940–41 had caused heavy damage to vessels and hence serious loss of importing capacity. The shipping authorities, as early as May, had sought to avoid a recurrence of the same trouble next winter by proposing that more steel be loaded during the summer months, any arrears thus created on the cereals programme to be made up later. The Ministry of Food, however, was not willing to

M

allow this adjustment to be made before July loadings, i.e., for August arrival, on the ground that stocks of wheat and flour would only then have reached a safe level. They had in fact just passed through a crisis.

II

Almost the first result of the shipping crisis the previous autumn had been to reopen the discussion of the minimum safety level for wheat stocks, fixed at thirteen weeks' supplies by the War Cabinet in December 1939.[1] In November 1940, though steadily falling, they were still above this level; and the Ministry's import programme, as recast in that month, proposed deliberately to run them down to it in order to bring in more animal feeds to tide over the period until the rationing scheme for animals could come into operation. Against this proposal the Cereals Division protested strongly. The thirteen weeks' minimum was barely adequate, they said, now that so many mills had been destroyed by air raids. This, and the disorganisation of distribution resulting from it, necessitated keeping a larger reserve of flour; nevertheless, wheat stocks must not be allowed to fall correspondingly, lest with arrivals of ships irregular and air attack constant, the flow of wheat to the mills be impeded.

Moreover, the Division was convinced by past experience that to aim at the minimum was unsafe. The Ministry of Shipping, even under far more favourable conditions than the present, could not be relied upon to fulfil its programme; existing stocks were only high on account of windfall shipments after the fall of France.[2] Events appeared to confirm this view; by mid-December, prospective cereal loadings for that month and the next were no less than twenty per cent. below those demanded by the new reduced programme to which the Ministry of Shipping was now supposed to be working. Wheat was apparently being sacrificed to steel.

Early in January sample figures from the Ministry of Agriculture's half-yearly returns came in which suggested that stocks of home-grown wheat on farms might be as much as 300,000 tons less than had been counted on. This wheat, instead of being obtained for

---

[1] For this decision and its context, see above, Chapter V.

[2] In the Division's own words: (11th November 1940) 'During the past year promises of tonnage were so much above actual facts that we found ourselves left with large balances of grain unshipped'; (26th November 1940) 'The satisfactory stock we now hold has been built up from supplies diverted from the Continent . . . If we acquiesce in accepting the minimum there is . . . no margin of safety for the tendency will be to aim at the minimum thus resulting in something less'. (13th December 1940) 'I do not believe that in one single month [since the war started] have they lived up to their programme . . . the surprising part of the matter is that it is . . . the Northern Range programme that the Ministry of Shipping cannot fulfil and have never done so'.

milling, was thought to have been fed to animals. (It later turned out that some of it, at any rate, had been reserved for seed.) No measures now taken were likely to secure much more than 200,000 tons of home-grown wheat for the mills during the rest of the season. So far, therefore, from programming for extra feeding-stuffs, the Ministry would have to use all available ships to make up the deficiency in human food; and the cereals programme was revised in January so as to provide for building-up stocks of wheat and flour to fifteen weeks' supply at the end of June. No sooner was this decision reached, however, than it was challenged by another claimant for shipping space; coal exports to the Argentine. Imports of wheat on the scale required could only be achieved by taking none from Australia, and from the Plate only sufficient to provide a reasonable amount of soft wheat in the millers' grist. To switch tonnage to this extent, however, meant that insufficient ships would go out to the Plate with coal—and protests were at once heard from the Board of Trade and the Mines Department. The Ministry, however, refused either to take more grain from the Argentine than it needed or to abandon the claim that thirteen weeks' supplies of wheat were a minimum.

In March, moreover, the disquieting fact came to light that flour consumption had gone up ten per cent.—presumably owing to the cut in the meat ration. As a result, wheat and flour stocks *had* fallen below the thirteen-weeks level, even in terms of the old rate of consumption; in terms of the new, they would suffice for 11·5 weeks only. Moreover, forward estimates of loadings for March and April were still below what was required on the old basis; and continued air attacks had further reduced flour milling capacity. Thus, in addition to the tonnage required for wheat, to make up deficiencies in the current programme, more ships were needed to import flour. These additional flour shipments could only be avoided by raising the extraction rate to eighty-five per cent.—the optimum figure prescribed by the scientists—thus enabling existing mills to produce all the flour needed to meet the current rate of consumption, without increasing the programme for wheat imports. It would also make existing stocks of wheat go further; roughly speaking eight weeks' supply would become nine weeks'.

Compulsory wheatmeal bread, however, would certainly be unpopular with the millers and the public. The Ministry's National Wheatmeal Loaf, despite advertising on a national scale, was making little headway. To some extent this may have been due to the reluctance of the trade to supply it, and to counter-propaganda in the trade press; but it is clearly imputing too much power to the trade to suppose that it would have been able to withstand a really strong public demand. Nor did the millers' opposition to eighty-five per cent. extraction necessarily lose force because it could readily be imputed to prejudice and self-interest. It was, of course, true that if National Wheatmeal was made compulsory, the public might come to prefer it to white bread on the one hand, and the proprietary and more expensive 'germ' breads (*Hovis*, *Turog*, etc.), on the other. The good-will of these brands, the profitable trade in wheat germ for vitamin preparations and wheat offals for feeding-stuffs might be prejudiced, and yet more milling machinery become redundant.[1] But these facts, while they might explain the attitude of the millers, did not dispose altogether of their arguments. These were, briefly, that the gain on paper would be largely offset by (*a*) greater waste through staling; (*b*) the illicit feeding of flour and bread to livestock in place of the lost offals; (*c*) more bread being eaten to replace the livestock pro-ducts that would be lost through a reduction in the supply of wheat-feed. Experience alone could show the extent to which these conten-tions were valid.[2]

Another objection to raising the extraction rate was the effect on feeding-stuffs supplies. There was indeed little scientific support for the belief, held in some quarters, that the milk output would suffer if cows were deprived of the supplies of fine wheatfeed which a seventy-two per cent. extraction provides; anyhow, there would be sufficient of this, even at eighty-five per cent., to meet the estimated require-ments of the dairy herd. In practice, however, what would mainly matter would be the diminution in the total supply of *controlled* feeding-stuffs. Unless drastic steps were taken to control home-grown grains, pigs and poultry—still rather too numerous—might be fed at the expense of dairy cows; and these drastic steps everyone concerned wished to avoid.

Nevertheless, it seems clear that the chief reason why a decision to raise the extraction rate—despite the persistent advocacy of the Cereals Division from March to May 1941—was put off time and again, was the belief that psychologically this was a bad moment to make the change. Shortages of other foods—meat, milk, cheese, jam —were at their worst. Future supplies, thanks to Lend/Lease and the greater allocation of shipping to food, looked brighter. Moreover, arrangements to fortify white bread with synthetic vitamin B_1 were well in train; the Ministry might look rather foolish if these had now to be abandoned. Hence it chose rather to increase flour imports, while putting up the extraction rate slightly, i.e., from seventy-three to seventy-six per cent. This policy of 'wait and see' was endorsed by the Food Policy Committee on 22nd May, when it deferred decision on a recommendation from the Scientific Food Committee that the

---

[1] Before the war, in spite of rationalisation schemes on the one hand and bread advertis-ing on the other, milling capacity was twenty-five per cent. above requirements.

[2] In practice, the reduction in wheat usage proved to be commensurate with the rise in the percentage of extraction.

time had now come to go over to compulsory wheatmeal.[1] This secured for white bread a further respite. The destruction of one more large mill, or a worsening of the shipping situation, could not but have turned the scales; but neither of these things happened just then. On the contrary, heavy air raids ceased, sinkings fell, and stocks, which as late as the end of May had only just struggled back to the thirteen weeks level, rose in June and July beyond all expectation.

III

The scare over wheat supplies led to an attempt to give greater statistical precision to the 'danger level' of wheat and flour stocks, in consultation with the Ministry's advisory committee of millers. Notwithstanding the fact that no stoppage of mills had occurred when total stocks fell to 11·5 weeks, it was decided to reaffirm the thirteen weeks' stock—in terms of flour consumption—as a minimum. The proportion of wheat and flour in this total was to be determined by milling capacity. Wheat should not be less than would suffice to keep the mills going for nine weeks—at this time (August 1941) equal to eight weeks' flour consumption. This gave a minimum figure for flour stocks of five weeks' consumption (excluding the millers' working stocks); this would need to be increased if milling capacity were reduced for any reason. But a further loss of milling capacity would not *per se*, it was now asserted, entail an increase in the extraction rate, provided that there was sufficient shipping to bring in the flour.

This might be true on paper; but in fact heavy destruction of port mills by air attack would inevitably be accompanied by destruction of and delays to shipping in port—in other words, by circumstances in which the extravagance of flour imports above the minimum could not have been afforded. As the Cereals Division was itself to point out later on, flour takes longer to load and unload, stows less economically and stores less readily, than wheat in bulk. It is clear that the new formula, no less than the old, proposed to hoist the danger signal well ahead of the actual danger level. Notwithstanding that the 1941 home crop was likely to be both larger and under reasonably effective control, it was still not fully taken into account.[2]

---

[1] The Minister of Food told the Committee that he favoured a 'policy of gradualness' so far as National Wheatmeal was concerned. Certainly the Ministry achieved gradualness. At the end of April 1941 the output of National Wheatmeal was some three per cent. of the total; by December, after more than a year of propaganda, costing some £35,000, it was to reach four per cent.

[2] Thus in estimating the number of weeks' supply represented by a given stock figure, whether spot or forward, the Ministry worked in terms of total consumption. The flow of wheat from the home crop was disregarded, i.e., put on the same footing as if it were on the other side of the ocean. Thus the estimates became more and more misleading; as the proportion of home-grown to total supplies increased, the hidden margin of safety increased also. But the Ministry continued to insist on a visible margin greater than that of 1939. See below, Chapter XIX.

While the Ministry of Food thus inflated its minimum requirements, the Ministry of War Transport contended that a large stock of
wheat was unnecessary, since it was always possible to restore the
position at short notice on the shortest haul. For the Ministry of
Food, however, the past performances of those responsible for shipping were bound to be more convincing than any *a priori* argument,
however reasonable. If less steel was imported in the summer of 1941
than the Ministries of Supply and War Transport would have liked,
that was because more had been shipped the previous winter than
the agreed ratio between Food and Supply programmes would have
allowed. It was hardly reasonable to expect the Ministry of Food to
be penalised in the summer, because it had been penalised in the
winter. Behind all the controversies one fact stood out; for whatever
reason, the system by which tonnage was allocated and operated had
yet to prove itself so efficient as to justify any importing Department
in putting forward actual minima and actual danger levels as a basis
for its demands on shipping.

The Prime Minister had coupled with his March re-allocation of
shipping an instruction to the Ministers of Food and Agriculture to
concert an eighteen months' programme for food supplies. Early in
July the Food Policy Committee approved a programme covering
the period March 1941–August 1942, in which 'first priority' imports
were put at 14 million tons annually. ('Second priority'—including
some maize, extra fats and sugar, and some miscellaneous items—
amounted to a further one million tons; but these were not included
in the accompanying estimate of total supplies.) The Treasury was
inclined to quarrel with so large a figure, arguing that no animal
feeding-stuffs as such ought to be imported,[1] that the arduous and
expensive food production campaign ought by this time to enable
food imports to be reduced to 13 or even 12 million tons, and that,
once Mr. Churchill's formula had allowed food stocks to be built up
to proper levels, it was reasonable to expect that it would be revised
in favour of the munitions programme. This argument gains some
support from an analysis of the programme figures, which not only
deliberately under-estimated the likely yield of home produced wheat,
potatoes, and sugar beet, but also provided for increasing stocks of
wheat, oilseeds, sugar, and canned meat. This procedure may well
have accounted for the best part of a million tons over the year,[2]

---

[1] i.e., apart from those, such as oilcakes and wheat offals, that were by-products of
imported human food.

[2] In discussions with the Treasury and for internal Ministry purposes the programme
was set out for the third year of war, instead of the calendar year 1942, making it difficult
to estimate exactly how much the programme presented to Ministers was inflated. It was
later admitted in the Ministry that the third-year programme allowed for wheat and sugar
supplies in excess of current consumption by 800,000 tons. To this must be added the
wheat equivalent of an under-estimate of potato production below average, say 125,000
tons. On the whole a total of one million tons does not seem too much.

mainly devoted, moreover, not to increasing rations, or improving the variety of the diet, but in effect insuring against the programme not being fulfilled.

The Ministry admitted that if there were overriding shipping difficulties some reduction could be made in these demands. But throughout the summer of 1941 the shipping prospects seemed to be getting better rather than worse. Hopes of American shipping help were running high; a figure of 34 million tons or even more was spoken of as a possible import for the calendar year 1942. Neither the shipping authorities nor the other supply Departments were as yet prepared to press for a share of imports over and above that given them by Mr. Churchill's formula. There was thus no pressure on the Ministry of Food to put forward a minimum programme of requirements. When in October the 'import budget for 1942' was discussed, by the Import Executive, the Ministry proposed a programme of no less than 16 million tons (15 million tons first priority), which it defended on the ground that the diet was insufficiently varied, and that, in particular, the sugar and fats rations ought to be increased. Even so, it is clear that the programme was inflated, since it provided for no decrease in wheat and flour imports beyond that to compensate for increased home production, while blandly admitting that more abundant supplies of other foods would be likely to reduce the consumption of flour. Moreover, some of the miscellaneous items were not certainly available in the programmed quantity.[1] In fact, the Ministry had already devised a 14 million-ton programme which provided for the more important 'extras'; and reductions even as low as 12 million tons were being contemplated on paper. Even these, it was thought, were not inconsistent with retaining the extra fats and sugar rations, though they would entail a wheatmeal loaf, possibly 'diluted' with potato flour, with its consequences for livestock production.[2]

Nevertheless, the Import Executive, the Prime Minister, and the Lord President's Committee were all content that the Ministry should have 15 out of a prospective 33 millions (Supply 16·5, Board of Trade 1·5) of imports.[3] Towards the middle of November, however, it became clear that competing claims upon shipping, particularly of supplies to Russia and the Near and Middle East, were likely to jeopardise the United Kingdom programme, and that

---

[1] The 'priority II' claim got short shrift from the Import Executive; three-quarters of it consisted of wheat, which it was claimed could serve either for human or animal consumption.

[2] The Ministry nevertheless dismissed as 'light-hearted' the suggestion by the War Cabinet Office economists that current standard of consumption could be maintained on $13\frac{1}{2}$ million tons of food imports, or $12\frac{3}{4}$ with wheatmeal bread.

[3] Mr. Churchill again showed concern that the meat ration should be improved, but no amount of optimism could make the refrigerated tonnage position capable of this.

Services demands on shipping were likely to increase. On 3rd December, three days *before* the attack on Pearl Harbour, Lord Leathers warned the Import Executive that imports in the first quarter of 1942 might not exceed seven million tons. It was agreed that, for the present, Ministry of Food plans should be based on an annual import of 13 million tons. The Japanese attack, however, made it even less possible to look so far ahead; as in the previous winter, the Ministry must expect to rely on improvisation.

CHAPTER XIII

The Meat Shortage and Livestock Policy,

1940-41

I

DURING the winter of 1940–41 the main preoccupation of the Government, so far as home food production was concerned, was with the adjustment of livestock numbers to the reduced supply of feeding-stuffs. As in 1917–18, controversy arose between those who would leave the adjustment to the discretion of farmers, and those who held that positive measures of compulsion were required if too many animals were not to be kept alive, but unproductive, on too little food. Once again scientific experts were ranged on one side, those who would have to carry out the measures on the other.[1]

The issue might seem to be a cool one of fact and forecast; concerned with probable deficiency and margins of error. But its discussion was anything but cool, and in the end its resolution turned hardly at all on the merits of compulsory slaughter, but almost entirely on the expediency of carrying it out. Moreover, the debate was complicated by another problem—the shortage of meat for the ration—with which it had really very little to do, and which itself was sharpened by accidents of circumstance and errors of judgement in the management of the generally efficient meat and livestock control.

The difficulties on the side of meat supply began, as they had in the autumn of 1917, with a glut of animals for slaughter that could be forecast but not prevented.[2] The rush of entries threatened to overwhelm the collecting centres and slaughterhouses; the Ministry had to refuse as much as one-fifth of the cattle and two-fifths of the sheep entered for slaughter. In order to relieve the pressure, imports of fat stock from Eire were restricted by nearly one-half, and on 30th September 1940 the meat ration was increased from 1s. 10d. per head per week to 2s. 2d. Stocks of imported meat in cold store began piling up as less and less was released for consumption.

Just at this time London and the East Coast ports were closed to refrigerated ships, so that all meat had to be handled at the West Coast; the railways were unable to provide enough insulated wagons

---

[1] Chapter VI, Section I.
[2] Ibid. Section III.

to clear the meat from the quays,[1] and the shipping authorities complained of delays in the turn-round of ships. They therefore pressed for a reduction in home slaughterings and a greater usage of imported meat; but these the Ministry of Food resisted. It pointed out to the Food Policy Committee on 29th October that the benefit to inland transport of moving imported meat direct to the consumer instead of into cold store was doubtful; that the home-produced beasts would go out of condition if not marketed when ripe for slaughter and that in any event the glut would soon be over. 'Thereafter', it said, 'weekly consumption of imported meat will exceed the average arrivals'.

These words have been quoted because they constituted a plain warning that the meat ration would have to come down in the near future. Before that very meeting of the Food Policy Committee was a warning to the same effect from another angle, that of the supply of refrigerated ships. Thanks to requisitions for the Services, there would not be enough of these for more than four-fifths of the Ministry of Food's second-year-of-war programme. That meant—since imports of dairy produce had priority over meat—that meat imports must be cut by more than four-fifths.

One might have expected, therefore, that the ration would have been reduced to its former level, or below it, as soon as the autumn glut ceased and stocks in cold store began to fall. This process set in at the beginning of November; but only on 4th December was the Food Policy Committee formally warned that the ration might have to come down—and not until the 16th—when stocks were half what they had been six weeks earlier—did it revert to 1s. 10d. Next day the Ministry of Food produced an analysis to show that even if Service rations were cut by one-quarter, and caterers' allowances by one-third, the civilian ration would still have to come down to 1s. 4d. (including offal, hitherto ration-free) in the new year.

A gradual drop to 1s. 4d. would be unpalatable enough—a sudden drop might cause a political storm to descend upon the Ministry. Feverishly it looked around for ways and means of scraping up more supplies—paying higher prices for Eire fat cattle and sheep, robbing bacon to secure pork, speeding up marketings of home-produced cattle by raising the price of the less forward beasts. Someone even suggested that the cut might look better if the price of meat were raised at the same time. On 6th January the ration was reduced to 1s. 6d. or 2d. more than the figure suggested by the Meat and Livestock Division. Meantime the stocks position had become worse;[2] heavy air attacks on Liverpool had slowed up discharging facilities for imported meat, while home marketings had dropped heavily. The

---

[1] For the solution of this problem, see Chapter XVI.

[2] It was in any case worse than Ministers had been told; for the estimates of 17th December made no allowance for the large proportion of stocks in cold store that were 'manufacturing' meat, not suitable for issue against the ration.

Division was not able, in fact, to issue more than seventy-five per cent. of a 1s. 6d. ration. It was at last decided to grasp the nettle; on 8th January Lord Woolton secured the Prime Minister's concurrence in a 'flexible' ration, to be varied between 1s. and 1s. 6d. weekly. The ration was not to rise above 1s. 2d. for several years.

Moreover, the drop was even more severe in fact than it looked on paper, for it was accompanied by a general tightening up of the permit system by which butchers secured their meat. Within a month the country had passed from a ration so high, and so slackly enforced, as to be almost nominal, to a position of real stringency. During most of January and February 1941 even the 1s. 2d. ration was only maintained by including in it a proportion of corned beef. Foot-and-mouth disease in Eire brought about the exclusion of all imports thence, whether of stores or fats; heavy snow over the whole country reduced home marketings and hindered distribution. Failing an improvement in overseas supplies it became evident that the ration must fall to 1s. after March, and on 31st March it actually did so.

Given the diversion of refrigerated tonnage, given also the rise in sinkings and the delays resulting from heavy enemy air raids, a fall in the ration was unavoidable. But the miscalculations of the Commodity Division had contrived to make the drop more sudden and more unexpected than it need have been. The Minister himself shared in the surprise and took energetic steps to ensure that it should not be repeated. From this time dates his insistence that Commodity Directors should themselves be unequivocally held responsible for the supply of the food in question, and that he must be warned in time of any difficulties that were likely to arise. As with the launching of points rationing a year later, he was adamant that the Ministry's reputation must on no account be tarnished by the appearance of hasty improvisation or want of foresight. From this time also dates the preoccupation with the safety level of all stocks that was to characterise the Ministry in later years.

II

The shortage of meat was to lend force to the Minister's advocacy, during the first six months of 1941, of a compulsory reduction in the numbers of beef cattle. Both Lord Woolton and the Prime Minister appear to have entertained the notion that there was a 'reserve of meat on the hoof' which could be drawn on at will, so to speak, to relieve a shortage of imported supplies.[1] This belief rested on a mis-

---

[1] On 24th March, on his return from Chequers to ask for more shipping, Lord Woolton wrote: '. . . We must continue the 'slaughter policy'; I have told the Prime Minister that we require the meat from it during the next six months, if we are to maintain the ration'. Hence, no doubt, the Prime Minister's reference, in his ruling on shipping of 26th March, to 'drawing as may be necessary on our meat reserves on the hoof to cover the next six months'.

understanding. The number of beasts ripe for slaughter at any given time is but a proportion of the total animal population; any attempt to increase this proportion substantially by accelerating slaughter is bound to mean killing immature beasts that are not merely lighter, but have relatively less flesh and more skin and bone. A 'slaughter policy' yields little present gain to set off against future loss.

The policy's official advocates realised this. What they held was that the animal feed position offered no alternative; that the rationing of feeding-stuffs, now scheduled to begin on 1st February 1941, the prohibition of the feeding of home-grown wheat to animals, and the prospect of a rise in the extraction rate for flour, all meant that the situation of 1917-18 was repeating itself. They were particularly concerned lest an attempt by farmers to maintain too many beef cattle should lead to a further fall in yields of milk, a food of supreme value that could not readily be replaced by imports. In an attempt to reach an agreed policy, a Livestock Policy Conference, representing the interested Departments together with the War Cabinet's Scientific Food Committee, was set up at the end of 1940.

There was substantial agreement among the members of this Conference that though the numbers of sheep, pigs, and poultry were still too high for their prospective feed supplies, the trend of those for sheep and pigs was in the right direction, along which it might be pushed by feeding-stuffs rationing and a certain amount of price manipulation. (No one could suggest any way of enforcing a fall in the numbers of poultry.) On cattle there was apparently irreconcilable conflict between the calculations of the experts and the observations of the 'practical men'. The statisticians produced elaborate estimates to show that, for want of concentrates,[1] a 'catastrophic'—that was the word used—fall in milk and meat production would take place between February and May, unless the number of animals was immediately and drastically reduced. The Ministry of Food's Economics Division advocated, therefore, an immediate and heavy slaughter of two-year-old steers and calves, enforced if necessary by requisition.

The Ministry's Meat and Livestock Division, which was in day-to-day touch with conditions in the country, did not agree. It held, with the Ministry of Agriculture, that if the situation was as bad as the statisticians made out there would have been loud complaints from farmers, whereas in fact there had been none. This view prevailed for the moment; early in February Ministers accepted recommendations that the import of store cattle from Eire should be restricted,[2]

---

[1] 'Concentrates' are that part of the animal's diet—cereals, milling offals, pulse and oilcake—on which its output of meat or milk largely relies. They constitute its 'production ration' as distinct from its 'maintenance ration' of grass or roots. Experience was to show that bulk foods could be substituted for concentrates to an extent not previously thought to be possible.

[2] They had already been totally stopped on account of foot-and-mouth disease.

that fat cattle prices should be further adjusted so as to discourage excessive fattening, that something should be done to reduce the number of bull calves, and that the Ministry of Food should buy up store cattle for immediate slaughter. Farmers were to be exhorted not to try and maintain pre-war numbers of cattle if output of meat and milk would thereby suffer, and should be warned that the shortage of imported feeding-stuffs would continue.

In March fresh calculations of feeding-stuffs supplies and requirements gave further impetus to the compulsory slaughter campaign. On the more favourable of two sets of assumptions about the third year of war, it was reckoned that there would be feed, at pre-war standards of consumption, for but ninety-five per cent. of the existing dairy herd, eighty-three per cent. of sheep, and eighty per cent. of beef cattle. But cattle numbers as revealed in the quarterly agricultural returns showed no signs of diminishing. The production catastrophe promised for the spring had not materialised and farmers showed no signs of expecting one. Slaughterings, except for calves, were rather below normal; the market for store cattle, partly because of the exclusion of stores from Eire, remained so firm as to preclude the Ministry of Food from buying them up for slaughter.

The advocates of slaughter urged that farmers must be saved from themselves; the Ministry of Food, supported by the Lord Privy Seal, got the Food Policy Committee to agree and to instruct the Agricultural Departments to produce plans for the compulsory culling of twenty per cent. of beef herds. (The Ministry acquiesced, though with reluctance, in a five per cent. culling of dairy herds, which appealed more strongly to the Agricultural Departments.) By this time, May 1941, the experts had produced yet another set of calculations, according to which a heavier rate of slaughter might be necessary now that the feeding of wheat to livestock had been forbidden.

The Agricultural Departments were not unwilling to weed out unproductive beasts (as was proposed for dairy herds), but disliked very heartily the enforcement by requisition, or threatened requisition, of the slaughter of sound beasts; for this would imply taking feeding-stuffs from those owners whose animals had been sacrificed, and handing them over to other farmers. Such measures, the Departments thought, would throw upon their local representatives the responsibility for invidious choices that might set the whole farming community by the ears.

The Minister of Food, for his part, had pressed the slaughter policy so long as it promised—as he thought—to provide some extra meat for the ration. But when he realised that it was only likely to produce sausages and pie-meat, and when, thanks to the summer improvement in the shipping situation and the measures taken to release meat ships, imported supplies threatened to choke the cold stores by the end of August and impelled, despite the shortage of home-killed meat, a rise in the ration from 1s. to 1s. 2d., he seems to have felt disinclined to go on supporting what was, after all, a matter not of food but agricultural policy. When, towards the end of June, the Agricultural Departments came back to the Food Policy Committee, and argued that experience had shown the experts' forecasts to be mistaken, that there were not too many but too few fat cattle for the flush of summer grass, and that there was no likelihood of an autumn glut, the Ministry of Food raised no objections to a complete reversal of the policy approved by Ministers in the spring. Farmers were now to be told that, owing to the improved supplies of imported meat, it was no longer necessary for them to offer a larger number of sound beasts than usual. Since they had never shown any signs of complying with earlier Government exhortations to accelerate slaughter, the reversal of policy had no practical effect.

In September the Livestock Policy Conference was called together for a *post mortem* on the policy based on its calculations, and made a comprehensive meal of its own words. There was, it admitted, no autumn glut of fat cattle, but on the contrary a strong demand for stores. The Meat and Livestock Division had been right when it prophesied that there might be not enough sheep to consume all the root crops; the reduction in pig and poultry numbers had gone far enough.

Non-expert Ministers and administrators might be forgiven if they found these transactions more than a little bewildering. How was it possible for figures with such expert authority behind them, and put forward with such conviction, to be proven false within so short a space of time? The answer is to be found in the calculations themselves: because they pointed to a sizeable reduction in beef cattle, it appears to have been assumed that the reduction would release a significant amount of feed for the remaining classes of animals. This conclusion will not stand up to analysis. Take concentrates as an example: even on the less favourable of the two assumptions about third-year-of-war supplies used by the statisticians, the paper saving to be gained was equal to 4·5 per cent. of total supplies; on the more favourable, it was three per cent.[1] Moreover, these estimates made no allowance for the

---

[1] A full analysis of the whole problem belongs to the separate monograph on agriculture in this series. It will be sufficient here to quote the figures immediately relevant to the compulsory slaughter proposal. These are (in millions of tons, starch equivalent):

A. Estimated supplies of concentrated feeding-stuffs .   .   .   . 3·6 (or 2·5)
B. Estimated requirements of a beef herd eighty per cent of that at December 1940   .   .   .   . ·45
C. Therefore, requirements of the twenty per cent. by which beef herds would be reduced   .   .   .   . ·1125
   C as percentage of A: roughly 3 or 4·5, according to the assumptions chosen.

fact that the country was not one large farm, and that there must be difficulties and losses in transferring from one farmer to another the feeding-stuffs rendered surplus in theory by a slaughter policy.

On a cool appraisal of the statistical evidence, therefore, the case for compulsory slaughter at this time must have been set down as 'not proven'. No one could propose so great a disturbance to the agricultural industry for so meagre a result, commensurate only with the likely error in the estimates themselves.[1] Cool appraisal, however, was not forthcoming; the statistics were used, not to elucidate the problem, but as camp-followers in a war of principles. Compulsory slaughter became not an expedient to be judged on its merits, but a dogma, a symbol of old conflicts renewed. The very language used by some of its proponents has a flavour of drama, as if the fate of the nation were at stake. Only in these terms can one explain the expenditure of time and energy upon a proposal that, but for its historical antecedents, could scarcely have been regarded early in 1941 as of first importance.

III

More than six months of argument had left relations between the Ministry of Food and the Agricultural Departments so strained that Lord Woolton felt the need for a *détente*. On 3rd July he made a 'personal statement' before the Food Policy Committee disclaiming any intention of interfering with the means by which the Agricultural Departments sought to pursue the ends of policy. The Committee had itself decided that milk production should be put before meat; but the responsibility of seeing that enough milk was provided was the Agricultural Ministers'. So too it was not for him, as Minister of Food, to make plans for controlling the numbers of livestock offered for slaughter. Henceforward it was to be clear that while the Minister of Food might state his requirements from home production, the Ministers responsible for agriculture must say how far and in what way those requirements might be supplied.

This '*concordat*' frequently irked the more ardent spirits in the Ministry of Food, and there were to be minor breaches of it in later years, for instance when the Ministry insisted in 1943 that farm prices for milk should be increased by more than the amount the Agricultural Departments thought necessary to maintain production. But there were to be no more of the major tussles that had enlivened the proceedings of the Food Policy Committee—indeed, for want of them

---

[1] They were stated, however, to the nearest thousand tons, i.e. to within ·1 per cent.

the Committee was to fall into desuetude. The stabilisation policy, by divorcing producers' and consumers' prices, removed what had been a recurrent occasion of conflict. The most important implication of the *concordat* was the ruling out, except in those hypothetical circumstances generally called 'siege conditions', of crop requisition as a weapon of policy. That meant limiting the amount of home-produced food marketed to the amount that farmers were willing to sell; or to put it another way, reducing the population of farm animals only to the extent that rationed feeding-stuffs could not be replaced by fodder grown on the farm itself. Thus, although the agreed cropping programme for the harvest of 1942 allowed for considerably increased sowings of wheat, potatoes, and sugar beet for human food, farmers were still urged to become more self-sufficing in feeding-stuffs.

The case for not attempting to coerce the farmer is too obvious to need emphasis here. Some in the Ministry of Food were inclined to chafe at the restriction that seemed to be imposed on its freedom to push economies in supply, and equalities of distribution, to their logical conclusion. One can understand the Ministry's feeling of frustration when, in the summer of 1941, it could not buy at the controlled price enough home-grown oats, out of a harvest of several million tons, to satisfy the needs of oatmeal millers and 'essential' horses, and rather than offer an extra bonus to get them, preferred to obtain 72,000 tons of maize under Lend/Lease. (The Treasury refused sanction for the import of 10,000 tons of rolled oats: 'I cannot', wrote the Financial Secretary, 'regard the provision of porridge . . . for human beings during the summer months as an essential requirement'.) This particular difficulty was got over the following year by making forward purchases of home-grown oats; but it illustrates a limitation that was to crop up again in the more important context of flour 'dilution'.

The very fact that the Ministry of Food had not been given responsibility for the food production campaign was bound, of course, to make its members the more fertile in proposing stern measures for getting the last ton of food off farms, and devising means for curbing the cottager's pig and the backyarder's hen. Their dealings with the Agricultural Departments over such matters as these might be summed up in the words of Macaulay:

'. . . those behind cried "Forward!"
And those before cried "Back !" '

Sometimes one cannot but feel that small economies were sought as a sort of moral compensation for the want of big ones. In fact, by the end of 1941 there was only one important saving to be made, namely, to raise the extraction rate of flour. The considerable further economies in imports that were achieved in later years must be credited to increased home production.

If there was little scope left for economy, through further extensions of control and improvements in marketing home-grown crops, there was still room for controlling price and rendering distribution more equitable. From mid-1941 onwards the Ministry of Food made a series of experiments in this hitherto unexplored field, with varying success. Some of the more important of these will be examined in a second volume of the present study.

CHAPTER XIV

Food Prices and the Stabilisation Policy

I

URING the autumn and winter of 1940–41 considerable progress was made towards defining the Government's food price policy. In August 1940 the War Cabinet had committed itself to subsidising 'essential' foods, and 'restraining' a rise in the cost-of-living index; it had also resolved that 'luxury' foods should be allowed to find their own price level. But the precise meaning of these commitments was left for future definition. Where was the line to be drawn between luxuries and essential foods? Bread is a necessity, smoked salmon a luxury,[1] but what of coffee, custard powder, lemon curd? Should subsidies be confined to foods included in the cost-of-living index, or extended to those, like oatmeal, whose consumption needed stimulating on account of its food value? Did 'restraining' a rise in the cost-of-living index mean that a gradual rise, say of two points per quarter, could be permitted, or must the index figure be completely stabilised, and if so, what of seasonal variations in prices, of, for example, eggs and potatoes?

To these problems the Interdepartmental Committee on Food Prices addressed itself, against a background of continually rising food prices. Already before the Cabinet's decision, the high price of new potatoes, coupled with increases in the price of eggs, milk and fish, had caused a sharp jump of ten points in the food index between 1st June and 1st July 1940; in August sugar was put up by a halfpenny a lb. (to meet increased costs) more than offsetting the decline of potato prices from their midsummer peak. In September the Treasury insisted that no further losses should be incurred on tea and milk, and that their prices should go up accordingly. Clothing prices were still rising, thanks largely to the Treasury's own purchase tax; the cost-of-living index was expected to be about seven points higher on this account alone. The Interdepartmental Committee urged that to peg the index, if it prevented a rise in wages, would still be worth while even at an apparent cost considerably higher than the £55 millions a year which was then being spent on it—though the Committee indicated ways by which, through a rearrangement of subsidies among different foodstuffs, the Exchequer could save

---

[1] See, however, Chapter XVII.

money. Subsidies might be needed in addition to cheapen foods like oatmeal and potatoes, whose value in war-time was specially great. Some part of this expenditure would, it was hoped, be recouped from the profits on luxury foodstuffs, as well as from increases in direct and indirect taxation. These views prevailed with the Treasury,[1] and found public expression in the Chancellor's budget statement of April 1941; they had been put into effect, however, in December, when the rise in milk prices already decided on for January was deliberately offset by a cut of 1d. a pound in retail sugar prices.

Simultaneously a beginning had been made on the other half of the programme; for the price of sugar to manufacturers was raised by 1d. The Ministry of Food followed this up by raising the price of West African raw cocoa and imposing a levy on cocoa from other sources, as from 1st March 1941; in April, on becoming the sole importer of rice, it deliberately raised prices of the better grades so as to earn an average extra profit of 1d. a pound. Cocoa, rice, and manufacturing sugar, however, were to be the only foodstuffs whose prices were deliberately increased by Ministry action; an elaborate scheme to raise the price of the dearer cuts of meat while reducing the cheaper never came to fruition, partly because it would have meant altering the way in which meat was rationed. On the other hand an oatmeal subsidy was introduced on 16th December 1940. (Coupled with an advertising campaign, it proved all too successful; oatmeal rapidly became unobtainable.) A project for providing the poor with specially cheap potatoes came to nothing.

The budget speech for 1941, the Treasury held, publicly committed the Government to maintain the all-items cost-of-living index number at a fixed level of 201½ points (base 1914 = 100, or thirty per cent. above the September 1939 level). The Board of Trade undertook to control clothing prices, which stood at ninety per cent. above pre-war; but the administrative work involved would obviously take time, and meanwhile the season for new potatoes was all too rapidly approaching. Fish, which the Ministry of Food had left alone since the withdrawal of its distribution scheme in September 1939, was still uncontrolled;[2] egg prices would go up on 1st August unless something was done. Meantime the non-food items in the index were still rising. In response to Treasury entreaty the Ministry accelerated its plans for controlling fish and eggs; a Maximum Prices Order for the former, and a revised scheme, including a subsidy, for the latter, were rushed through during June. A special subsidy was applied to potatoes so as to keep prices of the old crop stationary; in addition,

---

[1] Though, at its express request, they were deleted from the final version of a report by the Interdepartmental Committee. Apparently it was not thought fitting that the Treasury should appear to be taking advice on subsidy policy from other Departments.

[2] Except for herrings, kippers and bloaters, which had been brought under price control in October 1939 (S.R. & O. (1939), No. 1426).

the Ministry of Labour was persuaded of the advantages of an improved statistical technique in compiling potato prices. Instead of a
simple average of old and new potato prices, a weighted average was
taken, which gave emphasis to old potatoes as being more plentiful.
By these various means the situation was saved.[1]

From the Treasury point of view these manœuvres were eminently
successful; for while the food index was artificially lowered (to 167
in July 1941 as against 173, its peak, the previous November) the
all-items index remained virtually stationary. To the Ministry of
Food, however, the prospect of continually manipulating food prices
in the name of a sacrosanct all-items number was not alluring. To
stabilise the *food* index was both convenient and reasonably in accord
with the nutritional aims that the Ministry was beginning to set
itself; even the Scientific Food Committee, which had proposed to
subsidise the cost not of a specific 'basket' of foodstuffs, but of procuring, no matter how, essential food needs in terms of calories, had
been persuaded to accept this as a reasonable practical compromise.
The objection to stabilising the total index figure instead was not so
much theoretical as practical. Clearly the level of the whole cost of
living is more important than that of the separate items in it; cheap
food is of no avail if clothing and shelter absorb an undue proportion
of the household budget. (In so far, indeed, as 'drink' and tobacco
are necessities to most families, the taxes on them offset the artificial
reductions in food prices.) So long as the total index figure remained
stable, changes in the food figure were unimportant but for the fact
that they carried with them extra work for the Ministry of Food.
Every change in retail prices meant a complete revision of traders'
margins; changes downwards aroused compensation claims from
traders for book losses on stock already bought at the higher price,
while changes upwards meant that traders would enjoy an unearned
increment.[2] The Ministry felt that other Departments ought to take
their share of this burden.

---

[1] The Ministry of Labour jibbed, however, at the suggestion that milk supplied under
the National Milk scheme should be taken into account in computing the Index; arguing
that to do so *now* would lead to suspicion that the Index was being 'manipulated'. Nor
did it feel, later on, that an adjustment should be made in the price of margarine for
index purposes, although the proportion of 'special' (i.e. more expensive) margarine had
been increased.

[2] This question of traders' stock profits and losses, resulting from changes in the price
of Ministry-owned foods, had cropped up at intervals since the initial requisitioning of
stocks at the outbreak of war. At that time it had been decided to allow traders to retain
any profits arising from the difference between the price paid on requisition and the cost
price of the stocks, in order that the Government might better be able to resist claims
for compensation for losses.

Later the Ministry had sought to cushion traders against loss by 'staggering' price
reductions, i.e. reducing first-hand and wholesale prices in advance of retail prices, so
that stocks bought at the higher price might be cleared; or paying compensation to traders
on the basis of a 'notional' stock level. In one case (the reduction of sugar prices by 1d. in
December 1941) special claims for compensation were allowed from those whose stocks
Continued on page 185

II

While the pegging of the cost-of-living index was to affect the price of controlled commodities more and more as time went on, it had no very considerable influence in extending the scope of the Ministry of Food's price control activities. Already in the autumn of 1940 it seems to have been generally accepted, at any rate by the non-trade element in the Ministry, that price control would have to be extended very shortly, not merely to all the goods which the Ministry directly or indirectly controlled[1] but to all the miscellaneous 'manufactured foods' that form so large a part of the grocer's stock-in-trade. In response to public clamour the Ministry had as early as October issued a Maximum Price Order for onions, which neither ranked as an essential foodstuff nor were included in the index; on 1st November a similar Order was issued for rabbits, and on 16th December for turkeys. These measures were a departure from the principle that price control should be accompanied by control of supplies and distribution; and their effect was not such as to encourage further departures.

The task of fixing prices for the 2,000 or so items in the wholesale grocer's list, each of them multifarious in quality, style and weight of pack, was formidable and could certainly not be tackled by the Ministry's existing machinery under which each proposal had to be worked out by the commodity division concerned, and then run the gauntlet of three separate committees.[2] It might be possible to deal with a good many of these on the lines of margarine, i.e. by getting the industry itself to standardise 'lines' and prices, and marking these on the container.[3] But such indirect price-fixing was unlikely to work with such things as home-grown fruit and vegetables; effective price control for these would obviously involve a major reorganisation of the trade.

Nor was this all. Even supposing that, by one means or another, an extension of price control on this scale could be enforced, it might lead to chaos in distribution. For price control necessarily implies

---

Continuation

were in excess of the notional level. This led to criticism from the Committee of Public Accounts that too much compensation had been paid to the trade.

The prospect of a series of 'cost-of-living' reductions in food prices led the Ministry to enter into negotiations with the trade to secure an agreed procedure that should exclude the payment of compensation. These negotiations were inconclusive, but the upward turn in food prices put the problem into cold store for the time being. As late as 1947, however, it was to recur and again no solution of universal application could be found.

[1] Besides the 'staples'—meat, bacon, eggs, butter, cheese, cooking fats, milk, tea, potatoes, sugar—the following were already subject to Retail Price Orders : pulses, oranges, lemons, glucose, dried fruits, herrings, canned salmon, frozen cod fillets, and condensed milk.

[2] Namely, the Orders Committee, the Margins Committee, and the Interdepartmental Committee on Food Prices.

[3] See below, Chapter XXIV.

fixing prices at a point where supply and demand do not balance. That means substituting queues and under-the-counter sales for high prices; it means too that scarce goods will be marketed near the place of production on account of varying transport costs. Already home-produced eggs and rabbits had disappeared from the larger towns for this very reason. If, that is to say, the Ministry were to impose price control, it would also have to take responsibility for allocating scarce goods. To do this by giving each wholesaler a proportion of his pre-war sales would be unsatisfactory, on account of the population movements that the war, and particularly the great air raids, had brought about. On the other hand, individual tastes and requirements of these foods varied so greatly that the conventional rationing methods would be useless. In short, the times demanded new techniques, not only for price control, but for distribution and rationing also.

Meantime something had to be done at once, in the hope of keeping the situation in hand. In imposing a general standstill Order freezing the prices of a large number of groceries at the price charged on 2nd December 1940, the Ministry was under no illusion that this could be anything more than a temporary palliative. Its Legal Adviser roundly declared that such an Order would 'from the legal point of view combine every vice': it would be incapable of effective enforcement, inasmuch as it could be readily evaded by altering the quality of the goods sold, as had notoriously been done with tea; it would penalise the honest trader who had kept his prices down as long as possible, while exempting the racketeer who had raised his in advance of the 'appointed day'; there would be no uniform current price to which appeals could be made where a trader was not selling the article in question on that day. Moreover, since an independent decision had been taken to raise the price of manufacturing sugar on 1st January, a current prices Order could not be applied to sugar-using industries. It was in deference to these objections that the scope of the Order, though still wide, was limited to a score or so of commodities.[1] During the course of 1941 almost all these, together with numerous others, were to be brought within the scope of specific Maximum Price Orders. But this process—involving, as it must, costings investigations and the fixing of margins—was necessarily slow, and the position meanwhile was, from a legal point of view, far from

---

[1] S.R. & O. (1941), No. 23. The foods specified in the schedule to this Order were: coffee (including coffee essence, and coffee and chicory), cocoa powder, cocoa butter, and drinking chocolate; canned and bottled vegetables, canned pork and beans; honey; meat, fish, poultry and other edible pastes; meat and other edible extracts; shredded suet; dead poultry; rice, tapioca, and sago; macaroni, etc.; biscuits, rusks and crispbreads; soups—tinned, bottled and powdered; processed cheese; pickles, sauces, and relishes; custard and blancmange powders, table jellies; edible nuts.

Cereal breakfast foods had had an Order to themselves some days previously (S.R. & O. (1940), No. 2180) which provided for licensing manufacturers, as well as a standstill on prices.

satisfactory. The importance of the omnibus Order, indeed, lies less in its administrative effectiveness than in its public avowal of the Ministry's intentions. From then on, the Ministry's prestige was inseparable from an all-round application of price control to all foodstuffs in common use.

That this implication was accepted by the Government as a whole might be inferred from the passage in the Chancellor's 1941 budget speech, declaring that efforts would be made 'to prevent substantial increases in the prices of other articles in common use'. While this declaration was not formally in conflict with the previous Cabinet resolution that 'luxury foods shall be allowed to find their own price level', the definition of luxury foods had been very considerably narrowed. (One official remarked that it was as difficult to define a 'luxury food' as to define a 'heavy worker'.)

The Interdepartmental Committee, reviewing food price policy in August 1941, concluded that prices of all the more important foods not included in the index should be stabilised at about the April 1941 level, that is at the prices prescribed either in the Current Prices Order or in the Maximum Prices Orders then in force. The Committee recognised that to control some foods, particularly home-produced fruit and vegetables, might be so difficult as to be not worth while; and it continued to favour differential subsidies to foods such as potatoes and carrots, in order to prevent under-consumption. It also recommended that the problem of the poor consumer should be further studied, since the war-time rise in earnings had not benefited everyone. This last recommendation, however, seems to have been still-born; and indeed this Report was the Committee's swan-song. Henceforth food price policy was to be discussed less formally, but no less effectively, between Departments as occasion arose.

Besides the pressure of public opinion and the needs of the stabilisation policy, one further influence was at work impelling an extension of price control—the arrival of Lend/Lease foodstuffs. The Ministry could not set up a special system of distribution for these; but it was obviously obliged to see that private traders did not profit by American generosity. American anxiety on this score was allayed by a public statement[1] that no food obtained on Lend/Lease terms would be sold at uncontrolled prices, and that traders would only be allowed a reasonable profit in return for their services in distributing the goods. The difficulties of ascertaining what was a reasonable profit were got over by assuming that margins appropriate for other goods were also appropriate to Lend/Lease goods.

Price regulation by Order or otherwise is of course perfectly possible without price stabilisation by means of subsidies; but subsidies cannot be effectively applied under war-time conditions of shortage unless

---

[1] Mr. Eden—Ambassador Winant, in Cmd. 6311 (September 1941).

price control can be enforced. The first and most important steps in price control had been made by the Ministry of Food as part and parcel of its control of supplies and distribution. The decision to tie the consumer of rationed goods to the retailer in itself implied prescribing the price at which they were sold.[1] The very thoroughness of food control made the stabilisation policy possible; that policy in its turn contributed towards the completion and shaping of the food control edifice. It gave the Treasury an influence on food policy far transcending the powers it in any case enjoyed by reason of its control over departmental staffing and finance; in particular, the Treasury acquired a direct financial interest in the size of the margins allowed to traders under control, for these would affect very considerably the cost of food subsidies. Even the technique of margins-fixing was bound to be affected, since subsidies made the retail price, and not the first-hand price, the basis, avowed or otherwise, from which this process must begin. In short, the stabilisation policy meant that the Ministry of Food, so far as the prices of essential foods were concerned, became little more than the hand-maiden of the Treasury; its very success in control made it more dependent than more laggard Departments.

III

There is no real break in the history of food prices from 1941 till the end of the war. Their movement took a course which viewed in isolation would appear irrational, largely divorced as it was from food costs and the needs of food policy and dominated by the trend of non-food prices. These continued to rise until the summer of 1942, and they were responsible for a further reduction of 1d. a pound in the price of sugar (December 1941) and of 6d. a dozen for eggs (April 1942). By the autumn of that year, however, the Board of Trade scheme for utility clothing and its exemption from purchase tax would have to be reckoned with. The Treasury now looked forward to a gradual fall—of about six points—in the index, which would be only less embarrassing than a rise; and it consequently asked that food prices should be gradually put up again.

The situation created by this request was typically complicated, for a number of other price changes were being mooted at that very moment. There was the seasonal rise in milk prices; the Oils and Fats Division were proposing to raise the price of soap; the Fish

---

[1] The Ministry often laid stress on its prescribed retail prices being *maxima* only; but clearly where the customer is tied to the retailer, prices will tend to the maximum, except where price-cutting is resorted to in order to attract registrations—a practice publicly deprecated by the Ministry.

Division had in preparation a new Order which would reduce the price of certain kinds of fish. It was difficult to find a suitable candidate for the 'stabilising' price rise. The Eggs Division feared that if the price of eggs were restored to its former level there would be a demand from producers for higher prices; even if this could be resisted the incentive to market through the packing stations would be less. Cheese, just then very plentiful (thanks to Lend/Lease) was difficult to get rid of even at the existing price. The Treasury favoured a halfpenny on the 4-lb. loaf, but Bread Division objected that this would give an awkward price, and suggested 1d. with a corresponding increase on flour. This, taken in one leap, would affect the index too much; so the Ministry suggested that it should be coupled with a reduction in the price of potatoes, which would fall in conveniently with the eat-more-potatoes campaign. Whether the demand for potatoes would be affected by their price was extremely doubtful; Lord Woolton's personal view was that the potato subsidy was only necessary on cost-of-living grounds. But the device had other advantages; it would save the Treasury money, might discourage waste of bread and (since flour was to be put up less in proportion) would tend to ease any grievance which those who baked bread at home might feel at the special subsidy on flour for bread making. The Ministry of Labour was inclined to demur to so great a rise in bread prices, but was eventually persuaded to agree. On 20th September the maximum price of the 4-lb. loaf was raised to 9d., that of flour by $1\frac{1}{2}$d. per 7 lb., while potatoes were reduced to 1d. a pound.

This, however, was only a beginning. Next month, October, bacon prices were raised by an average of 2d. a pound; meantime news from the Ministry of Labour statisticians at Southport was anxiously awaited. The food index for October stood at 62, to the nearest whole number, which was what had been intended; but it was fractionally below instead of fractionally above that figure, since the whole of the permitted rise in flour prices was not being passed on by the trade to the consumer. It looked as if the November figure might be, despite bacon, below 62·5, in which case it could not be published as 63. (In the event, it came out at 62·56, saving the situation by ·07 of a point.) Again the Treasury pressed and again the Ministry agreed to a rise in food prices, this time of 1d. a pound on butter, to operate by 1st December. Still, however, clothing prices continued their inexorable fall, far exceeding all forecasts. It had originally been expected that higher wages in the clothing trades would be reflected in retail prices, but the Board of Trade now maintained that the task of revising the price schedules—which admittedly were complex in the extreme—could not be faced and that an offsetting subsidy on raw materials was preferable. (The Treasury had previously declared such a subsidy to be impossible.) The Ministry of Food was asked to agree to further rises—tea, sugar, and bread were suggested.

The Ministry had not unnaturally become exceedingly restive by this time; it felt that so rigid an adherence to a specific index number was not merely an unmitigated administrative nuisance, but might defeat its own ends by causing people to think that the Ministry had lost its grip on food prices. The Ministry of Labour was equally doubtful. Accordingly the matter was brought before the Lord President's Committee which, while accepting as a matter of urgency an increase of 4d. in tea prices on 1st February 1943, deferred decision on the other proposed increases pending an official inquiry into the way in which the cost-of-living index was calculated. Could it, for instance, be published quarterly instead of monthly? Could it be based on the maximum prices issued by the Ministry of Food, instead of actual prices collected by the Ministry of Labour investigators? The latter suggestion would save staff and avoid troubles such as had been caused by the failure of flour prices to conform to schedule; the former would not only save frequent price changes, but might be used to dodge awkward months like July, with its new potatoes. The officials favoured, and the Lord President's Committee accepted, both these suggestions; the *ad hoc* collection of the prices of eight main foodstuffs[1] was to be discontinued, and the Trade Unions and Employers' Organisations sounded on the possibility of quarterly publication. But Ministers still remained unwilling to raise food prices and particularly the price of bread further.

This reluctance the Treasury attempted to overcome by an elaborate display of evidence. 'The war-time distribution of the available goods and services', it argued, 'leaves in general no likelihood of hardship (as distinct from inconvenience). It may, indeed, seem to have laid the foundation for an improved nutritional standard for the nation as a whole, especially when account is taken of the special schemes such as the National Milk scheme . . . run by the Ministry of Food'. Family expenditure, thanks to rationing, had risen less than the rise in the index; the average increase in earnings had been considerably more. Therefore, there was no need to modify the existing policy of keeping the index steady at 99–100; and since the index was likely to go down a rise in bread prices was indicated. To show that this would do no harm it cited evidence collected by the War-time Food Survey about the average food consumption, not merely of sample working-class families, but of sample special groups in the population, such as families including heavy workers and families of men in the Forces. The average consumption of each of these groups was, it was said, satisfactory, compared with the experts' estimates of nutritional requirements. (All this sounded impressive; but in fact it was largely irrelevant, unless the extent of deviations from the

---

[1] Meat, milk, bread, butter, margarine, cheese, eggs, and sugar.

average was also known. Evidently, a satisfactory average figure might conceal a considerable number of individual cases within each group who were living at or below the nutritional margin, and on whom an increase in the price of bread, the cheapest of all foods, would press very heavily.)[1] Moreover, the Treasury argued, world wheat prices were likely to remain so high after the war that a 9d. loaf would be quite uneconomic; the sooner therefore that people became used to 10d. as the normal price, the better.

The Lord President's Committee was not convinced that the 10d. loaf was either an economic necessity or in strict accordance with social justice. While it accepted the need to balance the index by a further rise in food prices, it referred the choice back to officials. The Treasury persisted in pressing for an early increase in bread and flour; eggs were considered, only to be rejected in the face of earlier objections and the fact that the spring flush was the worst time of the year to alter egg prices. A decision was postponed for some time by the discovery that the Treasury, in forecasting the movement of the index, had forgotten to allow for the extra tax on tobacco imposed by the 1943 budget. Early in May, however, the Chancellor of the Exchequer secured Lord Woolton's agreement to a 10d. loaf in August and preliminary discussions on ways and means were once more set in train. They had yet to reckon, however, with the Minister of Labour. Early in June Mr. Bevin, who had at first opposed the rise to 9d. but had seemed disposed to accept 10d., finally seems to have made up his mind that bread must not go up; and he was unmoved when the Treasury put forward its argument about post-war wheat prices. The only practicable alternative seemed to be sugar; 1d. a lb. on sugar prices would have the same effect on the index as 1d. on the 4-lb. loaf, and although it would save the Treasury less money, it would bear less heavily on the poor. At 4d. a lb. sugar would still be cheaper than it was at the earlier stages of the war; moreover, the difference between the price of 'household' and 'manufacturing' sugar, which had been an incentive to fraud, would be lessened. The choice between bread and sugar went to Ministers, who decided for the latter.

Meantime the attempt to reduce the index' nuisance value by publishing it quarterly had encountered a fatal stumbling-block in the opposition of the Trade Unions. Though it remained steady during the rest of 1943 (not without alarums and excursions about the effects of changes in the price of hake and potatoes) fresh trouble lay ahead in a proposal to raise the pithead price of coal and to permit further increases in the price of gas. If the rigid stabilisation policy were to be adhered to, food prices would once more have to take a downward

---

[1] A similar misuse of the arithmetical average is to be found in the Ministry of Food's argument that the cost of the increase in bread would be under 1d. per head per week.

course. But much to the relief of the Ministry of Food, the Treasury now concluded that some slight rise should be allowed in the index, not only in order to ease the financial burden of subsidies (already likely to grow heavier as world prices rose), but also to siphon off the increased purchasing power resulting from the latest wage increases. The Lord President's Committee, not without some hesitation, agreed that the index should be allowed to take its course for the time being. But Mr. Bevin pointed out that if it rose above 203, wage increases amounting to some £40 millions would automatically follow; and the Chancellor agreed to reconsider the matter before that point was reached.[1]

Meantime the old problem of the appropriateness of the index had been raised again, this time by the investigations of Mr. Seebohm Rowntree,[2] who had come to the conclusion that it underestimated the extent to which the cost of living had risen. Officials reporting to the Lord President's Committee had little difficulty in showing that Mr. Rowntree's calculations not only exaggerated the extent of the rise, but were not strictly comparable with the index inasmuch as they measured, not changes in the cost of a given basket of commodities, but the minimum cost of providing a minimum diet. (It was this cost which the Scientific Food Committee had suggested should be stabilised.)

Admittedly the index was out of date, but to revise it in war-time would be impracticable. For this could only mean basing it on a 'basket' determined not by what would normally be bought by a working-class family, but what supplies were available. A new and uncertain element, the supply position for the various commodities, would thus have to be introduced into the index, if the new figure were not shortly to become as arbitrary as the old. The change-over from old to new would raise endless difficulties over collective wage agreements. It would be impossible to project the calculations back to the beginning of the war. Most important of all, the adoption of current accurate 'weights' for all the items in the index—tobacco for example—would completely 'stultify the stabilisation policy'. The Government would be obliged to counteract the increased taxation it had imposed on working-class luxuries by granting extra subsidies on the remaining items in the index. In short, though officials did not say so, the success of the index as a basis for the stabilisation policy was due to its imperfections as a measure of the rise in the cost of living.

---

[1] The Treasury was still, it will be seen, preoccupied with the money cost of subsidies. But so long as the Government was the purchaser of the vast bulk of manufactures, it would have to bear the cost of any wage increases brought about by allowing the index to rise. Moreover, the subsidies on some index items were more than outweighed by the taxes on others; the tobacco tax alone yielded more than the total cost of food subsidies.

[2] Privately communicated by him to the Ministry of Labour.

The net effect of these 1944 discussions was to leave the index where it stood; a nuisance, but (it still seemed) an indispensable nuisance now that policy had been based on it so long. The new latitude given the number might serve to keep food prices stable for a time;[1] but sooner or later the problem must be faced again, perhaps this time in the more difficult conditions of the period after an armistice. In retrospect it is clear that much trouble would have been saved if the Treasury had from the first felt able to allow the index to vary, say, within five points each way of a given figure, e.g., from 195–205. The picture of officials gravely pondering whether a halfpenny on the price of hake would not have a 'trigger effect' on the index is hardly edifying; nor could the Ministry of Food welcome a policy which caused the most efficiently controlled prices to move up and down in apparent aimlessness. As for offsetting seasonal rises by special administrative dodges, one can hardly not sympathise with the high official of the Ministry who in 1941 described the Treasury's request for this as 'stupid and unreasonable' and its alarm about new potatoes as 'just silly'. But it was three years before the Treasury admitted that these criticisms were substantially right, and that stabilisation and rigidity were not the same thing.

The dominance of food prices by a rigid cost-of-living index was a prolific source of irritation to the Ministry of Food; but it seems unlikely that the adjustments in food prices were considerable enough seriously to affect the position of the poor consumer, or to force more people below the nutritional margin. Nevertheless, it would be going too far to conclude that the nutritional margin no longer existed, and that the poor consumer was no longer with us. The number of people unable to afford an adequate diet was indeed likely to be at its lowest under war-time conditions of full employment; and the subsidy policy was calculated to benefit in particular those whose money income had not risen as a result of the war, and for whom price control without subsidies might have been insufficient. The policy did not preclude such devices as the artificial cheapening of potatoes; and it was supplemented by the National Milk Scheme, which (since poverty is most frequently associated with large families) not only helped those who needed help most, but stimulated consumption of the one staple foodstuff for which demand appeared to be really elastic. How far a hard, if small, core of poverty and malnutrition remained, despite both general and differential subsidies, is a problem on which more information is needed.

---

[1] The announcement of the changed policy in the 1944 budget speech was almost universally assumed by the Press to mean a rise in food prices.

CHAPTER XV

Distribution Problems and the Extension of Rationing

I

TOWARDS the end of 1940 it became clear that the Ministry of Food would be obliged to do something about the distribution of those foods still remaining unrationed; more particularly once it had committed itself to a wide extension of price control. The lesson of the last war, that control of prices is idle without control of distribution, had been rubbed in by experience with onions, rabbits, and turkeys. The shortage of milk and the abrupt fall in the meat ration at the New Year increased the demand for cheese, cake, and sausages, as well as for bread. The shift of population from bombed cities to the safer areas upset the system whereby allocations of 'manufacturing meat' for sausages, or fats and sugar for cakes, were related to the pre-war population, as reflected in the 'datum line' of manufacturers' and retailers' usage. Increased bread consumption brought with it a clamour for jam and other spreads at a time when, owing to Service and N.A.A.F.I. demands, there was less of them for civilians. Air raids and the destruction of cooking facilities had led to an increased demand for ready-prepared foods like canned salmon and chocolate.

These problems of supply and distribution were associated with and exacerbated by the more general problem of a threatened inflation. Increased purchasing power among the masses, thanks to the rise in earnings, was outrunning the supply of consumer goods even where, as with chocolate and sweets, this had not already been diminished. Thus while traders and administrators within the Ministry of Food debated ways and means of improving the distribution of individual foods, the Treasury and the economists of the War Cabinet Secretariat were pointing to the need for measures to restrict spending power generally. Not only increased taxation and forced loans, but more direct action, was held to be necessary. As early as January 1941 the economists advising the War Cabinet were urging that rationing of further foodstuffs, even if it were practicable, would not go far enough. Two alternatives were outlined; rationing of all food consumption by value, or 'the German point system'.

The former was given preference, since it could 'enclose' any specific rationing provisions that seemed desirable on nutritional or other grounds, would be a complete safeguard against a general rise in the price level, and would not bring with it the problems of management inseparable from the points system.

There was little disposition at the Ministry of Food to explore the possibilities of expenditure rationing; it was felt to be if not politically impracticable, at any rate a matter for the Government as a whole. The Minister himself declined to sponsor it. Meantime a Committee was set up in Colwyn Bay not specifically to promote further rationing schemes, but to undertake a comprehensive study of the distribution of unrationed foods; a remit which was at first held by its members to preclude them from recommending the extension of straight rationing. This extreme attitude on their part did not last very long, but it was departed from with considerable reluctance and misgiving.

To understand this attitude one must recall the traditions of the British rationing system, dating back to 1917. Rationing meant the guarantee of a fixed quantity, neither more nor less, to each individual consumer; it connoted a controlled system of distribution, beginning with Ministry ownership and ending with the consumer-retailer tie. The rationing of any food was therefore a serious and intricate process, not to be lightly undertaken; and only foods possessing certain qualifications might be admitted to a rationing scheme. They must, to avoid overloading the mechanism, be necessities; they must preferably be non-perishable, to avoid the problems of sale off-the-ration; they must be in regular demand, and be capable of even supply, week by week; and the variation in demand for them as between individuals must not be so wide as to make a uniform ration inappropriate. (The last case is exemplified best of all by tobacco, which many adults do not want at all—it must be remembered that the sale of rations was taboo, indeed illegal.)

By these criteria, there were not many foods left that were fit for rationing; tea had already been frowned on as not really suitable, and the manner of its distribution, without registration, was regarded as dangerously heterodox. Cheese, whose consumption by individuals was believed to vary very greatly, had always been held to be unrationable; so had eggs, on account of the difficulty of controlling the home-produced article. But there was a large class of foods none of which was sufficiently important to justify rationing it separately, but which might be grouped together for distribution purposes. It was suggested that the 'preserves group'—jam, marmalade, honey, etc.—might be a suitable subject for experiment. In order that the Ministry might not be obliged to control the whole supply, a 'minimum share' was proposed in lieu of a fixed ration. Consumers would be tied to retailers, and the registrations would be used as a basis for allocating supplies; the Ministry would announce the individual minimum share—representing say two-thirds of the total supplies available. It would not, as with ordinary rationing, be an offence to sell or obtain supplies in excess of that minimum.

This scheme is reminiscent of the attempt, in 1917, to avoid sugar rationing by introducing sugar registration; and it met with the same fate. The commodity division responsible for jam would have preferred a full rationing scheme, but the Ministry went ahead with the minimum share proposal, and secured a rather grudging approval from the Food Policy Committee and the War Cabinet itself. The scheme came into force on 17th March 1941, and rapidly proved to be unworkable. 'Everybody felt they wanted some of this mythical surplus, and the retailer was left in just the same invidious position in disposing of it as he had before the scheme was introduced. We abandoned it for an official maximum ration in June'.

Meantime the Committee in Colwyn Bay busied itself with further schemes for dealing with specific foods. A proposal to include cheese in a group-ration with eggs and canned fish was abandoned in favour first of a minimum share for cheese alone, and then of a straight ration by which means alone supplementary rations for priority classes of consumer could be provided for. (They were necessary because the standard ration was at first tiny—1 oz. per head per week.) A similar scheme for rice, tapioca, and sago, was first postponed and then rejected by higher authority within the Ministry on the ground that supplies of rice had so improved as to render it unnecessary. Rationing of canned meat, fish, etc., was rejected because supplies would only admit of a 'derisory' ration. The problems of chocolates and sweets, and of biscuits, were referred to the trade associations. An orthodox ration, with registration, was proposed for currants, sultanas, and raisins. Sausages might be included in the meat ration.

This variety of expedients, even if they proved to be workable, obviously did not touch a great number of foods whose distribution was causing complaints. These the Ministry proposed to deal with by itself entering into the business of distribution. It established, in July 1941, an Unrationed Foods Division, which was to set up Depots in each of the Food Divisions, in which would be accumulated stocks of a large variety of unrationed foods, ranging from canned fish to pickles and cornflour, under the direct control of the Ministry. These depots, which were in effect a revival of the 'Consumer Depots' debated in the summer of 1940,[1] were intended to be drawn upon, not only where cases of local shortage were reported, but also to supply deficiencies that might arise through enemy action, and to meet the

---

[1] See Chapter X.

needs of canteens and other establishments that, because they had no 'datum usage' of unrationed foods, had difficulty in obtaining supplies.

This scheme had barely time to get started before it was super-seded by the passage of events. But it indicates the lengths to which the Ministry was prepared to go in order to avoid extending ration-ing beyond very narrow limits. It was still wedded to registration as a *sine qua non*; one of the recommendations of the Committee on Un-rationed Foods was that registration should be applied to tea—a request repeatedly put to, and as often rejected by, the Minister in subsequent years.[1] Indeed, the Ministry's attachment to registration had been strengthened since it had recently abandoned the cutting out of ration coupons by retailers, on the ground that it was irksome and—since the coupons were seldom counted by the Food Office—ineffective. This rediscovery of the fact, laid down by the Beveridge Committee on Rationing in 1936,[2] that the essential piece of the rationing mechanism was the counterfoil, meant that any move in the opposite direction, that is to say retaining coupon-cutting but scrapping registration, would be quite contrary to the trend of rationing administrators' thoughts and actions.

The comments of the Ministry Committee on value rationing, which had been independently suggested by the London Divisional Food Officer as an expedient in an emergency, such as enemy invasion, illustrate its general outlook very clearly. Its members did not believe that such a limitation of purchasing power would of itself assist equitable distribution. 'Supplies can only be assured if demand is controlled in detail as well as in total'; the larger the group to which a monetary limit were applied, the more likely a scarcity of the more popular items. Moreover, it was said, consumers would be deflected towards the cheaper articles in the group, while retailers would tend to replenish stocks with those that showed the most profit—both working to the detriment of the poorer consumer. This argument the economists had met in advance; it assumed, they said, that under value rationing the dear goods would remain dear. On the contrary, the reduction in the spendable income of the rich was likely to bring down the prices of luxuries and hence discourage their production, while any shifts in general demand would be reflected in price changes. Any temporary dislocation while price adjustments were still going on could be met by allowing the sale of 'expenditure coupons'.

---

[1] This will be discussed in Vol. II.
[2] See Chapters I and III.

O

II

Whatever economists might think of the Committee's findings, the Minister of Food himself could scarcely reject them lightly, coming as they did from leading administrative and trade experts. But it was now June; and Lord Woolton was under pressure from his colleagues to do something more positive. There had been criticism of 'piecemeal rationing' in the Food Policy Committee back in March; in April the Lord President's Committee had endorsed the economists' view that the 'inflationary gap' could not be closed without a further extension of rationing. On 15th May it had asked the Minister of Food to submit positive proposals for rationing. When, in response, he put forward the recommendations of his advisers, they were roughly handled; it was said that they did not indicate 'any general policy except that of leaving things alone until difficulties arise'. The Ministry was accused of being too tender with the food trades, and the Minister was asked to inquire whether, as then organised, they were capable of securing equitable distribution. As for rationing, the Committee asked him to 'try again'.

These general questions were referred to a fresh Committee[1] set up in Colwyn Bay; the specific task of elaborating a points rationing scheme was entrusted to a small group drawn from the Ministry and the Economic Section of the War Cabinet Secretariat. The economists journeyed to Colwyn Bay to expound their proposals to the administrators and trade experts there assembled; but failed to carry conviction. The Ministry Committee, while admitting that the food trades as then organised were not capable of distributing unrationed foods equitably, opposed the introduction of a 'points' scheme. It argued that information on which to fix and vary points values could not be obtained with enough reliability and rapidity; that the scheme would provide no certain basis for allocating supplies; that there were insufficient stocks to act as a cushion to demand; and that the freedom of the retailer to seek supplies where he wished would hinder any attempt to economise food transport. Moreover, the scheme would confuse both consumer and retailer, cause delays and difficulties in shopping; even if it got rid of queues they would only be replaced by pilgrimages from shop to shop. Instead, the Committee proposed a wide extension of rationing, based on the consumer-retailer tie, to no less than six groups of foods, namely, 'canned meals'; dried fruits; pulses; biscuits; oatmeal and other breakfast foods; and rice, sago, macaroni, etc. For chocolates and sweets alone was the Committee prepared to dispense with registration.

---

[1] Several of its members, however, had belonged to the former Committee.

But this group-rationing scheme, no less than the point-rationing scheme, bristled with difficulties, as the advocates of 'points' hastened to show. It would involve far more regimentation of retailer and consumer; it would divert demand for, e.g., dried fruit, from other types of retailer to grocers; it would play into the hands of the shops that were accustomed to carry a wider range of goods; and it would necessitate the extension of stringent control to a large number of miscellaneous manufactured foods. Six extra registrations, with corresponding provision for removals and other changes, would put an intolerable strain on the local Food Offices. Moreover, some of the criticisms of a points scheme either exaggerated the difficulties—it was unlikely, for instance, that retailers would allow their stocks to be depleted in advance if replenishment depended on the number of coupons they could acquire in exchange—or rested on simple misunderstanding; if the points price of, say, canned fish, were put sufficiently high not only would a run on it be impossible, but anyone who judged the price worth paying would be able to get some.

In face of these arguments and counter-arguments, it was decided that both schemes needed working out in more detail before a decision could be reached. News of the points scheme reached the Prime Minister, who welcomed a 'flexible' coupon system. But this very flexibility aroused in Colwyn Bay fears which were nowise allayed by a second visit from the Economic Section. Every Commodity Director opposed a points scheme; the Wholesale Trade Adviser held that it would break down distribution, the Retail Trade Adviser that it would cause chaos in the trade. One only among the Divisional Food Officers supported it. As for the Rationing Division, which would have to prepare the documents and coupons, it found the practical difficulties appalling[1] and strove to mitigate them by suggesting either that points be combined with registration, or that some system be adopted which would allow coupons to be cancelled instead of cut out.

Nevertheless it was by no means clear that group rationing was not open to the same objections that had been raised against 'points'.

---

[1] 'I am appalled both at my desk and in the shop at the frightfulness of what we have envisaged so far:

    (*a*) the number of points and coupons involved is so colossal;

    (*b*) the cutting itself is dreadful to contemplate;

    (*c*) the counting is even worse;

    (*d*) the exchanging [i.e., of coupons for vouchers to be used at the wholesale and subsequent stages] is bad;

    (*e*) the use of paper is prodigious;

    (*f*) the printing and distribution are nightmares . . . I think these practical difficulties might well wreck the best devised scheme'.

(Memorandum dated 13th August 1941.)

Even in the simplified form now proposed, which by jettisoning canned vegetables, macaroni, and semolina, and grouping together incompatibles like breakfast foods and rice, reduced the number of new registrations to three or possibly two, it would still impose a considerable burden on Food Offices. Moreover, it left the problem of allocation within the more heterogeneous groups extremely vague; and thus was weak on the very point where a properly run points scheme would be strong.

The Minister himself was clearly attracted by the points scheme, once it had been fully explained to him, and when after all he decided to put forward group rationing for approval to the Lord President's Committee, he did so merely on account of the misgivings of almost all his advisers. But the advocates of 'points', though supported by a tiny minority in the Ministry, had the ear of Sir John Anderson, and the Lord President's Committee followed the strong lead given by its Chairman. The extension of consumer registration was particularly condemned as favouring the larger shops and making the consumer feel he was at the trader's mercy, while the points system was supported because it not only avoided these evils, but provided a means of controlling demand. Moreover, as the Lord President urged, points rationing could if it broke down be replaced by group rationing, but not *vice versa*, since group rationing alone involved a Ministry guarantee of supplies. These arguments were effective. The Minister, after reconsidering the problem, proposed and the Lord President's Committee and War Cabinet agreed in September 1941 that points rationing should be tried on a limited scale, i.e., for canned meat, fish, and beans; and that if it succeeded, it should be extended to other foodstuffs.

This decision was a signal victory, as it seemed, for economists over the *soi-disant* practical men. It was certainly a victory that was deserved on the merits of the case as argued. For while the supporters of the points scheme never denied that it would present practical difficulties in operation, and indeed attempted to demonstrate how these could be overcome, its opponents appeared to be incapable of grasping the principles on which it would function. There could be no better example of the gulf that can separate men of ability who have been inured to different habits of thought. To the majority of those who would have to work the scheme now it was adopted, it was almost inconceivable that it should not fail, and above all, should not put the stocks, for which they were responsible to the Minister and to the public, in jeopardy. Had points rationing been launched, not with mingled loyalty and misgiving, but in the enthusiasm born of understanding, its history might have been very different.

III

The practical difficulties, though perhaps no greater than those that would have attended any large extension of orthodox rationing, were considerable enough. A fresh ration book must be designed and printed in a hurry; means must be found to get it to consumers. The destination of the coupons, once the retailer had cut them out, must be settled, and their cancellation and exchange provided for. An initial schedule of 'points prices' must be drawn up. On the other hand, commodity divisions concerned must take steps to ensure that sufficient stocks were in the shops at zero hour; and dealers must be prevented from disposing of them in advance. A new Rationing Order would be needed, as well as a standstill order on these ear-marked stocks; and all this, it was thought, must be done as far as possible in secret. (Those who pointed out that traders would hoard, instead of dissipating stocks ahead of points rationing, were ignored, though they were to be proved right later on.)[1] And, of course, proper publicity must be secured at the right time.

The distribution of books caused much anxiety. The Post Office, even when appeal was made to the Postmaster-General himself, would not distribute them 'over the counter', pleading that this would be too much for their already overworked staff. The Board of Education, for similar reasons, declined to lend either teachers or school buildings. So the Ministry had to rely on its own local offices; the new book was to be issued on presentation of the standard book, and Food Executive Officers were invited to use their ingenuity to arrange times and places of issue most suited to the locality concerned with entirely successful results. Doubtless the lively public interest in the new scheme helped; but the very simplicity and flexibility of the arrangements probably accounted for their success. Simplicity indeed was the keynote of the book itself with its three differently shaded coupons, lettered instead of numbered for ready variation of value, and so devised that coupons of a given value could be cut out together.[2]

Relatively simple at the retail end, the scheme became more complex as one passed up the chain of distribution. After some debate it was decided to make the coupons exchangeable at local food offices into vouchers representing 100, 1,000, or 10,000 points respectively.[3] For every four-weekly period the points surrendered by any retailer

---

[1] When rationing of sweets and chocolates was introduced in July 1942, an early announcement produced a pre-rationing famine.

[2] It was actually worked out on a railway journey between Glasgow and Colwyn Bay; and its simplicity was at any rate in part due to lack of time for making it more complicated. Ideally the Ministry would have preferred four sorts of coupons, differently coloured.

[3] The 100 point vouchers could be cut in half—the 10,000 point vouchers were compounded of ten 1,000s.

would be rounded off upwards to the nearest 100 points. Vouchers, unlike points coupons, would be valid indefinitely; the retailer would be free to order any points goods he chose from the wholesaler, provided he sent vouchers with the order. Suppliers might not give points credit. (Catering establishments and institutions received not coupons, but vouchers corresponding to a fixed entitlement to all points foods.) The vouchers would pass by one or more stages of distribution to be finally 'killed' by the Ministry or its agents.

In theory, distribution would be governed entirely by consumer preference as translated by the retailer into his orders and regulated by the 'points prices' that the Ministry would fix for each commodity. The scheme, as a going concern, would thus be automatic; but it was not, of course, self-starting. Stocks of points foods must be got into the shops in advance; and these must be ample—so as to meet a rush on any particular food in the first four weeks, when the points price schedule would be wholly experimental—and evenly distributed between retailers, since any who were short of stock would be unable to collect coupons for replacement.

The Ministry had, therefore, to find a satisfactory way of making its initial allocations for the three groups of food—canned fish, canned beans, and canned meat—that were to launch the scheme. For canned beans and canned meat it was decided to base the allocation on permits issued by Food Offices according to the number of registered customers each retailer had for sugar, bacon, or butter, whichever was the greater. Special arrangements were made for butchers and others who had no registered customers for these foods. The distribution of canned beans was undertaken through the Heinz organisation, but controlled by an *ad hoc* company—*Candisco*—in which all the manufacturers were represented. Imported canned meats, which formed the whole of the initial canned meat allocation, were to be released through another *ad hoc* body, the *Association of Canned Meat Importers* (*ACMI*), which would distribute supplies to its members and so down the chain to the retailer. For canned fish, on the other hand, allocation was to be made, as it had hitherto unofficially been, in proportion to pre-war performance, adjusted to some extent for population movements. By these various means it was hoped to get into the shops by 17th November, the date for which the scheme was set to start, four weeks' supplies for 130 per cent. of the population.

This sounds—like all the figures connected with the points scheme —an operation of astronomical scale.[1] But it was the simultaneity of

---

[1] In its public statements on the scheme, the Ministry showed the same consciousness of mere size that had caused such distress to the Rationing Division. But (as was pointed out at the time) *any* scheme for 45 million people was bound to involve large numbers. The number of coupons handled by any given shop assistant in any week would be quite manageable.

its parts rather than its size as a whole which created difficulties; delays occurred, not at the centre, but at the periphery. One weakness was that the canned fish was stored in, and the canned meats had to pass through, buffer depots[1] that were often in isolated places and in improvised quarters, like derelict factories and at least one disused coal mine. Congestion in these depots led to considerable delays. Some Food Offices were slow, perhaps unavoidably, in issuing permits. The pooling arrangements through *ACMI* did not work as smoothly as had been hoped. The formation of *Candisco* took up valuable time whose loss offset the distributive efficiency of the Heinz organisation. Despite the most strenuous efforts, official hopes—perhaps too long maintained—that the food could be there in time were disappointed and on the 14th, in face of a clamour from many retailers that they had no supplies, the Minister decided that it must be postponed for a fortnight, till 1st December. Points available to the consumer, which were to have been sixteen per head, were halved for this period. The respite sufficed; and though the postponement caused much heart-searching the instant popular success of the scheme more than compensated for any momentary loss of prestige. What was in any case a venial error of judgement rapidly took on its true proportions.[2]

IV

The sharp deterioration in both supply and shipping prospects after Pearl Harbour meant that the extension of the scheme to other foods, always intended, had to be speeded up. As early as 28th January 1942, dried fruits and pulses were added; four weeks later, on 23rd February, canned fruit, tomatoes and peas; on 6th April, breakfast cereals and condensed milk. These additions were made without serious administrative hitch; but their implications for the economics of the scheme were confusing. It could not be expected that the initial simplified schedule of points prices would succeed in accurately balancing consumer preference against supply, or that the first revisions of it would hit the mark. In fact, consumers rapidly distinguished between foods of varying quality or attractiveness offered at the same points price; there was a run on red salmon, and to a less extent on the new American luncheon meats such as 'Spam', while canned pork sausage meat, and beans 'in gravy' languished in

---

[1] See Chapter XI.

[2] The special inquiry into the causes of the 'breakdown' (as it was termed) makes it clear that the postponement was made necessary by nothing more sinister than the causes here adduced. The only thing for which anyone could be blamed was a too sanguine estimate of the prospects, and hence a failure to warn the Minister in time. Nevertheless, the change in the official management of the scheme that ensued may not have been without effect on the struggle between flexible and rigid systems of allocation.

the shops. The pointing of *all* salmon, including the unpopular pink, upwards from sixteen to twenty-four points a pound failed to check demand; moreover, both the Meat and Canned Fish Divisions, in order to prevent depletion of their stocks pending a proper adjustment, continued to restrict first-hand allocations to the original *datum* basis. Evidently a considerable proportion of wholesalers' demand would thus be forcibly diverted to other points-rationed foods.

When dried fruits, for which straight rationing had been proposed before 'points' were seriously thought of, came in on 26th January, the system was not yet in equilibrium; and it was still unbalanced, despite up-pointing of both canned meat and fish, when the Dried Fruit Division moved from its initial voucher-free allocations to allocations governed solely by voucher demand. Symptoms evident on the first of these, when only eighty-five per cent. of vouchers could be met, became alarming in April; and they had this significant feature, that while demands from wholesalers dealing only in dried fruit remained normal, those for other wholesalers increased so much that only half the demand could be met. Yet dried fruits were not moving so quickly in the retail shops as to justify a rise in their points price, and this was rightly rejected as likely to lead to loss of fruit by deterioration. The Dried Fruit Division fell back on the expedient of allocating on a *datum* basis, only to meet with protests from the trade; reverting to allocations against vouchers, it found itself once again swamped with applications. The problem of what was to be done brought the whole problem of allocating points goods to a head.

The conclusion drawn was of capital importance for the working of the whole points scheme. It was recognised that the system of allocating freely against vouchers could not work for one commodity alone; but the real cause of the disequilibrium was never diagnosed. Because the allocation of all other commodities was working smoothly, it was assumed that there must be something wrong either with the pointing, or with the allocation, of dried fruit, or that traders were not playing the game.[1] But it was not really necessary to make any such assumption. If, as was common knowledge, demand for canned fish and meat exceeded the restricted supply, whereas other things would not sell at their existing price, this in itself suffices to explain the apparent run of wholesalers on dried fruit as a forced choice,

---

[1] Even those who were unhappy about the reversion to *datum* allocations failed to see that dried fruit might not be at fault:—'It has been the most troublesome addition to the points scheme, largely because we did not take a firm enough line with the Commodity Division and insist on substantial increases in points values as soon as the trend became evident. The present system of allocation is exerting an unsettling influence throughout the whole points scheme'. To argue thus was to confuse symptoms with causes. The suggestion that the Economic Section should be consulted was not followed up, in the belief that 'the judgment of people who have had practical experience of the working of the scheme is sounder than that of anyone who has to depend on theory'.

imposed on them by the rigidities in the rest of the scheme. The *datum* allocations of canned fish and canned meat protected the Divisions' stocks against the results of pointing too low, at the expense of their colleagues in Dried Fruit.

Two other contributory causes of confusion were also present. The granting of short-term voucher credit, as practised by both Meat and Canned Fish Divisions, harmless and even necessary in a properly adjusted system, tended in existing circumstances to increase the excessive demand for dried fruit. So, too, when retailers naturally, if not quite honestly, made use of coupons deposited with them but not spent by the customer, effective demand for points goods exceeded that recorded by a consumer survey. From the Ministry's point of view this was a dangerous malpractice; true, it could not lead to any increased consumption of points goods, but (it was argued) 'unpopular' lines would pile up in the shops and occasion a demand for down-pointing. This argument, however, boiled down to a tautology; *ex hypothesi* an unpopular line was pointed too high, a popular one too low. When all the facts are taken into account, the inflationary tendencies within the scheme, so far from being, as was alleged, inherent in it, turn out to be no more than the necessary result of the Ministry's toleration of restricted releases of foodstuffs undervalued in points. The remedy adopted—namely the general recourse to arbitrary allocations—was Procrustean.

By the summer of 1942 the points scheme, devised by economists and accepted by Ministers as a means of escape from rigid control over a large number of miscellaneous foods, had become for departmental officials a reason for imposing that control.[1] The original plan that the flow of goods should be regulated by voucher demand had not broken down; it had simply never been tried under conditions that gave it any chance of working, i.e., over the scheme as a whole. It is, of course, possible that a flexible scheme, run by people less wedded to tight systems of allocation and more willing to take economic advice, might yet have encountered insuperable difficulties. But the premature ossification that actually set in must be put down to prejudice—not of a baseless or ignoble sort, but prejudice nevertheless.[2]

Henceforward, that is to say, the Ministry was in fact to transfer

---

[1] As early as 10th January, but six weeks after the scheme had started, those immediately concerned with it were arguing 'that for the effective operation of the Points Scheme, it is essential as a general principle that the Ministry should own all the goods included in the scheme at the first stage of distribution': from which it might seem that control through points prices alone was rejected not on its merits in practice, but on purely *a priori* grounds. For, clearly, the only reason for Ministry ownership was to have absolute control over allocations. On the other hand, the vacillations over dried fruit do not suggest that the Ministry's mind was made up so early.

[2] Expressed most picturesquely by the official reporting on the postponement: 'no one can enjoy a fortnight's respite in a condemned cell'.

one of the main purposes for which the scheme had been conceived—
securing fair distribution of individual points foods between one
customer and another—to the shoulders of the retailer. This would
no doubt have been inevitable to some extent from the sheer difficulty of making fine adjustments in points values. But the general
resort to fixed allocations, coupled with a reluctance to change values
promptly and often because it upset the trade, erected it into a principle. The legal point that, unlike straight rationing, points rationing
conferred no entitlement to specific foods, was used in reply to those
who complained that they could not get what they wanted with their
points. The ideal whereby any points food should be available on
production of the requisite coupons was set aside even as an aim.

In the first few months of the scheme, the troubles to which this
was to lead lay in the future. The public rejoiced for the moment not
only in the substitution of fair shares for allotment by favour, but in
the new additions to the diet—mainly from Lend/Lease supplies—
which had given the points scheme so rewarding a send-off. With
points, the Ministry retrieved the reputation that had been somewhat
smudged, during the summer of 1941, by the difficulties it had encountered with eggs, fish, and onions.[1] If much of the credit taken by
the Ministry for points should properly go elsewhere, the reception of
the egg control scheme, which, as the Minister himself said, was 'a
heroic measure', but 'called forth nothing but abuse', may serve to
restore the balance.

---

[1] These will be discussed in Vol. II.

CHAPTER XVI

Port and Transport Problems, 1940-41

I

IN September 1940 the long-expected shipping diversion was put into effect, just as the enemy began his series of heavy air raids. Within a few weeks, delays in and around the West Coast ports had become acute; and the Ministry of Food thus found itself faced with a transport problem no less serious because it was expected.[1]

With the important exception of frozen meat, the major food cargoes were not seriously affected by diversion, nor did they become involved in the general congestion that prevailed on the Clyde and Mersey. Enough grain ships, for instance, to keep mills going were allowed into the Port of London throughout the period of diversion, and the elaborate plan for railing grain across country had never to be put into regular effect. The destruction of flour mills in London, Southampton and elsewhere threatened to reduce milling capacity to a point where the extraction rate would have to be raised[2] and did compel the Ministry to import more flour and less wheat. But the situation of the mills and silos in the vulnerable dock areas did at any rate ensure that the discharging of wheat, by far the greatest of our imported foods, was reasonably expeditious. Oilseeds and sugar, the next imports in order of importance, do not appear to have caused general and widespread difficulty, chiefly because, like grain, they mainly came in as whole cargoes.

Serious trouble began with frozen meat, for several reasons. No refrigerated ships were allowed into London for several months; on the other hand there was not enough cold storage space elsewhere to allow the Meat Division to reduce stocks in London to a level sufficient only for feeding London's population. Furthermore, the beginning of diversion coincided with an exceptionally heavy autumn glut of home-killed meat, which had to be put into consumption immediately.[3] Less meat, therefore, was being released from cold store than

---

[1] Full discussion of the problem of port congestion belongs to other histories in this series. It was hardly at all due to air attacks on the West Coast ports themselves, but rather to the effect of air-raid conditions on railway working.

[2] Chapter XII.

[3] Chapter XIII.

was being put into it, and the West Coast stores rapidly became completely full.

Unprecedented amounts of frozen meat had, therefore, to be moved by rail from West Coast ports to cold stores in and around London, at a time when London and its railways were under almost nightly bombardment. There soon appeared to be an acute shortage of refrigerated and insulated wagons, particularly at Liverpool; as a result, the turn-round time of refrigerated ships rose from a normal of ten days to as much as thirty days. Ministry of Shipping complaints led to a joint Departmental inquiry, as a result of which it was agreed that all insulated vehicles, whether road or rail, should be brought under a central operating committee, working from the Railway Clearing House at Amersham. On this Committee would be represented road operators, railways, 'MINDAL' (the war-time association of meat importers) with a Chairman from the Ministry of Food. The new arrangements came into operation on 6th December 1940 and their success was immediate. Transport of meat from the ports inland was never again to be hampered by lack of vehicles.

It was comparatively easy to arrive at a solution of this particular problem, because so few interests were concerned. The Ministry of Food envisaged its extension to other goods, including those controlled by the Ministry of Supply, and pointed out that for this purpose it would be necessary to pool all the long-distance road transport of the country.[1] The need was urgent, for the congestion that had begun with cold-store commodities had spread to others; tea, edible oils, fish, fruit, and most kinds of mixed cargoes. There was, said an official brief for the Minister of Food on 18th November 1940, an acute shortage of wagons and wagon sheets at the ports; 'the immediate vicinity of the ports is crowded with wagons under load which cannot get away and with wagons full of export commodities waiting to be unloaded . . . the railways are faced with a major operational problem and . . . there is no authority whose business it is to consider the problem as a whole, apart altogether from the interests of the individual companies and peacetime practices in determining the routes over which traffic shall travel'. Road vehicles and spare parts were scarce; it was virtually impossible, in the absence of a general road transport pool, to mobilise large fleets of vehicles to come to the aid of the railways at the ports; road haulage rates were rising rapidly. As for canals, there was a shortage of craft and of labour. Coastal shipping rates were fixed above rail rates, so that traffic that could have gone by coaster was consigned by rail. The

---

[1] The Ministry of Transport had long been working on this problem; but the difficulties of organising the trade were very great.

Ministry of Food urged that all these matters should be considered together by experts.[1]

Inter-departmental discussions on the inland transport position became increasingly active, but did not pass from specific points of complaint to a general analysis of the situation. The Port and Transit Standing Committee and the Economic Policy Committee did not get beyond particular points of detail, such as the supply of cranes and railway wagons at Liverpool; pre-entry under the Customs regulations; and the increase of demurrage charges for detention of railway wagons.[2] At the end of December a special Committee of Ministers was appointed to make recommendations on improving Port Clearance, and once again the Ministry of Food pressed for a wider and more expert approach to the problem. Once again it was denied; three major proposals did indeed emerge, but all of them related to the local situation at the West Coast ports. They were, the appointment of Regional Port Directors, responsible directly to the Minister of Transport, to co-ordinate the working of the Clyde, Mersey and Bristol Channel port groups; the 'decasualisation' of dock labour; and the construction of large sorting depots in the hinterland of the West Coast ports. About the first and third of these the Ministry was sceptical, not to say suspicious; it was afraid that port 'czars' would interfere with established departmental procedure, and was not convinced that the steel and equipment required for the inland sorting depots had better not be used, e.g. in the construction of more railway wagons. It argued that if wagons or some other railway equipment were scarce, the construction of depots would increase, instead of ease congestion. In any event, the depots could not help in the current crisis.

Believing that it had set its own house in order, the Ministry of Food was increasingly critical of the way in which the problem of transport in relation to shipping turn-round was being tackled. Early in 1941, it undertook an inquiry into the delays sustained by ships carrying food cargoes, which disclosed an astonishingly miscellaneous list of causes of delay:—separate ports of discharge for food and raw material; interference with ships in port by Service Departments; waiting for berths; damage to vessels; degaussing; bad stowage; air-raid warnings; shortage of labour or refusal of men to work in the black-out; disputes about overtime; shortage of railway

---

[1] 'I was at pains', wrote a senior official of the Ministry, 'to get the discussion off the plane represented by senior administrative and highly inexpert officials on to that of the experts who quite obviously knew what they were talking about'. The observation attributed to a Minister at the Economic Policy Committee that 'the real problem of internal transport was clearly congestion at the ports' accounts perhaps for a further comment of the same official: 'No worthwhile scheme for improving inland transport or port clearance will be devised by Ministers or administrative officials. It is an "expert" problem'.

[2] Meantime, a separate series of inquiries into railway congestion was occupying a different group of Ministers, the Lord President's Committee.

wagons; waiting for convoy—none of which were in the control of the Ministry itself. 'There was surprisingly little that we could do to influence the rate of turn-round. Peacetime customs of the food trades in the earlier days undoubtedly did interfere with the discharge of vessels, but these have long since been taken up firmly with the Supply Divisions. . . . If anything further can be done, it lies within the province either of the Ministry of Shipping, the Ministry of Transport, or the Ministry of Labour'.[1]

The Ministry of Transport came in for especial criticism, particularly for its handling of the railways. 'The extent to which the Ministry of Transport interferes with the Railway Executive Committee', Lord Woolton was told, 'is almost negligible'. The railway managers, it was alleged, were allowed to display a commercial outlook wholly inappropriate in war-time; one of the groups was trying to insist, as a condition of leasing land to the Ministry of Food on which to build new cold stores, that only that particular line should be used in bringing produce to it, despite the fact that this would mean a long detour from certain ports. The companies had defied instructions from the Ministry of Transport on the subject of exceptional rates for Ministry of Food traffic. Nothing had yet been done about the shortage of wagon sheets. So, too, it was only under pressure from the Ministry of Food and other Departments that something had been done about the canal position. In short, the Ministry of Transport's attitude towards the problem of organising transport to meet war-time needs remained 'almost as disappointing as it has been since the early days of planning'.

These general strictures clearly over-simplified what was a complex problem. There were several reasons why the analogy they drew between food control and transport control could not be pushed too far; the very different type of trade organisation, the fact that food control had a long tradition and two years' start in its favour, the dependence of the Ministry of Transport on other Departments for the essential information on which to assess transport demands. One cannot altogether acquit the Ministry of Food of applying a more severe standard to the shortcomings of others than it did to its own. It was certainly less willing than it might have been to give credit to

---

[1] The list of causes and the quotation are from a minute in response to a suggestion by the Minister that a man should be appointed specifically to watch the turn-round of food ships. Lord Woolton's further comment is worthy of quotation also:

'Clearly my suggestion is superfluous. But we must not rest whilst other Departments fail . . . until we *demand*—as we can do—that our ships shall not be kept waiting, this process of starving the nation will go on. I listen, until I nearly expire, to all the explanations of waiting time, etc. I want *us* to run a raging campaign against what I regard as a most dangerous failure to grip this serious problem. And we needn't bother about being tender; effectively they are our ships and these other Ministries are there to serve us'.

In response to this minute, Colwyn Bay set up a small 'War Room' in which detailed records of every ship carrying food, from arrival to departure, were kept. Throughout the summer of 1941 the Minister maintained his special interest in this question.

the very real improvements in the turn-round of ships that followed the appointment of Regional Port Directors—improvements that could scarcely be attributed wholly to the increased hours of daylight.[1] But the fundamental criticism of transport policy, that it wanted a unified and comprehensive view of what was a single economic problem, must be judged to hold good.

II

In May 1941 the Ministries of Shipping and Transport were merged as the Ministry of War Transport. This could not be expected to produce immediate and dramatic results on the organisation of inland transport,[2] though it did manifest almost at once that broad approach to the problem for which the Ministry of Food had so long pleaded. Ministerial discussions at the Import Executive and elsewhere continued on the old inexpert plane of local detail. The Chiefs of Staff suddenly took alarm at the concentrations of food stocks in port areas, and the Ministry of Food had once again to explain that these were first, inevitable, and second, not so vulnerable as might have been supposed; air-raid experience had shown that bulk wheat and sugar, for instance, were extremely difficult to destroy by bombing, and that much of the food damaged by the fire-fighters' water was capable of salvage. At one time the Regional Port Director at Bristol endeavoured to stop all sorting of goods to marks in the transit sheds and had to be called off by direct ministerial intervention.

The building of inland sorting depots went on, but was delayed by shortage of materials and labour; the first was not to be ready till early 1942. The decasualisation scheme for dockers had numerous teething troubles, particularly at Glasgow, where it was alleged that the men would not work on difficult cargoes, such as frozen meat. By August 1941, however, it appears that most of these difficulties had been overcome; Transport Division reported in that month that discharge of food ships everywhere had been consistently good. From this time onwards there were no complaints by the Division of delays in turn-round from any cause but one—shortage of labour. Even allowing for this trouble, which remained endemic for another year, the improvement was permanent, and must be attributed partly to

---

[1] The accusation about wagon sheets was on the verge of becoming unwarranted. As early as December 1940 Transport Division had claimed that the West Coast ports had already been cleared of foodstuffs and indeed were 'empty'. This was attributed to a fall in arrivals which meant that no more food ships had to be handled on the West than had been handled since the war began. Clearly, however, the Ministry of Food experience cannot have been typical; otherwise the drastic step of appointing Regional Port Directors would never have been taken. A detailed analysis of the effect of their appointment belongs to the history of shipping.

[2] Indeed, it delayed the formation of a single road haulage organisation which the Ministry of Transport had been on the point of completing at the time of the merger.

reorganisation at the centre, partly to a multitude of improvements in the detailed working of existing transport resources.[1] It may be significant, however, that the disappearance of complaints about turn-round coincides with a *crescendo* of reports about railway embargoes, which were to plague Transport Division for the rest of the war and indeed long after it ended.

One source of irritation to the Ministry of Food was brought to an end in the summer of 1941; a long controversy over railway charges. During the first year of war the Ministry of Food had obtained from the companies numerous 'exceptional rates' for goods consigned in bulk, treating the railways and being treated in precisely the same way as any commercial concern. Meantime, the Ministry of Transport had revived the pre-war discussions about special rates on all Government traffic. In May 1940 it set up a Government Traffic (Railway Charges) Committee, on which the Service Departments and the Ministry of Supply were represented. (The Ministry of Food did not come in till later.)

To this body the railway companies proposed a scale of reductions on standard charges, which, though tolerable to other Departments, was quite out of keeping with the concessions the Ministry of Food was actually obtaining for its traffic. The Ministry therefore asked to 'contract out' of the negotiations. The companies, however, who were now becoming inundated with applications from various Government Departments for special rates for their traffics, refused to quote any further exceptional rates for Ministry of Food traffic at all, on the ground that the matter was now *sub judice* and that all Government traffic must be treated alike. For several months they ignored the expostulations of both Ministry of Food and Ministry of Transport, until in February 1941 they were told by the latter that all negotiations would be broken off unless they made efforts to meet the special requirements of the Ministry of Food.

As soon as Transport Division actually got round a table with the goods managers, progress was quite rapid. In April it was agreed in principle that a flat rate per ton for all Ministry commodities, irrespective of distance, should be adopted as soon as sufficient data existed on which it could be calculated, i.e. as soon as a *modus vivendi*

---

[1] In April 1941, a 'Central Transport Committee' began to meet regularly. It was composed originally of representatives of the Ministry of Transport, the Ministry of Shipping, the principal Departments using transport, and the Railway Executive Committee. Its aim was to provide a medium through which prospective Departmental demands and the ability of transport to meet them could be considered. The various detailed improvements will be examined in the histories of shipping and inland transport. Among them may be mentioned the effective pooling of railway wagons and sheets, the establishment by the Ministry of Supply of a Transport Directorate, a greater use of road and coastwise transport, port improvements, particularly in Glasgow, and some increase in rail track mileage, particularly in South Wales. It should also be remembered that air raids virtually ceased after the invasion of Russia, and that much more use was made of London and East Coast ports than had originally been contemplated.

on the discount question could be made effective. Meanwhile the Government Traffic (Railway Charges) Committee had agreed with the goods managers on a first step towards overcoming the difficulties in granting exceptional rates for Government traffic. From 1st June 1941, a system of percentage reductions from standard charges, varying with the class of traffic, was applied to all goods consigned on Government account; the Ministry of Food should receive a further discount of five per cent. on the total bill. In September 1941, following the Government's second financial agreement[1] with the railways, the Committee was able to carry this process of simplification further; a system of flat rates was adopted for all Government traffic. The flat rates represented broadly the average rates for traffic in July 1941, taking account of the rates of discount that had been recently agreed. These simplifications undoubtedly meant that the Ministry of Food trading account would have to bear increased charges in respect of transport—charges that could not be passed on to the consumer because of the stabilisation policy. But the loss to the Treasury must have been offset by the fact that all railway net earnings over and above the guaranteed revenue now accrued to the Government.

---

[1] Cmd. 6314.

P

PART IV

CHAPTER XVII

The Zenith of Food Control

I

THE introduction of points rationing all but coincided with an event of a very different order of magnitude—the Japanese attack on Pearl Harbour. Their conjunction was apt, for if the second presaged more demands on the ingenuity of the food controllers, the first indicated that they would not be found wanting in that quality, or in the resolution and self-confidence without which it would go for little. From that time onwards, one may say, the Ministry of Food conducted itself as one having authority and mastery in all things that concerned it.

Mastery in day-to-day operations, for the principal foods which had been comprised in its original control plans, had long been the rule. Ministry trading, though requiring no less than private trade continual watchfulness and adaptability, was by now established as of routine; 'straight' rationing, though continually under improvement, amendment and simplification, was no less so. But there had been a reluctance either to depart, except perforce, from the important but limited range of food control's initial activities, or to embrace new and (as it seemed) less perfect methods of control. It was a reluctance not confined, of course, to the Ministry of Food, or for that matter shared by all the Ministry's members. But up till now it had been sufficiently widespread to give a tentative air to some of the extensions of control that had actually taken place. The scheme for controlling home-produced eggs; the first attempts to 'ration' milk to non-priority consumers;[1] the first moves in the direction of concentration of industry and transport economy; and the approach to the problem of 'manufactured foods'—all these have something of the spirit that had resisted so strongly the introduction of points rationing itself.

By the spring of 1942 that caution was no longer in the ascendant, for reasons that are easier to surmise than to substantiate with chapter and verse. It is true, of course, that the war prospects were such that heroic measures might win recommendation almost on the ground of heroism alone. The Ministry had often to restrain the quixotry of those—both within and without its ranks—who would have set the

---

[1] These will be analysed in Vol. II.

public by the ears for the sake of some fractional saving. It is true also that the waters of extended control had not turned out to be so cold as the controllers had feared, and that points rationing in particular had won unbounded popularity. These imponderables—together with that other, the establishment of the Minister himself as a symbol of what one contemporary termed 'not paternal, but avuncular' government—may well have been more important than any specific changes in the administrative machine itself.

Certain developments within and around the Ministry during the year 1941 help, however, to explain its growing self-assurance. A fresh reorganisation, affecting two of the major Departments into which the Ministry was divided, took place in the summer of 1941. The Supply Department—that is to say the trading divisions and their ancillaries—was not changed in fundamentals. But the split of responsibility between traders and civil servants within each division was ended by placing it primarily on the Trade Director. Moreover, a leading Trade Director, who some months previously had been designated 'Commercial Secretary' and entrusted with the task of overseeing the commodity divisions' management of their stocks,[1] was now made head of the Supply Department, with power to report direct to the Minister in all questions concerning the organisation of food supply.

This change was, perhaps, mainly of psychological importance, reflecting as it did a feeling that trading in food was for business men and methods rather than those of the Civil Service. For in practice it was only possible—and only willingly assented to by civil servants themselves—because by this time the Trade Directors had become accustomed to working, not indeed on Civil Service lines, but within the canons that ministerial and departmental responsibility imposed. For that matter, the Ministry's career civil servants, few but influential, could scarcely be put into Sir Frank Coller's 'mandarin' class; some of them might, in no derogatory sense, be put in his other class—'adventurers'.[2] (By this time—so far had the process of interpenetration gone—it is often difficult to detect the background of the author of a particular minute or memorandum.)

Of more real importance, perhaps, was a change in the committee system at Colwyn Bay which at once reflected the wider field of the Ministry's interests and the need for closer integration between policy and day-to-day action. The old Overseas Purchases Board was replaced by an advisory *Food Supply Board*, composed of senior members of the Supply and General Departments, and having a series of com-

---

[1] This was after the meat ration had been brought down at a run by the exhaustion of stocks in cold store. See Chapter XIII.

[2] Coller, *op. cit.* p. 55: 'The public (in 1917) wanted a Food Controller with a free hand and a courageous temper in charge of a Department staffed by adventurers, not by mandarins'.

mittees to cover imports, home supplies, utilisation (i.e. such questions as the amount of fats and sugar to be allotted for cakes, biscuits, and other manufactured foods), distribution, and consumption. The secretariat of the Board and its committees was drawn from the General Department also.

The purpose of these changes was to put an end to the reproach that the Minister's own complaint of the previous summer[1] still held good. As late as February–March 1941 a Ministry official could still point to the lack of a 'co-ordinated nutrition and consumption policy', exemplified in a 'general vagueness and uncertainty . . . about the nutritional, dietetic and household aspects of the Ministry's job of feeding the public adequately. . . . Rations are cut, new foods are rationed or priorities granted without reference to . . . the implications and repercussions of such changes on the general food situation'. A colleague, agreeing with him, quoted Wordsworth: 'As with many another Ministry of Food policy, where nutrition is concerned we have

> The blank misgivings of a creature,
> Moving about in worlds not realised'.

These criticisms reflected, not any deficiencies in the scientific advice at the Ministry's disposal, nor any want of willingness to use it, but the difficulty of bringing it to bear effectively on a multitude of problems whose scientific implications might not be realised by the administrators or traders handling them. The Food Supply Board and its committees did, in practice, provide a means for ensuring that changes affecting the nation's food supply, both large and small, were scrutinised for consistency with each other and with the requirements of a rationally determined food policy. Commodity Directors and others were successfully indoctrinated with the need to refer even small decisions to a nutritional context. The extensions of control that took place in the later years of war were, more than ever before, deliberately reasoned out.

II

This latest stage in the development of food control as a whole marks the achievement of a revolution in the attitude of the British State towards the feeding of its citizens. The nature of that revolution has sometimes been over-simplified and its accomplishment dated too early. It is emphatically not the case, for instance, that food policy was scientifically *determined* from the outbreak of war, or indeed at any time. To talk, as a memorandum presented by the Ministry of Food to the Interim Commission of F.A.O. in 1944 did, of the 'nutri-

---

[1] Chapter IV above.

tional plan devised by the Ministry of Food', and to adduce as among the 'principles' in this plan such obvious war-time expedients as the rationing of meat, fats, and sugar, was quite unhistorical. The choice of foods for rationing, and the initial ration levels, were determined without professional advice on the basis of the supply situation; their scientific antecedents went back to the experience of 1914–18. Even the principles of food policy adopted by the War Cabinet as late as August 1940 contained no scientific references beyond a guarded obeisance in the direction of the Basal Diet, unless one counts, what the scientists would certainly have approved, the eschewing of any deliberate measures to restrict consumption.

Nevertheless, the revolution was already under way. To find its origins one must go back to the world economic depression of the nineteen-thirties; for it was this, bringing with it the appearance of 'poverty in the midst of plenty', that perhaps more than anything else changed the problem of better feeding for all from an academic study to one that clamoured for practical application. With millions unemployed, minimum-cost diets became a pressing question in social welfare; the piling-up of surplus wheat, sugar, and other agricultural products suggested the possibility of reviving agriculture through a marriage with nutrition. New attempts were made to draw up optimum standards of diet, notably under the auspices of the League of Nations and the United States Department of Agriculture.[1] In Great Britain the work of Sir John (now Lord) Boyd Orr, *Food, Health and Income*, aroused much discussion by adducing evidence from surveys of food consumption that the diet of a large number of poor people was inadequate, often grossly inadequate, for health. From this time onwards the call for active measures to promote better feeding was continuous; it became a plank in the platform of social reformers, among whom some of the leading experts in nutrition were numbered.

Though the British Government had, through the Medical Research Council and other agencies, financed or assisted much of the basic research on which this campaign was based, and had appointed, as early as 1931, the first of two advisory committees on nutrition, the official attitude to the question before the war was distinctly guarded.[2] In the 1936 discussions of the Committee on Food Supply[3] the references to nutrition were almost perfunctory. The Food (Defence Plans) Department was indeed charged with the duty of consulting with the Medical Research Council (as well as with the

---

[1] Leitch, I. 'The Evolution of Dietary Standards'. *Nutrition Abstracts and Reviews*, Vol. II, p. 509 (1942).

[2] It is well exemplified by the fact that the only reference (paragraphs 43 and 44) to *Food, Health, and Income* in the official *First Report of the Advisory Committee on Nutrition*, published in 1937, was so covert as to be unrecognisable. (In the second edition of *Food, Health and Income* Sir John Boyd Orr pointed it out (p. 5).)

[3] Chapter I.

Ministry of Health), where this would be appropriate in making its plans. But in practice its contacts with nutrition experts were sporadic and confined to specific questions. Its whole approach to the problem of food in war might be held to preclude any deliberate attempt to plan supplies beforehand in a way that would have admitted scientists into full and continual consultation. In any event, to have superimposed elaborate calculations of nutrient values on the un-sophisticated pre-war estimates of supply prospects[1] would have been futile. The want of recourse to scientific help was not a failure to plan in one specific respect; it was a symptom of the general absence of strategic planning in the civilian sphere.

The first signs of a changing attitude appear in the Ministry of Health's strong reaction, in the autumn of 1939, to the rationing proposals; in the National Milk Scheme, originating from the same source; and in the emphasis on milk in the Food Policy Committee's resolutions on the food production campaign. As early as December 1939 leading physiologists were telling the Minister of Health (Mr. Walter Elliot) that 'a change in the diet of the people was highly desirable and the war presented an opportunity . . . to bring about some reform of dietary habits'. Milk and potato consumption, they said, should be stimulated, and calcium might be added to bread in the form of chalk.

Nevertheless, as late as April it was possible for the House of Commons Select Committee on National Expenditure to elicit from official witnesses an admission that inter-departmental discussion on nutritional matters was informal and (in the Committee's view) 'sporadic'; and to express doubts whether the position of the Ministry of Food's Scientific Adviser was such that he necessarily gets the opportunity of seeing all the matters handled by the Ministry that 'might be identified as scientific problems' and so to suggest the initiation of research work on them.[2]

The Select Committee recognised that these questions were largely a matter of organisation; and it was to be a full year before the influence of scientific advice could be said to penetrate to every corner of Ministry activity. But no time was lost in applying it to the main lines of policy, particularly in the field of imports, for which a second-year-of-war programme was even then being drawn up. To the first draft of that programme, completed a few weeks before the fall of France, there was appended a *Survey of War-time Nutrition* that set out, in detailed and quantitative form, the sort of nutritional strategy that the Ministry would require to pursue.

The survey began by accepting as axiomatic that the pre-war diet

---

[1] Chapter V.

[2] *Fourth Report from the Select Committee on National Expenditure.* Ordered by the House of Commons to be printed: 7th May 1940 (pp. 42–45).

of as much as half the population, and that the poorer half, was deficient in varying degrees in those nutrients that are essential, not indeed to life, but to vigorous health. There was a sufficiency of energy-producing foods, and probably of protein, available to everyone; but despite a general increase in the consumption of the so-called protective foods, particularly butter, eggs, fruit, and vegetables, over the last twenty years, many people were going seriously short of calcium, iron and the vitamins A, B and C. War conditions, the survey declared, were, on the analogy of last-war experience, likely to lead to a steady deterioration in the quality of the national diet, more particularly in that of the poor.

Ways were indicated in which this danger might be averted. Prospective shortages of Vitamin C and iron respectively might be offset if people would eat more potatoes, and bread made from high-extraction flour. If it were desired to retain white flour in deference to public and trade preference and the usefulness of wheat offals as an animal feeding-stuff, vitamin B_1 could be synthesised and added to flour. Loss of vitamins A and D from butter could readily be made good by adding them to margarine. Calcium deficiency, which appeared to be the most spectacular of all, both pre-war and in prospect, should be met by encouraging milk production and importing cheese in large quantities. Increased home production and consumption of potatoes, green vegetables, and oatmeal, were all desirable, as were imports of canned fish (particularly salmon), condensed and dried milk, and pulses. Fruit (other than oranges and lemons), nuts, and eggs in shell, were uneconomic ways of using shipping. Last, but not least, there was reiterated the truth, often insisted on but as often forgotten, that there was no prospect of reducing to any worth-while extent the amount of energy-providing food consumed by the population at large, and that attempts to persuade people to eat less might have disastrous effects upon health. It followed that bread rationing should be undertaken only as a last resort.

The principles underlying this survey were, scientifically speaking, in no sense novel; though—as the Minister of Health had found in discussing sugar rationing the previous autumn—they were by no means universally familiar. It is an important landmark, however, for two reasons. It was the first example of successful collaboration between food scientists and the statisticians engaged in drawing up forward programmes—the first application of nutritional principles to a piece of economic planning. It was, that is to say, eminently a practical document—not a statement made, so to speak, in the air. More important, perhaps, its acceptance as a basis of planning by the Ministry of Food and the Government as a whole conceded, perhaps not explicitly, the principles of food welfare for which pre-war reformers had striven. The restrictive, anti-inflationary, public-safety machine of food control was to be converted, through the application of dietary standards, into an instrument for doing in war-time what no modern government had attempted even in peace. The initiative that had begun with the National Milk Scheme was to run through the whole of subsequent food policy.

This would hardly have been possible had not the Ministry of Food developed its own internal machinery for acquiring and transmitting scientific advice, instead of being content to rely—as it had in the first few months of its existence—on consultation *ad hoc* with the Ministry of Health, the Medical Research Council, and other agencies. The setting-up of its Scientific Adviser's Division, so far from depriving these bodies of their influence on food control, was an indispensable condition of that influence being continuously effective; for only thus could they be kept in touch with circumstances. Indeed, the time that passed before the Division itself was effectively integrated, through the General Department, with the Ministry of Food's organisation may itself partly account for the want of impact of the original Scientific Food Committee of 1940–41, compared with the Standing Interdepartmental Committee on Medical and Nutritional Problems that in effect succeeded it as the final source of advice to the Government on these matters. (The chairman of this Committee was the Chief Medical Officer of the Ministry of Health, whose primary responsibility for these scientific questions was reaffirmed by Ministers in 1941.) As with many another problem of the war economy (shipping and inland transport, for example), the appointment of a high-level committee was no substitute for effective departmental organisation, though it might help to bring it about.

III

One may classify scientific knowledge as applied to food control into, broadly, nutrition—the principles of proper feeding—and food technology—the use of scientific techniques in the preparation, transport and preservation of food. The two categories are not mutually exclusive, because the *nutrients*, i.e. the substances having food value, present in a food may be affected by its technical treatment, just as they are by varying methods of cookery. Applied nutrition, that is to say, covers a wide field, from the devising of import programmes to the encouragement of better cooking.

Scattered throughout this history will be found examples of the influence of scientists on the course of policy.[1] They were chosen

---

[1] For instance, the choice of Lend/Lease shipments (Chapter XVIII); bread policy (Chapter XX); the Basal Diet (Chapter VI); and Food Standards (Chapter XXIV). Further examples will appear in Volume II.

because of their intrinsic importance rather than to illustrate that influence in operation, and perhaps are not altogether representative of it. Much of the scientists' work was of a useful, unspectacular kind that touched no major issue, though it might be of great value in the day-to-day activities of the Ministry. The work of the specialists on infestation of food stocks by rats, mice and insect pests—a problem that grew as the stocks themselves piled up—may serve as an example. Another, in a different field, was that of the Special Diets Advisory Committee set up by the Ministry of Health and the Medical Research Council. It advised on the general ration allowances that should be made, on production of a medical certificate, to particular classes of invalids, and also adjudicated on individual claims for extra rations that could not be categorised in advance.

Some developments in food processing, for instance 'dehydrated' or desiccated vegetables,[1] and ready-to-eat or emergency food packs, were mainly useful in special applications, such as use by the armed forces, or contingencies that in fact never arose, as in the case of food dumps for people cut off by enemy invasion. Much of scientific activity was necessarily directed to meeting hypothetical circumstances of this kind. It is at least possible that the use of dehydrated minced meat might have made a substantial contribution to the saving of shipping. It was claimed that this meat, reconstituted, was indistinguishable from freshly-cooked minced meat. But the refrigerated tonnage position never became so bad as to compel the British civilian to put this claim to the test.

Of the various 'ship-saving' contrivances that were explored intensively from 1941 onwards, two are specially noteworthy. The first —spray dried egg powder—is a remarkable instance of the application of scientific method at speed. A whole new industry was developed in the United States, in the course of a few months, to prepare and pack dried egg by a process worked out by British scientists of the Department of Scientific and Industrial Research, and with their active supervision. Not only the technique of drying, but difficulties arising from the resistance of harmful bacteria (*salmonella*) to the drying process had to be faced. The result was an addition to the country's food resources, the value of which was perhaps only fully appreciated when, as a result of the cessation of Lend/Lease after the war, supplies were cut off before those of shell eggs could be restored. (On the other hand the claim that reconstituted dried egg was equal in all respects to shell egg appears to have been sanguine, even from the scientific point of view, and was perhaps never taken very seriously by the public.)[2]

---

[1] The technical (though not the economic) aspects of vegetable dehydration are exhaustively reviewed in *Vegetable Dehydration*. Ministry of Food Scientific and Technical Series, H.M.S.O. 1946.

[2] These matters will be fully discussed in Vol. II.

Some idea of the saving in shipping space on account of dried egg alone may be given by a calculation made in November 1942. During the first eight months of that year nearly 47,000 tons of dried egg powder was imported into the United Kingdom; it occupied about 6¼ million cubic feet of ordinary shipping space. The equivalent in shell eggs would have been over 200,000 tons, requiring 25 million cubic feet of refrigerated shipping space, and being also far more difficult to handle.

The other principal contribution to ship-saving was by the boning of imported beef before shipment and the 'telescoping'[1] of frozen mutton and lamb carcases in the refrigerated holds. In the calendar year 1939 only about one-tenth of beef imported was boned; in the twelve months ended September 1942 more than nine-tenths of the beef was boned, and all mutton and lamb telescoped. The average stowage factor for all meat was reduced from 100 cubic feet to 85 cubic feet; only by this means were imports maintained at the pre-war level despite an acute shortage of refrigerated shipping. In addition, various devices—including such details as the removal of 'many tons of hooks and chains'—were employed to improve the lifting power of ships. The greater density of boneless beef compared with chilled whole carcases made it possible, and indeed necessary, to dispense with pig iron ballast that had formerly been necessary to keep some vessels stable.

These experiments in improving the stowage factor of food cargoes were not the simple thing the layman might suppose. There is, for any ship, an optimum relation between the weight of cargo and the space it occupies, which finds expression in the classification of commodities as 'weight' or 'measurement' cargo. Ideally a ship must be both full and down to her marks when loaded. There is no advantage, that is to say, in increasing the *density* of the cargo to a point at which the ship has to sail with some holds empty. For vessels carrying food alone this point was obvious enough; but many, including some fitted with refrigerated space, carry mixed cargo, and only the shipping authorities could decide whether a further increase in food densities would be useful. Thus in November 1942 the suggestion that dried egg and milk powder from North America should be compressed into blocks was discouraged by the Ministry of War Transport 'for the moment' because already ships were tending to sail with some space to spare, though down to their marks. The particular virtue of dried egg, that is to say, consisted in the fact that it not only occupied one-quarter of the space that would be taken up by an equivalent quantity of shell eggs, but was nevertheless of the same order of density.[2]

---

[1] 'Telescoping' consists in cutting the legs off and inserting them in the carcases.

[2] Spray-dried skim milk powder, imported in place of canned evaporated milk, showed a substantial saving of tonnage, although its stowage factor was actually less favourable —105 as against 47 cubic feet per ton.

The point of these economies, from the point of view of nutrition, was that they were concentrated on what was thought to be one of the most vulnerable features of the United Kingdom food situation—the supply of animal protein. Another prospective deficiency against which, on expert advice, the Ministry of Food took special measures was that of Vitamins A, C, and D, particularly in the so-called 'vulnerable groups'—young children, and expectant and nursing mothers. Their needs were met, from December 1941 onwards, by the issue of what came to be known as *Welfare Foods* at cheap rates or free—cod-liver oil and concentrated orange juice, the latter obtained under Lend/Lease from the United States. Another 'welfare food', though issued in a different way, was 'National Milk-Cocoa', prepared by the Ministry for consumption by adolescents engaged in industry, as a protein supplement.

Besides these and other specific contributions to food control, the Scientific Adviser's Division, together with others in the General Department, consistently strove to assess not only the food value of the national diet as a whole, but the effect that it might have on people's health and well-being. Information was collected from a variety of sources, official and private, ranging from clinical observations of individuals or groups to press and censorship reports. A market research agency was employed to conduct a running monthly survey of working-class, and occasionally middle-class, food purchases.

In 1943 the Ministry started a Body-Weight Survey, collecting periodically the weights of a representative sample of the population. In the same year, as a result of controversy about the respective consumption levels of the United States and the United Kingdom, the first of a series of attempts to calculate the comparative levels of food supplies available to civilians in the two countries and in Canada was undertaken, under the auspices of the Combined Food Board.

The value of this evidence to the historian seeking to assess the results of food policy will be briefly discussed later.[1] But it must be said here and now that as an accurate and immediate guide to policy-makers the calculations fell short of what was sometimes claimed for them. Moreover, this was due, not merely to the state of nutritional knowledge or the limitations of the supply statistics even under control, but to a want of rigour in the formulation of the questions it was desired to answer and the handling, meticulous in detail though it often was, of the numerical material.

Thus, quite apart from any difficulties of statistical detail, the Body-Weight Survey must be held to fail as a means of detecting early signs of calorie deficiency, because the third variable in the

---

[1] Chapter XXIX; and Appendix B.

equation—activity, which might also be affected by an insufficient supply of food—was not amenable to measurement. A fall in industrial output would be a much more likely sign that something was wrong. The War-time Food Survey of household purchases was open to another objection, namely that its principal activity, or at any rate that which had the widest circulation within the Ministry, was embodied in a form—namely an arithmetical average—that is the least sensitive index of food welfare or the success of food control measures. One may have to take it—as in calculations derived from the total supplies of food available—in default of anything better. But deliberately to compute it from the observations of individual cases is to blur what is required to be made distinct.

The levelling-down effect of food restrictions, and the levelling-up effect of the war-time expansion in employment and earnings, could not but make the average working-class consumption standard approach much nearer the national average than it had in peacetime. A picture of the deviations, for one reason or another, from that average figure would have thrown a real light on inequalities of distribution and differences in food habits; the reduction of the average itself to terms of nutrients was but an arithmetical exercise. Few facts could be more certain, or less useful, than that the average consumption of a sufficiently large sample of the population would, errors and omissions excepted, conform to the average *per capita* figure of available supplies. So far as the great majority of supplies were concerned, this latter figure was controlled; hence for these the survey was doing little more than arguing in a circle.

The possibilities of the survey technique, as some of the specialist inquiries it undertook demonstrate, are such that one cannot but regret this mistaken emphasis. Such inquiries as those into vegetable consumption in different areas, or variations in the take-up of the cheese ration, might have been extended to a point at which they furnished more than sporadic hints about the pattern of consumption. A more rigorous and methodical approach to these problems might have yielded results both convincing and influential.

However that may be, the study of nutrition, as applied by the Ministry of Food's advisers, was not so much exact science as art. Their contribution did not rest on fine calculation but on the application of quite broad general principles and what one can only call a feeling for the nutritional situation, reinforced by a continual watchfulness for indications of danger. The acceptance of optimum, rather than minimum, standards of feeding as the aim of policy, and the stabilisation of the general supply situation during the later years of the war, offered full scope for activity that was something more than a holding of existing positions. Indeed, it was easier for the experts to claim that such and such a positive measure would be beneficial, or a useful safeguard, than to show that a particular cut would be disastrous. Attack was the best form of defence.

One must beware, moreover, of attributing to scientific influence changes that resulted from the pressure of events. What is generally claimed to be the greatest single improvement in the quality of food during the war, the introduction of high-extraction flour, was made solely on supply grounds; the part nutrition experts had in it was the secondary, though by no means unimportant task of determining the best level of extraction. This example illustrates very fairly the point at which the influence of the scientists ceased and considerations of general policy took charge. So long as their proposals impinged on no strong existing prejudice, and meant no major regimentation of the consumer, they were not only listened to but welcomed and encouraged. But all the merits of wheatmeal bread did not suffice to secure its willing acceptance; and the earlier proposal to fortify bread with synthetic vitamin B_1, which was actually in train when the shipping crisis forced the Government's hand, was an attempt to circumvent opposition too strong (it was thought) to be dislodged by a frontal assault. The subsequent reversion for a short time from eighty-five per cent. extraction to one of eighty per cent. which, thanks to improved milling techniques, resulted in a loaf having sufficient of the valued ingredients of wheatmeal together with many of the attractive features of white bread, struck a nice balance between nutritional ideals, shipping stringencies, and the known preference of the consumer.

Such compromises were possible because, partly for reasons outside the Ministry of Food's control, but partly because of the skill with which, helped by the scientists themselves, it argued its case for sufficient shipping and made the most skilful use of it, the food situation never reached the point at which science must have been called in to dictate, instead of to improve, the national diet. Recognition, therefore, of the scientific contribution to food control must never lose sight of the fact that the latter's main achievement has to be assessed, not in terms of nutrition alone, but as a piece of war-economic administration.

IV

One can measure the importance of good and complete organisation in everything—within and without the Ministry of Food—bearing on the supply of the essential foods to the consumer, by the quite astonishing stability of ration levels from 1942 onwards. Although, for the eighteen months after Pearl Harbour, the shipping situation was at its worst; although a shortage of almost every foodstuff except wheat developed before the war ended, the British household was scarcely affected, so far as the necessities of life were concerned. The task of achieving this stability remained a strenuous one, demanding unremitting exercise of forethought, ingenuity, and skill in negotiation. But the manner of its accomplishment was such as to leave no longer the same margin for debate and argument.

The Ministry of Food so to speak expanded beyond its basic task in all directions:—taking part, through the Combined Food Board and other bodies in organising food supplies internationally; bringing a new and expert hand to those problems of international commodity control that even war could not set wholly on one side; putting into the common pool its own ideas on national and international reconstruction; and, on the other hand, venturing into new fields of minute regulation of secondary foods such as the pre-war planners had barely envisaged and which some old hands still regarded with apprehension. The spirit of the Ministry in those years is not something that can be documented. The historian none the less must record, though he cannot convey, the sense of adventure that prevailed; as if it had been recaptured from the days of Lord Rhondda. There was nothing in those years so difficult, or (one must in honesty add) on occasion so remote or even unimportant, that someone was not ready to put his hand to it.

This self-confident zeal was not without its critics in the Ministry. 'Controller's Itch', wrote a leading trade director, was a highly contagious disease; more kindly, Lord Woolton himself warned officials against going to 'vast labours to produce schemes which can yield but small results' and against a 'craving for perfection' which, he said, was a besetting sin of Government Departments. Hence the numerous cases in which some cherished plan or—as officials might think—unanswerable reform, be it the rationing of coffee, the 'pooling' of tea, or a scheme for providing cheap vegetables for the poor, was trodden upon from above. With food control, to solve one problem was to raise another; the question of where to stop could not be decided by logic and often was settled by an accident of temper or circumstance.

Much of what the Ministry undertook in these later years was not at its own behest. It was not to serve the cause of improved supply or more equitable distribution alone that it applied 'concentration' to food industries, or devised transport zoning schemes. These measures arose from the diversion, actual or prospective, of labour, transport and storage space to war requirements; they were the contribution of food traders and food consumers to the national effort. If these shortages stimulated fresh controls, that of paper, their basic raw material, sometimes restrained them and—in the case of rationing— impelled simplifications of procedure.

By 1942 the various interdepartmental bodies concerned with food policy had faded; first the Committee on Food Prices, then the War Cabinet's Food Policy Committee and Scientific Food Committee. So too the Import Executive and the Battle of the Atlantic Committees of the War Cabinet had been replaced by a Shipping Committee which reported on facts—an important function—but did not decide on policy. These changes are evidence of the maturity of departmental collaboration; the machine of economic control had come to operate without many of the frictions that had earlier generated heat as a multitude of high-level discussions on what were often really matters of detail.

The central rôle of the Lord President's Committee of the War Cabinet, and its attendant economists and statisticians, in coordinating the Government's general economic policy, has been discussed in the introductory volume to this series.[1] In one instance—the introduction of points rationing—this central influence brought about a major decision of food policy. But in general it was restricted to matters—such as shipping and manpower—that definitely went beyond departmental competence. It is true that the economists of the War Cabinet office were often active on subjects—such as bread rationing, meals rationing, and minimum stock levels—that might be held to be on the far side of the invisible barrier of responsibility. But it would be difficult to find an occasion on which, when they clashed with the judgement of the Ministry of Food, the latter did not prevail. Nor is this surprising, seeing that the Ministry had its own experts who were naturally more versed in the facts of the case and who—such is the common dislike of theorists—were able to exploit in argument the claim to superior wisdom based on practical experience. The logic of events, rather than the activities of a ubiquitous planning intellect, limited the Ministry's freedom of choice and at the same time restricted interdepartmental disagreement on the fundamentals of economic policy.

But though the conditions of victory were now seen more clearly and allowed to be more exigent than in the earlier years of war, it would be over-simplifying the picture to attempt to relate them directly with all the manifold activities of food control after 1942. No more can these activities be largely explained in terms of a philanthropic urge towards better feeding, expressed in the form of simple principles capable of universal application. It is better to acknowledge that they moved along separate though continually intersecting planes, under impulses that derived not only from the war situation and the war economy, but from the opportunism of reformers, the survival of peace-time problems and habits of thought, and the sheer

---

[1] Hancock and Gowing, *op. cit.* pp. 220–223.

Q

momentum of the control machine itself—to say nothing of political factors, transient or permanent.[1]

In the later years of food control, controversy or uncertainty about comparatively simple general principles largely yields to a greater preoccupation with minute technical detail, exercised on a scale that is world-wide. Mastery of these technicalities, arid though they may sometimes appear, is a condition of understanding its history, no less than of success in administration.

---

[1] One may detect these secondary motives variously at work in, for instance, the labelling reforms (Chapter XXIV); the international wheat negotiations (Chapter XXVII); the extension of price control to such things as smoked salmon (initially by S.R. & O. (1942), No. 1561) and goat meat (S.R. & O. (1941), No. 1851); and sumptuary regulations like the price limit on restaurant meals and the compulsory simplification of cakes.

CHAPTER XVIII

Food Supplies from North America: Lend/Lease and the Combined Food Board

I

THE coming of Lend/Lease began, and the entry of the United States into the war consummated, a change in the orientation of British policy that was no less decisive for food than for other sectors of the war economy. It did not, perhaps, as did the willingness of Canada to supply wheat and other foods on terms that the United Kingdom could fulfil,[1] spell the difference between subsistence and starvation; it did mean the provision for British civilians of a diet that was both tolerably varied and reasonably in accordance with the prescriptions of nutritional science. Lend/Lease enabled the maximum concentration of tonnage on the North Atlantic, consistent with other calls on shipping; it made up the loss of livestock products that resulted from the devotion of British farming resources to wheat, potatoes, and milk, for direct human consumption. In short, it, together with Canadian aid, provided the only resolution of the British food problem consistent with winning the war.

When the war spread, first to Russia and then to the Far East, the comparatively simple problem of supplies to the United Kingdom became merged in the wider problems of United States support for all the Allies and the evolution of United Nations' strategy. Food became, like shipping and manpower, a scarce asset to be husbanded on a world scale. It was a far cry from the days when the Food (Defence Plans) Department had been drawing up its schemes on the unspoken assumption that world food supplies in war-time would be virtually unlimited—an assumption that for a while, after the collapse of France, had seemed justified by the prospect of inexhaustible surpluses of food. Then, the problems of 'cash and carry' had been intractable; now the manner of their resolution was clear, if its details required continual and watchful attention. But—so had the war developed more than apace with the solution of war problems—the conquest of difficulties served only to unmask not merely fresh problems of the former kind, but others on a different plane.

---

[1] A summary account of financial help by Canada to the United Kingdom will be found in Hancock and Gowing, *op. cit.* p. 375.

Food procurement overseas had always had, must always have in the hands of Governments, an element of diplomacy. From 1941 onwards this element took command of all the others. The key position of the United States, the characteristic features of its political, administrative, and economic system combined to make Anglo-American relations, not merely in general but in day-to-day terms, the clue to the successful operation of British food control; which, in its turn, had no small contribution to make to the management of United Nations food problems. The Ministry of Food realised this when it picked the handful of men who were the British Food Mission in Washington, and who joined with United States and, later, Canadian representatives to run the Combined Food Board. Their work, more especially during the formative period of the Anglo-American alliance, was of a quality that it would be impertinent to praise, and that only a study far more detailed than the present could fully convey.

Up to the end of 1940 the United States had accounted for but a small proportion of British food imports. The Johnson Act and the Cash-Carry legislation made it impossible for the United Kingdom to obtain dollar credits; her stock of realisable dollar securities was limited; and essential munitions had the first claim on the exchange available. Dollar expenditure on food was indeed considerably more than the amount originally planned (under £10 millions for the first twelve months of war); partly owing to the slowness with which control was established over imports of such things as canned fruit and cereal breakfast foods; partly because the sudden and largely unexpected shipping stringency, coupled with the delay in rationing, compelled Britain to buy 'dollar sugar'; partly because political considerations combined with actual shortage of animal feeding-stuffs to bring about a large-scale purchase of United States maize (though at a very favourable price).

Nevertheless the Treasury continually strove to restrict the Ministry of Food's dollar expenditure. It banned, in the autumn of 1939, the import of American apples; it stipulated sugar rationing as a *quid pro quo* for releasing dollars for sugar in January 1940, and in May insisted that the sugar ration should go down to 8 oz. rather than that more dollar sugar should be bought. Even in the summer of 1940, when long-term import programmes were laid aside in order that stocks might be built up against a possible German onslaught, very little was spent on food from the United States. In August, the Exchange Requirements Committee vetoed altogether certain items (dried fruit, eggs in shell, and canned vegetables) that the Ministry was proposing to buy in the United States during the second year of war, and asked that the purchase of certain others (canned fish, evaporated milk, and starch) should be postponed till the New Year.

'I have only so much in the way of resources', wrote the Chancellor to the Minister of Food on 7th September. 'I must make them last a definite period of time and to prefer bacon to aeroplanes, aluminium or tanks seems to be impossible . . . the effect of unnecessary purchases in the United States on our diminishing dollar resources is a certainty; the political effect of such purchases . . . is exceedingly doubtful.'

Moreover, it was only prudent to conserve dollars until the result of the Presidential Election in November—a coming event that cast its shadow over all attempts to get round the exchange difficulty. Discussions with the Americans on barter schemes and other devices had been inconclusive yet had made it clear that if President Roosevelt secured his third term, he would seek to overcome the obstacles in the way of securing United States supplies, particularly surplus farm products, such as maize and even wheat. Meantime, however, the Battle of Britain was at its height, the destruction of food supplies by air attack began to be a serious, though never critical problem, and the worsening shipping situation meant that the Ministry of Food must turn increasingly to North America for supplies. In January 1941 the Ministry was obliged to ask the Treasury for permission to incur dollar expenditure up to a total of £15,000,000. It explained that the main commodities involved were likely to be cheese, lard, condensed and dried milk, canned meat, bacon, pulses, and possibly cereals. These purchases were essential if stocks and consumption were to be maintained at an adequate level; 'we cannot afford any reduction in our programme arrivals of human food'.

By this time events in the United States were moving rapidly, and early in February the prospect of obtaining food under the proposed Lease-and-Lend Bill became bright. On the 13th February Commodity Divisions were invited to supply details of the deficiencies in their existing programmes that could be made good from the United States and a rough estimate was drawn up in order of priority for submission to the American Government. It included cheese, condensed and dried milk, lard, canned fish, egg products, canned meat, oranges, pulses, bladders and casings, sugar, and last but not least bacon. The Ministry's Scientific Adviser recommended that United States supplies be used more especially to ward off a prospective shortage of first-class protein. Apart from meat and cheese, the Americans might be asked to supply also dried skim milk, spray dried eggs, and beans, especially soya beans.

It had now been decided that a British Food Mission should be sent to Washington. Proposals to do so had been mooted before the fall of France[1] and again in October 1940, but so long as British requirements were limited by exchange difficulties there was little

---

[1] In the form of a suggestion that an Anglo-French Purchasing Commission for food-stuffs should go to the United States.

point in sending a Mission. Occasional purchases, for example, of dried milk, had been made through the Commercial Counsellor, who employed the British Purchasing Commission as his agent; or as in the case of maize, ordinary trade channels had been used. The coming of Lend/Lease was obviously going to alter all this. Nor merely was the amount of foodstuffs involved going to be many times greater, but a United States Government Department, the Department of Agriculture, was to be charged with the duty of procuring supplies for the United Kingdom. Moreover, the problem of co-ordinating food and other requirements would need Ministry of Food representation in Washington, *vis-à-vis* the British Purchasing Commission under Mr. Arthur Purvis. The United States Secretary of Agriculture was reported to have strongly urged the dispatch of a British Food Mission and the Ministry was quick to respond; so quick, indeed, that the actual selection of the Mission has left very little trace in official records. The Hon. R. H. Brand, who was already in the United States, was asked to accept the headship of the Mission, and two senior officials of the Ministry were sent out to assist him. They arrived in Washington at the beginning of April, and shortly afterwards the appointment of the Mission was made public.[1]

It took some little time to get the machinery of Lend/Lease into working order; the technique was new and unfamiliar, and though the greatest goodwill and helpfulness was displayed by the United States Secretary of Agriculture and his colleagues, inevitably snags arose; for instance, the original terms of the Lease-and-Lend Act, strictly interpreted, would have prevented the British Government, as the beneficiary under them, from transferring Lend/Lease foodstuffs to the British consumer except through *ad hoc* channels of distribution. The actual procedure by which goods were obtained was somewhat complicated. The Mission would present a list of requirements to the Department of Agriculture, which would either invite tenders from the United States suppliers, or earmark the goods from surpluses already in its possession. The Mission would then 'requisition' specific quantities of earmarked goods as and when shipping became available. The administration of the necessary funds, which were voted from time to time by the Senate for the purchase of Lend/Lease goods, was undertaken by the Office of Lend/Lease Administration (OLLA). It was this body that certified the eligibility of goods for shipment under Lend/Lease, and accounted for the money spent and goods delivered.

Actual shipments were arranged through the New York offices of

---

[1] Though the head of the British Food Mission was a member of the British Supply Council, he remained directly answerable to the Minister of Food himself, even after the appointment to Washington of a Minister Resident for Supply, at the end of 1942.

the Ministry of War Transport, where a special food division was at once set up, with a small office actually in the Department of Agriculture. Within the Mission itself, arrangements were made for continual regular meetings with the United States authorities. An 'Operating Sub-Committee', on which representatives of the Department of Agriculture and the Mission sat, met three times a week; it discussed and revised the details of the Ministry's loading programme in accordance with the latest information as to supplies and transport available; soon, by arrangement, it came to do the same for cotton and tobacco, while it also discussed more general questions such as future supplies. At a higher level, and meeting usually weekly, was the Anglo-American Food Committee itself, attended by Mr. Wickard, Mr. Brand, and Dr. Parran, who as Surgeon-General of the United States was interested in the nutritional aspects of Lend/ Lease food shipments, together with representatives of other United States departments attending *ad hoc*. The Mission had also to maintain numerous other contacts; both with the other British Missions, and with the multitude of other United States Departments interested in food questions. It is a tribute to the efficiency of all concerned that despite the difficulties of building up a new organisation, and of war-time communication between London and Washington, over one million tons of Lend/Lease foodstuffs arrived in this country between May and December 1941.[1] This amounted to over one-fifteenth of the year's arrivals (one-sixth if grain, sugar, and oilseeds are excluded), and was mostly made up of foods of the highest priority; nearly 150,000 tons of evaporated milk, nearly 100,000 tons of lard, 80,000 tons each of dried beans and bacon, 70,000 tons of dried fruit, 50,000 tons of canned meat, 40,000 tons of cheese, and 26,000 tons of canned fish. The staff engaged on making these arrangements in Washington comprised less than ten senior officials. A considerable saving in subordinate staff was secured by pooling 'common services' with the British Purchasing Commission, and later with the British Supply Council.

II

The Mission had much more to do than simply make technical arrangements for shipments of food. The adoption of Lend/Lease had profound repercussions on the United States farm economy; it meant, for example, an increase in hog production comparable to the similar increase in 1917–18 with stimulating effect both on the price of hogs and of maize, their staple food. It was later to mean changes in the diet of the American consumer; a straw in the wind was the withdrawal by Mr. Wickard in August 1941 of butter from the 'blue

---

[1] A full list of Lend/Lease arrivals will be found in Table VII, p. 396.

stamp' plan, under which surplus foodstuffs had been distributed at specially cheap rates to necessitous United States citizens. Consequently the needs of the United Kingdom, its consumption habits, and its home production of foodstuffs, became necessarily and rightly objects for the closest scrutiny by American officials. The Mission, in the words of one of its members,

> 'could do no more than ask, explain, and if possible, persuade the U.S.D.A. . . . the United Kingdom had been given not a blank cheque but an expense account, the expenses had to be detailed, justified and audited before payment would be made'.

For instance, the Mission soon found itself involved in nutritional discussions; the Americans urging the fortification of bread with dried skim milk and offering vitamin concentrates on a large scale, the Ministry explaining that its use for these products was limited. American criticism of the cost of distributing Lend/Lease foodstuffs had to be answered.[1] Under-Secretary Appleby, of the Department of Agriculture, and other officials visited this country and informally examined food and nutritional problems. Informal contacts were also maintained through the Harriman mission in London.

Even before the United States had entered the war, a very considerable degree of collaboration had been attained, limited only by the political implications of United States non-belligerency on the one side, and on the other a certain diffidence in taking advantage of American generosity, and perhaps also a tendency to resent, if not to resist, American helpfulness about British domestic problems. While the entry of the United States into the war must have done something to remove these inhibiting influences, it raised fresh problems for the Mission. The needs of the British Commonwealth had to compete not merely with those of Russia and the other United Nations, but with the needs of the United States armed forces and increased United States civilian demand arising out of 'war prosperity'. Moreover, Japanese conquests in the Western Pacific had important consequences for the United Nations food supply. Philippine sugar, Burma rice, Japanese and Kamtchatkan salmon, East Indies copra, were all cut off; British Empire tea supplies threatened. It seemed evident that some sort of combined machinery would have to set up in Washington or London for food as for munitions, shipping, and raw materials.

It was some time, however, before what was readily agreed in principle could be accomplished in practice. There was not yet in the United States, as there had been in the last war, a single Food Administration to be the *vis-à-vis* of the Ministry of Food. Responsibility for production lay with the Department of Agriculture, but its powers in other directions were limited by those granted to other

[1] See e.g. Cmd. 6311 (1941).

agencies, including the War Production Board, the Office of Price Administration, and the Board of Economic Warfare. American officials recognised that this dispersal of responsibility needed to be remedied as the food situation became more difficult, and the Department of Agriculture was the most likely candidate for the task. But there were serious obstacles in the way of giving the Secretary for Agriculture, or any other single agency, the powers of a food 'czar', as was repeatedly urged. For instance, a suggestion that the Secretary for Agriculture should be given control over imported, as well as home-produced, oils and fats, in the interests of better co-ordination with the British, could not but conflict with plans being made in other quarters to 'centralise and consolidate' authority over the United States foreign relations in the economic sphere. Hence, a solution was sought in the setting-up, early in June 1942, of a Food Requirements Committee, under the Chairmanship of Secretary of Agriculture Wickard, which should co-ordinate the work of all the interested agencies. 'The Food Requirements Committee', to quote the American official historians,[1] 'did not prove to be an effective administrative device'; inter-agency difficulties arose which issued, six months later, in the designation of Secretary Wickard as Food Administrator. But the decision to set it up seemed to be a sufficient step forward for Mr. Brand to report to London, as early as 9th May, that the way was now clear for the establishment of a Combined Food Board.

Meantime two informal agreements on particular commodities were in process of completion. The Director of Oils and Fats in the Ministry of Food visited Washington and negotiated a Memorandum of Understanding, dated 13th May, by which the United States and the United Kingdom divided the world sources of Oils and Fats into two 'buying zones' in which the United States and the United Kingdom respectively would be sole purchasers on behalf of the whole United Nations.[2] On the 20th May a similar informal understanding was completed for the United Kingdom–United States purchase of South American canned meat. These agreements embodied the principle of exclusive purchase that had been found essential in the first world war and had been revived by the short-lived Anglo-French Food Executive. (They were not the first of their kind with the United States; even before Pearl Harbour the Ministry's Director of Sugar had visited Washington and concluded an agreement for the purchase of the non-Empire Caribbean sugar crop and the delivery of the United Kingdom's share of it through Lend/Lease. Sugar, however, was not yet scarce.)

---

[1] See the United States one-volume official history, *The United States at War*, pp. 328–330.

[2] This will be further discussed in Volume II.

The nucleus of a Combined Food Board already existed in the Anglo-American Food Committee; what was now done was, in effect, to widen that body's terms of reference and provide it with a formal secretariat. Little difficulty was encountered in drafting terms of reference, since both sides were agreed that they must be as wide as possible. Originally it was proposed to embody them in an Executive Order from the President: in the end, for reasons which do not appear in the British documents, no such Order was issued. Instead an announcement was made by Mr. Churchill on 9th June, on behalf of Mr. Roosevelt and himself, in the following terms:—

'In order to complete the organisation needed for the most effective use of the combined resources of the United States and the United Kingdom for the prosecution of the war, there are hereby established a Combined Production and Resources Board and a Combined Food Board. . . .

(The Combined Food Board) will be composed of the Secretary of Agriculture for the United States and the head of the British Food Mission who will represent, and act under the instruction of the Minister of Food. The purpose of the Board shall be to co-ordinate and obtain a planned and expeditious utilisation of the food resources of the United Nations.

The duties of the Board shall be to consider, investigate, enquire into and formulate plans with regard to any question in respect of which the Governments of the United States and the United Kingdom have or may have a common concern, relating to supply, production, transportation, disposal, allocation or distribution in or to any part of the world, of foods, agricultural materials from which foods are derived, and equipment and non-food materials for the production of such foods, and to make recommendations to the Governments of the United States and the United Kingdom in respect of any such question.

To work in collaboration with others of the United Nations towards the best utilisation of their food resources and in collaboration with any interested nation or nations to formulate plans and recommendations for development, expansion, purchase or other effective use of their food resources.

The Board shall be entitled to receive from any agency of the Government of the United States and any department of the Government of the United Kingdom any information available to such agency or department relating to any matter with regard to which the Board is competent to make recommendations to those Governments, and in principle, the entire food resources of Great Britain and the United States will be deemed to be in a common pool about which the fullest information will be interchanged'.

The question of the machinery of the Board was left open for the very good reason that it was still under discussion. On the British side, the problem arose of the relation of the Ministry of Agriculture and Fisheries to the Board. Mr. Hudson and his advisers would have liked the terms of reference amended to provide for consultation of a Ministry of Agriculture representative in Washington on any point affecting British agricultural production. They wished to appoint a permanent liaison officer there with the right to report directly to the Ministry. The Ministry of Food resisted this proposal; not only was it contrary to the principle that all Anglo-American food questions should go through one channel, but it would also mean advertising British inter-departmental differences to the Americans. Eventually a way out was found by setting up a Committee of the Board in London on United Kingdom Agricultural Production, comprising representatives of the Ministries of Food and Agriculture, the offices of the War Cabinet and the United States Agricultural Attaché. The Ministry of Agriculture thereupon agreed that there was no need for it to have a representative at the Washington end. Meantime a somewhat elaborate plan for the Board's Secretariat was being worked out in Washington during July and August. On 11th August the announcement was made of the appointment of two Executive Officers and two Deputy Executive Officers. It was proposed that the Secretariat should work through a series of expert committees, one for each commodity or group of commodities. In practice the Board itself only met for the formal purpose of approving recommendations.

III

The decision to set up a Combined Food Board had been taken without previous reference to Dominion or Allied Governments, and the problem now arose of how to fit them into the scheme; this was all the more urgent because the Ministry of Food had considerable commitments in the form of long-term contracts with overseas producers. The Ministry had already taken steps, in collaboration with the Dominions and Colonial Offices, to set up a number of informal *ad hoc* Committees to discuss Commonwealth and Allied requirements of certain commodities (oils and fats, tea, canned fish, and rice) likely to be scarce; and the scope of these committees had been extended to include the requirements of, for example, the Middle East Supply Centre. Considerable progress had been made towards agreement on these matters, and in particular on the need for co-ordinating Empire demands for foodstuffs produced in North America. Early in June, when the decision to set up the Combined Food Board was already taken, the Dominions Office suggested the setting up of a Commonwealth Clearing House for food, on the model already existing for raw materials; and this proposal was welcomed both in the Ministry of Food and by a meeting of Dominions representatives held there on 18th June. At further meetings on 15th and

31st July, and in cables between the Ministry and the Mission, the new organisation and its relation to the Board were more clearly, though never very clearly, defined. The London Food Committee, as it was to be called, was to be responsible for presenting to the Combined Food Board 'the complete Empire and, in some cases, complete United Nations picture of supplies and requirements of commodities which come up for consideration by the Board, and also for reviewing the Empire interest in other questions of a general or particular nature which are being discussed'. The London Food Committee would work through a series of commodity Sub-Committees, but whereas the Board met at regular intervals, it 'was not expected that the main Committee would need to meet very often'. The Parliamentary Secretary to the Ministry of Food was to be its Chairman, and that Ministry would also provide a Secretary.

It seems to have been contemplated at one time, at any rate by the Mission, that the Board should itself set up a number of Sub-Committees in London. In fact only two such committees were formed; the United Kingdom Agricultural Production Committee and a Committee on Tea.[1] The reason for the first has already been explained; the second sat in London because the British Empire was the sole producer, and the United Kingdom the principal consumer, of all the tea available to the United Nations. The objections to creating further such committees, or of making the London Food Committee itself formally a part of the Board were largely political.

Although the Board's advisory status and essential subordination to the respective national authorities were explicit from the start, it tended to have for outsiders and even for the Ministry of Food itself the aura of a super-national, external institution. Officials would talk of the 'authority' of the Board; of 'submitting' stock or consumption levels 'to' the Board. The Board, in reality, had authority to do nothing beyond collecting information and formulating problems for solution; it could not even arrive at, still less impose, its recommendations except by unanimous consent; it must not even criticise the facts and figures brought before it. This being so, the use of language which implied something different was calculated to arouse misunderstanding. Some regular machinery for reaching and registering inter-Allied agreement on food supplies was essential; there was everything to be said for formalising and where necessary extending the principles of exclusive purchase and combined allocation. Operationally the Board was admirable; politically it did not win such ready approval. The worst thing about it, as one critic[2] is said to have remarked, was its name. An 'Anglo-American Co-ordinating Committee' would have had a soothing sound; the word 'board' had

---

[1] The U.S.S.R. was directly represented on this Committee.
[2] An unnamed Canadian Cabinet Minister.

connotations—the word 'director' springs immediately to mind—
that could scarcely fail to arouse emotions—whether of hope or fear—
disproportionate to its intentions and capabilities.

Canada, with her special position *vis-à-vis* both Britain and the
United States, naturally felt apprehensions of this kind. The incep-
tion of Lend/Lease had aroused fears in Canada of a diversion of
orders from Canada to the United States. In February 1941 the
British Government was constrained to assure the Canadians that its
buying programme could not be 'appreciably modified' and in fact
the Ministry of Food, though not specifically concerned in this assurance, continued to place large contracts in Canada, notably for
bacon, cheese, and canned fish, using the machinery of the Mission
for this purpose. Nevertheless, it was inevitable that the Canadian
economy should be disturbed by Lend/Lease. The large purchases
the United States Department of Agriculture was making were
bound to have a stimulating effect on farm prices that could not fail
to be reflected across the border.

Thus alarm was expressed lest the higher price of hogs in the
United States should lead to a movement of Canadian hogs over the
frontier and endanger the fulfilment of the Canadian bacon contract
with the United Kingdom; and Canadian cheese producers looked
askance at the higher prices available in the United States. When
Mr. Brand visited Ottawa in June 1941 he found the Canadian
Government already of the view that the prices to be paid for
Canadian foodstuffs should be fixed by that Government, which
would make up the difference between its price and the price that
the British Ministry of Food was prepared to pay. From this point to
the thousand-million-dollar gift of late autumn was a logical step;
with it, the supply of food from Canada to the United Kingdom became in many respects analogous to that from the United States, and
the opening of a branch of the British Food Mission in Ottawa in
February 1942 was a logical, if belated, result.

Conscious that they were making, in relation to their population,
a far greater contribution than the United States to the food supplies
of the United Kingdom, the Canadians felt slighted by their public
exclusion from the Combined Food Board, whose discussions would
presumably affect them intimately. On 14th July they formally
demanded full membership of the Board in a letter complaining of
lack of co-ordination between Canada and the United Kingdom and
of the uncertainty of Canada's relationship to Lend/Lease supplies.
So far as the actual working of the Board was concerned, the claim
was based on misunderstanding and perhaps could have been disposed of easily, but that the Board's pretensions of themselves aroused
the question of prestige. The objections, both in Washington and
London, to granting the Canadian request were not so much to

Canada's membership in itself—her special position was readily admitted—as to the undesirable precedent it would form. If Canada were let in, would not others—particularly the 'L.F.C.' Dominions—want to come in too, and would not this hopelessly clog the Washington machinery from the outset? To these fears on the grounds of efficiency London added another—that, to use Lord Woolton's own words, 'If we give way to the Canadians there is a danger that all the United Nations are going to be represented on the Food Board at Washington. This will mean that the centre of gravity will move from London to Washington, and the Combined Food Board will determine the food policy of this country'.

Strenuous efforts, extending over several months, were made to get Canada to be content with something less than full membership. At the end of July Mr. Brand went to Ottawa bearing proposals that a joint United States–Canada Agricultural Production Committee be set up in Ottawa; that Canada should be directly represented on the relevant Board Committees; and that a Canadian representative should attend all meetings of the Board itself where Canadian interests were concerned. The Canadians, however, remained unsatisfied. By this time it had become clear that the food claim could not be separated from other claims put forward by Canada for representation on the Combined Raw Materials Board, and the proposed international joint organisation for European Relief. After it had been decided that Canada should be admitted to the Combined Production and Resources Board, Mr. Brand again journeyed to Ottawa, hoping to persuade the Canadians that this concession was sufficient. To the surprise of the Ministry, he was for the moment successful; the Canadian Ministers agreed that they need not press for membership of the Combined Food Board, inasmuch as it was not directly concerned with procurement of supplies, and would not affect existing arrangements. But it was not to be long before the Canadian claim was renewed.

CHAPTER XIX

The Later Years of the Combined Food Board

I

IT soon became apparent that the Combined Food Board could only fulfil its declared purpose of obtaining a planned and expeditious utilisation of the food resources of the free world if a sufficiently effective food control were established everywhere. Restrictions on the consumption of meat, sugar, oils and fats, and dairy produce, would become imperative both in North America and the Southern Dominions, if the minimum needs of the United Kingdom and the U.S.S.R. were to be met and some provision made for Relief. The United States Administration recognised, within a few months of entering the war, that consumer rationing there would become a condition of meeting its commitments to its allies and its own military and naval forces. The task of food control and rationing in the United States was a formidable one. A huge and heterogeneous population, spread over half a continent; a multitude of producers; a habitual popular mistrust of Government and particularly Federal Government interference—these were only a few of the broader problems.

At first, moreover, it was thought that meat rationing, for instance, would not be necessary for some time. In July 1942 it was stated to be a year off; in October, it was felt to be urgent and was actually announced for December. But technical difficulties, such as the printing and distribution of 130 million ration books, impelled postponement until the end of March 1943.[1] The result was to bring the Combined Food Board face to face with a serious crisis over supplies to the United Kingdom.

In August 1942 a proposal for a large-scale switch of refrigerated tonnage had been discussed by the Combined Food Board and the Combined Shipping Adjustment Board that, *inter alia*, meant supplying the United Kingdom with meat from the United States instead of the Southern Dominions. The Americans undertook to earmark 263,000 tons of meat per year, over and above the 195,000 tons already agreed upon; they expected that, provided the shipping arrangements could be made, deliveries at this rate could be achieved from the New Year onwards. It was understood that Southern Dominions shipments would be correspondingly reduced, that the

---

[1] This account is based on the one-volume official United States War History, *The United States at War*, pp. 358–369.

British would not increase the meat ration, and that as much as possible of the meat not shipped from Australasia would be canned or dried. This plan still held the field as late as December, when the Ministry's Director of Meat and Livestock visited Washington to complete the detailed arrangements.

Early in January, however, there began to be hints that all was not well with procurement in the United States. In mid-February the War Food Administrator indicated that he could thenceforth supply frozen meat at the rate of only 120,000 tons a year, and was unable to guarantee even this rate more than three months ahead. Even the hurried switch of tonnage back to the Southern Dominions could not mend the situation. Not merely was the American offer considerably less than the original pre-diversion programme; meantime large demands for the United States Army in the Pacific had cut into available Southern Dominions supplies of frozen meat, while supplies from the Plate had been depleted by increased demands for corned beef for Russia and the United States. The Ministry of Food reckoned that to maintain the 1s. 2d. ration and the existing production of sausages, meat pies, etc., it would need over 300,000 tons of meat from the United States in 1943. The only way to make up the deficiency would be to draw on the large British stocks of corned beef for civilian consumption; but this would be contrary to an existing agreement and would reduce the stock available for European relief.

The crisis took the acute form it did because increased demands on United States supplies of meat on behalf of Russia and the American armed forces coincided with the postponement of the rationing scheme. But it reflected a feature of food administration in the United States that was to be permanent, namely the incomplete control of meat slaughtering outside the federally-inspected plants of the big meat packers. Control of small slaughterers was, according to the American official historians, 'perfunctory'; and this led, as time went on, to a diversion of a high proportion of livestock away from the big packers who alone might send meat across State borders to supply the large cities, the armed forces and export requirements. 'The problems of meat supply and distribution which aroused so much concern in 1944 and 1945 were due in large part to the failure to solve the slaughter control problem in 1943'. Whereas, that is to say, meat rationing in the United Kingdom was superimposed on a complete system of supply and distribution, in the United States it was, in a sense, a substitute for such a system.

Even so, the coming of rationing greatly eased, at any rate for the moment, the difficulties of the United States Administration in meeting its commitments. In the months before, however, it was scarcely surprising that American officials should be exceptionally critical of British requirements. Now that air attacks on Great Britain had fallen off, there was a natural tendency to look on the Russians as bearing the brunt of the enemy onslaught and to regard their requests for food as the more urgent. (Moreover, Russian requirements were not subject to combined allocations, but were set out in separately negotiated protocols.) The whole Lend/Lease programme was to some extent affected by the recent Republican victories in the Congressional Elections. Moreover, there was very little accurate information in the United States about the food situation in the United Kingdom; and there were those in the Department of Agriculture, for instance, who maintained that the British were, on the average, as well off as Americans for meat and fats. Just as the British had already agreed to the setting up of a Combined Food Board Committee on United Kingdom Agricultural Production, so they would now be called upon to justify their rate of consumption and their stock levels.[1]

The specific problem of meat supplies was taken up with Mr. Harry Hopkins himself. At the Mission's suggestion, the Ministry undertook to reduce its demands for United States cheese in the hope that since cheese and meat were to be rationed jointly in the United States this might make it easier for the Americans to provide extra meat. On 5th April the Ministry began issuing one-seventh of the meat ration in corned beef. In the last week in April Mr. Hopkins produced an offer of a further 100,000 tons, making a total of 252,000 tons over the year.[2] The Ministry accepted this, stipulating, however, that it might still have to draw on corned beef till the end of September. This caution was justified in the event; for the Department of Agriculture found it impossible to increase the rate of supply immediately. At the end of May they could only promise 10,000 tons for July and 5,000 for August; early in July they confessed that their chances of fulfilling the programme were slender, A further *démarche* was made through Messrs. Stettinius and Harriman simultaneously. Towards the middle of August, however, the Mission was able to report that frozen meat procurement was going much better, and the Ministry felt justified in reverting to an all-carcase-meat ration on 18th September.

II

For some months during 1943 the work of the Combined Food Board was also hampered by comings and goings in Washington. In March Mr. Wickard, who had for several months doubled the posts of Secretary of Agriculture and Food Administrator, relinquished the latter to Mr. Chester Davis. But Mr. Davis failed to agree on the

---

[1] The Inquiry into Food Consumption Levels in the U.K., U.S.A., and Canada, whose results were published early in March 1944, was a result. See below, Chapter XXIX.

[2] The 100,000 tons came out of the theoretical allocation to Russia, which was apparently far above what could be shipped thither.

R

extent of his powers with the White House, and resigned in his turn in June. Judge Marvin Jones, who had been Chairman of the Hot Springs Conference, now became Food Administrator. But these changes did not affect the position of Mr. Wickard as the American member of the Board, nor of its American Executive Officer, with the result that the American side of the Board could no longer speak for those responsible for the country's food administration. Not merely the Board's day-to-day functioning, but its prestige and moral authority, would be undermined if this position continued. For although it continued to consider proposals and make recommendations, these were bound to cause political trouble in the United States if they could be plausibly represented as British dictation of the disposal of American food resources.

The need for more effective United States collaboration was another aspect of the same situation that provoked the now renewed Canadian demand for full membership. So long as the scarce foods subject to allocation[1] had been those imported from United Nations dependencies and satellites or from outside sources like Argentina, it was possible to deny the suppliers direct representation. But as soon as the Board began allocating United Nations' domestic production and to suggest rationing in the producer countries in order to safeguard the allocations, the Governments concerned would find it impossible to co-operate unless they were not merely consulted, but seen to be consulted, in advance. The very formality and publicity attached to Anglo-American co-operation in the Combined Food Board called for a comparable degree of punctilio in dealing with other United Nations. The Canadian Government especially felt this because of its close association with the United States and its new Mutual Aid proposals.

To the Mission the Canadian arguments seemed cogent; indeed, Mr. Brand urged that the admission of Canada would be of direct assistance in dealing with the United States. The Ministry of Food, however, felt that it would open the flood gates and mean the end, not only of the London Food Committee, but of the Board itself. But the Ministry found itself in a minority of one, for other London Departments had long been lukewarm in their opposition. It was agreed, though, that the admission of Canada would necessitate a change in the status of the London Food Committee. Hitherto, though its commodity sub-committees had done useful work, the main Committee had tended to fall between two stools. Meeting too seldom to be efficient as an operating committee, it was yet insufficiently dignified to serve as a façade that would offset the powerful attraction of Washington. A solution was sought in converting it into

---

[1] Strictly speaking, the Combined Food Board did not 'allocate' foodstuffs but registered recommendations about their allocations.

a London Food *Council*[1] with the Minister of Food himself as Chairman, and the appropriate Ministers and High Commissioners as members. The functions of this body and its undefined relationship to the Combined Food Board would be unaltered, and it would still have no secretariat other than that provided by the Ministry of Food, though there was some suggestion, never in fact carried out, that this secretariat should be full-time.

These twin proposals—the admission of Canada to the Board and the 'promotion' of the Committee—were put to the Commonwealth Governments in mid-July. India, South Africa and New Zealand agreed, but Australia's acceptance was not received till 26th August. A day or so earlier Mr. Law had received from Ambassador Winant a tentative American scheme for expanding the Combined Food Board to include Australia, New Zealand and perhaps other producer countries, each to be represented by the highest food authority. The Australian Foreign Minister, Dr. Evatt, was attracted by this plan, which would of course have brought the London Food Committee to an end. Had the American proposal reached a more formal stage, and had not the other Dominions already unanimously agreed to the British plan, the whole combined food organisation might have gone into the melting-pot. But for the moment it proved possible to persuade all concerned that there were sound practical reasons for keeping the London organisation in being, and not endangering the efficiency of joint planning by the 'quite new experiment' of enlarging the Washington Board. 'Our experience', it was urged, 'proves [the] great importance of plans first being put together in [the] centre where main purchasing and shipping arrangements for carrying out those plans are also centred'. The State Department, while prepared to give the new Council a chance, would not however agree to rule out for good the enlargement of the Board itself.

Another more immediate threat to the position of the Combined Food Board was finally disposed of in November with the successful launching of the United Nations Relief and Rehabilitation Organisation on a 'limited' basis. For many months controversy had raged between those who wished to give UNRRA power to allocate scarce goods and those who argued that it should be one among other claimants before the Combined Boards. The Ministry of Food had naturally been foremost in supporting the latter view, partly for the sake of efficiency—clearly only an organisation participated in by national food authorities would dispose of the information necessary to allocate international food supplies; and partly, of course, because the United Kingdom would, against an all-powerful UNRRA, lose the privileged position and even perhaps the power of veto that she had as a member of the Combined Food Board. So far as the privilege

---

[1] This was the name originally suggested for the London Food Committee in 1942.

went, this could be defended so long as war continued on the ground that the British people, as active participants in the battle, must be kept 'fighting fit'. For the rest, no Minister of Food would have for one moment thought of foregoing his ultimate right (so far as he had the power) to determine British food policy. The same applied to those Allies with overseas resources, whether in supplies of foreign assets, such as France and Belgium, even though their Governments were still in exile. The notion of a supreme yet all beneficent relief organisation was, whatever its advocates might say, only applicable to countries that war had reduced to administrative and political, as well as economic, confusion. The threat that an inflated UNRRA presented was not to the 'authority' of the Combined Boards, for they had none, but to national sovereignty itself. For that reason its fate can scarcely, when the time for decision came, have been in doubt.

Meantime the personal positions of Mr. Wickard and Judge Jones had at length been satisfactorily adjusted. The President had been unwilling to remove Mr. Wickard; Judge Jones was as unwilling as Mr. Davis had been to take his mind off pressing domestic food problems to participate actively in the work of the Board. At one stage the Americans proposed to get over the difficulty by appointing Lord Woolton as British member of the Combined Food Board, so that both he and Judge Jones could appoint deputies to do the actual work. Eventually it was decided that Mr. Wickard should become 'neutral' Chairman of the Combined Food Board, and that he should preside at what might be called plenary sessions of the Board. A more important change from the practical point of view was the appointment of a new United States Executive Officer who was directly responsible to the War Food Administrator.

III

The enlarged Combined Food Board continued during 1944 to deal effectively with the short-run problems of allocation, including the new problem presented by the shortage of inland transport for North American wheat, which necessitated the combined programming of a foodstuff that was still plentiful. But it failed to plan further ahead because the Ministry of Food and the War Food Administration could not agree on the prospective world food balance sheet for 1945 and later years. As early as the beginning of 1943 the Ministry had been apprehensive of a world food shortage appearing as soon as Europe was liberated, and its fears had been written into the Hot Springs resolutions.[1] In September of that year it embarked on an elaborate statistical analysis of the position. This analysis was not to be completed until July 1944; its results can be summed up in a brief

---

[1] See below, Chapter XXVIII.

quotation: 'the food consumption of the present free world at current rates would in 1945 equal or exceed production for every major foodstuff . . . only a small part of the prospective gap between 1945 production and requirements, including those for European relief, can be met by utilising surplus stocks'. It followed that unless production were increased, the budget could only be balanced by reducing consumption in the already free world. There was, the Ministry argued, imperative need to increase food production, to maintain combined allocation, and to continue to control consumption.

The detailed calculations adduced in support of this argument did not, in fact, add anything to it; indeed they might serve as an instance of the limitations of statistical forecasting as applied to policy. For the deficits they disclosed were, though absolutely considerable, not so large in relation to total supplies or requirements as to be incapable of disappearing under favourable circumstances. Thus the paper deficit in wheat was disposed of by yet another bumper North American harvest; the estimates of relief requirements, though 'official', were thought by many to be excessive either in themselves or in relation to shipping or the intake capacity of European ports; and (American critics were to point out) military requirements would not remain at their 1944 levels after the liberation of Europe. Moreover, American officials naturally put higher than British the possible contribution that United Kingdom stocks could make towards bridging any gap that did emerge.[1]

It was natural that the War Food Administration should be inclined to discount the possibility of shortages; to meet them by further restrictions on United States consumption would be unpopular and difficult,[2] while to stimulate production still further was to run the risk of embarrassing surpluses. Conversely, the British had nothing to lose and everything to gain by encouraging more production and less consumption in exporting countries. For the moment it was decided to compromise. The Combined Food Board's statement on world food prospects to the second meeting of the UNRRA Council at Montreal in September 1944 ran as follows:

'The Board has confidence that, given the necessary co-operation between governments, the problem of meeting overall requirements of Allied countries in Europe during 1945 can be solved. . . . Supplies of bread grains will be more than adequate. The supply of pulses is satisfactory. . . . Animal protein foodstuffs as a class continue to cause concern, but a reduction in military requirements should release some supplies of particular types. The supply of fats and oils is not abundant and meeting requirements in full will depend on the world crops of vegetable oil seeds during 1945. The sugar position is extremely difficult at present. . . . '

---

[1] See Chapter XXI below.
[2] The United States Presidential Election was due in November 1944.

The Allies were thus given a vague assurance that the position was very difficult but that everything would be all right on the night.[1] Thereafter things were allowed to drift for several months, while the Combined Food Board collected some more statistical material. The Ministry of Food's own inactivity during that autumn is difficult to understand. All this time nothing had been done to acquaint British Ministers with the problem; the War Cabinet had, indeed, received no report on the food situation since March 1944, and a proposal to bring the facts before it was held up for want of adequate figures—as if the world food shortage were an academic problem awaiting verification. Yet the Ministry had professed in July, and got the 'L.F.C. countries' to accept, that the situation was grave. Even more unaccountable than its acquiescence in the compromise statement was the United Kingdom's claim, now put forward, for increased allocations for 1945 in order that rations might be improved.

These equivocations were brought to a decisive end as soon as the Board got down to allocating meat, sugar, and oils and fats for 1945. For oils and fats, it did succeed in reaching agreement for the first six months of 1945, but only by estimating supplies at a level that no one in the Ministry, at any rate, believed they would attain; over meat and sugar it achieved complete deadlock. As late as the end of February 1945 the Ministry was hoping to reach agreement with the War Food Administration that the Americans would reduce civilian meat consumption towards the British levels, while still allowing the United Kingdom supplies enough to maintain existing rations, provided that it ate into stocks. Early in March, however, the War Food Administration came forward with a proposal that no United States meat should go to either the United Kingdom or the liberated areas in the second quarter of 1945: this would have entailed an immediate cut in the British meat ration (to 1s.) and 'tapering off' of supplies of 'points' canned meat. For sugar, notwithstanding that the gap between supplies and requirements was, after allowing for stock reductions, of the order of a million tons (enough to cover half the annual United Kingdom consumption), the American authorities seemed unwilling to take any action before May. The figures on which the oils and fats agreement had been based, moreover, looked more and more shaky; and here again the Ministry looked to the United States for action; 'a rationing scheme for soap in the United States', wrote the Minister of Food, 'would make a world of difference'.[2] It was in

---

[1] Assistant Secretary of State Dean Acheson the very next day drew the only possible inference. 'The time has come', he told the UNRRA conference, 'for UNRRA to put to one side worry about availability of supplies. . . . Somebody else has undertaken to meet that responsibility. If they fail, as they will not, we will know where the responsibility lies'.

[2] This was true enough in theory. In practice there were insuperable administrative difficulties in the way of introducing soap rationing, even of the loose British type, in the United States.

these circumstances that the War Cabinet, on Mr. Churchill's own initiative,[1] agreed that Mr. Lyttelton, as Minister of Production and a member of the War Cabinet, should go to Washington together with Colonel Llewellin to endeavour to secure the joint action that the combined machinery designed for the purpose had failed to achieve.

IV

How completely that machinery had broken down, in the absence of a top level 'agreement to agree', is apparent from the time-table of the ministerial visit to Washington. For although Mr. Lyttelton and Colonel Llewellin arrived there on 27th March, it was not until 18th April that a factual balance-sheet for the principal foods involved could be completed by officials from the three countries[2] and the negotiations proper be enabled to begin.

The facts now faced were at once simple and intractable. For sugar, there was, after allowing for agreed stock reductions, a deficit for 1945 of the order of a million tons, roughly equal to the estimated needs of the liberated areas. It was proposed that the main contribution to this gap should be made by reducing sugar consumption in all three countries to a level a little below that then current in the United Kingdom. This solution would have meant that the greater part of the cut would have fallen on the United States civilian population, whose consumption during 1944 had been at the rate of 89 lb. per head, compared with 71·5 in the United Kingdom, and the apparent cut would have been more than the real, since the higher consumption (far in excess of the United States allocation for 1944) would have continued during the first four months of 1945.

The War Food Administration felt that they could not face the political consequences of action that would mean that United States civilian consumption would actually fall below that in the other two countries, and they therefore asked—and it was eventually agreed—that the new principle of parity should operate from 1st April 1945. In practice this meant an increase over the year in the United States allocation of approximately 150,000 tons, or 2 per cent., mainly at the expense of the British whose civilian consumption would have to be further reduced by two-fifths of a pound per head per year—not a major concession to make in return for the principle of parity in the future.

For oils and fats a similar plan was agreed on, the chief point at

---

[1] The formal invitation to the Ministers from President Roosevelt should not be allowed to conceal the fact that the initiative came from the United Kingdom.

[2] Canada was persuaded not merely to join in the discussions but to reimpose meat rationing, lifted in February 1944 because of a temporary glut of supplies.

issue being how much contribution to the gap should come from a reduction in consumption in the three countries, and how much from the United Kingdom stocks and the hypothetical allocation to liberated countries. The first British offer had been a reduction of 245,000 tons (in terms of oil) but the War Food Administration declared that it could not face a consumption cut on the scale that this would entail. In return for agreement that the parity principle should be maintained up to at least June 1946, the Minister of Food undertook to give up a further 100,000 tons by that time, of which not more than 75,000 should be before the end of 1945. Even so, the United Kingdom would still be left with about 300,000 tons of oil equivalent, or well over 100,000 tons more than the minimum prescribed by the Ministry Committee of 1943.[1] Moreover, a considerable part of this stock represented savings for which the Ministry of Food was entitled to no credit, inasmuch as they arose from shipments in excess of previous allocations. (The United States was making a stock contribution of almost equal size in 1945, but her end-year stock would be thereby reduced to a very low level.)

The actual work of allocation was handed back to the Combined Food Board Oils and Fats Committee; thus the agreement left the exact extent of the ration reductions that would be required uncertain. The Ministry's Director of Oils and Fats, taking as he did the view that even now the Americans were being over-sanguine about supplies, and that the position would be worse in 1946 when inroads into stocks would not be possible on anything like the same scale, recommended cuts totalling 89,000 tons as against the 50,000 tons to which the United Kingdom was committed. To these—a ten per cent. cut in supplies to trade users and the halving of the cooking fats ration—the Ministry was shortly constrained to add a reduction of the adult soap allowance by one-eighth—a step which incidentally was to compel a drastic revision of the soap 'rationing' scheme.

An attempt to apply the same principle of parity in civilian consumption to supplies of meat and bacon encountered fatal stumbling blocks. For sugar, and oils and fats, it was possible to bridge the gap between supplies and requirements without raising directly the question of Forces' supplies or putting such a strain on the United States rationing scheme as would break it. For meat this was not possible, the root difficulty being that only two-thirds of United States meat supplies[2] (that passing through federally-inspected slaughterhouses)

---

[1] See Chapter XXIV below. These figures exclude the 'wasting asset' of whale oil which had not been included in the 1943 calculation, but was included in the total given in the documents for the end of 1945.

[2] This also applied to lard. But (a) the demands of the Armed Forces were less overwhelming, (b) compound cooking fat provided at any rate part of the United States civilian requirements.

could be drawn on for military supplies, for export, and for feeding large cities like New York, Washington, and Los Angeles, that were remote from the meat-producing areas. Increased exports, therefore, unless they came out of military supplies, must fall with disproportionate force on consumers in these large cities—so much so that, according to American officials, an average consumption of 120 lb. a head per year (slightly more than the United Kingdom rate at the end of 1944) over the whole country would mean only 70 lb. for the average eastern city dweller. (This is not quite so drastic as it sounds, for the consumption of poultry in the United States was far higher than in Britain.)

The War Food Administration was therefore unwilling to make a gesture comparable with those of the British and Canadians, who had offered to withdraw all canned meat from civilian consumption; but even had it been willing to do so, this and other conservation measures by the civilian food authorities could only provide half the savings required. The rest could only come from the military; and in the Anglo-American exchanges that led up to the departure of the Lyttelton-Llewellin mission it had been understood that military food requirements should come under review. President Roosevelt's sudden death, and even before that, the resignation of Mr. Justice Byrnes from the Office of War Mobilisation, had left the mission to negotiate with officials who had no authority to override the military or even to secure from them reasoned statistical justification of their claims for meat in terms of men, rations, and stocks.[1]

Only the new President's direct intervention could, it was clear, alter this situation, and the mission was naturally reluctant to press him during his first few days of office. When Mr. Truman saw the Minister of Production, just before the Ministers were due to return, he told them that he had the matter under investigation and would take a personal interest in it. In the meantime, however, all the British could do was to make the best terms for themselves, leaving the liberated areas' requirements in abeyance.[2] After some argument, the Americans agreed to supply an amount of carcase meat and bacon to the United Kingdom, sufficient to make up with other supplies the existing rations—on paper. But they could supply none

---

[1] How extravagant these military demands were can be judged from the following table, prepared during the negotiations, representing roughly the comparative standards of meat consumption:

U.S. Military .	400 lb. per head per year
British Military .	300 lb. per head per year
U.S. Civilian .	120 lb. per head per year
British Civilian .	106 lb. per head per year

[2] Apart, that is, from a contingent promise by the United States to supply them with 220 million pounds (carcase weight equivalent) of canned meat in the last quarter of 1945, if it were not required by the military, and a similar promise by the United Kingdom to release 90 million pounds if it were not required to maintain the civilian ration (which it would be in practice).

of this until the fourth quarter of 1945, which meant that, in order to conserve stocks, Britain would have to reduce the bacon ration to 3 oz. immediately and draw yet again on canned corned beef stocks for a proportion of civilian meat supplies. These and similar small sacrifices (no rice at all, less milk products and cheese) which the United Kingdom consumer would be called upon to make as contributions to the world food shortage were unpalatable rather than tragic.[1] To secure the principle of equal consumption for sugar and fats was a substantial gain to set off against them; even on meat the door was not completely closed. The ministerial visit to Washington had been successful in securing a vindication of the principle of combined allocation.

V

The use of words like 'breakdown' and 'failure' in connection with the Combined Food Board may seem too harsh. There can be no denying that a great deal of unobtrusive but very useful work was carried out under the Board's ægis, and that the principles of exclusive purchase and combined allocation for which it stood were wellnigh indispensable as a means of keeping down prices and securing 'fair shares'. Nor, again, can one doubt that its existence was valuable in securing joint consultation on all food matters as a matter of routine. The gain from such consultation was mutual, for if the United Kingdom was vitally interested in North American decisions, the other food authorities had much to gain from the pooling of Britain's invisible assets—experience, knowledge and comparatively integrated governmental organisation. Nevertheless, it remains true first, that in face of the larger issues of the world food shortage, the Board was only just saved from shipwreck; and secondly, that it aroused continuous, and in the end decisive, criticism from the remaining United Nations.

Leaving aside the question of the rightness of individual decisions on this or that occasion, one can perhaps diagnose the weaknesses of the Board along the following lines. In the first place (and this could not be helped) the United States and Britain were unequal yokefellows, with at any rate in appearance unequal interest in the Board's success. On the one hand, the Ministry of Food, unique in completeness and administrative mastery of its day-to-day trading problems, a mastery forced upon it, but also made simpler to achieve, by its dependence on imported supplies; on the other, an American food administration faced, for all its resources in actual food, with admini-

---

[1] 'It would be tragedy', the Minister of Food had written early in March, 'if we have to celebrate the end of the war in Europe with a cut in our already meagre and dull standards of consumption'.

strative and political difficulties of a kind London had never experienced and could not readily be brought to understand. For the one, the success of the Board seemed almost a matter of life and death; for the other, the Board was almost a marginal organisation.[1]

It is this contrast between the British and American food organisations that limited the powers of the Combined Food Board as soon as it passed from the discussion of particular foods to food in general. Combined allocation as a matter of routine, without controversy or feverish *ad hoc* negotiations, seems only to have been possible so long as it applied to those foods of which the United States was either a net importer or (as with dried egg, or on occasions lard or cheese) had a large export surplus. The British, desirous of planning their import programme a year at a time, and anxious to keep unsettling changes in rations to a minimum, were apt to be disconcerted and critical when confronted with American insistence on the changing facts of life. In all the Washington negotiations of 1945 there is nothing more revealing than the insistence of Judge Marvin Jones, the Food Administrator, that the Memorandum of Understanding which embodied their conclusions should not be considered legally binding. Allocations of foodstuffs in the United States, he pointed out, were only firm for the immediately following ninety days; for any greater length of time they were purely tentative.

American official historians have been no less critical of United States food policy than British officials were apt to be.[2] But on this point it was surely more realistic than the British. Long-term programming was no doubt a convenience to planners; but, looked at from the angle of a food-producing country instead of a food-importing one, was it not a chimera? Even from the British point of view, did it matter so very much if rations went up and down over short periods, and in any case were not the Ministry's stocks originally intended to be reservoir to even out the flow of goods to the consumer, rather than a moral support for the commodity director? Were not the British rather too wont to suppose that their own unique organisation was some sort of norm for other food administrations?

If the judgement implied in these questions be accepted, the Combined Food Board's troubles may be put down to a disparity between its pretensions and its capabilities. What it did, and did for the most part admirably, was a workaday job of adjustment; what it appeared to be doing, what it even claimed to do, was to plan Allied food supplies on the grand scale. The larger task was by the nature of

---

[1] 'The Combined Food Board', write the American official historians, *op. cit.* p. 339, '. . . provided information on world supply and advised on allocations of particular commodities'. The rest of their account of U.S. food policy, forty-nine printed pages, is devoted to domestic questions and may perhaps be taken as some indication of the attitude of many, if not most, U.S. officials.

[2] *Op. cit.* Chapter II, especially pp. 362–369.

things too much for it, and was made harder by the attempt to keep it exclusive. It could have been made a valuable symbol of the willingness of the Allies to submit the management of food supplies to a modicum of mutual discussion and criticism and to underwrite one another's food consumption at any rate to minimum standards. To make it at the same time an administrative device, and thus to introduce criteria of a different nature into the judgement of what its membership ought to be, was to allow day-to-day efficiency at the expense of moral authority. Perhaps the original attempt to form the Food Board on the analogy of other boards that were in essence operational and in whose case joint Anglo-American predominance corresponded more closely to the economic facts was itself a mistake. For it must be emphasised that it was not what the Board actually did, but its exclusive appearance that caused so many of the political difficulties.

VI

It was the Board's pretensions, too, that brought in their train the scarcely less elaborate organisation of the London Food Council. For some time after the setting-up of the Council the Ministry of Food appears actually to have thought that it could really be made something more than its predecessor had admittedly been—'a group of people who advised the Ministry of the effect of its proposed decisions on the territories they were representing'. A genuine attempt was made to get the Council to meet at regular intervals and discuss broad general issues of policy, such as the expected world food shortage.[1] There were some who visualised the Council as a possible substitute for the Combined Food Board, should the United States decide to abandon combined planning before the British judged the time was ripe. When in May 1944 Anglo-American discussions were started in Washington on the future of all the Combined Boards after a European armistice, and on the form in which other Allies might best be associated with the combined machinery, Ministry officials actually proposed that some countries be asked to join Council rather than Board commodity committees. This suggestion was only reluctantly dropped, on the Minister's explicit instructions, when the Mission pointed out that it would fatally offend the Americans, who had only tolerated the London Food Council because it was a purely Empire body, and that the manner in which other countries were associated with the Combined Food Board must defer to the overwhelming need for securing continued United States participation.

---

[1] The Council was also provided, as the Committee had never been, with printed notepaper of its own.

It was not indeed until August 1945 that the Ministry admitted to itself that there was no prospect of the Council showing any signs of independent animation; that, as one official put it, it might be best

'to abandon the attempt to have worth-while meetings every three or four months and regard the Council as a kind of ultimate and somewhat ethereal umbrella of authority for the practical work which the subordinate committees meeting more frequently do.'

The reason for the Council's ineffectiveness seems, however, even at this late date to have been imperfectly understood. It was not merely that 'co-operation between the L.F.C. Dominions and ourselves has proved too continuous and smooth to provide controversial topics for reference to a ministerial body'—other, that is to say, than the War Cabinet itself—true though that was. What took the life out of the Council was the inevitable preponderance of the Ministry of Food, not merely because it took the lion's share of the supplies allocated, but because it alone had the expert knowledge.

Even the effectiveness of the Commodity Committees was onesided, because the Ministry alone was able to propose overall allocations. The remaining members could discuss allocations to themselves, but had no means of judging the fairness of these to others. It would have been completely feasible for the Divisions concerned to make all the allocations by separate agreement, without ever calling the committees together at all. In short, while it was certainly convenient and sensible that detailed programming for the 'L.F.C. countries' should be handled in London, it was equally certain that the Council itself must be incapable of handling any major conflict of interest among its members, since this would *ipso facto* mean that the United Kingdom Minister of Food and his representative, the United Kingdom Member of the Combined Food Board, could no longer act as honest broker on behalf of the whole 'L.F.C. area'.

However, the existence of the London Food Council was never, after mid-1944, allowed to jeopardise Anglo-American co-operation, and the negotiations on the future of the Combined Boards were uneventful. In December 1944 the United Kingdom, the United States and Canada agreed that the Food Board should continue, unenlarged, as long as war needs existed, to allocate all essential supplies and that other countries should be admitted to the Board's committees as and when appropriate. The crisis of March and April 1945, culminating in the Memorandum of Understanding, was not allowed to affect this decision. Nevertheless, progress in admitting other countries was slow and some of them were showing signs of restlessness when the sudden end of the war with Japan necessitated a further decision about the future of the Board. Agreement was reached with Mr. Clinton Anderson, the new United States Secretary of Agriculture[1] and Board member, to continue the Board until further notice, reviewing the situation every six months.

By this time the world food shortage was evident, and the Anglo-American dissent about its likelihood, which had prevailed all through 1944, had been ended by events. But the very support of Mr. Anderson for combined allocation and international planning made him more anxious, rather than less, to have direct representation of the other Dominions on Combined Food Board committees; and though the Ministry in September 1945 brought out once more its old argument about operational efficiency, this had lost force now that it had been agreed that the Washington committees should be enlarged. When in October New Zealand expressed a preference for direct representation in Washington, the Ministry acquiesced; the end of the London Food Council was in sight, though it was to survive until mid-1946, when the Combined Food Board was to be transformed into a representative International Emergency Food Council.

---

[1] He took up his appointment on 1st July 1945.

CHAPTER XX

The Nadir of Food Imports: Wheatmeal Flour and Bread Dilution, 1942-43

I

THE most immediate result of the spread of war beyond Europe, so far as the Ministry of Food was concerned, was a threat to United Kingdom imports. The shortage of ships that, after a comparatively easy summer, had begun to develop during the autumn of 1941, was greatly sharpened by United States belligerency, which at once meant new opportunities for the U-boats and new military demands on tonnage, and only in the long run relief from the American shipyards.[1] By mid-January 1942, but a few weeks after the Japanese attacked, the Ministry of War Transport was counting on only 5¾ million tons *total* imports into the United Kingdom for the first quarter of the calendar year.

As always when a turn for the worse in shipping coincided, as it usually did, with the seasonal fall in arrivals and in food stocks, the Ministry of Food's first anxiety was breadstuffs. Stocks of wheat and flour at the end of August 1941 had represented nearly eighteen weeks' supply, with the new home crop still in prospect. This situation had permitted considerable imports of maize for animal feeding in September and October, at the expense of wheat; but in November, Cereals Division had already given warning that if imports of maize were to continue, stocks of wheat and flour would shortly begin to approach the danger level. The position, it was said, needed all the more careful watching because, with an increasing proportion of cargo space allotted in liners or so-called CAM vessels[2] that could not be diverted to East Coast ports, it was difficult to maintain supplies to the East Coast mills.

After Pearl Harbour, concern rapidly verged on alarm as prospective Northern Range wheat shipments for January shrank first to 300,000, then to 250,000 tons. It looked as though by the end of February wheat stocks would have fallen below the danger level on the Cereals Division's formula[3] and in March and April lower still. Even if home-grown wheat prices were manipulated so as to en-

---

[1] See Hancock and Gowing, *op. cit.* pp. 412–416.
[2] i.e. merchant vessels armed with catapulted aircraft. These were unable also to use some smaller West Coast ports, such as Swansea and Barry.
[3] See above, Chapter XII.

courage farmers to bring forward their wheat earlier, this would only postpone the crisis until April. The Division held that unless 200,000 tons extra wheat could be imported between January and April, the only alternative to drastic bread rationing would be to raise the extraction rate to eighty-five per cent. as soon as possible. The Minister himself asked the Ministry of Supply to 'lend' him 200,000 tons from their steel programme, but met with a refusal. There was nothing for it but to put the problem up for decision by Ministers, a step which the opponents of high extraction flour within the Ministry were very reluctant to take.[1]

On 16th January the Lord President's Committee took the initiative in asking for a statement of the effects, more particularly on the milk supply, of raising the extraction rate. The old ground of the previous year was gone over once more; the Ministry of Food and the Agricultural Departments painted a gloomy picture of the effect on home-produced meat, milk and eggs. The Minister of Food argued that in practice the loss would almost entirely fall on milk, that since this could not be allowed to happen maize would have to be imported to replace the wheat offals, and that as a result the saving in tonnage might be no more than 120,000 tons a year, representing the increased feeding value of maize compared with wheat offals. Though there were mitigating factors at the moment, their effect would be only temporary. Even were it possible to throw the whole loss on pigs and poultry, replacing the bacon and eggs by imports, the saving would not exceed 475,000 tons. 'I should not be justified in raising the rate except under the explicit instructions of the War Cabinet'.

The Lord President's Committee was divided on the matter, and on 6th February recorded no decision, pending a discussion on the whole import situation. But the argument for raising the extraction rate was put forcibly by the Lord President and the Minister of War Transport, and there can have been no doubt in Lord Woolton's mind that there would be no chance of getting *more* shipping, simply to maintain the white loaf. Opposition within the Ministry of Food therefore collapsed; and at the next meeting of the Lord President's Committee the Minister announced his support for compulsory wheatmeal. Only the Agricultural Ministers held out, and carried their opposition to the War Cabinet. This occasioned some further delay, while means of mitigating the loss of wheat offals were considered. Under pressure, however, the Agricultural Departments conceded that they could get through to the next harvest with an

---

[1] As the Permanent Secretary himself put it: 'There are of course people inside and outside the Government who, for reasons apart altogether from the supply position, would like to see the Minister take a decision to increase the extraction to eighty-five per cent. for the rest of the war . . . certain people may at once grasp this opportunity of giving wheatmeal a boost with the result that our wheat and flour stocks may be reduced not entirely for shipping reasons'.

extra 87,000 tons of maize; the Minister of Food modified his earlier refusal to draw on the 100,000 tons of maize, imported the previous year and held by the Ministry of Food as a 'milk production reserve'; and on 4th March the War Cabinet resolved that the extraction rate should be raised on or about the 1st of April. (It was actually raised on 23rd March.)

In all the discussions leading up to this decision there is no evidence that any but shipping considerations weighed with Ministers. The Minister of Health did indeed put forward the medical arguments in favour of high extraction; but even he made it clear that he would not have pressed for the change on nutritional grounds alone. The long-standing agitation in Parliament, and elsewhere, in favour of wheat-meal bread appears to have been utterly without effect. Indeed, one may question whether the decision would not have been again postponed—or at any rate more strongly contested—had it not been for the Cereals Division's fear of running down stocks. On analysis this fear appears to have been exaggerated by an over-cautious allowance for the flow of home-grown wheat off farms. Although wheat arrivals during the first three months of 1942 were less by 125,000 tons than the meagre expectations, stocks of wheat at end-March were fully up to forecast. At no time did they fall as low as in the previous winter, when proposals to raise the extraction rate had been defeated, notwithstanding that Britain was then under heavy air attack.[1]

The Allied reverses of the early months of 1942 also caused the ploughing-up campaign to be intensified for 1942–43. The Ministry of Food asked that a further 500,000 acres should be sown to wheat, 300,000 to potatoes, and 110,000 to other vegetables. The Ministry of Agriculture felt that this was too ambitious a programme, having regard to supplies of labour and fertilisers, and added that it would mean interference with sound farming practice, and cause loss to farmers in subsequent years through loss of fertility. Moreover, it criticised the already high apparent waste of the potato crop. In the end the Lord President's Committee decided that County War Agricultural Committees should be urged at once to try and get the wheat, but that the Ministry of Food's other proposals should be left over until the time of the spring sowings was nearer.

Any extra help from home agriculture would not, however, materialise until the 1943 harvest had been gathered and threshed, i.e. to all intents and purposes not till 1944. According to the estimates

---

[1] The forecast of monthly deliveries of home-grown wheat, upon which the Cereals Division had based its claim for 200,000 tons extra arrivals, was a rate of 75,000 tons from January-April, after which 'very little home-grown wheat can be expected'. The actual quantities delivered were, in thousands of tons:

January 167, February 195, March 201, April 166; total 729,000 tons, exceeding the estimate by more than twice the extra tonnage asked for. Moreover, a further 117,000 tons was forthcoming in May, making a total of 846,000 tons, close on three times what was forecast for the rest of the season.

S

of the War Cabinet Shipping Committee[1] the worst squeeze in shipping would come long before then, viz. in the first six months of 1943. Failing any further help from the United States, and on certain hypotheses as to losses, requirements of civil imports for other areas, and military demands, the total non-tanker imports into the United Kingdom during the eighteen months ended 30th June 1943 were forecast at 35 million tons; consumption of imported goods at existing rates over the same period would amount to 41·4 million tons. On the showing of the responsible Departments, the gap of 6·4 million could not be bridged wholly by running down stocks; even if these were to reach their minimum at the end of June 1943—and to let them do so would be extremely imprudent unless greatly increased imports could be counted on for the second half of 1943—the gap would still amount to over two million tons. Unless more help were got from America, or cuts were made in Service demands on shipping—the latter a step that the Committee did not feel able to suggest—further drastic economies in civil consumption were inevitable; and the Committee seems to have felt that most of them ought to fall on food.

The Ministry of Food insisted that no reductions in actual food consumption were now possible; the way of economy could only lie in raising the extraction rate still further, to ninety or ninety-five per cent., and by resorting to 'dilution' of flour with barley and oats. When allowance was made for the lower digestibility of higher-extraction flour, the low extraction rate that was possible from diluent grains, and the need to replace the livestock products which would be lost through lack of feeding-stuffs, the net saving was put at about 800,000 tons. This would be achieved only by resort to an unpalatable and less digestible bread, requisitioning oats on farms —a step that the Agricultural Departments had always resisted— and cutting the beer output in half.[2] Small wonder that Ministers recoiled from proposals so drastic and so difficult to carry out. The Standing Committee on Medical and Nutritional Problems reported unfavourably on raising the extraction rate to ninety per cent. and this was accordingly dropped; the other proposals of the Shipping Committee[3] were put aside while the possibilities of another diluent —potato flour—were explored.

---

[1] The Shipping Committee was a committee of officials under the chairmanship of Mr. Harcourt Johnstone (Secretary to the D.O.T.) charged with reviewing the shipping situation in all its aspects, and set up in April 1942. The contemporaneous disappearance of the Import Executive is significant—it was no longer thought necessary for a ministerial committee to discuss short-term import problems.

[2] The discovery that beer contains not inconsiderable quantities of two vitamins, riboflavin and nicotinic acid, was published in the following year (1943). See *Nature*, Vol. 152, p. 273, and 'Unconsidered Trifles in Our Diet' (Sir J. C. Drummond and T. Moran: *ibid.*, Vol. 153, p. 99).

[3] They included a paper economy of 100,000 tons to be secured by drawing on 'the reserve of meat on the hoof'. Once again its proponents disregarded the point that the carcases of any beasts so slaughtered would be largely skin and bone, fit only for manufacturing purposes.

II

The possibilities of diluting wheaten flour with other substances are determined by four main factors. The first and, of course, the most fundamental, is the availability of the diluent; the second, the technical problem of dilution; the third, the extent to which palatability and baking quality may be allowed to suffer; and the fourth, how far it is insisted that the national flour shall be uniform in quality. In the previous war the Ministry of Food had thrown palatability and uniformity to the winds, and had diluted up to as much as thirty per cent. with a variety of things—oats, barley, maize, beans, rice, and potatoes. This high rate of dilution, however, had been necessary, not in order to save shipping—in the majority of cases it was wasteful of shipping owing to the low extraction rate from diluents other than rice—but because these grains, particularly maize, could be obtained more readily than wheat. Neither home-grown grain nor potatoes had been used in the loaf on any large scale.[1] The 'war bread' so produced had been unattractive, but not it seems unwholesome, apart from some trouble with the infection known as 'rope'; and it might therefore be supposed at first sight that the only real limitation on pursuing a policy of dilution this time was obtaining a supply of diluents. Clearly, dilution would only secure a real economy of imports if it diverted to bread foodstuffs that would otherwise be wasted; but the implications of diverting barley from beer, or oats from livestock, were unwelcome. Potatoes appeared to offer an attractive alternative; the acreage for 1942 had increased so much, thanks to deliberate policy, that given even moderately favourable crop conditions, there seemed likely to be a surplus over present consumption. Could not that surplus be taken for bread?

Again, the example of the last war offered a parallel encouraging at first sight but in reality quite unhelpful. What had happened then was that in certain districts bakers had been obliged, on the orders of Food Control Committees, to mix cooked mashed potatoes into their dough. But this practice had never taken place on a large scale; it was unsuited to the large plant bakeries, which had greatly multiplied since 1918; it was held by baking experts to be a principal cause of 'rope'. Nevertheless it was an expedient to which recourse could have been made for the purpose of dealing with casual surpluses of potatoes, had the Ministry been prepared to throw uniformity overboard. The proposal now mooted was different; it was that potato flour should be specially prepared, for admixture by millers or bakers

---

[1] See Beveridge, *British Food Control*, pp. 98–100. His assertion (p. 98, note 2) that but for the Armistice the bread of 1919 would have consisted 'largely' of potatoes, is quite mistaken: even a ten per cent. dilution with potatoes would have absorbed two million tons or more, a quantity quite impossible to obtain even from a bumper crop.

at a uniform rate. No plant, other than a small experimental one, existed, but experiments had been made on a potato flour produced by crushing the dried potato slices, or 'cossettes', produced by the sugar beet factories in the off-season and used for feeding-stuffs. Tests at the Millers' Association laboratory at St. Albans as early as May 1941 appeared to show that two per cent. of this flour could be used as a diluent without seriously affecting bread quality, particularly when eighty-five per cent. flour was used. These experiments were not followed up by practical bakery tests, nor was any inquiry made into the possibilities of obtaining the 500,000 tons of potatoes that would be required for a national two per cent. dilution. But the results were given a certain amount of publicity in official and ministerial circles. It was put about that the problem had been solved and that plans were ready to put potato dilution into effect.[1]

Thus, though it remained the Ministry's official view that the best way to use potatoes was as a table vegetable and that dilution, if it was to be resorted to, had better be with oats, the contrary view gained currency among both Ministers and officials. It was strengthened by the exceptionally heavy apparent wastage of the potato crop of 1941—wastage the unavoidable nature of which was not generally understood. (The whole question of potato flour had been gone into fully in the spring of 1940, but the inquiry and its results were by now forgotten.) The short point is that it is extremely difficult to forecast a *certain* surplus of potatoes, even when the crop and the conditions of its clamping are known; and that the least likely period of the year to be able to count on such a surplus is from February to May, when the sugar beet factories are free for potato drying. That means that it would be a mistake to plan a reduction in wheat shipments on the offchance of having some potato flour later on. All that could be hoped for from potatoes was a possible windfall towards the middle of 1943, i.e. after the worst shipping squeeze was expected to be over; and the wheat equivalent of that windfall would be at the outside 100,000 tons. But these facts were neither grasped firmly by the Ministry as a whole nor in consequence put unequivocally before Ministers.

Hence the discussions that took place in the Lord President's Committee in the summer of 1942 were both protracted and unreal, as the true position only emerged by slow and painful stages. Thus on 24th June the Committee resolved that dilution with potato flour should begin 'forthwith' to the extent of the processing plant available, evidently supposing that this capacity, though limited, was sufficient to make the effort worth while. (In fact, it was negligible

---

[1] An official minute to the Parliamentary Secretary, in August 1941, ran as follows: 'We have already completed an enquiry into the possibility of adding potato flour to bread *on a national scale. Plans are ready for it* to be done to an extent of not less [*sic, sc.* more] than two per cent. to all bread flour, if such dilution is required.' (Italics mine.)

—less than 10,000 tons per annum.) On 10th July the Committee were told that supplies of potatoes were uncertain, but that the sugar beet factories would be able to produce sufficient flour after the beet campaign ended in January. The Minister of Agriculture made great play with the amount of potatoes alleged to be wasted, and suggested that the use of the sugar beet factories might obviate taking any of the 1942 oat crop for dilution. The gap till January, it was suggested, might be bridged by using what remained of last year's oat crop. On 24th July the Minister of Food said that he would prefer not to dilute with potato flour unless the amount of oats for a five per cent. dilution (the most that could be undertaken without affecting the quality of the loaf) would not be forthcoming and unless there was a manifest surplus of potatoes, but that given these conditions he would be prepared to replace up to two per cent. of oats with potato flour, provided this did not make the bread less palatable. The Committee were warned that it was as yet by no mean certain that the product of the sugar beet factories would be suitable for dilution.

This was the first hint that the technical difficulties of producing a suitable potato flour had not, after all, been overcome. The Ministry's technicians raised several objections to its use; unless a low sulphur coal were used, the beet factories' product would contain an excessive amount of sulphur dioxide; the grinding of the cossettes to a suitable powder presented difficulties, and most of the factories had no space for grinding equipment. In the face of this discouraging report, the Minister could only propose to his colleagues that potatoes be abandoned as a diluent altogether. He now suggested that the five per cent. dilution already agreed on should be carried out with oats, or failing oats, barley; and that any cossettes that it might be possible to produce from potatoes should go in aid of the feeding-stuffs ration. This cold douche was accompanied by the statement that even if a suitable potato flour could be produced, it would not be possible to use it in combination with oats or barley without impairing the quality of the loaf—a statement in flat contradiction of what Ministers had been told previously. Not unnaturally, the Lord President's Committee expressed suspicion of this advice, and asked that further enquiries should be made.[1] In fact, however, dilution with potato flour was buried from then on.

III

The proposal to put barley into flour was new; it arose because the barley crop of 1942 had considerably exceeded expectations that it would only suffice for existing uses, of which the chief was brewing.

---

[1] There is no record of any further report to the Committee on this subject.

Such a windfall was all the more welcome because barley is a better diluent than oats in all respects—effect on bread quality, ease of handling and economy in extraction. A given amount of wheat could thus be saved both more readily and with less diluent. Some oats would, indeed, still be needed, but not to an extent that would require the Minister to go back on his declared intention not to ask for their compulsory removal from farms. A sufficiency (some 300,000 tons over a year) could, it was thought, be made up from Ministry stocks of old-crop oats together with purchases in the open market, while the 200,000 tons of 'surplus' barley could be procured by making an Order requiring all sound barley not needed for seed to be sold to an approved buyer. The final disappearance of potato flour from the scene would not therefore interfere with the promised saving of 300,000 tons of wheat imports by a five per cent. dilution. This was the main, indeed the only genuine economy in the 800,000 tons of imports the Ministry had undertaken to save, without de-stocking, over the twelve months ended June 1943.[1]

Clearly, dilution must begin without delay if it were to save anything like the promised amount of shipping. But a variety of obstacles —no single one of them very serious, but cumulatively very effective— arose. The instruction to buy oats had first been given at the end of June; but a dispute arose about procedure. Should the Home-grown Cereals Division employ its own buyers, or operate partly or wholly through the port offices of the Imported Cereals Division? A solution to this interesting but hardly vital problem could not be reached till September. Opinions were divided on whether whole oats or groats (i.e. husked oats) should be put into the grist and whether or not kiln-drying of oats would be necessary. Until this was settled, on 27th August, no order could be placed for the special husking machines, since these could only deal with oats that had not been kiln-dried; there were further delays in getting Treasury sanction for the order, and the first of the machines was not to be delivered till December. Want of storage space, as well as instructions from higher authority that dilution should not take precedence over the needs of oatmeal millers and essential horses, hindered Ministry purchasing operations; in many districts the oat crop was late, so that deliveries lagged behind purchases. Even so it was lack of machinery rather than of oats which made it impossible to put them into the loaf on the appointed day.

The same sort of difficulties arose over barley, of which Ministry purchase had been authorised on 30th September. Three weeks were spent in internal discussions whether millers should purchase barley

---

[1] The remaining 500,000 tons was a paper saving got by assuming that this much more food would be provided by home production. Subsequently an import programme was agreed on by the Shipping Committee which provided for a certain amount of de-stocking.

direct, or whether, in order that they might have no excuse for not carrying out instructions, it should be purchased by Home-grown Cereals Division and allocated for milling through the Port Area Grain Committees. A decision in favour of the surer but slower process meant that buying operations could not begin until November; they had to be restricted to parcels that would keep till after 1st January, the date scheduled for dilution to begin; and this concentration on high-grade samples brought purchases for bread into direct competition with purchases for malting and flaking, i.e. for beer. A Direction to approved buyers that would have prevented barley flakers from buying high-grade barley unless it had been refused by the Ministry roused protests both from the trade and the Ministry's own Brewing Division, and had to be amended before it came into force on 14th December.

The Minister himself, who had been originally led to believe that dilution with oats might begin as early as October, and had been disappointed at having to tell his colleagues that 1st January was the earliest possible date, was much disturbed at the hint of further delays.[1] His energetic personal intervention was partly responsible for definite priority being given to dilution, towards the end of December, when an Order was issued requiring merchants to offer the Ministry one-third of all their purchases of barley from 1st January onwards. It must be added, however, that such a measure could only have been taken earlier at the risk of interrupting malting operations and perhaps causing local beer shortages; to introduce it now was to push open a door that was already ajar. It was indeed idle to place the main blame for the delay in introducing dilution on the various administrative hold-ups that had taken place. The Minister evidently thought the various Divisions concerned had prosecuted their tasks with less than all possible zeal. But even supposing this were true (the evidence is hardly conclusive), swifter action would itself have raised difficulties. Had speed been made the first consideration, the Director of Imported Cereals' proposals, namely to put whole oats into the grist and to instruct millers to buy home-grown barley direct, could have been adopted; and dilution begun in September or earlier with the old crop of oats the Ministry held. But this would have sacrificed bread quality and uniformity at once and before long have led to an outcry from brewers and maltsters that the millers were taking their barley. The Ministry could only move swiftly if it also moved drastically; dilution must either be given absolute priority over, or be the residuary legatee of, other uses for barley and oats; the maximum saving of imported grain must either

---

[1] It seems likely that the Divisions would have completed their preparations by December in any case.

sacrifice, or be sacrificed to, the palatability of the national loaf.[1]

By the time dilution was ready to begin in mid-January, the import situation had sharply deteriorated, thanks to the demands of the North African campaign on shipping and a severe rise in the sinkings of food cargoes. The import programme, finally agreed on by the Shipping Committee at 15·43 million tons for the eighteen months up to June 1943, itself provided for running down stocks to the presumed danger level, but at the end of 1942 it seemed prudent to discount the possibilities of the programme being fulfilled. The scope for major economies appeared to be limited to raising the extraction rate to eighty-eight per cent. and to an increase of dilution to ten per cent.[2] The Minister and his advisers, however, wished to avoid any dramatic cuts that would require Cabinet sanction, lest these result in a deliberate cut in the food programme which would leave the Ministry no better off than it was before. Sufficient barley for a ten per cent. dilution could only be obtained by withholding brewers' licences to acquire it; a further watering of beer would have to bear most heavily on the stronger brews sold in industrial areas. A reduction in beer output sufficient to save any considerable amount of grain would mean closing the public houses, say, two days a week or, in effect, rationing beer. From this prospect the Lord President's Committee unanimously recoiled. An ingenious way out was suggested—the 'dilution' of beer, not with water, but with oats and perhaps dried potato 'cossettes', which could replace the flaked barley that brewers had already been using up to some extent in order to save labour in the maltings. On 20th January the Minister met the brewers, who agreed to try and save up to ten per cent. of their barley usage in this way. Naturally it took time to adjust brewing methods, but thanks to the constant pressure of the Brewers' Society on its members, substitution to the extent of ten per cent. was achieved by July 1943.

The gloomy assumptions on which policy had been framed in January were to be dispelled with the spring. From May onwards there was a dramatic improvement in loadings and an even more dramatic fall in sinkings; mastery over the submarine coincided with the full results of the American shipbuilding campaign. By July

---

[1] An attempt to blame farmers, and hence the Ministry of Agriculture, for the delay, provoked a crushing rejoinder: 'The postponement . . . has been due . . . largely to your own decision to allow maltsters to take the cream of the market and to restrict your buying price to a maximum of £6 a quarter'.

[2] Apart from a saving of 25,000 tons by reducing the cheese ration, which was in any case to become necessary on supply grounds, the remaining 'economies' proposed were either to run down stocks of wheat and canned meats below the nominal danger levels, or to adjust imports, in the case of sugar, to the actual instead of the expected home production. The economists advising the Lord President were very active at this time in pressing for trifling cuts in food consumption, e.g. rationing restaurant meals or reducing the sweets ration. They also showed unwillingness to abide by the Shipping Committee's estimates, to which they had been parties; constantly laying stress on the possibility that these might be too sanguine.

wheat stocks had so much improved that the Minister could call for a review of dilution policy in order to improve the baking quality of the loaf. Experience had shown that the 'green' (i.e. not kiln-dried) groats, though the most that had ever gone into the grist was three per cent., had a more unfortunate effect on bread quality than anything else, particularly when they were associated with a great deal of 'weak' home-grown wheat. Moreover, since the effective rate of extraction from oats was only about forty per cent.,[1] it could be replaced by less than half the tonnage of wheat. The Divisions concerned were very ready to dispense with groats, but barley (and the minute amount of rye being used in some places) presented a more difficult problem. They could not be bought and stored, since they would need to be dried and drying capacity was lacking. To sell Ministry-held barley for animal feeding would arouse criticism and lose money; to leave it on farms would be to relax a control that might need to be tightened again later on; to replace it with wheat would not noticeably improve the loaf. It was decided to drop the use of groats early in August; the question of barley might have remained longer in abeyance had it not become clear that the 1943 harvest, splendid though it was, would show a sharp drop in the supply of oats. The Agricultural Departments' estimates, made in September, suggested that oats sold in 1943–44 off farms would be 350,000 tons short of the 850,000 required for essential uses. Only half the gap could be filled by throwing in the whole of the Ministry of Food's stock of old-crop oats, acquired for dilution but no longer needed. The only course open was to stop putting barley into bread and oats into beer. On 8th October the brewers were released from their undertaking to use oat flakes, and on 4th November the Lord President's Committee approved a proposal to discontinue the use of barley as from the end of that month. Once the millers' stocks of barley were worked off the only coarse grain to remain in the loaf would be a small quantity of rye, and that only locally.

In the nine months ended 30th September 1943, 302,000 tons of barley, 49,000 tons of oats and 8,000 tons of rye were put into flour, and some 280,000 tons of imported wheat thereby saved. This was not unsatisfactory in amount—the target had been 300,000 tons—even though most of it was made after the acute shipping crisis had

---

[1] One of the reasons why green groats were more harmful to baking quality than expert advice had led the Ministry to expect may have been that the shelling plants were only eighty-five per cent. efficient, i.e. quite a sizeable amount of husk found its way into flour. Oat*meal*, of which casual seasonal surpluses had also been used, was not objectionable. It is important to note that the composition of the loaf did not correspond to the composition of the grist from which flour was milled, owing to the varying rates of extraction from different grains, and the admixture (compulsory after January 1943) of varying proportions of imported white flour, as much as twenty-five per cent. in Scotland. A typical loaf at this time would have contained eighty-two per cent. wheatmeal flour, ten per cent. white flour, five per cent. barley flour, three per cent oat flour, apart from chalk and possibly milk powder.

passed. It is a striking comment on the activity of the previous year that nearly all this saving occurred from the barley windfall, and that the raid on the brewers and the use of oats accounted between them for not much more than 50,000 tons of wheat, or three days' supply. Even had all the oats the Ministry was able to purchase been put into flour, the saving would only have been of the order of 100,000 tons; and this would have caused an even worse shortage of feeding grains in the following season. Nor could it have been accomplished except by jettisoning refinements such as flour quality and uniformity, though this would have had the advantage of dispensing with the consequences of these refinements; an elaborate system of purchase and distribution and the procurement *ad hoc* of expensive husking plant. (Expense under this item alone accounted for £50,000.)

It was, in fact, the preoccupation with loaf quality that had reduced the effect of oats dilution to insignificant proportions. Dilution can be looked upon in two ways; either as a means of using casual surpluses that would otherwise be wasted, or as a desperate resort in acute crisis; in either event swift and decisive improvisation, rather than elaborate and detailed planning, is required. An elaborate plan for oats was doubly inappropriate since there was no likelihood of putting it into bread for any time unless recourse were had to requisition, and this would not be done except in so grave a situation as to make bread quality a very minor matter indeed. If the crisis did not justify giving the public less palatable (though not less nutritious) bread for a few months, it would have been better and cheaper to leave oats alone.

CHAPTER XXI

Imports and Stock Levels, 1943-44

I

A
T the end of 1943, thanks to a splendid harvest and a great improvement in imports, the Ministry of Food's bulk stocks[1] stood at $6\frac{1}{2}$ million tons; close on two millions more than they had been a year earlier. These substantial stocks were, in fact, the dominating feature of the food situation for the remainder of the war; they should have enabled the Ministry to take any likely fluctuations in imports in its stride. True, the shipping position was once again clouded by uncertainties; the prospective invasion of France might mean not only further military demands on shipping, but a recrudescence of the port congestion of 1940–41 or even (it was thought) a temporary stoppage of all civilian imports into this country.

Moreover, the United Kingdom import programme was still dependent on American help. At no time between June 1943 and the end of the war was the Shipping Committee able to forecast the total rate of import, even six months ahead, at all closely; for the year 1944, for example, its estimates varied between $24\frac{1}{2}$ and 26 million tons. Yet so easy was the stock position, not merely for food but also presumably for raw materials, that the Committee found no great difficulty in arriving at a budget which at worst imposed a nominal cut on food stocks, while cutting raw materials stocks by nearly a million tons; and this, be it noted, assuming an increase in the consumption of imports over that of 1943 of more than $2\frac{1}{2}$ million tons, of which a million was food. In the event, the shipping position was to be so little critical as to be of secondary interest; the reports of the Shipping Committee, which in previous years had called for such difficult decisions, sank henceforth to the level of routine statistical exercises.

With its stores overflowing with food[2] the Ministry might well have chosen to take life less grimly. The possibilities of easing the consumer's lot were indeed not great, inasmuch as every major foodstuff

---

[1] i.e. those under its effective control as distinct from (a) stocks on farms (b) stocks in the hands of the trade.

[2] Literally so, since raw sugar and oilseeds were being stored in the open under tarpaulins. It was this stock situation that was termed by the Shipping Committee 'fairly satisfactory'.

except wheat was now scarce, and indeed, subject to Combined Food Board allocation.

With relief demands ahead whose size was no less uncertain for having been estimated time and again, it would have been imprudent to make out of stocks ration increases that there was little hope of maintaining from future supplies. Some relaxations that might have been possible on supply grounds were ruled out by other shortages, for instance that of manpower. The one major improvement that did seem feasible was that for which the Prime Minister more particularly had been pressing since the summer of 1943, namely the diversion of some grain to begin the rebuilding of the livestock population. In November, Ministers had agreed that some of the barley freed by the ending of bread dilution should go to pigs and poultry; a further step would be either to resume, on however small a scale, the import of feeding grains, or to achieve the same object indirectly by a reduction in the flour extraction rate.

Such a course would be open to criticism as contrary to that very Article XIII that the British delegation had sponsored at Hot Springs;[1] any reduction in the rate of extraction would also be attacked as nutritional backsliding. To the first criticism the Ministry's reply would be that the United Kingdom had already pushed the reduction of livestock and the growth of cereals for human consumption beyond the point at which it could be maintained without permanent damage to soil fertility; to the second, that it had sponsored new developments in milling technique that enabled the production of an eighty per cent. flour that contained a sufficiency (though admittedly not as much) of the valuable ingredients in the eighty-five per cent. flour, and that was superior in colour, texture, and baking qualities.[2] Neither argument was perhaps as completely conclusive as the Ministry might have wished; but it delayed action for quite another reason, namely that the shipping uncertainties of the first six months of 1944 did not permit of budgeting for any increased cereals imports, while the Commodity Division would not hear of any deliberate inroads into stocks of wheat and flour. For these were already forecast to fall below the figure set as a *minimum prudent level*.

At very first sight this appears so impossible a paradox, so completely dissonant with the general stock position, as to require the closest scrutiny. The prescription of a minimum prudent level below

---

[1] See below, Chapter XXVIII.

[2] These developments were the result of research into the distribution of nutrients, particularly the B-vitamins, among the different parts of the wheat grain. See Drummond and Moran, 'The Scientific Basis of 80% Extraction Flour' (*The Lancet*, 2nd June 1945, p. 698); Moran, 'Nutrients in Wheat Endosperm' (*Nature*, Vol. 155, p. 205).

It must nevertheless be added that the medical members of the Standing Committee on Medical and Nutritional Problems were reluctant to acquiesce in reducing 'the margin of safety which National [i.e. eighty-five per cent.] flour provides'.

which the stock of any commodity should never be allowed to fall was itself new. For some time the Ministry had sought greater consistency and clarity in its stocks policy, which now more than ever called for reasoned justification. So long as it had merely to make good a case for shipping against the no better substantiated claims of other importing Departments, it could rely on 'danger levels' that were little more than informed guesses of individual Commodity Directors, likely to err on the safe side in varying degrees. Now, however, something less vulnerable was needed. The United Kingdom depended on American help both for shipping and supplies; and supplies were even scarcer than shipping. The United States Government would not be justified in imposing fresh restrictions on its own people in order to maintain excessive stocks in Britain—stocks which in some cases were obtained on Lend/Lease and which might strengthen the recipients' bargaining position against American traders when Lend/Lease came to an end. Moreover, United Kingdom stocks were the obvious, because the nearest, source from which to draw immediate supplies for European relief after liberation; an attempt must be made to assess how large this contribution could be. As early as May 1943 Commodity Directors had been asked to provide estimates in a common form; but it was found impossible to reduce their answers to a general basis of principle without further investigation and discussion, and in October a special committee of the Food Supply Board[1] was formed to undertake this task.

II

The difficulties were more than technical; the question of responsibility within the Ministry could only be avoided by the greatest tact. Since May 1941 the responsibility for maintaining supplies of any food had been specifically charged to the Commodity Directors by Lord Woolton himself; and it was natural and inevitable that they should maintain that they could only discharge it if the Minister for his part was content to rely on their advice of what the danger level for stocks really was. Even if they admitted his right himself to override that advice in particular cases, they would have denied statisticians or economists, say, any but a subordinate part in framing it. (They had to play some part, since the Directors' own views must otherwise remain statistically inarticulate.) The inquiry could only proceed, therefore, by question and persuasion aimed at elucidating or modifying existing opinions; in so far as it led to a whittling down of minimum requirements, this must be by agreement with the Division concerned.

---

[1] Chapter XVII.

The method adopted was to segregate the various purposes for which stocks of each food needed to be held, and prescribe a minimum for each separately. Thus *minimum working stocks* were defined as the lowest level at which processing and distribution could continue to function smoothly and uninterruptedly under 'normal' war-time conditions, i.e. allowing for difficulties of labour, internal transport, diversion of shipping, and so forth, but not for the direct consequences of enemy action. This level, expressed in terms of weeks' supply, was the sum of the minimum quantity required for immediate distribution to the wholesale trade, plus the amounts in the various earlier stages —processing, sorting, blending, packing, discharging from ship— that must elapse between the time a commodity 'arrives' in port and the time when it is ready for distribution. Obviously, working stocks so defined will vary widely from commodity to commodity.

To let stocks fall to this level deliberately would evidently be un-wise; and it was therefore proposed to prescribe a *minimum prudent margin* that should always be maintained in addition, to take care of abnormally high sinkings, air-raid damage, or similar contingencies. This margin, when added to the *minimum working stock*, would consti-tute the *minimum prudent level* of stocks for each particular commodity. Stock sufficient to cover a period of half the weighted average voyage time was taken to provide a reasonable prudent margin; on the ground that this period was roughly equal to the time it took to procure fresh supplies and/or position ships; which in its turn, allow-ing for stocks afloat, themselves covering a period equal to the average voyage time, would be the time required to replenish stocks in this country. This arbitrary and somewhat abstract argument was found generally acceptable not so much because it was convincing, or even generally understood, but because calculations based on it, e.g. for dried fruit, appeared to accord reasonably well with experience. Suitable exceptions to it were made to meet the circumstances of commodities like coffee, which not only had seasonable shipments, but was liable to have an unduly large proportion of its import programme at risk in a single cargo. Again, for 'processed' commo-dities (flour, refined sugar, margarine, and jam) arbitrary additions to the margin so calculated were made to allow for air attack on plant.

The *minimum prudent stocks* thus built up were supposed to make no provision for certain further risks, e.g. transport difficulties in the supplying country, the difficulty of varying the make-up of loading programmes at short notice, the danger that, for example, carcase meat from the United States would not be forthcoming, or increased demands for one commodity arising out of the shortage of another. To cover these risks, it was proposed to provide for a *general food reserve* equivalent to four weeks' consumption of imported food; rather less than half of this, or 350,000 tons, to be held as canned meat and milk, rather more than half, or 450,000 tons, as wheat, raw sugar, and oilseeds. In other words, the point, made by at least one Commodity Director during the discussions, that these staple foods should be given especially high minimum levels was conceded; though it might have been argued that those foods that could make no claim to shipping priority needed relatively larger stocks.

In principle all this discussion appears eminently reasonable, and the careful, almost meticulous detail in which the specific circumstances of each and every food were gone into was calculated to impress the critic. The estimates of prudent margins and general reserves carry conviction, for the most part, by the admitted element of uncertainty in them. Closer examination, however, of the figures for working stocks—the base of the whole structure—arouses doubt. There was, for instance, no sort of consistency in the stocks that Divisions claimed it was necessary to hold for immediate distribution, i.e. to cover allocations under the various rationing schemes and to manufacturers. Thus 'points' canned meat and canned fish were said to require eight and seven weeks' supplies respectively to cover an eight-weekly allocation, fruit pulp for jam makers only four, while starch, which was allocated every thirteen weeks to manufacturers, was only held to require four weeks' cover at this stage. Most Divisions held, in effect, that they could not be sure of honouring their allocations unless they had first-hand stocks to cover the whole allocation period.

Apart from the fact that these long allocation periods were purely a matter of convenience, it was surely a mistake to treat stocks at earlier stages of distribution as if they were not steadily becoming available all the time. Allocation needed to be regarded as a periodical accounting process, not a physical movement of goods occurring in spasms every four or eight weeks. Take canned fish, for example; the fact that the 'pipe-line' from ship to first-hand distributor was claimed to be as much as twelve weeks long meant that the Division held that much more cover against allocations, and deprived its claim for seven weeks' additional supplies to cover distribution (nineteen weeks' supplies in all) of plausibility. A more realistic minimum figure might have been arrived at for such commodities by prescribing that total working stocks should equal either the number of weeks' supply allocated at one time *or* the amount in the pipe-line up to the point of allocation, whichever was the greater.

It seems beyond doubt that many of the figures for working stock were inflated by assuming that stocks in the earlier stages of distribution did not constitute cover for the final stage, and that the segregation of purposes for which stock might be held in itself justified holding a separate stock for each purpose. Indeed, this inflation may well account for Commodity Directors' general acquiescence in minimum prudent margins calculated on an arbitrary and not over-generous formula. From their point of view there was everything to be said for including as much as possible under working stocks that by definition were sacrosanct; the narrower, relatively speaking, the prudent margin, the less the opportunity for imprudence—or argument.

The inadequacy of so purely tactical an approach to the problem becomes clear, however, directly the true purpose of stocks is considered. Working stocks, after all, were at best a necessary evil, and every ton of food unnecessarily earmarked for them was condemned to uselessness only less surely than if it had been destroyed. The only really valuable stocks were the genuine reserves that could be called upon to iron out short-term fluctuations in supplies. The greater the proportion of stocks claimed as working stocks, the less the control that the Ministry (as distinct from the individual Division) had over them, and the greater the probability of the consumer being sacrificed in the name, not of long-term supply prospects, but of the short-run stock position.

III

In the case of wheat and flour, even so cautious an approach as this broke down, and Division and Committee failed to agree on minimum stock figures.[1] In 1939 what was in effect a minimum prudent level for imported wheat and flour stocks had been fixed by Cabinet decision at thirteen weeks' supply, or rather over fourteen weeks', allowing for millers' working stocks of flour. In 1941 this figure had been reaffirmed by the Ministry's advisory committee of millers in a rather different form; 'the position', it was said, would 'be considered dangerous' if stocks fell below nine weeks' millers' usage for wheat, plus six weeks' stock of flour.[2] Again it is clear that a prudent minimum was intended. At the end of 1942 Lord Woolton had explicitly asked for[3] a genuine minimum figure to be given him; in reply there was propounded a figure (seven and a half weeks' supply of wheat, six of flour) which, allowing for differences in presentation, was only 65,000 tons, or half a week's supply, less than the

---

[1] See Chapters V and XII.

[2] The figures have been adjusted from those in the original statement to include millers' working stocks of flour (at one week's supply).

[3] 'I am concerned', he had written, 'at my own lack of precise knowledge as to the number of weeks' supply of bulk wheat that it is essential to have in this country in order to keep the mills going. There is, of course, on the part of the millers a natural tendency to put this figure high in order to encourage me to ensure our wheat stocks. I don't require this encouragement but I shall be glad if I might be given the danger level figure. By this I mean the time at which our distribution machinery might be disturbed and some reorganisation called for. In such circumstances we might, for instance, in order to maintain supplies, have to fall back on our stocks of flour to supplement the flour coming from the mills'.

previous estimates, notwithstanding that almost one-half of total supplies were now home-grown.

This new estimate was, however, accompanied by a very revealing historical analysis of the problem which made it amply clear, short of saying so outright, that the figures did not constitute a working minimum in the sense which the Ministry was henceforth to use the term. This might indeed be inferred from the very fact that the minimum stock of imported wheat was put at nine weeks' cover (in terms of the maximum seasonal usage), while that of home-produced was put at only three weeks. For it would be clearly illogical to argue that the mills would stop unless they had at hand a greater proportion of one element in their grist than of another; and the difference (amounting to some 300,000 tons of imported wheat) was far too great to be attributable to unloading from ship and delivery to mill.[1] More striking than this, however, was the revelation that the level of *available* wheat stocks in November 1939, when some East Coast mills had been stopped,[2] was not 600,000 tons but 260,000; the remainder being the Government security stock which was never released to millers. (It was not held in those ports where difficulties arose.) In other words, from the point of view of maintaining distribution, the remaining 340,000 tons of Government wheat might just as well not have been there. This admission in effect torpedoed the reasoning that had been built on the experience of 1939. That experience had been generally held to justify the necessity of working stocks in excess of 600,000 tons; but, on the contrary, it went to show that mills could be kept going on a total stock far less than this, even under difficult conditions of shipping diversion. The significant point was not that a few mills had been stopped but that the great majority had continued working.

It is uncertain whether those who approved these earlier submissions to the Minister fully realised that such inferences might have been drawn from them, or whether he himself observed how strong an element of prudence was concealed in the figures. At all events, by October 1943 the arguments had disappeared from view and only the figures remained. These were put forward anew with but one qualification, namely, that four weeks' out of the six weeks' stock of flour was now regarded as a prudent margin. The whole of the wheat, however, was claimed as a working stock; a further 350,000 tons, or nearly five weeks' maximum usage of imported wheat, was put forward as a prudent margin. These levels were, of course, quite out of line with those built up *a priori*, in the way already described, by the investigating committee. The initial estimates of the prudent level differed by as much as half a million tons; the Committee made

---

[1] Most imported wheat was discharged by suction directly into the millers' silos.

[2] See Chapter V above.

T

numerous concessions in an effort to meet the Division's point of view, but the Director of Cereal Products would not abate his require-ment of 1,200,000 tons of wheat by even the 100,000 that was all that separated the Committee's final recommendations and his own. The Committee's figures, he protested, were entirely academic; the Minister had instructed him 'to wear a belt and braces' where wheat and flour stocks were concerned. It had to be agreed to differ, which meant that in practice the Division's view prevailed.

All that the effort at compromise had succeeded in doing was to reduce the overt difference of opinion so far as to make a show-down from which the true position might possibly have emerged—impos-sible. Those who insisted, in all sincerity, that milling was in danger of interruption immediately stocks of wheat fell below 850,000 tons were the victims of a myth, born of experience imperfectly under-stood, and thereafter unconsciously exaggerated over four years of war. It was a harmful myth, because it seems to have been responsible for the Division conducting its affairs in a state of anxiety that was hardly less inimical to wise decision than an unreasonable optimism would have been. In point of fact, the margin of safety represented by any given stock of wheat had been at least doubled since 1939, when the original thirteen weeks' minimum had been laid down, by the increases in home production and in the extraction rate. Any increase in transport and labour difficulties was small by comparison, and the Division on its own showing was now able, as it had not been on the occasion of the mill stoppage in 1939, to direct grain ships to ports of its own choice.[1] History was in fact repeating itself. Sir Arthur Salter, pleading in 1937 for a storage policy in time of peace, had argued that large stocks would make Ministers feel safe and prevent the recurrence of what happened in 1917–18 when 'the character of this danger [i.e. of starvation] several times led to the actual gravity of the transport and supply situation being greatly exaggerated'. The Ministry of Food had the stocks this time; but, for cereals, at any rate, it gained little from them in peace of mind or increased ability to pursue a calm and reasoned policy.

IV

The caution that dictated a postponement of any return towards white bread until the beginning of 1945 was most evident over the specific commitments for short-term relief supplies into which the Ministry had entered in January 1944 at the request of the Supreme Commander, Allied Expeditionary Force. The Civil Affairs section

---

[1] This admission had itself been forgotten by March 1945, when the Division produced, for the Minister's use in Washington, a new, cogent, but at all material points false justification of its position.

of SHAEF had formulated its requirements from United Kingdom stocks to cover the first ninety days after the beginning of operations on two alternative hypotheses: the first ('Overlord') assuming that the enemy would resist and liberation be gradual; the second ('Rankin C') that there would be complete collapse of the enemy without fighting. On the former hypothesis the quantities asked for (with the not very important exceptions of coffee, cheese and pulses)[1] were wholly negligible compared with total stocks in the United Kingdom; yet Cereals Division insisted on whittling down a flour requirement of 109,000 metric tons[2] to 50,000, and actually proposed to mill 100 per cent. extraction flour in provender mills to meet the deficiency;[3] moreover, even this offer was made subject to replacement within ninety days of withdrawal. Under collapse conditions contributions would be larger, though hardly disproportionately so; and here the amount of wheat and flour the Ministry was prepared to contribute was certainly substantial, more than 400,000 tons, without replacement; though this was only the measure by which its prospective stocks exceeded the '*minimum prudent level*'. In every case the Ministry reserved the right to modify its commitment at ninety (or for those commodities for which replacement was demanded, thirty) days' notice.

Early in May 1944, Cereals Division asked that ninety days' notice be given to cancel the wheat commitment under 'Rankin C' conditions, on the ground that a reduction in North American cereal loadings in May and June would bring stocks down at the end of July to only a little over one million tons. Opinion elsewhere in the Ministry was opposed to this course; it was pointed out that the commitment in the improbable event of its coming into force at all would do so before the notice expired; furthermore, to give notice would involve an American inquiry into United Kingdom stock levels. These would be difficult to defend for (it was bluntly and truly said) 'we had some 600,000 tons of wheat and flour up our sleeves'. Nevertheless it was at one moment decided to cancel the commitment in so far as it concerned wheat (i.e. up to a maximum of 373,000 tons); later this was modified so as to leave a commitment of 100,000 tons only. Notice was served on the War Office in this sense, only to be suspended at the latter's urgent request for reconsideration; moreover, the shipping authorities weighed in with the view that cancellation, even in part, would only make matters worse, since the American military would simply make up the deficiency by shipping

---

[1] The amount of coffee asked for exceeded total United Kingdom stocks. Canned meat or fish was offered and accepted in lieu of cheese.

[2] The original estimates were all made in metric tons, but in practice the Ministry worked on the assumption that metric tons and long tons were identical.

[3] The 100 per cent. flour was offered at the rate of not less (*sic, sc.* more) than 5,000 tons a week. It was refused by SHAEF on the ground that it would not keep.

wheat themselves, thus taking tonnage away from the civilian programme and probably causing worse port congestion than was
already expected to occur.

At this point of the argument, the Allied landing in Normandy
occurred to render the whole 'collapse' commitment academic; and
the Ministry was thus enabled to cloak its cancellation notice as a
new offer on the hypothesis of 'collapse following operations'. Towards the end of June agreement was reached on the basis of a total
commitment of 225,000 tons of wheat, 146,000 tons of flour, and
56,000 tons of biscuits; out of which not more than 59,000 tons of
wheat, 68,000 tons of flour, and 48,000 tons of biscuits might be
drawn *before* the collapse of Germany.

The weeks of hectic negotiations and minute calculation and re-
calculation of stocks, requirements and prospects that preceded this
agreement are an excellent example of the kind of thing that a
generous accumulation of stocks is designed to avoid. The case of
wheat and flour was unique in that the figures on which the Ministry
based its policy convinced no one outside the Division itself; for
other commodities the stated minimum stock levels were at once
more plausible[1] and perhaps less tenaciously believed by those who
put them forward. Nevertheless it was not to be expected that even
these would impress outside opinion, least of all American officials
who had plenty of motives for regarding the strongest case with
suspicion.

'There is', reported the British Food Mission in June 1944, 'a
widespread and critical attitude regarding the Ministry's statement
of what constitute minimum stock levels. Every time a M.E.A.L.[2]
stock report comes out, and every time during the discussions of a
particular allocation we have to defend a stock level higher than the
pre-war, we are conscious of this general suspicion or dissatisfaction'.

The reasons for the American attitude were explained as three-
fold; a desire to maintain United States civilian consumption of
scarce goods like canned milk; a fear (which was shared in Canada)
that the United Kingdom might use its stocks to force down the price
of certain exports in the post-war period; and a belief that Lend/
Lease funds could not properly be used to maintain stocks essential
during the period of heavy submarine and air attack but excessive
once these risks were removed. Those who held this last view, indeed,
would sooner have the British eat the stocks than maintain them
intact. The Mission urged in vain that the Ministry meet this

---

[1] That for oils and fats, only mildly inflated in October 1943, underwent considerable
further inflation during 1944. It escaped serious criticism, mainly perhaps because oils
and fats did not compete for tonnage on the North Atlantic.

[2] These letters stand for the United States *Mission for Economic Affairs in London* which,
under first Mr Averell Harriman and then Mr Philip Reed, prepared a series of reports on
the United Kingdom stock position.

criticism by offering now or soon to reduce its stocks substantially directly Germany collapsed. In December, when it looked as if a further powerful effort would be needed to finish the European war, American criticism became more vehement; the United States War Shipping Administration itself appealed to the British for more ammunition with which to defend the United Kingdom import programme against the attacks of the United States War Department. There was to be no escape from yet another stock enquiry.

The findings of this inquiry, carried out in January 1945 by officials of M.E.A.L. and the Ministry of Food jointly, need not be examined in detail. The Ministry made some concessions to criticism by re-ducing some of the more vulnerable prudent margins, e.g. those for canned meat and canned milk. What it was really doing here was abandoning, for the sake of argument, the provisions against uncer-tainties of supply. Apart from this, and from adjustments to meet changing rates of consumption, the Ministry had not changed its ground. The critics were, of course, placed at a tactical disadvantage throughout by the emphasis on working stocks; for they could always be belaboured by the expert opinion of the Trade Director, who was thus judge in his own cause. Nevertheless, the Ministry yet again failed to produce arguments conclusive enough to end the contro-versy; for the report that had been agreed with M.E.A.L. had scarcely been transmitted to Washington before the Foreign Economic Administration made proposals for cutting United Kingdom stocks to meet an expected shipping squeeze that went far beyond what had been just agreed as practicable. These proposals were successfully beaten off during the Yalta conference, and the German collapse took away their *raison d'être* only to substitute another, less transient one—the world food shortage. Even so, the stock reductions to which Britain agreed, following the visit of the Ministers of Production and Food to Washington in March 1945,[1] did not compromise the Ministry's basic arguments.

V

The foregoing analysis does not seek to endorse the arguments used against the Ministry of Food on any given occasion, nor to deny the strength of the case for maintaining high stocks in the United King-dom even after the end of hostilities. It is possible to argue that the policy of insurance through stocks had been pressed to a point at which warehousing difficulties (for instance the need to take excep-tional measures against vermin) and upkeep costs represented too high a premium. (As against this, the Ministry must have made a

---

[1] Chapter XIX.

considerable profit on the rising market after the war.) Moreover, one should not forget that, except for whale oil, of which by this time there was hardly any left, it is not practicable to accumulate stocks of the major foods sufficiently large to insure against failures, as distinct from small fluctuations, in supply; there could, that is to say, be no question of protecting the level of consumption by drawing on stocks for any considerable period of time.

The best level of stocks, even so, may be conceded to be a matter of broad judgement rather than calculation, on which it is better to be safe than sorry. But there is much less to be said for basing one's notions of the optimum on misleading ideas about the minimum; a world of difference between asserting that the highest possible stocks are desirable, and continually exaggerating the imminent danger of distribution breaking down. To force minimum levels higher and higher in relation to risks was to compromise the claim that large United Kingdom stocks were in the general interest. It was cold comfort for the Allies to be told at one and the same time that stocks were safe in the United Kingdom against loss through control leakages, but that they could not be diminished because of the dangers to which the country was exposed. In particular, the enhancement of minimum working stocks merely sterilised food by preventing either the Ministry or anyone else from putting it to use. Acknowledgement that the United Kingdom did release one million tons of food to Europe before the end of 1945 must be tempered by the comment that it could certainly have spared more, had need been shown.

One must recognise the difficulties in the way of a realistic calculation of minimum stocks. To allow the Commodity Director the last word on them was, given the organisation of the Ministry, almost inescapable; yet it was almost to guarantee that they would be set too high, if only because each commodity would be treated in isolation. Moreover, a Director might argue thus: 'I shall be expected to put forward a figure greater than the real minimum; therefore I must for my own safety comply with that expectation, lest higher authority force me below it'. As long as that reasoning was conscious it may be admitted that the Ministry suffered no disadvantage beyond a series of statistical contests that might perhaps have been difficult to evade anyhow. But the example of wheat and flour shows clearly how a safety-first policy may be at any rate partly frustrated through self-deception. The obstacles to establishing minimum stock figures that were at once sufficient insurance and yet not vulnerable to criticism were great; but they had to be surmounted if the Ministry were to get full value, both in peace of mind and ability to manœuvre, from its own prudence.

CHAPTER XXII

Ration Changes and Projects, 1942-45

I

IN mid-November 1941 the total fats ration was raised from 8 ounces per head per week to 10 ounces; and the sugar ration from 8 ounces to 12 ounces. On 12th January 1942 these allowances reverted to their former levels, at which they had stood since the summer of 1940. The two changes, together with the withdrawal of a tea ration from children under five, in July 1943, make up the sum total of the effect of the ups and downs following Pearl Harbour on the basic rations of the British household.[1] They measure the effectiveness with which the Ministry of Food defended its minimum standards, and the impossibility, in the growing world food shortage, of improving on them.

Changes not greatly affecting the nominal value of rations or the total food issued were more frequent. In October 1941 the Ministry introduced a milk supply scheme that gave effective priority to children, expectant and nursing mothers, hospitals, schools, and certain classes of invalids, and secured, at any rate, rough justice as between the remainder of consumers. In June 1942 dried egg in packets made its first appearance. In February 1942 a loose rationing scheme for soap, rather on the lines of that for tea, was introduced, in order that fats and oils might be diverted for food. In April the tea scheme was tightened up by enforcing the 'cutting-out' of coupons, which had been abandoned in favour of 'cancellation' in January 1941. (Since the tea consumer was not tied to a retailer, cancellation had proved an inadequate check on consumption. It was not, however, till December 1942 that the cut coupon became the basis for replacement, saving a million pounds of tea a week, or rations for eight million people.)[2] In July, chocolates and sweets were rationed, and in August biscuits were put 'on points'. These last changes illustrate the trend of policy in the years of planned stringency. The large economies had all been made; but, confident in its own machinery, no longer willing to regard any saving, however small, as

---

[1] Cheese is an exception. A flood of supplies from the United States impelled the ration upwards from 2 ounces (June 1941) to a peak of 8 ounces, far above actual consumption, in July 1942. Early in 1943 a fall set in, and from May of that year to the end of the war and after, the ration fluctuated between 2 and 3 ounces.

[2] These arrangements will be examined in Vol. II.

unworthy if it could be fairly spread, and recognising that savings of labour, transport, and 'ancillary materials' such as packing paper, were now perhaps more urgent than those in food itself, the Ministry carried out a process which may best be described as 'paring' food consumption wherever it could be assured that the game was worth the candle. Not all the little economies that were canvassed, or even adopted, may have justified the effort, unless one accepts the argument that in time of national adversity self-denial should be practised on grounds of morale. At any rate, one may allow differences of opinion about minor adjustments to secondary foods. Certainly none of the changes that were made approach in importance the two that went near to being adopted in the worst period of shipping crisis —bread rationing,[1] and the rationing of restaurant meals.

In the last war scientific experts and administrators alike had regarded an unlimited supply of breadstuffs as the foundation of food policy. Sir William Beveridge, in his review of policy in 1936, had gone so far as to make this the one indispensable axiom, given which the level of other rations did not matter. In 1939, Mr. W. S. Morrison, the then Minister of Food, had told the War Cabinet that bread rationing would be 'the last resort of a starving nation'. Everyone agreed, of course, that it would be necessary to ration bread under those extreme but ill-defined circumstances generally termed 'siege conditions', when rationing bread would in effect be rationing hunger, though the Ministry had never really got down to producing a scheme for doing so. The shipping situation in 1942 was not conceived by the Shipping Committee in such apocalyptic terms, and the long debate on bread rationing at this time was really concerned with the problem of waste. It was the economists of the War Cabinet Secretariat, fresh from their successful advocacy of points rationing, who were now eager to suggest that new techniques might render old maxims obsolete even where bread was concerned; and that a substantial economy in flour usage could be achieved by rationing without depriving anyone of sufficient to eat.

The Ministry of Food found these suggestions unconvincing but difficult to refute. Bread rationing might be, as one official said, a steam hammer to crack a nut, or as the Minister himself wrote, 'a suggestion that appeals only to the ignorant'; the difficulty was to prove it so, especially when so many other belligerents had resorted to it as a matter of course. The notion that there was over-eating on a large scale, thanks to the continued production of cakes and pastries, was scouted by the Scientific Adviser, mainly on the ground that there was no evidence that large numbers of adults were putting on weight. Such calculations as could be made of average supplies of food related

---

[1] The introduction of mild bread rationing in 1946 falls outside the scope of the present volume.

to requirements indicated no more than a reasonable margin to cover
inevitable losses, e.g. in distribution and cooking; the country as a
whole, it was urged, was neither over-eating nor otherwise wasting an
undue proportion of its food supplies. The trouble with this type of
argument was that it tended to prove too much, as in an estimate
which showed flour requirements, allowing for no waste at all, at
six per cent. above the actual consumption. Moreover, it rested at
bottom on assumptions about the activity of the population as a
whole (and hence its demand for calories above the minimum to
maintain health[1]) which were incapable of being verified within
sufficiently narrow limits to affect the case. Suppose, for example, a
ten per cent. cut in bread consumption to be imposed; that would
have meant a four per cent. cut in total calories on the average. If
this could have been spread out evenly, it could scarcely have done
harm to anybody; some of it would have been taken up by a reduction in avoidable waste, such as the feeding of bread to hens and
dogs, some more by the consumption of the remaining unrationed
foods such as potatoes, some more by simply eating less and (if necessary) doing less work. How much scope there was for this sort of
squeezing might be argued; but no one could effectively deny that
there was some; and its application might even help to throw light
on what proportion of waste and unnecessary consumption still
remained.

There was force, however, in the view that conventional rationing
methods were incapable of the fine adjustments that would be required. It was axiomatic that bread rationing would have to differ-
entiate between heavy workers, adolescents, young children, and even
perhaps between men and women. This would involve difficult
though not insuperable problems of classification, especially where
heavy workers were concerned; it was for this reason that organised
labour had always set its face against differential rationing. More
difficult to overcome was the variation in requirements between

---

[1] The calorie requirements of an individual depend in general on his or her physical
size and activity combined. The importance of activity is illustrated by the following
table of recommended dietary allowances, drawn up by the National Research Council
of the United States Food and Nutrition Board:

	Man weighing 70 kg. [11 stone approx.]	Woman weighing 56 kg. [8·8 stone approx.]
Sedentary . .	2,500	2,100
Moderately active	3,000	2,500
Very active .	4,500	3,000

(The figures represent net calories per day.)

Evidently the requirements of a whole population can be assessed very differently according to the degree of activity attributed to the various individuals in it. Hence the Scientific
Adviser's express unwillingness to be drawn into argument about average levels of
consumption; he preferred to rely on the argument from body-weight. But this was also
a shaky foundation (apart from the technical difficulties in securing a representative
sample of body-weights over a period); for while over-eating would probably be reflected
by an increase in weight, under-eating might be compensated (within limits) by a fall
in activity, leaving weight unaffected.

individuals of like stature doing the same type of work. In order that the big eaters should not go short, the ration for each category would have to be fixed near the maximum probable requirement. Experience had shown that people tended to take up their rations whether they needed them or not; hence, its opponents argued, bread rationing would either lead to waste (with no reduction or even an increase in total consumption) or cause actual hunger, with all its repercussions on industrial morale and war production. (To the suggestion that potatoes could be used to make up the deficiency, the Ministry replied that there could be no guarantee that the potatoes would be available. Bread and flour constituted the only reliable 'buffer'.)

In principle, this argument was incontrovertible; in practice it assumed that to prescribe an individual ration was to limit individual consumption. It is true that the Ministry had always set itself this aim, and had gone so far as to prohibit the sale or exchange of rations lawfully obtained. Even apart from the ordinary give-and-take in households there was no reason to suppose that this safety-valve of any rationing system had in fact been successfully closed. Hence the picture of widespread hunger following a mild dose of bread rationing was overdrawn. Moreover, the inflexibility of any system based on fixed rations could, the economists urged, be met by putting bread 'on points'. That all breadstuffs should be so treated never seems to have been put forward seriously, but a combination of straight and points rationing had obvious theoretical attractions—for instance the possibility of dealing with special categories by giving them extra points. The Ministry's first reaction was of violent opposition; it was still very anxious about the points scheme, which had only been running a few months; the advent of bread and flour suggested a new disturbance with possibilities of large-scale inflation in demand for bread.[1] Some thought that to put bread on points would make any saving impossible; on the other hand one critic feared that the switch away from bread to other points goods would be troublesome. The Lord President's Committee was firmly told in July that the points scheme was unsuitable for necessities like bread, since the Ministry could not guarantee supplies under it.

There the matter might have rested but for the intervention of the Prime Minister, who suddenly called for a bread-rationing scheme to put an end to waste (which he boldly estimated at half a million tons) using the points system. The War Cabinet itself called for further inquiry by the Lord President's Committee; and the Ministry of Food, while reiterating all the previous objections to rationing, was constrained to admit that a combined scheme of straight and points rationing could be made to work—given time. But the savings to be

---

[1] The supposed inherent tendency of points rationing to inflation is discussed in Chapters XV and XXIII.

expected of it, especially at first, were so problematical that it could not be relied upon to save any shipping at all then and there. The Lord President's Committee agreed that to ration bread immediately would be inexpedient; but the Ministry (without, it seems, specific instructions from Lord Woolton) nevertheless decided to get down to producing a detailed scheme. Reflection seems to have made officials somewhat less chary of points and somewhat less sure that waste was insignificant; there were even one or two who were inclined to support a 'double decker' scheme merely for its psychological effect. The Ministry had still to prepare a last-ditch scheme; perhaps the two tasks might be successfully combined.

The delaying tactics the Ministry had practised from February 1942, when bread rationing was first mooted, till August, when it really got down to work, were inspired less perhaps by the arguments that were avowed, than by consciousness of the administrative difficulties of devising a workable scheme, particularly a mild one directed against waste. However justified, this could not be pressed far by administrators *against* economists, if only because all were agreed that if the worst came to the worst a rationing scheme there must be. The Ministry's efforts during the winter of 1942-43 were concerned with detail rather than with principle. An elaborate scheme combining registration with points was eventually jettisoned in February 1943 in favour of a separate points scheme for breadstuffs alone, under which the cut coupon would serve as the basis for replacement. This was a reversion to first thoughts, for registration had been rejected as unworkable by the very same Division of the Ministry in March 1942.[1] The wider economic issues that bread rationing would raise appear to have been left almost untouched.

For instance, no mention was made of one fundamental difference between rationing bread and rationing other things, namely that one basic product, flour, appears in the shops in various guises with varying degrees of perishability. There was no attempt to consider the effect of rationing on the relative demand for bread, flour and cake; no account was taken of the fact that cake is mostly sold in shops whereas bread is largely delivered to the door. No one considered the implications of the difference between bread-eating England and scone- and cake-eating Scotland. True, the problem of oatmeal was ventilated (perhaps because the Ministry's Director of Bakeries was a Scotsman) but this was a solitary exception. The Ministry might have

---

[1] Bread is bought so frequently that the problem of consumers away from home would be far worse than with any other rationed food. This alone would probably have made a consumer-retailer tie unworkable. Furthermore, bread, flour, and cake, are often habitually bought from different shops. Separate rations and registrations for each of these would be rigid and cumbersome and anyway inappropriate since allocation would have to be in terms of flour. A single registration would distort the pattern of the trade in favour of those who already sold all three varieties of breadstuff.

explored such matters more thoroughly, perhaps, had its dislike of the whole idea been less profound.[1]

The improvement in overseas supplies put an end to bread-rationing proposals for the time being; but in 1946, when bread rationing was thought to be urgently necessary, most of the details had to be worked out afresh, against time.

II

The same criticism—want of a broad economic approach—must be made of a scheme for rationing main meals in restaurants,[2] elaborated in detail during the spring and summer of 1942. The pre-war plans had always envisaged that half a meat coupon (i.e. one-quarter of the weekly ration) would have to be surrendered for each meat meal taken in a restaurant, and the decision not to require this, in 1940, had been almost casual.[3] On various occasions since then the inequity of coupon-free meals had been criticised; but the Ministry had been less and less willing to reverse its decision as time went by and as the habit of eating out became more widespread. The policy deliberately adopted after 1940 of fostering works canteens and communal feeding centres appeared to run clean contrary to any attempt to make the individual eater-out surrender part of his rations. Furthermore, it provided, by means of differential allowances to canteens serving heavy workers, or school dining-rooms, a means of giving these classes of consumer extra food without the invidious complexities of a differential domestic ration. Coupled with the various sumptuary and price regulations directed at luxury establishments, it enabled the Ministry to make out a reasoned case for continuing its policy of

---

[1] The atmosphere is most vividly conveyed in the following letter, written in February 1943:

'A very comic meeting yesterday with the Scientists. They looked with great interest at all the tables in . . . [X's] . . . paper, and looked learned and said, "are these all right?" to which . . . [X] . . . replied, "Yes", and then they took the tables for granted, so that as far as scientific advice was concerned they really contributed nothing. However, when given their heads they all got very interested in policy and quite a number of them said, "What is the object of all this? It seems clear that it will save no bread, so how does it improve on the existing situation, why do it'?"

'At this the Ministerial end of the table sat and smirked and found it rather difficult to reply, since it really reflected the Department's views. No very convincing case was put up by anybody for the scheme at all. [Y] . . . tried lamely to suggest that it might possibly have a one per cent effect, and might be keyed up to produce more saving later, and . . .[Z, an economist from the War Cabinet offices] tried to be convincing. He alone urged that the inclusion of the points element . . . had merit in introducing elasticity.

'In so far as it produced a contribution, the debate will probably serve to defer bread rationing'.

[2] i.e. those containing meat, bacon, poultry, game or fish.

[3] See Chapter VIII.

restricting supplies to the establishment, while leaving its meals coupon-free. Inasmuch as the total rationed food consumed in catering establishments other than factory, school and similar canteens was of the order of three per cent. of all supplies, the Ministry could maintain that such luxury feeding as remained consumed such an infinitesimal amount of food as hardly to justify the administrative complications of the coupon.[1] In short, to demand coupons for meals would inconvenience the trade and the public without saving any food worth mentioning.

The force of these arguments will be evident; their weakness lay rather below the surface. For instance, the Ministry held that to exact the surrender of meat coupons in restaurants would not enable it to curtail supplies to butchers, because it could not know how many of each butcher's customers would elect to eat out in any given week and must therefore issue him enough meat to supply them all. Yet Rationing Division had all along insisted, and was to continue to insist, on a periodic return of stock and sales by butchers designed for no other purpose than the adjustment of buying permits to actual sales instead of to nominal entitlement.[2] Even had this not been so, the proportion of eaters-out, though it would vary from locality to locality, would certainly not do so from week to week, or from butcher to butcher, so much as to make it impossible to apply a suitable cut to local permits.

For all its show of firmness the Ministry was less than happy about coupon-free meals; their existence was an affront to officials rightly proud of their achievements in fair distribution. Moreover, there might come a time when the critics could no longer be put off. If differential rationing of bread, or perhaps other foods, had to be introduced, coupons for meals must, it was felt, come too. Indeed, as officials worked simultaneously at schemes for all these, they developed a conviction that the meals scheme should come first.

To link coupons for meals with the newly-introduced points scheme provided a way of evading the dilemma, that had hitherto seemed to face administrators, namely that to grant meals coupons to everyone over and above the domestic ration might merely increase the consumption of meals, while to make them an alternative to it might lead to the accumulation of surplus rations and their illicit sale by the retailer. It was not thought possible to put meals directly 'on points', because this would complicate the allocation machinery, both for points goods and for caterers' supplies; moreover, the 'sudden death' of points coupons at the end of each ration period,

---

[1] The Economic Section of the War Cabinet Office suggested meals rationing as a contribution to shipping economy.

[2] It is true that there was no means of verifying this return, but the Division would never admit that it was without value. This question will be further discussed in Vol. II.

and their physical attachment to the ration book, made them an inconvenient form of meals currency.

Some sort of token, to be bought with points coupons, presented obvious attractions; but neither the Plastics Control nor the Mint could offer much hope of producing several hundred millions of tokens quickly. The shortage of raw material and of suitable plant were both serious obstacles. Pressed to think again, the Plastics Control was able to suggest a firm that could produce tokens of dyed celluloid in a matter of months; and it was thereupon decided to ask the consent of the Minister and the Treasury to place an order for the tokens as a precautionary measure in advance of securing Cabinet sanction to introduce the scheme. So sure were all concerned that coupons for meals were inevitable and the scheme workable that consent to the expenditure (estimated at £35,000)[1] was readily obtained. The order for 200 million celluloid 'washers' (an accurate description as well as a convenient subterfuge) together with wooden rods and stands on which they could be threaded, was placed in July and completed towards the middle of December 1942; they were distributed in stores throughout the country.

Meantime the scheme itself underwent various refinements and alterations of detail. Lord Woolton was not to be hustled by his now enthusiastic officials into putting the scheme before his colleagues earlier than the time he judged to be ripe. His initial reason for holding it up was the fiasco of the Beveridge fuel rationing proposals in the spring of 1942; and several times later in that year he repressed efforts to bring it forward again. It was well that officials were granted this extra time for thought, for, as the chief architect of the scheme himself put it, 'the number of little problems is legion'. Some of them concerned its mechanics, for instance whether the 'purchase' of tokens should take place elsewhere than at the food office or sub-office and what the caterer was to do with them. Others comprised consequential amendments to the existing control of establishments; for instance, the meat allowance in respect of 'subsidiary', i.e. coupon-free, meals would disappear, and the 'five night rule' under which persons staying more than five nights at a hotel had to surrender all their rations for a week, would necessarily have to be amended to a 'seven night rule' or alternatively be abolished altogether. Again, there were such questions to settle as whether extra points, and if so how many, should be given to special classes of consumer; whether the Ministry could now dispense with that thorn in its flesh, the special cheese ration given to manual workers not having access to canteens; and what could be done about members of H.M. Forces fed in mess, who would have no points with which to buy tokens.

---

[1] This was an underestimate, since it did not allow for the stands and packing. The actual cost was a little under £50,000.

III

Problems of this sort were easily tackled by Rationing and Catering Divisions. But there were two major features of the scheme that must have given trouble in practice. The first was the indefinite validity of the token, compared with the four weeks' life of the points coupon for which it was interchangeable. Evidently tokens would provide an attractive means of hoarding points purchasing power and hence an unbalancing factor in the points market. An attempt to raise points prices might result in a flight into tokens; a reduction in points prices, or the introduction of an especially attractive points food, would cause the disgorging of token hoards in order that full advantage might be taken of current points entitlement. The Ministry was much exercised about inflation within the points scheme; yet this proposal was likely to undermine the chief safeguard against it.

One's doubts about the wisdom of introducing an undated ration currency linked with points are reinforced on studying the discussion about the rate of exchange of tokens for points coupons.

> 'Any sort of comparison' wrote the official mainly responsible for the scheme 'between the constituents of a meal and the equivalent point purchase of anything else is quite irrelevant; our only object at first is to fix a price which makes it possible for the eater to eat out, and is on the other hand noticeable. From all our points statistics, the Points Branch view is that almost any price, however low, will be most definitely noticeable. The take-up [i.e. of points-rationed foods] is very heavy and the world will know it is giving up something when buying its meal ticket'.

A few weeks later he had shifted his ground:

> 'All my expert colleagues . . . have been very emphatic that the one point per meal which we have fixed so far is much too cheap . . . They are quite right about this. Nevertheless I have hung on to the point figure because without it we should not succeed in letting people have nearly a meal a day, and that would make the scheme so unpopular that it would give us a bad start'.

Even at this low price, however, it was obviously impossible to confine the exchange of tokens to the twenty or twenty-four points coupons alone, since many people would not be able to get enough for their needs; and this led to unequal treatment of those who required a few meals out and those who required many. Six meal tokens it was proposed might be obtained by surrendering a week's points; but four more by surrendering coupons and registration for meat; while hotel residents, obliged to surrender all their rations, would get five more tokens, or fifteen in all per week, to be used either in or out of the establishment.

The economic implications of this arrangement will become apparent when it is remembered that the number of points in circulation in any ration period would be something like six times the number of main meals served during that time. There would, that is to say, be plenty of scope and every incentive for a large-scale traffic in tokens in order to avoid sacrificing the meat ration.[1] Existing malpractices, such as the inflation of caterers' returns of meals served, and the evasion of the rules for hotel residents, would be encouraged; the caterer-retailer in particular would enjoy endless possibilities of manipulating tokens and points. Any shrinkage in demand for points foods would be offset by an increase in demand for precisely those straight rationed foods that the Ministry was most anxious to husband. The plan could not but draw attention to the excellent food value represented by even an inferior restaurant meal. Experience had demonstrated the consumer's keen eye for a points bargain; to put meals on points, though indirectly, was to bring them into the foreground of his conscious calculation—a position too delicate to be exposed by any anomalies in their price.

The admission, however belated and reluctant, that the points price of meals was too low must logically have led to a reconsideration of the whole scheme, had it ever been considered on the plane of economic strategy. But no one had thought out the economic implications of rationing meals, i.e. of establishing by forced exchange some equilibrium between the eater-in and the eater-out; in this broader field of policy there had only been retrogression from the original simple proposal that half a meat coupon be surrendered for each meat meal. That (which had survived as a somewhat incongruous part of the new scheme) had the very solid merit that it neither disturbed the remainder of the rationing scheme nor was inconsistent with the reasonable requirement that he who takes all his meals in a hotel shall surrender all his rations. Indeed, these two taken together might have provided the basis for a solution of the problem of eating out that was both equitable and economically workable.

Such a solution, however, would have been far too drastic for ready acceptance at this late stage of the war, as the reception of the tokens scheme by the Trade Union Congress Advisory Committee, to whom it was submitted early in 1943, clearly showed. The last thing the representatives of organised labour wanted was equality between the eater-in and the eater-out. Their idea of a suitable *quid pro quo* for the abandonment of coupon-free meals was a bonus of ten extra points per month for all 'gainfully occupied workers', instead of

---

[1] This traffic was bound to arise, of course, merely by reason of the limitation of exchanges to the food office. At the time the scheme was abandoned the Ministry was considering modifying this requirement.

the four extra points for manual workers proposed by the Ministry.[1] By the time their comments were received (April 1943) the improvement in shipping prospects was about to render any scheme otiose. The tokens were held in store until August 1944, when, in response to an appeal from the Ministry of Supply for the storage space they occupied, it was agreed that they might be disposed of—'for grinding down'.

---

[1] This was in addition to the four extra points per head per month to be given to all consumers to offset the introduction of a new commodity (meals) into the scheme.

CHAPTER XXIII

Points Rationing, 1942-45

I

THE main lines on which points rationing was to operate for the remainder of the war had been settled as early as the summer of 1942.[1] Various foods, of which the most important perhaps was biscuits, were to be put on points during the remainder of the war; defeated candidates for inclusion ranged from kippers to bread and flour.[2] The one major change, affecting the public only remotely and incalculably, but the trade intimately, was the scrapping of the voucher system and its replacement by what was known as 'points banking'.

Points banking was something more than an ingenious administrative device; it was an attempt to solve an economic problem that had been troubling officials ever since their unhappy experiences with dried fruit. The indications of general points inflation that were held to be apparent at that time were put down to the perennial validity of the voucher. Retailers, it was thought, would tend to hoard vouchers until they smelt a points 'bargain', and thus render the scheme liable to be upset by a sudden rush of demand. This fear that any latitude given the consumer or the trader might leave the Ministry powerless in the grip of incalculable hostile forces does not appear to have been warranted. No doubt, retailers, like housewives, would spend their points income as wisely as they could; why should not they? The Ministry, by its control over points values and total new issues of points, had automatically the last word; it could at any time squeeze out any excess that seemed to be piling up in the shops, or protect its stocks against depletion. This control was in no real sense weakened by the impossibility of making an exact count of the vouchers outstanding in the hands of the trade at any moment, nor did it need reinforcement by administrative restriction of supply; moreover, none of the 'points foods' were necessities of life. Even so, the Ministry—its 'trade' element no less than its 'official' element— was mistrustful of such indirect and flexible methods, and uncomfortable without the sense of having things well in hand that is furnished

---

[1] Chapter XV.

[2] Bottled mussels, on the other hand, were for a long time included. 'I don't think', minuted an Assistant Secretary in October 1943, 'we could possibly consider taking bottled mussels off points for the country as a whole'.

by a plenitude of statistical information. A search began very early for means of replacing the unaccountable voucher by some sort of banking system that would show exactly where each trader stood, and provide means of tying the inflation bogey hand and foot. A further attraction of such a scheme was found in the thought that it would save paper.

An opportunity for experiment presented itself in the scheme for rationing chocolate and sweets, which was to come into force at the end of July 1942. This had originally been worked out by the trade during the summer of 1941, when the group *v.* points controversy was in full swing; and it had been approved by Ministers as early as 29th August, only to be held up while the possibility of rationing tobacco jointly with sweets was explored. At the end of November the Lord President's Committee had decided that sweets rationing should not wait on tobacco, but the Prime Minister then stepped in and vetoed the sweets rationing scheme. In April 1942 the war situation caused the tobacco rationing project to be revived; and this time Mr. Churchill agreed that a 'personal points rationing' scheme[1] might be introduced that could start with sweets and be extended to tobacco if the need arose.

It was this projected combination that gave sweets rationing its official title and brought it under the control of those responsible for points rationing proper. As introduced, it was a straight ration by weight with cut coupons and no registration, just like the revised system for tea introduced in April 1942: it lacked the one salient feature of points rationing, adjustment of supply to demand by differential points prices. Moreover the manufacturing side of the trade was thoroughly well organised. A non-voucher technique was, therefore, at its least hazardous; and especially attractive to Points Rationing Division because, owing to the size of container in which wholesale confectionery is packed, vouchers would have had to represent forty-eight or sixty-four points—awkward numbers to manipulate.

The Ministry had no difficulty in persuading the trade to agree to a rudimentary form of banking system for 'personal points.' Each retailer would have an account at the food office, which he would replenish once every four weeks by depositing the coupons he had collected. He would then draw 'cheques' (transfer forms) against this account in favour of his supplier; the period of validity of these cheques was limited, and he might not draw more than twenty in any one period. A wholesaler would operate in the same way through the Divisional Food Office, into which he would pay the transfer forms obtained from retailers. The responsibility of recording these trans-

---

[1] 'Personal', as distinct from points spent by the housewife on behalf of the whole family.

actions lay, however, not with the 'bank' but with the trader himself. Each period he was given a deposit slip, showing the amount he was entitled to spend; he had to enter his disbursements and payees on this slip, and return it to the food office with the next set of collected coupons. There was no means by which the 'bank' could prevent overdrawing, though it could be penalised after the event by 'docking' the account, or in bad cases by compelling the trader to attend at the food office and have his cheques certified. Furthermore, the food office took the trader's word for the number of coupons paid in; only a sample check was applied to them.

So loose a system was acceptable to the Ministry mainly because the War-time Associations of the industry exercised a tight grip over manufacturers' output, and any increase in demand from lower down the chain of distribution would at once arouse suspicion and inquiry. The points scheme proper presented far more complications, on account of the number of different commodities and types of trader it covered. The Ministry's first thoughts—put on paper before the introduction of sweets rationing—had embodied taking advantage of the proposed limitation of suppliers under the Sector Scheme,[1] adding to it a limited life for retailers' and possibly wholesalers' points cheques, and the validation by the food office of each cheque. (Even so, the food office would not have counted the coupons surrendered, but merely verified that the trader was not overdrawing their points value as declared by him.) Retailers' protests brought about a postponement of the Sector Scheme and thus undermined the banking proposals; retailers also objected to the suggestion that they settle their points accounts only once each ration period; this, they pointed out, would lead to points being frozen in the hands of wholesalers whenever an order could not be fulfilled.

The Ministry thereupon offered to do without cheque validation by the food office (except as a sanction for an offending trader) and to allow up to say thirty cheques to be drawn each period. The majority of retailers' representatives were now prepared to accept the scheme; but an outcry arose from wholesalers, who claimed that the existing voucher system was working satisfactorily and that the proposed banking procedure was too rigid and too complicated.[2] Again the Ministry hesitated to put so unacceptable a scheme into force:

'I have thought and thought' wrote one official to another 'about what would be the right answer. My mind goes round in circles. Somehow or other I cannot bring myself to disregard the almost

---

[1] Chapter XXVI below.

[2] It was a retailer, however, who made the most pungent criticisms; 'it would', he said, 'impose enormous additional work on the local food offices; the scheme as it has run for the past ten months is too simple for the Ministry and with their usual utter disregard for paper and labour must have a more complicated one. . . . To talk too of points inflation is sheer nonsense . . . any shortage of points goods is easily remedied by the alteration in number of points required and the supply and demand thereby stabilised'.

unanimous and oft-repeated warnings of the wholesalers. . . . Your discovery that banking will actually involve more paper than vouchers has also somewhat unnerved me'.

It was agreed (October 1942) to wait and see how banking of personal points worked out in practice.

The original motive for introducing points banking—fear of inflation—had, by the spring of 1943, been replaced by its opposite; a feeling that there was insufficient credit in existence to guarantee free movement of points foods. Trade representatives were now vociferous in their complaints of a 'points shortage'. One would, indeed, expect that over a period of time accidental losses of vouchers and mistakes in calculation would of themselves bring about a gradual reduction in the available points currency, for all that it was offset by the 'rounding-up' process whereby odd numbers of coupons were exchanged for vouchers valid to the next 100 above. A similar process of gradual credit shrinkage was to make itself apparent in the personal points scheme, where there was no complicating factor of points pricing. Nevertheless, it seems probable that the apparent deflation, like the apparent inflation of the previous year, was mainly a symptom of maladjustment between the supply and points price of particular foods. Then, a run on dried fruit had resulted from a refusal to supply the full demand for canned meats and fish; now, the overpricing of certain unpopular lines was absorbing the trade's purchasing power and making it impossible for it to take up the goods the public wanted. The remedy lay either in reducing the points price of the hard core of unsaleable stocks or in raising the price of the remainder: the disease could not be cured by manipulating the total amount of points currency in circulation. But the zealots for points banking within the Ministry were now reinforced by retail grocers' representatives who had become convinced that a banking system would end the points shortage, and who objected to frequent changes in points values as disturbing.

By April 1943 officials had evolved a new version of points banking that eliminated the main bugbears of the earlier scheme—the freezing of unspendable points higher up the chain and the limit on the number of retailers' transactions. The retailer would still have his points account at the food office, made up monthly. But it would be debited, not by a cheque drawn in favour of the supplier, but by a points invoice sent by the supplier to the retailer on a prescribed form, after despatch of the goods. Any unspent points would be carried forward to the next period; and any credit adjustments that the Ministry might desire to make could be based on the evidence of, and readily operate through, traders' accounts. Under this system a retailer would be able to order quite freely within the limits set by the state of his account; even at the beginning of a ration period, when his total credit had yet to be determined by the food office, he would be safe in ordering up to the points value of coupons collected in the previous month. (This enabled the Ministry to delay the balancing of points accounts by food offices to the second week of the ration period, the personal points accounts having to be dealt with in the first week.) The new proposals were welcomed by the trade generally (though some wholesalers were sceptical or openly hostile)[1] and points banking duly came into operation on 19th September 1943.

II

The advocates of points banking had all along claimed that it alone could throw a clear light on the problem of points credit; but in practice its introduction had the opposite effect. The reasons for this can only be brought out by a close, and necessarily complicated analysis. (Those who wish to omit such technicalities should turn at once to Section IV, p. 304.)

It must be understood that the changeover from 'cash' to 'credit'— from voucher payments to four-weekly accounts settled in arrears— in itself necessitated an initial grant of credit to traders other than retailers. The retailer's position remained unaltered,[2] since he continued to collect points which he could begin to spend immediately after the end of a ration period. (In practice, indeed, there was nothing to prevent him ordering goods for future delivery against points with which he would be later credited.) The wholesaler, however, was not able to use points owed him by the retailer in respect of any one period until the next period but one, i.e., four weeks after they had been debited to the retailer's account and eight weeks after the latter had 'paid them in'. There was, that is to say, no clearing system providing for the almost simultaneous settlement of Divisional and Local points accounts; as if a joint-stock bank were to insist that four weeks must elapse between paying a cheque into one's account and drawing against it.

For multiple shops with a central buying organisation, special arrangements had been made for the transfer of points between branches and the head office. The Ministry, to meet criticisms that to treat these multiples in all respects like a wholesaler and his retail

---

[1] These were mainly provincial wholesalers whose organisation had, through an oversight, not been consulted at an early enough stage in the proceedings.

[2] There was one exception to this, which accounts in part for the grant of initial credit to *all* retailers. It arose where a retailer had been accustomed to exchange coupons into vouchers more often than once a month and would therefore enter the banking system with less than one month's vouchers in hand. Such retailers might find their buying capacity curtailed in the first four weeks of the scheme, if their other points assets (e.g. vouchers in suppliers' hands) were not, as they often must have been, large compared with those of other retailers.

customers, and to require head office to forward a points invoice to each branch in respect of each consignment of points goods, would mean unnecessary paper work, had agreed that they need not maintain an exact balance between the points drawn from any individual branch account and the goods supplied to that branch. At a firm's option, the points account slip (on which a wholesaler would invoice a retailer) might be used as a cheque drawn by the branch in favour of its head office. Though this would save a good deal of duplicate accountancy within the firm concerned, it would not affect the time-lag in the transmission of points:—

POINTS BANKING TIME TABLE

Four weeks' ration period	*Retailer-wholesaler nexus*	*Centrally-buying multiple*
1.	RETAILER collects coupons against goods sold.	BRANCH collects coupons against goods sold.
2.	RETAILER lodges coupons with Food Office and gets credit; places orders with WHOLESALER. WHOLESALER despatches goods, sends account slip (P.C.L.2).	BRANCH lodges coupon with Food Office and gets credit, against which it draws 'cheque' (P.C.L.2) in favour of HEAD OFFICE.
3.	Food Office pays points to WHOLESALER by P.C.L.3.	Food Office pays points to HEAD OFFICE by P.C.L.3.
4.	WHOLESALER lodges P.C.L.3 with Divisional Food Office; acquires credit.	HEAD OFFICE lodges P.C.L.3 with Divisional Food Office; acquires credit.

The eight weeks' delay in settlement meant that wholesalers and centrally-buying multiples, if their trading position were to remain unaltered, would need to be given a 'starting credit' equal to eight weeks' current turnover, in addition to the value of any points assets or stock in hand when the scheme opened. This credit would be automatically wiped out at the end of the eight weeks (except in so far as any of it remained unspent), and hence needed to be distinguished from any credit that it might be desired to give traders for other reasons.

Officials had neither drawn a clear distinction between the two types of credit, nor assessed correctly the effect of the delay. They supposed that a wholesaler's existing points assets (estimated at four weeks' cover on the average) could be used to help bridge the gap, and thus estimated wholesale and multiple credit requirements at only four weeks instead of eight. Since, however, they proposed to give two weeks' extra credit to all traders, the initial grant to wholesalers and multiples was put at six weeks' turnover, calculated, moreover, not on current trade but on the base period 10th January–3rd April 1943. When one wholesaler rightly pointed out, before the scheme began, that so far from granting him credit, the Ministry was restricting his supplies and forcing him to eat into stocks, it was suggested that he did not know what he was talking about.[1] A week or so later

---

[1] A leading multiple raised the same point on 6th September 1943 without effect.

the Ministry discovered that he was right and hurriedly made a grant of three weeks' further credit to wholesalers and centrally buying multiples.[1] It did not admit its mistake publicly but passed the grant off as one to enable traders to take up extra points foods it was releasing. Thereupon the association of independent retailers clamoured for an extra week's credit to them, and 'for the sake of peace'[2] was given it.

This exacerbated the effect of another error that had been made, namely, supposing that the branches of multiples did not require the retail credit given to the independents, but that it had been allowed for in the grant to head offices. This overlooked the patent fact that any credit given to a retailer must in due course accrue to his suppliers.[3] Thus a multiple head office having a basic turnover of say 40,000 points every four weeks would get an initial grant of 90,000 points. After the initial eight weeks of the scheme it would (assuming its turnover to remain constant) have left 10,000 points, which added to the 40,000 points accruing from four weeks' branch trade would give it a total permitted turnover of 50,000 a four-weekly period. A wholesaler similarly placed would be able to collect no less than 70,000 points (four weeks' actual trade *plus* three weeks' starting retail credit) from his retailers, making a total permitted turnover of 80,000 points.

Where a multiple's stocks were ample, or its points trade stationary or declining, these provisions might be slow in making themselves felt. The first to feel a squeeze would be those multiples whose turnover had increased between 3rd April and 19th September 1943 and whose stocks were not high enough to allow them to be run down, i.e., converted into retail sales that would yield points income to swell the banking account. (It was an anomalous result of the banking scheme that it penalised any liquidation of stocks that had occurred before its introduction, and encouraged subsequent liquidation.) It is this, and not an organised agitation as the Ministry hastened to suppose, that explains the especially loud outcry that arose in the Northern Division centred on Newcastle-on-Tyne. Multiples there seem to have been exceptionally short of stock; as early as 22nd November the

---

[1] The Ministry supposed at this moment that to secure parity all round it needed to give four weeks' supplementary credit, but—'We had always been frightened at the size of the multiples' central accounts and if they had been given eight weeks' working credit at the beginning they would have been able to swamp the market and clear out all the choicest lines made available in ration period 3 . . . partly because we were afraid of too many points and partly because we foresaw trouble with . . . [the independents] . . . we gave only three weeks' credit'. The element of truth in this argument conceals a fundamentally confused notion of the problem. The way to prevent multiples from stealing a march on independents was to grant them the eight weeks' credit by instalments, not to shrink its total amount.

[2] These are the words of the senior official responsible.

[3] This had been pointed out as early as March 1942 in a discussion on the possibility of inflation through the grant of extra voucher credit.

Divisional Food Office reported that nearly all of them were in a precarious points situation, and was empowered to deal with it by granting temporary 'loans' of points to those in difficulties. But (as might have been expected) this did not mend the position, and there were complaints that multiples and co-operatives were unable to take up the first-hand allocations of points goods that had been made to them. The Divisional Food Office again appealed to Headquarters to allow a grant of say two weeks' points to firms showing need, and pointed out, truly but vainly, that it was the denial of credit to their branches that had put them in this position.

To this Headquarters replied by arguing that there was no question of an allocation to 'multiple or any other retailers' (forgetting that a multiple head office acts as a wholesaler); that an increase of credit to multiples would involve a similar grant to wholesalers; and that any general further increase in points credit would upset distribution. This last argument was, indeed, to be the Ministry's main prop in its refusal to do justice to multiples; yet it amounted to no more than a confession of weakness. The weakness was more real than apparent, since officials thought of themselves as making a concession to multiples instead of remedying a mistake; a true diagnosis would have forced them to brave the criticism of the rest of the trade and at the same time provided them with a convincing reply to it.

The multiple and co-operative national organisations, however, were themselves unaware of the true nature and extent of the dis-crimination; they asked for only one week's extra credit, the equiva-lent of the extra week that had been given to the independents. Even this the Ministry refused; instead it offered a concession under the new procedure it was introducing for the review of individual re-tailers' points capital. Any retailer or multiple[1] claiming to be short of points would be able to make a return of stock on a prescribed form (P.C.L.7). If the points value of this stock, together with the trader's 'bank balance' did not equal a certain minimum figure, the Ministry undertook, provided the trader had not himself been at fault, to make up the deficiency. This figure was fixed at nine weeks' basic turnover for independents, ten weeks' for multiples using a central depot; but though multiples and co-operatives accepted this as fair, it was far from being so. For the total stock of a multiple, both at headquarters and in the branches, was set off against its minimum points capital; as if a retailer should be asked to count towards his minimum a proportion of his wholesale suppliers' stock equal to his share of their turnover. The extra week granted with one hand was more than taken away with the other. Having already placed a lower ceiling on the multiple's turnover, officials were now insisting that it must sink lower than an independent before the Ministry would

---

[1] A similar procedure was applied to wholesalers in November 1944.

come to its assistance. The full effect of the first decision is difficult to measure by reason of the second, but in spite of the harder terms of relief, over half the multiples in the country were estimated to have received refresher grants of points under the P.C.L.7 procedure between June 1944 and April 1945. Only one-eighth of independents qualified for relief during the same period.

There is no need to look further for an explanation of the lower proportion of 'points trade' to registrations among multiples and co-operatives compared with independents, that occasioned so much complaint from the former. What the Ministry attributed to consumer preference must in part at least have been due to its own action in creating an initial maldistribution of points credit. It was the merest good fortune that had placed the greater burden on those whose integrated organisation was best capable of bearing it. No doubt multiples could and did maintain a lower ratio of stocks to turnover than could the retailer-wholesaler nexus; though they failed to maintain their position completely, they did well enough for the Ministry to escape violent criticism.

The discrimination against multiples, coupled with the reference of initial credits to a performance figure already six months' old,[1] accounts also for such phenomena as the overdrawing of points accounts by nearly half the multiples in the London Division by March 1944—no doubt the result of a desperate effort to maintain trade that had expanded by more than the margin of twenty-five per cent. allowed over the datum. Overdrawing, though not on this scale, was to become chronic in the points scheme; and though the Ministry was careful to select only the most heinous, inexcusable and repeated cases for prosecution, it found difficulty in convincing many courts that anything more than a technical offence had been committed.[2] Indeed, it had no ready reply to the trader who should claim that his overdrawing was to meet demand, not to stimulate it, and that there was no good reason why the Ministry should compel him to turn away lawful custom. To say that overdrawing tended to dislocate distribution was no more than to assert, without means of proof, that the existing pattern of distribution was something more than arbitrary—was, in fact, right.

Resentment at these prosecutions led trade representatives who had been foremost in clamouring for the introduction of points banking to lament publicly the passing of the voucher and accuse the Ministry of creating unnecessary crimes. Officials, naturally resenting

---

[1] It is only fair to add that it was the retailers, including a majority of multiples, who rejected a Ministry offer to re-assess credits on an up-to-date basis.

[2] One frequent occasion of overdrawing was unsolicited or excess deliveries by suppliers, to return which could not only have occasioned waste of transport but might injure the retailer's chances of obtaining further supplies. Asked to advise what a trader should do in such a case, the Ministry declined to reply.

this attack, more especially from such a quarter, replied that points banking was a necessary control like any other; that traders who overdrew were, in effect, poaching on other traders' preserves; and that anyway, the law had got to be obeyed. No doubt the majority of those prosecuted deserved it, for the Ministry sifted its cases with great care and patience.[1] What is more doubtful is whether it would not have done better to allow more latitude by, say, balancing accounts over three or four ration periods, and thus get rid of a good deal of the minor harassing of petty offenders that had to go on. Such rigidity in small matters accorded ill with the rough and ready basis on which the whole structure had been built.

III

As a result of these controversies, the Ministry built up a theory of points credit by which it sought to justify its treatment of different classes of trader, and the periodic adjustments it made to meet, for instance, changes in the total points allowed to consumers. It would indeed be surprising if such a theory, worked out after the event, should stand up to logical analysis, for it could only do so if the decisions it sought to justify had been, by good fortune, wholly reconcilable one with another. And, in fact, for all its diagrammatic explanation and special terminology, the Ministry's treatment of the problem was over-simplified.[2] Three different factors—a trader's physical stocks and unspent balances, his four-weekly points turnover, and the delay in settlement affecting wholesalers and multiple head offices—were all lumped together and referred to as constituting 'points capital'. Thus it was laid down that while an independent retailer required eight weeks' working points capital, a wholesaler needed twelve, and a centrally buying multiple sixteen. The ten weeks' minimum cover in stock and points, prescribed for multiples and wholesalers under the P.C.L.7 procedure, were spoken of as being really equal to eighteen weeks' and fourteen weeks' respectively.

This addition of the delay in settlement to the presumed resources of certain classes of trader served only to darken counsel, for all that it was qualified by an explanation that the extra capital was 'frozen in the pipeline'. What had not been realised was the transient nature of the original starting credit, which only increased a trader's purchasing power to the extent that it was in excess of the delay in settling accounts. Despite the disclaimer implied in the statement

---

[1] The sanction originally proposed, namely, the operation of an offender's account by the food office, was not used, perhaps from lack of staff. To impose a fine in points —another possible penalty—might hurt innocent customers as much as the retailer.

[2] A shortened exposition is to be found in the Ministry's 'Explanatory Notes' on the Scheme (F. 718 and 718A) circulated to the trade.

about frozen credits, officials never grasped this fact, as is clear from their practice. They tended on the one hand to exaggerate the amount of credit available to wholesalers and particularly to multiple head offices; on the other, they under-estimated the decisive effect at the wholesale stage of any adjustments in retailers' accounts, whether by the grant of extra credit or by a change in the total points allowed to the consumer.

This led to undue complication in the management of traders' points accounts. To give but one example: early in 1945, the points ration was reduced by one-sixth (i.e., from twenty-four to twenty points a four-week period); a change that was, of course, reflected at once in points collected by retailers, and eight weeks later in whole-salers' and multiple head offices' points receipts. Considering the number of uncertainties affecting traders' purchasing power, the Ministry could surely have afforded to ignore the temporary enhance-ment of it that would result; more particularly as traders would know that a shrinkage in demand was coming and might be ex-pected not to spend up to the limits of their accounts. Nevertheless, it not only wrote down the current accounts of wholesalers and multiples by one-sixth immediately, but also deducted an equal amount from the first four weeks' points accruing to them at the reduced rate (i.e., for one period they received only sixteen points to cover a twenty-points entitlement.) The intention was to force them to liquidate part of their points reserves to bring these into roughly the same ratio as previously to their turnover. This device was certainly ingenious, but equally certainly ill-suited to the Ministry's real purpose, namely to reduce excessive stocks. For the larger the stock in terms of turnover, the less it would be affected by a levy calculated on turnover, and *vice versa*; that is to say, discrepancies of stock as between one trader and another could not but be increased.

IV

It may be granted that the points banking system settled down to work tolerably well for all its underlying misconceptions. That it would have worked better if its creation had been informed by a less narrow type of expertise—that of the economist, say, instead of that of the accountant—is beyond doubt. Even so, it seems questionable whether it could ever have achieved an accuracy, certainty, and adaptability that would give it a decisive advantage over vouchers. If it had embodied a scientific regulation of credit, based on an exact knowledge of the points position of each trader and related to his current needs, its utility would have been undoubted; overdrawing would not only have been condemned as stultifying the bases of calculation, but as manifestly unnecessary. Any approach to this perfection was out of the question from the outset. Lack of manpower compelled the Ministry to take the word of the trader for all but a small sample of points paid in—which made the occasional warning or prosecution appear the more arbitrary.

An elaborate structure of statistical returns, built up on shaky foundations, had thus to serve as the basis for the deliberate manipulation of effects which, under the voucher system, would have been automatic. For a complete self-regulating adjustment of demand from the retail end was substituted a system requiring positive intervention to meet all but the most gradual changes, e.g., in population within a given district. The routine handling of pieces of paper which, however numerous, were simple to understand, was replaced by a procedure which at its simplest required the application of ingenious arithmetical formulae (e.g., the P.C.L.7 calculations) and in its more refined forms required more concentrated mental effort than busy officials were capable of giving it. Want of accuracy in detail was necessarily matched by vagueness in total; for instance, the amount of points credit unspent, or immobilised by reason of delivery delays or inability to fulfil orders, could only be guessed at. In short, points banking, so far from clearing up uncertainties, contributed some fresh ones of its own. Its latent inflationary possibilities were greater, not less, than those of the voucher system it had superseded. Indeed, it was wholly inconsistent with the maintenance of any direct relationship between consumer demand, as reflected in retailers' buying policy, and the proportion of different points foods released to the trade. So much loose credit lying about could only be tolerated on condition that the amount of food issued by the Ministry was rigidly controlled both in total and in detail.

Points banking was thus at once a result of and an occasion for the inflexibility that had come to be characteristic of the whole points rationing scheme. Though this inflexibility must be attributed in great part to the want of conviction with which the scheme had been introduced, it must be recognised that the Ministry would have encountered considerable obstacles if it had persisted with freer methods. One was the concentration and zoning proposals,[1] which implied the fixing not merely of national, but also regional quotas of production for such goods as biscuits, cereal breakfast foods, and syrup and treacle. While distribution of these was regional, their points price, for obvious reasons, must be national; and the most watchful adjustments of supply must therefore constantly be made if local shortages or gluts were to be avoided. Again, frequent changes in points values disturbed and confused the trade; each time anything was reduced in points price, the Ministry was faced with a clamour

---

[1] See Chapters XXV and XXVI.

for compensation for loss of points, clamour which, as a general rule, it firmly resisted, since any sustained losses could be redressed under the P.C.L.7 procedure for individual traders.[1]

Fine adjustments were in any case impossible in a system whose units of account—for reasons of simplicity—were so large in terms of individual income. The smallest possible change in price, e.g., of one point up or down—was equal to one-twentieth or one-twenty-fourth of a whole four-weekly points ration—as if a shilling were the smallest coin in a system where nobody was allowed more than £1 a month. Since there was a general feeling that pointing should be more or less by weight, this was apt to lead to great swings in the values of high pointed items like canned salmon.[2]

Persons living alone were especially hit by changes in price and by the indivisibility of canned and 'pre-packed' articles. Considerations like this made inroads into the logic of the points price system for items like canned milk. Were the Ministry to market canned milk at its economic points price, these 'singletons' could only get it at a disproportionate sacrifice of other goods for that particular period; if it chose on the other hand to keep the points price low, they did at least get the chance of an occasional 'bargain' by favour of the grocer. Rather than compromise the scheme, it might have been better to devise *ad hoc* arrangements for such commodities. Semi-perishables like biscuits went stale if pointed too high, under the counter if pointed too low. The Ministry was to confess failure in these matters very early when it withdrew its disapproval of the reservation of points goods for a trader's registered customers; a more obvious symptom was the prevalence of queues for biscuits at chain stores. Again, it was a denial of the original intentions of points rationing that a housewife, tendering the points value of say, a pound of sultanas, should be told she could only have half a pound. These maladjustments, later experience was to show, could be much reduced by a deliberate effort to create a 'buyer's market' in points foods.

If the undoubted popular success of points rationing appears somewhat dimmed in the light of close analysis, the explanation lies largely in the first months of its existence, when it was deprived of skilled nursing. That it represented a great improvement on the anarchy that preceded it is undeniable; but so would have any device that restricted individual expenditure on a wide range of foods. The

---

[1] Though this was obviously the right, and indeed the only practicable course, one of the arguments used to defend it was dubious, namely, that traders' buying policy was at fault if they found themselves overstocked with unpopular goods and had to take a heavy points loss on them. For (*a*) the trader frequently had to take what he could get, (*b*) the miscalculation of points values was not his, but the Ministry's.

[2] The smallest significant change in the points value of a pound of red salmon would be eight points; the least possible four, if quarter-pound tins were to move in proportion. (There was considerable indignation when, for a time, a pound and half-a-pound of pink salmon were given the same points value.)

reason for adopting points rationing, instead of the numerous cumbersome alternatives that had been proposed, was that it offered to the consumer freedom of choice, and to the controller and trader an absence of minute regulation. In practice the first advantage was restricted and the second nullified. The 'flexible coupon system' that Mr. Churchill had welcomed had been converted into a complex of detailed ingenuities that contrived to enmesh the retailer in paper returns while leaving largely to him the scheme's main job—fair distribution of points foods between one customer and another. Later efforts, strenuous though they were, to remedy what came to be admitted as a defect were hindered by the legacy of the past.

CHAPTER XXIV

The Control of Manufactured Foods: Food Standards and Labelling Reforms

I

THERE could be no better example of the distance the Ministry of Food was to travel from the original concept of limited liability for a comparatively few 'principal foods', or of its mixed motives and feelings in the process, than its dealings with the very numerous secondary foodstuffs, such as biscuits, custard powder, pickles and sauces, soft drinks, and flavouring essences, that make up so large a portion of the grocer's stock-in-trade. Step by step it moved from merely supplying all or part of the raw materials used by these 'manufactured foods'[1] to an almost complete control of their ingredients, output, packaging, labelling, and price. Sometimes it rationed them also. In doing these things, the Ministry was influenced by stringencies of supply; by the need for economies in labour and transport; by the need to protect the public against exploitation in prices or quality; and by an enlightened opportunism which saw in the very existence of war-time controls a means to make permanent reforms in the standard of manufactured food offered for sale.

Control of food manufacturers began from early 1940 onwards, with control of their raw material, notably fats, sugar, and starch, supplies of which were furnished through permits issued by the Commodity Division. But the principles on which permits were granted to different classes of 'trade user' were at first rough and ready and unco-ordinated. Allowances were simply based on a more or less arbitrary proportion of pre-war usage, determined by the supply position of the raw material and the particular Division's notion of the importance of the final product. Little or no regard was had to the relation, for instance, between supplies of sugar and fat for cakes and biscuits, or sugar and raw cocoa for chocolate.[2] No control

---

[1] 'Manufactured foods' is taken here to exclude such products as flour, margarine and refined sugar, although they, no less than say baking powder or table jellies, are manufactured. The border-line is one of convenience rather than logic.

[2] This situation was noted by the Select Committee on National Expenditure (*loc. cit.* p. 44) in the spring of 1940:
'We were told that . . . chocolate makers had been allotted seventy per cent. of their normal requirements in sugar as compared with only sixty per cent. to the boiled sweet makers. The Ministry, it was stated, could not go further than this because it would have meant too much dislocation in existing business. The Minister had himself received a deputation from all manufacturers using sugar and of course there was a "pull devil, pull baker business between condensed milk, boiled sweets, pastry cooks and all the rest of it."'

was exercised over the use manufacturers made of the ingredients allotted to them, the quantities of the finished product they produced, or the prices charged at any stage of distribution.

In June 1940, when the re-introduction of control over margarine and cooking fats raised for the first time the problem of co-ordinating the release of supplies for trade use, the Ministry took over as a going concern the Allocations Control that had been set up for sugar by the Food Manufacturers' Federation and the Manufacturing Confectioners' Alliance, with the intention of using the experience so gained for the benefit of other Commodity Divisions. But the powers of this body remained purely advisory; it had no authority over individual commodity directors, nor was there as yet any means of formulating and enforcing a policy of allocations to secondary food manufacture. A proposal, put forward about November 1940, to abandon the pre-war datum basis of allocation in favour of a system which related a firm's supply of raw materials to the quantity and character of its output, was not pursued because of trade opposition and the formidable amount of work and staff entailed.

So long as supplies remained reasonably ample, minor anomalies and general slackness in the system might be tolerated. But the shortages of raw material, the pressure of demand on manufactured foods as supplies of rationed foods shrank, and the maldistribution resulting from population movements all impelled the Ministry, during the winter of 1940–41, towards a reluctant change of policy. The hasty introduction of a general standstill Order on food prices, the long debates on the extension of rationing that culminated in the introduction of points rationing nearly a year later,[1] were paralleled by a slow, and as yet still piecemeal extension of control at the supply end. One measure, the making of special arrangements to secure priority in raw material supplies to manufacturers of food for the Services, N.A.A.F.I., and Civil Defence, may even have had the effect of further shrinking supplies to the ordinary civilian, by attracting demands for priority that otherwise would not have been made. As early as September 1940 the trade was told of the Ministry's intention of discouraging merely luxury lines and encouraging cheap ones; but during that winter substantial progress in this direction was made only in the well-organised chocolate and sugar confectionery industry. During the first half of 1941, the Ministry could not but debase the quality of certain foods, whether by reducing allocation of raw materials, or as with liquid milk, prohibiting their use except for essential purposes. The future was indeed sketched in more clearly with the avowed adoption during 1941 of national measures designed to save man-power and transport, for these would necessitate interference with the food industries in a detail that few officials had yet contemplated.

---

[1] See Chapters XIV and XV.

W

II

The first impulse to action, however, came from public outcry about the extreme case of the general trend in food manufacture, namely the pullulation of numerous and mainly worthless substitutes for foods that had become scarce during the winter of 1940–41. Some degree of adulteration was indeed forced on food manufacturers by the sheer pressure of unrationed demand, unless they chose, as some reputable firms did, to limit their output or even to withdraw some products from the market altogether. There was a sense in which the manufacturer who used his ingenuity to stretch scarce ingredients by the addition of, say, a little wheat flour was performing a public service. But there was nothing at all to be said in favour of milk substitutes, made of flour, salt, and baking powder, and sold at 5s. a lb., or of onion substitutes containing merely water and a smell. Even products that could claim to be useful, such as egg substitutes made of rice flour or cornflour, colouring matter and baking powder, which was sold even before the war, or meat substitutes composed of yeast extract, cereal filler, and perhaps soya flour, might still be misleadingly labelled and excessively priced.

In theory, the makers could be prosecuted by local authorities under the Food and Drugs Act of 1938;[1] but that Act had come into operation after war had broken out and no labelling Regulations had been made under it that would assist would-be prosecutors to determine whether a *prima facie* case for action existed. Local Authorities were hesitant, therefore, to take offenders to court; a single prosecution that failed might, in effect, secure immunity for the product over the whole country; and in any event the penalties provided were not a sufficient deterrent in face of scarcity profits. Moreover, of course, the Act did not provide for any control of price. In October 1941, after consultation with the Health Departments that were primarily concerned, the Ministry of Food made an Order[2] to come into force almost immediately, forbidding the manufacture or sale of any substitute food except under an individual licence prescribing formula, label and price.

The Substitutes Order[3] was effective in arresting the trade in worthless substitutes claiming to be substitutes; but it could readily

---

[1] 1 & 2 Geo. 6. ch. 6. Local authorities might prosecute for *false* labels before the passage of this Act; it added a power to prosecute for misleading labels, and also empowered the Minister of Health and the Secretary of State for Scotland, the Ministers responsible for the enforcement of the Act by Food and Drugs Authorities, to make labelling regulations generally.

[2] As late as August 1941 officials were still taking the line, apropos of providing ingredients for egg substitutes, that it was not the Ministry's business to enforce the law of foods and drugs.

[3] S.R. & O. 1941, No. 1606 (11th October 1941).

be evaded by re-labelling. The Ministry was soon embarrassed by having to inform makers of unsatisfactory products that these were outside the provisions of the Order, thus pointing out the loopholes in its own regulations. Anomalous cases arose of an identical product being marketed under different labels only some of which required to be licensed. Those immediately responsible for working the Order were not long in concluding that effective protection could only be given to the public if all manufactured foods were required to comply with the same conditions of licence after scrutiny. Elsewhere in the Ministry the magnitude of such a task aroused apprehension; in the summer of 1941 it was still hesitating on the brink of a wider extension of rationing, or indeed of further controls of any sort, and still had hopes that by giving manufacturers of, for instance, cakes and biscuits more raw materials, and encouraging the production of more economical varieties, it could bridge the gulf between supply and demand. Even before the darkening import prospects at the end of that year put paid to these hopes, the demand that the food trades should surrender more man-power, and pressure on the Ministry to get on with concentration schemes[1] meant that it must make up its mind which food industries it wanted to keep in being and what level of output was desired from each. It could not even begin to do this on the knowledge already in its possession; but fear that a full inquiry might be unwieldy as well as unpopular, combined with the need to get some sort of figures as early as possible, limited the scope of its first approach to manufacturers. Only the leading firms, and those already licensed under existing control orders, were asked to furnish details of output and man-power; they were not asked what ingredients they employed.

When, therefore, the Food Supply Board[2] prescribed, for the guidance of executive divisions, a series of tonnage figures to which the total production of a number of manufactured foods should conform in the calendar year 1942, it was relying largely on guesswork. Moreover, there was no means of ensuring, for those manufactured foods not yet controlled other than by allocation of certain raw materials, that actual production would correspond even reasonably closely to the levels laid down. It was indeed decided that, for foods that should be included in the points rationing scheme that had just been introduced, the output of each manufacturer should be determined in advance and not be allowed to adjust itself to consumer demand as regulated by points price—a decision which was, perhaps motivated largely by the wish to make the points scheme foolproof. During 1942 the output of canned beans and more especially biscuits was limited under this rule; the rationing of chocolates and sweets in

---

[1] Chapter XXV.
[2] Chapter XVII.

July carried with it a similar limitation on another large user of raw materials. But it was not until November 1942 that the Ministry began an inquiry into standardising the procedure of allocation of raw materials for all manufactured foods, and not until the end of February 1943 that the results of the inquiry were ordered to be put into effect. Even so, much detailed work had to be done before the principle, only now generally laid down, that each allocation of raw material should be conditional upon its use in a specified final product, could be made legally binding and the structure of control completed.

From the point of view of economy in ingredients, this tidying up process meant little or nothing; the last supply cuts of any size were those for biscuits and sweets in the late summer of 1942. From then on the variations in manufacturers' supplies, though they might affect individual products severely, were of small account otherwise. Some of them, such as the withdrawal of sugar allocations from cereal breakfast foods and sweetened flour mixtures,[1] that might have been intelligible as part of a policy of ruthlessness with inessentials, became little more than gestures by themselves. Could it really be said, at the time of Pearl Harbour and the fall of Singapore, that the production of colourings and ready-packed cake and pudding mixtures must go on for the sake of 'morale', 'consumer convenience', or 'variety in diet'? And if so, was not the decision that the axe should fall on table jellies and ice cream[2] alone, as being the only truly dispensable foods, all the more invidious?

In fact, the obstacles to ruthlessness were more formidable than either the apostle of austerity, or the gourmet shuddering at the thought of custard powder and bottled sauces, might willingly admit. For instance, the Ministry could not very well leave the rich man his coffee and take away the poor man's coffee essence; still less could it take away one food manufacturer's livelihood and spare another's without arousing storms of protest. A more technical difficulty lay in the great variety of products a single manufacturer might produce, so that to ban some of them as superfluous might do no more than cause him to work short time and increase his overheads (and hence the cost of the products that remained). For the less well-organised trades, the Ministry still had not sufficient information on which to make distinctions of this sort. Nor was it able to escape into a benevolent neutrality in small matters, if only because the demand for economies in manpower and storage space called for individual decisions about the national importance of this or that firm's pro-

---

[1] The total pre-war usage of sugar in cake and pudding mixtures had been 3,000 tons annually. The import of sugar at its lowest, in 1942, was 774,000 tons.

[2] Ice cream was prohibited in order to save transport. See Chapter XXVI below. Even table jellies were not banned until 1943 (under the Manufactured Foods Order).

duction. At a time when the call was for austerity and the putting of first things first, it must preoccupy itself more and more with a multitude of tiny details that could not be left to settle themselves.

III

While the Ministry as a whole moved slowly towards a general policy for manufactured foods, individual Commodity Divisions had not been idle in promoting control Orders dealing with particular parts of the field in which they, as responsible for a raw material, were interested. To take three examples: Cereals Division administered an Order covering flour mixtures for cakes and puddings; Starch Division one for custard and blancmange powders; Fruit and Vegetable Products Division one for 'soft drinks.'[1] By the summer of 1942 the overlappings and inconsistencies of Orders sponsored in different parts of the Ministry at different times and embodying often pointless and always confusing variations in details of drafting, had become a major nuisance to administrators themselves. From May of that year an approach to uniformity had been secured by making the panel of expert officials concerned in administering the Substitutes Order a focus for consultation with Divisions administering analogous Orders for starch food powders and flour mixtures; but that only made the legal anomalies themselves more manifest.[2] It was, therefore, proposed to introduce a comprehensive order that should replace or forestall piecemeal legislation, and bring not only manufacturers, but packers of food ready for retail sale, under control. Hitherto the exemption of subsequent possessors of a food from the conditions binding the manufacturer had been a frequent source of abuses. Not only was it difficult for a food and drugs authority, faced with an unsatisfactory product, to trace it back through four or five

---

[1] Respectively: The Flour and Flour Mixtures (Licensing and Control) Order (S.R. & O. (1942), No. 348); The Starch Food Powders (Control) Order (S.R. & O. (1941), No. 1742; The Soft Drinks (Licensing and Control) Order (S.R. & O. (1942), No. 1337.

[2] A hypothetical example was given to the Ministry's Orders Committee in May: 'a product consisting of twenty-six per cent. flour and seventy-four per cent. soya flour, if sold as a milk substitute, would come under the Flour Mixtures Order if the manufacturer produced more than ten tons of flour mixtures per annum, but under the Food Substitutes Order if he produced less than ten tons. . . . If . . . sold as a cake improver it would come under both the Soya Flour and the Flour Mixtures Order if the manufacturer produced more than ten tons per annum, but under the Soya Flour Order only if he produced less than ten tons per annum. If the product consisted of twenty-four per cent. flour and seventy-six per cent. soya flour it would come under the Substitutes Order if sold as a milk substitute, but under the Soya Flour Order if sold as a cake improver. . . .' Furthermore, 'it was difficult to determine within one or two per cent. the precise composition of such products'. Again, an egg substitute based on rice flour was licensed under the Substitutes Order; a competing product based on wheat flour under the Flour Mixtures Order. Worse still, a lemonade powder refused a licence as an unsatisfactory lemon substitute might get one from another Division under the Order controlling soft drinks.

agents to the original makers, but such a chain of transactions could not but result in an artificial and exorbitant retail price.

In deference to those who feared that the sheer task of taking returns from, and subsequently licensing, every manufactured food might be overwhelming in extent and perhaps difficult to justify by its tangible results, the new Order, issued in September 1942,[1] was ingeniously drafted so as to give traders the minimum of trouble and the Ministry the maximum freedom of manœuvre. Those not already licensed under an existing control Order or otherwise controlled were obliged to complete a standard form of return giving details of ingredients, processes, packages, prices, current (and where appropriate pre-war) output, and to submit specimens of labels. The making of this return of itself would permit firms to continue manufacture without a specific licence, provided they did not alter formulæ or labels, unless and until the Ministry should appoint a day by Order after which one or more types of product should be licensed, in which case price, formula and label conditions would be imposed by the terms of the individual licence. Any new product, and any change in an existing product, would require to be licensed under the terms of the principal Order. In effect the measure had three objects, apart from tidying up the law. It would enable the Ministry to find out what the facts about manufactured and 'pre-packed' foods were; it would prevent further changes without permission; and it would provide for any further action that might be required.

The intention of the draftsmen had been that the full application of the Manufactured Foods Order to different classes of product should be accompanied by the revocation of the various specific Orders whose overlappings and inconsistencies had caused such confusion within and without the Ministry. Objections to the making of so comprehensive an Order had been overcome partly by the plea that it would lead to a great simplification of control. Various attempts in this direction were made by the Ministry's Orders Committee during 1943, but met with seemingly insuperable, though seldom obviously conclusive, objections. A proposal to revoke the Substitutes Order, for instance, was not pursued because the Ministry's legal advisers could not convince their lay colleagues that all substitutes already licensed could be classified as manufactured foods, and that there was no danger, not merely that the Ministry might lose control of them, but that products already covered by the Manufactured Foods Order might escape by claiming to be substitutes. The majority of Commodity Divisions apparently preferred

---

[1] The Manufactured and Pre-packed Foods Order (S.R. & O. (1942), No. 1863). 'Prepacking' was defined as the packing of food (other than by a retailer for sale on the premises) 'in advance ready for retail sale in a wrapper or container'. ' "Pre-packed" shall be construed accordingly' and did not, as its form might suggest, refer to food *before* it was packed.

to go on working an Order already in operation. The status of foods already under control in September 1942 remained, therefore, for the most part unaltered.

The extension of control, on the other hand, was hindered by difficulties of definition and classification.[1] The five or six thousand items for which returns had been made defied reduction to a number of groups that should be at once all-embracing and manageable. Such things as seasonings and gravy preparations might be grouped either according to composition or to purpose; and it was not easy to say in advance which grouping would best serve the Ministry's ends. Hence the application of the full licensing provisions was both gradual, and in the event, partial; by the end of 1943 only a few commodity-groups had been brought in, of which the most important was baking powder.[2] Even so, the task of imposing price control on one group[3] of over 400 individual items proved too heavy and licences had to be issued without price-fixing conditions. A proposal to bring bakers' sundries within the Order was turned down, as a matter of policy, on the ground that they were not sold by retail.

The principles that should determine the maximum prices to be imposed by licence under the Manufactured Foods Order and the Orders it had been intended to supersede had given much food for thought. When the Substitutes Order had been rather hastily put into force, there had been no time for elaborate investigation of the costings of individual firms, and maximum prices had been set by rule of thumb, based on expert knowledge of the food trades generally and the cost of the ingredients making up the product in question. Such a method, rough and ready though it was, had proved acceptable mainly because it was dealing with new products made on a small scale, and the question of pre-war prices did not arise. If price control were now to extend to goods that were on the market before the war, would the Ministry be justified in approving the pre-war price without more ado, more particularly for branded goods whose price had been heavily inflated by advertising, covert or overt? Hitherto, in deference to general Government policy, it had generally refused to allow advertising costs as an expense in computing margins of profit. If, for goods produced by national advertisers, it took the established pre-war selling price as a starting-point it was open to the

---

[1] And also by a decision from higher authority that a licence should in no case be refused for products already being manufactured during the year ending 30th September 1942.

[2] A shortage of tartaric acid had compelled manufacturers to resort to the cheaper, though no less efficient, aerating agent, acid calcium phosphate. The less honest had merely reduced the active ingredients. Other foods brought under the full provisions of the Order during 1943 were 'stuffings' composed of herbs, flour, etc., edible extracts (e.g. of meat or yeast), gravy preparations, powdered soups and factory-made Christmas puddings.

[3] Compendiously described as 'edible extracts, soup mixtures and gravy preparations', 439 licensed products in all (at January 1945).

charge of inconsistency; but the alternative, to base all permitted prices *de novo* on costings, would mean a great deal of extra work which might not in the end provide firm ground to go upon.

Moreover, to force manufacturers of non-essential foods, under conditions expected to be temporary, to reduce prices that the public had cheerfully paid before the war was, the prevailing view urged, 'unreasonable'; any saving on advertising had far better go to the Exchequer through excess profits tax than to the consumer. Where it was proposed to take account of advertising was in dealing with applications for price increases. For products having a turnover of £20,000 a year or less, an increase would be allowed to the extent of the rise in ingredient costs compared with pre-war; for those having a larger turnover, the manufacturer would have to show that the increase in costs had in fact swallowed up his pre-war advertising expenses.[1] Such a policy, discriminatory though it might be in favour of established extravagance, had more in its favour than administrative simplicity and the avoidance of trouble with big business. Had the Ministry deliberately set itself to shrink the customary costs of large advertisers, it might have found itself challenged in Parliament and the Courts for going beyond what was necessary to the prosecution of the war. Apart from this, the Ministry could scarcely press traders further than the more enlightened of them were voluntarily prepared to go. Even in carrying out its price control policy, it sometimes solely relied (as with salt) on a gentlemen's agreement with the trade. The commonest method of operation, however, was for the manufacturer's or packer's licence to specify a maximum retail price to be stated on the label, while an Order made it illegal for the retailer to sell above the marked price.

IV

Even before the Manufactured Foods Order was made, and long before the various obstacles to putting it into full and comprehensive operation had become manifest, the Ministry had decided, with the consent of the Health Departments, to tackle the problems of food standards and misleading labels by itself taking powers similar to those conferred on the Ministry of Health by the Food and Drugs Act of 1938, so that it could make comprehensive regulations covering the labelling and composition of food. (These would, of course, cover a much wider field than the provisions of the Manufactured Foods Order.) This course, officials felt, would be more satisfactory

---

[1] To please the Treasury, the Ministry undertook, in reviewing any application for price increases, to take into account the return the applicant firm was getting on its capital. I can find no evidence that this undertaking was ever put into practice, nor is it easy to see how it ever could have been in relation to but one out of numerous products made by the average food enterprise.

than action under the existing law by the Ministry of Health at a time when a Ministry of Food was in existence, or alternatively the transfer of permanent powers to a war-time Department. At first they proposed to proceed by simple Statutory Rule and Order under existing Defence Regulations, and during the winter of 1942–43 much effort and consultation with interested parties were spent in preparing a suitable text.

The powers to be taken were very wide, and to those unacquainted with the provisions of the Act of 1938 might well seem novel and alarming; there were members of the House of Commons who were making it their business to pounce on any encroachments by the Executive. It was necessary, therefore, that Ministers be consulted before the Order was issued; and in March 1943 the Lord President's Committee, while sympathetic in principle, felt that a Defence Regulation rather than an Order was the appropriate legal instrument. The work of drafting was now taken over by Parliamentary Counsel; but when, after no less than eleven efforts, satisfactory draft Regulations were brought before the War Cabinet's Legislation Committee, they were turned down as likely to arouse serious opposition in the House. Instead, the Committee suggested that all but the more urgent provisions be embodied in a Bill.

The prospects of further delay filled officials with alarm; the evidence of the returns made under the Manufactured Foods Order strengthened their conviction that action was urgent, and further experience with other Orders, such as the Substitutes Order, revealed all too clearly the deficiencies in the existing law. Moreover, they felt that, perhaps owing to faulty presentation, the Legislation Committee had been daunted not so much by the content of the proposed Regulations as by their sheer bulk, and had not realised that the principles underlying them had already been approved by Parliament before the war. They persuaded the Minister to let them make a third attempt; after consultation with the Solicitor-General a fresh set of Defence Regulations, based on the Act of 1938 and empowering the Minister to make detailed Statutory Rules and Orders on the lines embodied textually in the previous Draft Regulations, was duly approved by the Lord President's Committee and the Legislation Committee during October. The Defence (Sale of Food) Regulations were signed in Council on 28th October, to come into force on 1st January 1944; at the instance of the Legislation Committee a White Paper[1] explaining them was issued in November.

In anticipation of getting its powers considerably earlier, the Ministry had set up in September 1942 an advisory inter-departmental committee on food standards, the work of which had progressed so far that the first individual standards orders—for mustard,

---

[1] Cmd. 6482.

shredded suet, self-raising flour, baking powder, and what the trade
had been persuaded to agree should henceforth be called 'golden
raising powder' (i.e. so-called egg substitute)—were ready to be
issued in January 1944. At the same time a Food Standards (General
Provisions) Order was issued making it illegal to market any food not
complying with the standard prescribed for it. In the attempt to make
it watertight, however, this general Order had been so drafted as to
confuse not only enforcing authorities but the Ministry itself; as
became apparent in discussion of the proposed standards for table
mustard and liquid coffee essence. For these would apply, under the
terms of the general Order, not merely to any food product sold under
these or similar descriptions, but to anything, howsoever described,
that was in fact mustard or coffee essence. Though this in nowise
weakened the force of the Order against products sailing under false
colours, it was likely to cause trouble in administration; and in June
1944 the general Order was amended so as to make it clear that it
applied only to foods purporting to be the food for which a standard
had been fixed.[1]

A more important class of difficulties arose in determining the
standards themselves. In a time of general shortage of ingredients and
extensive use of substitutes, to fix pre-war standards would be idle;
and the Ministry was often torn between its desire to economise raw
materials and its wish to secure that the purchaser obtained a worth-
while product. Again, Commodity Divisions' custom of allocating
raw materials only to manufacturers who had used them before the
war meant that a variety of different ingredients might go to make up
products selling under the same description; to set up a standard for
this description might throw Ministry and trade into confusion. For
such things as margarine, the Ministry was itself varying the ingredients almost from week to week in accordance with the supply
position. Yet another difficulty might arise from the lack of published
research on analytical methods of determining food composition; in
the case of baking powder, for instance, the Standards Order itself
had to prescribe in detail the appropriate method of analysis; and an
attempt to prescribe a standard for sausages had to be abandoned
because the trade could not be brought to agree that the method by
which it was proposed to determine meat content was infallible.

V

Except for a few relatively simple items of food, therefore, the
prescription of standards proceeded but slowly after the first few
months after the Regulations came into operation. So too, in spite of

---

[1] S.R. & O. (1944), No. 42 (14th January 1944); amended by S.R. & O. (1944),
No. 654 (1st June 1944).

the swiftness with which the Ministry's new Food Standards and Labelling Division prepared a draft Labelling Order, it was to be nearly two years before the Order could be put into full force for every section of the trade. The principles of such an Order were simple, and largely derived from the practice of the United States Federal Food and Drugs Administration. Ready-packed foods were henceforth to be labelled with the name and address of the manufacturer or packer, the 'common or usual' name of the product, a list of the ingredients, and the minimum quantity, by weight or measure, of contents present. If any claim were made for the presence of ingredients of especial food value, such as certain vitamins and minerals, the amounts present must be specified. Discussion within the Ministry of the foods that must, for one reason or another, be exempted temporarily or permanently from part or all of these provisions occupied some time; discussion with trade interests and local authorities' organisations took even longer, one reason being the need to overcome local authorities' objections to the proviso that the Minister's prior consent was necessary before action could be taken against an offender (action for false weight or measure excepted). The authorities felt this as a restriction on their freedom of action that was not imposed by the existing law; but the Ministry insisted on it advisedly under war-time conditions, if only to protect a trader from being prosecuted for something he had done with Ministry consent or even under Ministry instructions.

In the six months between the issue of the Order[1] and the proposed date for its operation, 1st January 1945, the Ministry found itself, indeed, constrained to undertake a complete review of the labels proposed to be used by manufacturers licensed under one or other of the control Orders for which Commodity Divisions were responsible, few of which contained specific labelling provisions. The great majority of labels so scrutinised failed to comply with the Order, and it became clear that, what with the difficulty of printing new labels and the waste that would ensue if existing stocks of labels were not worked off, the date of operation of the Order would have to be postponed.

This scrutiny also revealed the need for certain relaxations and amendments in the Order even before it should come into force. It was decided, for instance, to exempt protective inner containers, enclosed in a duly labelled outer package, from the need to bear any sort of label. Foods consisting of a single ingredient were found to be insufficiently covered by the Order, since it did not specify whether the 'common or usual name' was that of the material of which the food was composed or the use to which it should be put.[2] Again, it

---

[1] S.R. & O. (1944), No. 738 (29th June 1944).

[2] e.g. a 'baby food' might consist either of semolina or dried milk.

was not the Ministry's purpose to insist, as under the Order un-amended it would in fact have insisted, that the mere disclosure of the presence of a scheduled mineral (e.g. calcium phosphate in free-running salt) should of itself oblige the further disclosure of the exact proportion used. The amendment of the Order for these various purposes carried with it the need to postpone its operation still further —until 1st May 1945 for manufacturers and correspondingly later for wholesalers and retailers. Even so, large numbers of temporary dispensations had to be granted by individual licence; and for custard powder and free-running salt, where proposals to fix standards by Order, which would automatically exempt these foods from the liability to disclose ingredients, had been discussed and then abandoned, a General Licence to use up old labels had to be granted.

These were technical matters; the question of disclosing on labels the use of preservative raised a moral problem for the Ministry. The existing law[1] permitted the use of only two types of preservative, sulphur dioxide and benzoic acid, in scheduled types of food, for some of which the disclosure of preservative was already obligatory. To this the Food Standards and Labelling Division proposed merely to add the requirement that any food not exempted from disclosing ingredients, or covered by the existing preservatives regulations, should disclose the specific preservative used. This would mean that the Ministry's concentrated orange juice, distributed to children under the Welfare Foods Scheme, would have to admit that it contained sulphur dioxide—a requirement, ironically enough, from which war-time standardised soft drinks were exempt, though they had virtually no food value and it was regarded as an essential supplement to young children's diet. Those who feared that suddenly to reveal the presence of a preservative would depress the already unsatisfactory take-up of orange juice, proposed that a standard should be prescribed for it—taking a leaf from the book of some traders who had pressed for a standard in order to avoid disclosing the composition of their products. But this could scarcely be decently done for orange juice unless a standard was prescribed for other Vitamin C preparations, such as blackcurrant syrup and purée, and even rose hip syrup; and the variety of concentration, acidity and Vitamin C potency among these was so great that a single standard for all was thought to be impossible. Reluctantly it was decided that both blackcurrant syrup and Ministry orange juice must comply with the Order—a salutary lesson for the Department of the effect of its own regulations. There is no evidence that the consumption of orange juice suffered as a result.

---

[1] S.R. & O. (1925), No. 775 as amended by S.R. & O.s (1926 No. 1557, (1927) No. 577, (1940) No. 633.

A similar difficulty had occurred over the labelling of margarine to show its vitamin content, inasmuch as one manufacturer used the 'pro-vitamin' carotene to provide Vitamin A, whereas the others used the vitamin itself. If the presence of carotene as such had to be disclosed, the source of the margarine might also become evident —and the 'pooling' of margarine be undermined. After considerable technical argument it was agreed to amend the Order so as to allow carotene to be referred to by its Vitamin A equivalent.

The long delay in enforcing the Order had not meant that a beginning had not been made with actual labelling reforms. As early as January 1944 a suggestion by a local authority that proceedings be taken in respect of a product labelled 'cream custard' had led the Ministry to initiate a voluntary review of custard and blancmange powder labels. As a result the trade agreed to adopt a 'code of practice' deleting any pictures or references that might mislead the buyer into supposing that these preparations (composed mainly of maize starch) contained cream or eggs. Some 200 manufacturers and packers submitted their labels and packages for scrutiny—a process which itself took several months. Voluntary co-operation on these lines between the Ministry and the trade had from the first been the object of those administering the new labelling regulations, and prosecution was regarded only as a last resort. It was, in fact, the Ministry's close relations with the food trades that gave it so great an advantage in matters of this sort, compared with a normal peace-time Department. Indeed, the small group within the Ministry, headed by its Manufactured Foods Adviser, who had from 1941 worked steadily, ingeniously and unremittingly to put teeth into the 1938 Food and Drugs Act, had realised from the first the outstanding opportunity the Ministry's very existence gave them of making a permanent and long overdue step forward in food and drugs legislation.

There is, of course, a sense in which concern for custard powder and coffee essence might be mocked at as itself making a mockery of the phrase 'total war'; and it is certainly true that in this, as in many other instances, the intention to make short work of *minutiæ* had at length turned into preoccupation with them. The later rejection by the Ministry of the time-honoured designations 'digestive biscuits' and 'tonic water' might seem straitlaced to others besides the manufacturers; but the worst that could be said about it was that it took over-seriously something that had become too conventional to be misleading. When the larger measures of food control should come to an end, the Ministry's reforms in the field of standards and labelling would stand out as a solid gain, unobtrusively snatched from the years of austerity.

CHAPTER XXV

'Concentration' and the Food Industries

I

CLOSELY tied up with the process by which the Ministry of Food, from mid-1941 onwards, evolved a tight control over all the food industries from raw material to finished product, was the application to them of the policy known as *concentration*. This policy had originated in the Board of Trade during 1940 to deal with the results that were expected to flow from restriction of supplies and/or output in the industries supplying the home market. If—the supporters of the policy argued—these industries were left to themselves, the reduced production would be spread over all the firms in it; there would be widespread part-time working and waste of labour and factory space. Operating costs would rise, leading to a demand for higher prices and profits; the less efficient firms would be forced into bankruptcy from which recovery after the war would be impossible; the yield of labour and other resources to the war effort would be slow and disorderly.

Concentration proposed to avoid these evils by a planned readjustment of resources to output. Within an industry, certain firms would be classified as 'nucleus' firms, to work full time, and to enjoy protection for their labour and space and a guarantee of supplies of materials. The remainder would be, in due course, closed 'for the duration', with compensation from the profits of the nucleus firms and a guarantee of reinstatement. The Board of Trade appears to have envisaged a series of mutual assistance pacts or marriages negotiated by firms themselves; neither the Government, nor even a trade association, would be charged with deciding which factories should close and which remain open. But the Departments would insist that concentration arrangements be so made as to release labour in those places, of those sorts, and at those times, that would be most convenient from the point of view of the munitions industries that were to absorb it. The same applied to factory space.

From the very first, that is to say, concentration was not just another word for rationalisation, as it had been understood before the war, or as it had been applied, very drastically, to slaughter-houses under the Meat and Livestock Control Scheme. The main, if not the only criterion of a successful concentration scheme was its yield in labour and space to the war effort. Neither was concentration

322

a synonym for contraction. It pre-supposed contraction to an extent sufficient to bring about a surplus of resources—a surplus that without concentration might not be fully diverted to war purposes. 'Proposals may be expected from industry', wrote the President of Board of Trade in February 1941, 'that labour should be surrendered on a quota basis, each manufacturer contributing a proportion of his labour force . . . such dissipation of labour and production must be checked'—by concentration.

The policy had such an obvious logic, and chimed so well with the shortages of manpower and factory space that were rife in the spring of 1941, that it was promptly and publicly adopted by the Government for all industries, including the food industries. So far as the Ministry of Food was concerned, ready assent to the principle preceded serious and detailed examination of its consequences. It clearly could not be applied to major industries, such as flour milling and oilseed crushing, that were fully employed and, indeed, dangerously short of reserve capacity against air attack. The Ministry had little detailed information at this time about the minor industries. Reduced allocations of raw materials, such as sugar, starch, glucose, and fats, to them had not, so far as it knew, been matched by falls in output or a widespread resort to short-time working. Substitute materials, particularly that versatile and unrationed product, wheat flour, had apparently replaced the scarce ingredients. The prospect of applying control to, or even collecting information from, a great number of miscellaneous industries, none of them using much material or employing a large labour force, was one that the Ministry was only gradually and reluctantly being brought to consider.[1]

During the summer of 1941, partly perhaps because of the changes in internal organisation within the Supply Department,[2] very little was done in the Ministry about concentration. It was, perhaps, too much to expect Commodity Divisions, who had plenty of problems of their own, to show great zeal about projects that appeared to be likely to confer small and not altogether certain benefits on other Departments.

The Oils and Fats Division did, indeed, very promptly concentrate the dripping, otherwise the edible fat melting, industry. But this was a measure that was in the interests of control; it reduced a chaotic industry to order, cut costs and removed a strong incentive to sell on the black market. The scheme was really a rationalisation far more drastic than anything contemplated in the White Paper on concentration,[3] and it aroused complaint from the Ministry of Labour that they had not been sufficiently consulted about it.

---

[1] Chapter XXIV.
[2] Chapter XVII.
[3] Cmd. 6258 (March 1941).

However active the Ministry of Food had been, it could scarcely have produced results that would have made a show beside those being claimed by the Board of Trade, because the industries in which contraction was possible were in total much smaller, and the possible reduction of output much less, than in the industries for which the Board of Trade was responsible. But since this was not generally realised outside the Ministry, the apparent want of activity on its part incurred the more blame; in December 1941 the Minister of Food was criticised in the Lord President's Committee[1] and specifically asked to arrange for closer collaboration with the Minister of Labour. A small·committee of senior officials, the 'Concentration Panel', had just recently been appointed to oversee the production of concentration schemes; and in January 1942 definite instructions were given to each Commodity Director that he must either produce 'a scheme to achieve the maximum economy in production of the products under his control', or satisfy the Panel that there was no scope for it. A good many proposals were put up by Divisions as a result; but only five industries—bacon curing, biscuits, chocolate and sugar confectionery, soft drinks, and starch food powders—were expected to yield an 'appreciable amount' of labour or space. (For instance, 10,000 operatives were expected to be released from chocolate and sugar confectionery, 4,000 from soft drinks, 1,000 from starch food powders.) Sixteen more industries were scheduled for possible concentration, more it seems from a desire to treat all alike than because sizeable savings were expected.[2]

Because the Ministry of Food by this time had accepted responsibility for maintaining a prescribed level of output in these five industries, and had rationed or was proposing to ration three of them (bacon, sweets, and biscuits), there could be no question of either leaving the initiative to individual firms, or imposing a concentration scheme without consultation with the industry as a whole. Where a representative trade association did not exist that could be entrusted with the details of a concentration scheme, as with soft drinks, the first step was to create one for the purpose. So, too, only bacon curing, out of the five, conformed to the 'pure' concentration pattern of the White Paper, i.e. the closing down of whole factories consequent upon a reduction in turnover. Since the reduction here arose from the fall

---

[1] One senior official had foreseen this. 'It is time', he had written in April 1941, 'we got a move on, otherwise we shall find that we are lagging behind the Board of Trade and being hauled over the coals by Ministers for not doing anything'.

[2] These were: Cheese-making, Cheese 'processing', Cider, Distilling, Egg-Packing, Food-Canning, Glucose Manufacture, Margarine, Pepper and Spice Grinding, Pickles and Sauces, Provender Milling and Compounding, Rice Grinding, Sausage and Open Meat Pack Manufacturing, Seed-crushing (in Hull only), Soap-Making, and Technical Fat Melting. A good many of these might better be described as rationalisation schemes undertaken for the Ministry's own purposes, and cited to the Lord President's Committee purely as window-dressing.

in the pig population for want of imported feeding-stuffs, it was irrevocable and likely to last for the duration. For the other four, prior decisions had to be made on the level and type of output that would be permitted, i.e. on the contraction, if any, in tonnage or number of varieties of, say, biscuits, that was required, before a concentration scheme could proceed. This point is important, not only for the timing of concentration, but in considering the estimates that were made of its effects, both before and after the event. Estimates of the labour yield of the bacon scheme, that is to say, may be referred to concentration alone; those for biscuits, sweets and soft drinks must relate to all the measures of enforced economy including concentration undertaken after 1942.

The Concentration Panel had, therefore, to walk warily between two pitfalls. On the one hand, it did not want to cause 'undue and unnecessary dislocation' to the food industries: 'I should not like the Minister to think', wrote the Chairman of the Panel in March 1943, 'that the food industries have been thoughtlessly rushed into unwise schemes for concentration'. On the other hand, it did wish to satisfy the claims of other Departments for labour and space. As with transport economy, there could be no short cut to a solution, and each trade was to some extent a law unto itself. If, to the Panel itself as well as other Departments, Commodity Divisions appeared sluggish and obstructive, they for their part often felt that the instructions they received from the centre had been drawn up without regard to the idiosyncrasies of their particular industry.

II

This could scarcely be said of bacon-curing, for the industry had been fully controlled since the outbreak of war and was evidently ripe for concentration. Nevertheless it was not until June 1942 that the Ministry got down to the task of selecting the factories that should be closed—a task that curers' representatives had declined.[1]

To avoid any accusation of bias, the selection was entrusted to three officials, none of whom had any connection with the industry; the method adopted was to invite the Board of Trade and the Ministry of Labour to submit lists of factories they would like closed, and to compile the provisional closing schedule from these, excepting only any factory deemed by the Division to be essential. This pro-

---

[1] One reason for the delay was that a new and reduced margin of profit for bacon curers was being negotiated. The Bacon Division secured general agreement that concentration could not go on until the amount of the margin had been reduced; but once it had been agreed (a) that existing capacity was excessive, (b) that nevertheless the new margin should be based on past costs, and the profits used to compensate closed firms, the actual amount of the margin was (one might have thought) irrelevant to the decision to concentrate.

X

cedure would enable the Ministry to tell any aggrieved curer that his factory had been closed because its labour and/or space were particularly required for the war effort; but it did not suffice to prevent it from running into political difficulties.

Among the factories that for geographical reasons had been marked by the Ministry of Labour for closure were two belonging to the Co-operative movement—one at Winsford, near Crewe, the other at Kilmarnock. They were efficient modern factories, and Winsford in particular had exceptionally low labour usage per unit of output; the total labour employed by both on bacon production was only 122, but between them they accounted for close on two-thirds of Co-operative curing capacity. One might have expected the Ministry of Food to walk very delicately where they were concerned; on the contrary, not only were they unhesitatingly and rapidly scheduled for closure, but Winsford was pressed upon the Board of Trade for storage purposes.

However good the technical reasons may have been for taking this line, it was politically maladroit. Not only the Co-operative movement, but the Trade Unions were up in arms at once, and appealed to the Deputy Prime Minister. Matters were made worse by the fact that many displaced workers from Kilmarnock were transferred to other and, as was alleged, less desirable bacon factories. (The Ministry of Labour subsequently withdrew them for munitions, but the harm was done.) In the ministerial discussions that ensued the Ministry of Food succeeded in sustaining a not-over-strong case; partly perhaps because the Co-operatives put forward the quite indefensible claim that in any concentration scheme the proportion of capacity they should give up must not exceed that by which the whole industry was contracted. But the odium it had incurred, coupled with the almost negligible release of labour that resulted from the bacon-curing scheme, made the Ministry distinctly less willing to fall in with the behest of the other Departments on later occasions.

In this instance, all three Departments had been at one in rejecting the Co-operative contention that the most efficient factories should be given nucleus status on principle, without regard to location. This rejection was implicit in the White Paper, and the Ministry of Food had taken a similar line in concentrating the biscuits and sweets industries. It would have been perfectly possible to produce all the chocolate for which the Ministry was prepared to allocate ingredients in the factories of the eight biggest firms. Several of these, however, were in 'difficult' labour areas; to concentrate in this way would have completely destroyed the existing structure of the trade; a similar course would not have been possible for sugar confectionery where such giant firms did not exist; and additional transport would have been required. For these reasons the Minister had, in February 1942, approved a process of ordered shrinkage rather than concentration, based on, but rather severer than, proposals put forward by the trade. This meant fixing a limit of five workers per ton of output, beyond which no protection would be given to a firm's labour; the limit—which was to be achieved by stages from month to month—would be such as to make impossible the production of luxury lines or packings. It was proposed to meet the Board of Trade's space requirements by compressing production into part of each factory, though the Ministry was also prepared to release a limited number of complete factories. Departments agreed that no firm should be closed outright except where its whole labour or space were required for war purposes. The scheme began to be put into force in April 1942, and a month later a scheme on similar lines was applied to the biscuit industry.

No sooner had the biscuit and sweet schemes got started, however, than the Minister decided that a cut in the production of each must be made, as a contribution to the shipping 'gap' and a sop to the advocates of austerity. Biscuits were to go on 'points' from August 1942, and their output was to be cut in half; the proposed four-ounce ration for sweets was to go down to three ounces. These changes implied a drastic—and in the circumstances especially unwelcome—contraction of both industries.

Meantime shortages of labour for war work had become more acute, especially in certain districts. The Ministry of Labour was particularly anxious for the complete closure of factories in difficult labour areas, because this (it thought) would release for war work a great deal of labour that was not subject to statutory direction. It would have liked the Ministry of Food (a) so to arrange its concentration schemes that these factories would be declared redundant, irrespective of other considerations, (b) to withdraw their raw materials forthwith. The Ministry of Labour asked that the revised scheme for chocolate and sugar confectionery should completely eliminate several large and efficient firms in north-west London, and almost completely stop production at Bournville, the largest factory in Great Britain, which was within the Birmingham munitions area. Similar proposals were made for the biscuit industry.

The Ministry of Food felt that these proposals for biscuits and sweets must be resisted. They would not, it maintained, release sufficient useful labour to outweigh the increased calls on transport, the wrecking of the proposed zoning schemes, and the enhanced difficulty of getting back to normal after the war, that must result from the complete closing of the big firms. It would be impossible to defend them to the trades. But the Ministry also contested the Ministry of Labour's claims in principle. It was, and had always been, perfectly willing for firms whose production was not essential to have their factories requisitioned or their directable labour withdrawn. But it was not willing to withdraw their raw materials in order to release undirectable labour. There could be—it argued—no guarantee that the labour so released would go to useful work; it might just drift away altogether. If that happened, odium would fall, not on the Ministry of Labour, whose policy had brought about the closure of the factory, but on the honest broker, the Ministry of Food. (Moreover, the most efficient factories in the biscuits and sweets industries could, even if all their directable labour were withdrawn, still produce at a lower rate of labour per ton than the others.)

The Ministry of Labour was obdurate. Its officials took their stand on the 'principles of concentration' said to have been embodied in the White Paper of March 1941. According to these principles, a concentration scheme was not a concentration scheme unless certain factories were closed; they might never close unless their raw materials were withdrawn; therefore the Ministry of Food must accept the logic of concentration and close them. The Board of Trade supported the Ministry of Labour: at a meeting of Ministers on 3rd November 1942 the Minister of Food was constrained to accept the majority verdict, though with certain safeguards. It was agreed that in future schemes forward dates should be fixed for the closure of certain factories, so that labour could be withdrawn in orderly fashion before those dates when the allocation of raw material would cease.

III

As if to illustrate the point for which the Ministry of Food had unsuccessfully contended, there occurred shortly afterwards an occasion to show what the urgent national need, in the name of which the principles of concentration had been invoked, might mean in practice. Among the factories scheduled for closure in the concentration scheme for starch food powders had been that of Carltona Ltd., at Willesden. It was a large, modern, and efficient factory which the Ministry of Food had only agreed to close at the specific request of the Ministry of Labour and the Board of Trade. (It was in a 'scarlet' area, i.e. the most difficult of all for labour supply.)

The firm showed fight, and endeavoured to protect itself against total closing by securing, unknown to the Ministry of Food, a War Office contract for packing salt; in November it began legal action to restrain the Ministry of Works from requisitioning the factory. Nevertheless, the Ministry of Food agreed to make arrangements to withdraw allocations of raw material and transfer production, if the Ministry of Works would fix a date for its requisition; indeed, it went further and pressed that this action should be taken lest other firms be encouraged to postpone closing by issuing writs likewise. Carltona Ltd. were given a month's notice that the factory would be closed on 31st December 1942, and were invited to make arrangements, through the Food Manufacturers' Federation or otherwise, for another firm to manufacture on their behalf. They ignored this request, and were then warned that in their default the Ministry would make its own arrangements, i.e. withdraw not merely the factory's, but the firm's allocation of ingredients. This, too, was ignored, and finally the allocation was withdrawn.

The company, however, continued to function with its existing stocks after the scheduled date; when, on 2nd February, its action came before the High Court, it still held the factory and at least some of its labour; and this remained the position at the end of February, three weeks after Mr. Justice Hilbery found in favour of the Departments. Nor was this all; the best use the Board of Trade could find for the factory was for the storage of baby carriages, while of twenty-seven workers employed there all but two turned out to be undirectable part-timers. It was indeed fortunate, as a Ministry observer remarked, that the High Court was prepared to accept the Crown's plea that the Defence Regulations gave the authorities absolute discretion. The Ministry of Food had been put in a false position; it had been the decisive instrument in closing a factory which it did not wish to close, and which, on the facts that transpired ought not to have been closed. The moral victory lay with the company, obstructive and disagreeable though it may have been.[1]

Another firm was more successful in its resistance. This was the Toro Soap Company, a non-nucleus firm under the soapmakers' concentration scheme. As early as July 1942 the Board of Trade had asked for this firm's premises at Castle Bromwich, and had been told that Oils and Fats Division would not object to their requisition, even though the concentration scheme was not yet ready. In December the Air Ministry, to which the factory had been allocated, came to an agreement with the firm to take only part of their space; and the Division therefore agreed that they might carry on in the remainder, if they could run the gauntlet of the Ministry of Labour. In March 1943 the Division was informed that the whole of the firm's labour would be directed elsewhere, and arrangements were accordingly put in train for the transfer of its production. The firm, however, maintained that its labour was non-directable and appealed to the Lord Mayor of Birmingham to intervene. After hedging for several

---

[1] The company's appeals failed both in the Appeal Court and the House of Lords. By this time it had accepted the inevitable and made arrangements for the transfer of its production to other firms, through the good offices of the Food Manufacturers' Federation.

months[1] the Ministry of Labour admitted that only three workers out of twenty-one were directable, though ten more could readily be placed elsewhere. None the less the Division would have been prepared to enforce closure by withdrawing the company's licence, had not doubts about the legality of so doing led to reference upwards, and eventually to an exchange of letters between Lord Woolton and Mr. Bevin, in which the latter decided not to press his Department's point.[2] The Toro Soap Company, by refusing to budge, had triumphed over three Government Departments.

Meantime, the Ministry of Food's objection to a rigid concentration procedure had been met. Shortly after the ministerial ruling of 3rd November, in deference to which the Carltona factory had been closed, the Board of Trade ran into a political storm when it proposed to concentrate the Luton hat industry out of existence. Early in December the President of the Board of Trade put up to the Lord President's Committee what amounted to an endorsement of the Ministry of Food's doctrine; small firms, he urged, should not be closed down unless the materials or premises they used were required; labour should not be withdrawn from firms resisting concentration unless local investigation showed that it could be employed on more important work. Ministers thereupon called for a fresh codification of concentration policy. In the inter-departmental discussions that followed the Ministry of Food took no part. They resulted, in March 1943, in a new statement of principles, in which the 'withdrawal of personnel on an ordered plan' was accepted as an alternative principle that might be applied for the remaining Board of Trade industries to be concentrated. The original principle was not denounced, but it was agreed that it should not be used.

There could be no question, therefore, of another Carltona case being forced upon the Ministry of Food; and in fact, even before Ministers had adopted the new statement, the Ministry of Food had been able to persuade the Ministry of Labour that, after all, a satisfactory arrangement on the 'ordered withdrawal' principle was

---

[1] On 31st March 1943 the Ministry of Labour were reported as saying that they proposed to take up the whole of Toro's labour force. On 10th May they wrote 'the workers employed by this firm are suitable for transfer to more essential work and no difficulty is expected in placing them'. On 24th July they wrote that the Regional Controller had been asked to begin withdrawals from 31st July onwards. On 4th August they wrote, 'It is quite possible that the labour is not "directable". . . . You will appreciate that, under concentration, withdrawals are not confined to "directable" classes but includes [*sic*] any workers suitable for transfer'. Only on 13th September was the true position elicited from Ministry of Labour Headquarters.

[2] The legal point at issue was whether the power to license manufacture taken by the Ministry of Food could properly be used for the ends of another Department. The soap concentration scheme was a voluntary one and of itself provided no means of enforcement. There can be little doubt, nevertheless, that if the Ministry of Labour had stood firm the licence would have been withdrawn, in which case the legal point might have gone to court.

possible for chocolate and sweets. Biscuits were now settled on the same lines. In each case the trade's response to the drastic demand for closure had been to produce counter-proposals for contraction, demonstrating that a comparable amount of directable labour could be released in this way without disturbing the traditional structure of each trade. The sole effect of the interdepartmental controversy had been to delay releases by several months.

The settlement of the biscuit scheme was followed by the completion of what had been in some ways the most troublesome of all—that for Soft Drinks. The Ministry's habitual technique of 'leaving it to the industry' had been hampered here by the fact that there was not one trade association, but three, and that the interests of the different sections of the trade—table waters, squashes, and cordials—were too divergent for them readily to agree on a voluntary scheme. It was, therefore, necessary to apply a modicum of compulsion, by licensing all sizeable manufacturers of soft drinks on condition they joined a war-time association specifically formed to impose the concentration scheme. For the purpose of this scheme a figure of total production was drawn up, to be reached in stages; the first stage consisting in a simple cut of aerated drink production by one quarter, to be compensated by an increase in the production of concentrated drinks.

On this basis the newly constituted Association went to work on its scheme, in May 1942. Meantime, however, the other Departments were pressing for some releases 'on account', and the Ministry therefore agreed to close first twenty-three, and then a further two hundred-odd factories in advance of the complete plan. This concession caused a great deal of trouble. The first twenty-three had been asked for by Board of Trade headquarters, in several cases without proper co-ordination with the regional offices of the Factory and Storage Control. Sometimes it turned out that not all the factory was really required; sometimes that to stop mineral water manufacture would bring, say, beer bottling to a premature end. Protests and appeals to M.P.'s were frequent; several orders for closure had to be withdrawn. For the remaining advance releases local investigation was made an essential preliminary, but even so progress was slow and the possibilities of obstruction considerable. As a result of the Ministerial meeting of 3rd November, the Ministry was prevailed upon to fix 31st December as a closing date for all the factories in this list.

By this time the Association had completed the concentration scheme proper, the most thoroughgoing of any sponsored by the Ministry of Food. It provided not only for the designation of nucleus factories and a pool for compensating firms, but specifically for deconcentration 'when the emergency should be over.' In order mainly to save transport, zoning was introduced, brand names and makers' labels were suppressed, and ingredients and prices standardised as from 1st February 1943. Thereafter the way was open for a further closure of factories on an ordered plan, and this proceeded with greater smoothness than the haphazard 'first stage' of concentration had done. Now, however, the uproar resulting from the hasty application of ill-prepared proposals led to Departmental caution in applying sound and orderly principles; although a firm lost practically nothing by being closed, it was allowed an appeal first to an independent tribunal and then to the Minister. This procedure was a fruitful cause of delay; another, that could not be avoided, was the need to adjust production in some regions to meet the demands of the American forces for soft drinks. Throughout 1943, and perhaps even later, numerous non-nucleus firms remained in production, and it was not until January 1944 that the adjustment of output to the limits set for the various types of drink was even reasonably complete.

IV

In March 1943 the Minister of Food put in to the Lord President's Committee a report on the results, actual and prospective, of concentration in the food industries, which claimed that there was little further scope for action. In fact, no further schemes were initiated, and although the schemes in train were not complete until the end of 1943 there was no later effort by the Ministry to assess their results. So far as factory and storage space was concerned, the figure of releases to December 1942—about $4\frac{1}{2}$ million square feet—must have been improved on during the remainder of 1943. Even so, it must have been small compared with the 70 millions yielded (up to March 1944) by the Board of Trade industries, and the 220 millions requisitioned by the Factory and Storage control after mid-1941, 37 millions of which was allocated to the Ministry of Food.

The figure of labour releases, given in March 1943 as upwards of 30,000, is more difficult to interpret. It was claimed at the time that the figure, like that for storage space, related only to the direct results of concentration schemes; but other evidence makes it clear that this claim was only a matter of dates, and that in fact it included all labour losses to the industries concerned, from whatever cause, during the period of concentration. If one compares the estimate for chocolate and sugar confectionery—11,500 for the original scheme, 2,000 for the revised scheme—with the Ministry of Labour figures of insured persons in the industry, whose numbers fell between July

1942 and July 1943 by 11,000, and by a further 1,000 in the ensuing year, the matter seems beyond doubt.[1]

This may explain the enormous discrepancy between the Ministry of Food estimate of concentration releases and that computed from Ministry of Labour records—rather more than 10,000 up to 3rd March 1943. Thereafter, complete figures from this source are lacking; but later releases from two of the three industries from which most were expected seem to have been exceedingly small—600–650 for biscuits, about 150 for soft drinks. The yield from the third—chocolate and sugar confectionery—may have been more substantial. Even so, total releases on account of food concentration may have been as little as half the Ministry of Food's 1943 estimate, i.e., about 15,000 insured workers.

Whatever figure one takes, it still overstates the positive gain of labour to the munitions industries. Many workers released by concentration schemes were for one reason or another not suitable for transfer to munitions; elderly men, juveniles, women with household responsibilities, could none of them be directed and were frequently difficult to 'place' locally. Others might be physically unfit. What residuum of labour actually reached war work directly or indirectly is conjectural.[2]

It is, moreover, not strictly correct to attribute these labour releases to concentration alone, except for the 300 released from bacon-curing. For biscuits, and chocolate and sugar confectionery, which between them accounted for more than three-quarters of the labour estimated to have left the 'concentrated' food industries, the drastic cuts in output, and reduction in the number of separate 'lines' must of themselves have meant considerable labour savings. The fact that they were combined with a concentration scheme presumably made it easier for the Ministry of Labour to take up workpeople made redundant, and allowed some choice of the location of releases that would not otherwise have been possible. But even without such a scheme, some releases must have fallen in the most suitable places from the Ministry of Labour's point of view. *Mutatis mutandis* this argument applies to space also.

While, therefore, the economies imposed in the name of concentration were meritorious—for biscuits and soft drinks, even apart from releases of labour and space—concentration of the food industries *per se* made no significant contribution to the war effort, except in so

---

[1] A minute dated 24th March 1943, covering a draft of the paper submitted to the Lord President's Committee, remarked: 'The figures compiled by the Board of Trade . . . must, to a large extent, include releases that would have been effected quite irrespective of any concentration procedure. *It all depends upon the date as from which you compute the releases*'. (My italics.)

[2] These difficulties were common to non-food industries; but the amount of 'unsuitable' labour being employed by the food industries appears to have been exceptionally high.

far as it may have made orderly what otherwise might have been more haphazard releases of labour and space. (It certainly did not make them swift or easy.) Whether this in itself was sufficient reward for the effort put into concentration schemes by Departments and trade alike may well be doubted. Nor does it seem possible to argue that the smallness of the dividends, particularly in labour, was due to over-caution or want of zeal in the Ministry of Food. Ministry officials who were in no way identified with the prejudices of a particular Commodity Division pointed to the Carltona case—which was by no means isolated—as justifying a wary attitude towards the demands of other Departments, which were frequently found to be based on inadequate or out-of-date information.

Even if it be granted that there was something in both these contentions—that, in short, the interdepartmental machinery might have worked better—it still seems true to say that the conditions for a spectacular success just did not exist. It was unfortunate that, at the time when the policy was first formulated, those in the Ministry of Food who sensed this were not in a position to prove it, from sheer lack of information about the minor food industries. The apparent success of the Board of Trade, in circumstances that were not really comparable, was used against the Ministry by those who knew even less of these industries. Still more unfortunate was the short-lived attempt to elevate concentration—which was, after all, only an expedient—into an economic dogma to which appeals might be made in the event of interdepartmental disputes, and that ought to be applied to industries regardless of their size and structure.

Had the hopes reposed in concentration been more modest—as they must have been if the conditions of individual industries had been better understood—and had, in consequence, the preparation of schemes been limited to those industries where sizeable rewards could be expected, or where the requirements of food control imposed some form of rationalisation, the release of resources would have been not markedly less, and the savings in administrative effort very great.

CHAPTER XXVI

The Pursuit of Transport Economy, 1941-44

I

THE port and transport crisis of 1940–41 had brought the whole Government to realise the need not merely for improvements in the management of inland transport, and particularly its co-ordination with shipping, but for widespread measures of economy in its use. It was no longer sufficient to concentrate on savings in motor fuel, and hence on cutting down road transport; all forms of transport were, and would be, under intense strain, particularly in the dark winter months. The very real economies in transport *supply*, such as had been made by the road transport pools of the biscuit and sweet makers, and the pool of insulated rail wagons, must be supplemented by cutting down total *demand*. Unnecessary movement of goods, long hauls and cross hauls, needed to be cut out.

The Ministry of Food's transport experts needed no prompting to make them aware of the need. The Minister himself was quick to respond to the formal invitation of his colleagues, in the summer of 1941, to introduce economies:

'It is necessary' (he wrote) 'that we should call upon both distributing manufacturers and wholesalers to organise their business in such a manner as to use the minimum of transport. . . . There is no time to lose. . . . I should like complete plans to be ready for operation during the first week in August'

and, a few days later:

'the whole plan should be in operation by 1st September of this year'.

One is irresistibly reminded of Sir William Beveridge's comment on the Government's potato policy of 1917: 'It is the business of civil servants to translate into complicated prose the simple raptures of their masters'.[1] In this case, as in the similar one of concentration, the response of Colwyn Bay was to set up a Transport Economy Committee without mandatory powers; a course scarcely likely to provoke swift action from the Commodity Divisions, but almost inevitable at a time when measures for the integration of Ministry policy had only recently been introduced, and when its control, and therefore its knowledge, were limited to relatively few bulk foods. To apply economy measures to these was comparatively simple; to move

---

[1] Beveridge, *op. cit.* p. 154.

further and deal with manufactured foods, the wholesale trade, and retail deliveries was to wrestle with a complex unknown. Moreover, it was thought to require new legal powers. Officials felt, therefore, that any action by the Ministry of Food ought to be taken within the framework of an announced Government policy applying to all transport alike. Whether from pressure of work, or simply from the difficulties inherent in finding an interdepartmental formula, it was not until nearly the middle of October that the Lord President's Committee was enabled to authorise Lord Leathers to declare publicly that economy of all forms of transport was essential in the national interest.

Thereafter the Ministry of Food acted with dispatch. By an Order[1] dated 28th October, powers were taken to control the movement of any foodstuff owned by any food undertaking in Great Britain. Henceforth, the Ministry could prescribe how far, and by what means, any food or even any particular consignment of food should travel, and the time or place at which it should be loaded or unloaded. The Transport Economy Committee was wound up, and a positive instruction given to Supply Divisions to initiate transport economy schemes forthwith, in conjunction with Transport Division.[2] If schemes could not be produced within a reasonable time, Transport Division itself could propose plans. In either case agreement with the trade should be reached if possible, but failing it recourse would be had to compulsion.

These steps were too late to have great influence on transport difficulties during the winter of 1941–42, except for certain bulk traffics. During 1941 the distribution of refined sugar and cattle cake had been zoned, and considerable further economies made in the transport of meat. The Divisions concerned with home-grown cereals, potatoes, tea, and dried fruit, were preparing economy schemes but for none of these was there sign of swift or drastic activity. For a whole further set of products—biscuits, chocolate and confectionery, beer, wholesale bread—little or nothing had been done. Wholesale distribution of groceries and provisions appeared to be particularly wasteful of transport, inasmuch as there was no restriction on the number of wholesalers from which a single retailer might draw his supplies, or on the distance over which wholesalers might send their goods. The new egg control scheme had been planned without thought of transport economy. On the retail side, milk and bread offered obvious possibilities of saving.

In principle all this was clear enough; but the task before the

---

[1] The Food Transport Order (S.R. & O.(1941) No. 1694). At a later date this Order was held to be superfluous since adequate powers already existed under Defence Regulation. Nevertheless it was not revoked.

[2] Cf. the similar order about concentration (Chapter XXV).

Ministry was in detail immense. Hitherto such economies as had been effected had either been for goods in the Ministry's own control, or had been indirectly brought about by fuel restriction. The movement of every foodstuff was individual to itself; detailed fact-finding was an essential preliminary to action. As with concentration, impatient pressure for quick results indicated nothing but unwareness of what the problems were. Nevertheless, progress appeared to be disappointingly slow. The only important zoning schemes introduced in the first half of 1942 were mild ones for biscuits and jam, both highly organised trades which were consequently easy to deal with. In August a 'Sector Scheme' for wholesalers of grocery and provisions divided the whole country into nine self-contained regions. Retailers and caterers within any single sector were henceforth prohibited from obtaining a variety of groceries and provisions from wholesalers (or multiple depots) outside that sector. At the same time a beginning was made on the long overdue task of restricting the number of wholesalers from whom a retailer might draw his rationed supplies.

Though the Sector Scheme was no doubt considerably better than nothing, it could scarcely be regarded as radical; cross hauls within sectors were still possible and some sectors were sufficiently large to allow journeys of over 100 miles.[1] Moreover, any journey of less than forty miles, even over sector boundaries, was still permitted. Even so, the scheme met with trade resistance, and its introduction was followed by a flood of claims for exemption, many plausible in themselves but taken together subversive of the whole. The summer of 1942 saw also zoning schemes for tomatoes, soft fruit and plums, and various restrictions on the movement of new potatoes. Though numerous other economies were being pursued all the time, another winter was approaching with but one major advance to register, namely the White Fish Zoning scheme, which came into operation on 17th October.[2]

II

During the autumn of 1942 the whole problem of simplifying distribution was exhaustively reviewed, and in December fresh instructions at last gave the experts in Transport Division, instead of the Commodity Divisions, the initiative in preparing zoning schemes. Vigorous work during the early months of 1943 brought to completion a whole series of them—factory-made cakes (May), biscuits (an

---

[1] Thus Scarborough, Caernarvon, Leeds, Liverpool, and the Isle of Man were all in Sector 6, and Sector 8 comprised the whole of Scotland.

[2] This scheme will be discussed in Vol. II. There was a tendency to claim too much in public for the Ministry's achievement to date.

improved scheme), chocolate and sugar confectionery, and self-raising flour (June), and bulk flour (July). A zoning scheme for ice-cream was completed, only to be superseded by a decision to ban ice-cream manufacture altogether on transport grounds. Central and Divisional joint Committees were set up with the Brewers' Society to secure further economies in transport. In short, the objectives laid down by the Minister eighteen months previously were at last being actively pursued, so far as home-manufactured foods were concerned. More activity was also manifest elsewhere; an ambitious scheme for superseding all first-hand suppliers of groceries and provisions by an *ad hoc* Company on the lines of those set up for bacon and meat importers was indeed rejected as too radical and likely to take too long, but both first-hand suppliers and wholesalers were instructed to form regional war-time associations for the specific purpose of economising transport and manpower. Milk Division's schemes for rationalising farm collections and retail deliveries also made good progress, the latter being virtually complete for the larger urban areas by the summer of 1943.

By this time, however, zeal in high places for austerity had dimmed as the war situation looked more promising. A straw in the wind was the decision of Ministers, in March 1943, to lift the ban on the transport of cut flowers by passenger train. The Ministry of War Transport appeared lukewarm, at least so those preparing food zoning plans felt, to any schemes not involving a large tonnage. Enthusiastic, even pressing, about beer, it was inclined to dismiss such things as pickles and sauces, for which a scheme had been prepared after months of labour, as a small matter. To the Transport Division such backsliding was dangerous; the improvement in the transport situation might easily only be temporary, and halting the advance of economy schemes might lead to actual retreat, if not collapse.[1] The pickles and sauces scheme was in fact a test case; its own savings were not negligible, estimated as they were at one and a half million ton-miles, but a much greater prospective saving on all sorts of other things, from tea to salt and cereal breakfast foods, hung on it.

---

[1] Transport Division regarded the railway managers as being responsible for this attitude. Since the Ministry of War Transport was entirely reliant on the companies for technical advice on rail matters—i.e., it had no independent railway experts on its staff—the suspicion was bound to arise and must be difficult, if not impossible to dispel. The anxiety of some of the railway operators to get back to normal is clear; one group was actually canvassing for traffic as early as 1944.

An example of what Transport Division regarded as weakness with the railways is the case of a firm of sweet-makers who were accustomed to send their goods by rail from London to a depot at Falkirk, leased from the L.N.E.R. They were willing, when approached, to send them by sea, via Grangemouth; but to send otherwise than by rail was contrary to the terms under which the depot was leased from the company. Despite pressure, the Ministry of War Transport declined to order the 'controlled' railway to waive this clause in its agreement. This particular movement was stopped by zoning, and was in any case small in tonnage; but Transport Division's feelings about it can well be understood.

In July 1943 the Minister himself called for a review of zoning policy; in effect Transport Division was called upon to justify continuing the course on which it was set. The result was a compromise; Lord Woolton agreed that zoning of pickles and the revised schemes for preserves and cereal breakfast foods should proceed; and that further discussions should take place with the trade on oat products, vinegar, and salt. But he wholly declined to agree to a National brand of tea, without which major transport economies in tea distribution were impossible;[1] and he insisted that any future schemes should be submitted for his personal approval before the Ministry was committed to them. Statutory schemes for pickles and cereal breakfast foods were at length introduced in October and November, but trade protests were successful in bringing about a further postponement of the preserves scheme, and it did not come into operation till April 1944. A number of minor voluntary schemes—cider, biscuit flour, cereal filler for sausages, and empty biscuit tins—were also introduced during this period. In May, a revised scheme was introduced for soft drinks.

It had taken three years for transport economy schemes to reach their zenith—an obstinate fact that must weigh heavy in the balance against all the praise which is their due. The greater part of the delay must be put down, not to technical difficulties, for these though very real were overcome with great ingenuity, but to the opposition of vested interests that were very ready to thrust the consumer before them as a shield. The question of how far consumer choice ought to be preserved in war-time is not, indeed, easy; opinions will always differ on such points as that of National Tea, against which the Minister stood so firm. To be deprived of a favourite brand of chocolate, pickles, or cereal breakfast food is a real though minor grievance; and one may wryly applaud, at any rate on psychological grounds, the decision to allow one breakfast food widely used as a laxative to be sent anywhere in the Kingdom. Ministry procedure in these matters, however, was far from being consistent; even pooled and standardised commodities were treated differently. On the one hand, the separate identities of soft drink manufacturers were almost completely obliterated;[2] on the other, the standard pack of canned beans was not only marketed under a variety of brand names, but was not zoned at all. The completeness of a transport economy scheme clearly depended as much on the resoluteness of each individual Commodity Director and the willingness of the trade to co-operate, as on its intrinsic merits or technical ease of accomplishment.

---

[1] Even allowing for the preservation of brands, more economies in tea distribution could have been secured but for the mutual mistrust of the two largest firms, which proved a fatal stumbling block to a pooling of deliveries, on the lines of those for biscuits.

[2] Almost, but not quite, since each manufacturer was given a code letter which could not be kept entirely secret.

Turning from zoning schemes to other measures of transport economy, the same phenomena are apparent. While milk deliveries in the large urban areas were drastically dealt with at a relatively early stage, the only restriction on bread (apart from that imposed by petrol restrictions) was a limitation of deliveries to three a week. Further restrictions were constantly mooted but came to nothing, chiefly it seems because Bread Division was unwilling to propose the tying of customers to a single baker, without which any local zoning of deliveries would be unworkable.[1] Yet it is surely clear that no more hardship would have been imposed on the consumer by this than by the drastic curtailment of all other retail deliveries, worked out by the Ministry of War Transport with the consent of the Ministry of Food, and in one town[2] imposed on an unwilling minority by Order, after prior agreement with the traders. Since maximum prices Orders forbade any charge for delivery, there was a strong incentive for retailers to abolish deliveries altogether, and the Ministry had on occasion to issue warnings not to go too far.[3]

III

The Ministry's conciliatory approach to zoning schemes in no way detracts from their technical interest; indeed, it called for greater skill than more ruthless methods might have done. Broadly speaking, the preparation of a zoning scheme was begun by calling together representative traders, and inviting them to prepare plans on lines laid down by the Ministry. For many industries, such as jams, and pickles and sauces, the Food Manufacturers' Federation, with its expert officials, was called in. For beer, central meetings with the Brewers' Society were supplemented by local meetings in every Food Division. When a scheme had been hammered out, it would either be announced as a voluntary scheme, which the trade association and the railways would combine to police, or more often, especially for trades where a large number of manufacturers were concerned, would

---

[1] A contributory influence here may have been the feeling that registration of consumers for bread would be a step easing the introduction of bread rationing, which all but a few enthusiasts were eager to avoid. The Order limiting bread deliveries was S.R. & O. (1943) No. 1653.

[2] St. Andrews, where a proposal for a voluntary scheme, agreed to by the trade, evoked much local agitation. The Ministry of War Transport was unwilling to enforce the scheme by Order, but the Ministry of Food undertook to do so. Since a few non-foodstuffs were involved, the Order (S.R. & O. (1942) No. 901 S.28) was made under Defence Regulation 55 instead of the Food Transport Order, a proof, incidentally, that the latter was legally superfluous. The objectors, however, continued their agitation, and the Principal of the University and the M.P. for East Fife were drawn in. After being amended in March 1943, the Order was finally revoked in July on the understanding that the restrictions would be voluntarily maintained.

[3] 'We have no powers', the Ministry remarked on one occasion 'to compel traders to deliver'. One ingenious trader in N.W. London got over the maximum price difficulty by hiring a taxi, his customers sharing the cost.

either be made the subject of a special Order, or included in the provisions of a general Control Order. The principle on which zoning
was undertaken was to secure that each zone should supply its own
needs, if possible; that zones having a surplus should not import at all,
nor should deficient zones export. Since the location of factories was
different for every foodstuff, ranging from the extreme dispersion of
breweries to the extreme concentration of margarine, oatmeal and
ice-cream, each group, if not each individual food, had to be zoned
separately—a complication which gave not only the Ministry, but
manufacturers of several products and still more wholesalers, a great
deal of work. A fruitful source of anomalies was the need, on administrative grounds, to make zone boundaries coincide with those of
Food Divisions or local government areas, neither of which had any
significance for food distribution.

The sort of problem that arose may be shown by one simple illustration. Barnoldswick, a small town in the extreme west of Yorkshire,
gets its food supplies through wholesalers in Colne, over the Lancashire
border. Under the Cereal Breakfast Foods Zoning Order, it was lawful for Barnoldswick retailers to sell product A, but not product B;
contrariwise, Lancashire wholesalers might sell B, but not A. To prevent the consumer in Barnoldswick going without altogether (A and
B being the only 'biscuit' breakfast cereals on the market) the Ministry
had not only to issue a licence, allowing the wholesalers in question to
handle A solely in transit to their customers over the border, but
arrange with the makers of A to supply them. A more general anomaly,
more insidious because traders might seize upon it to attack a whole
scheme they disliked, lay in the fact that wherever a line was drawn,
it could always be claimed that it eliminated a few economic hauls
along with the uneconomic. The Ministry strove to meet all bona-fide
difficulties by the issue of licences; but each individual case needed to
be considered not only on its merits, but with regard to the precedent
it might create.

The Sector Scheme for wholesalers, which had preceded the introduction of separate zoning schemes, and still remained in force,
offered similar difficulties. A firm of self-raising flour manufacturers
in Newcastle had been accustomed, under the Sector Scheme, to
distribute their flour in Scotland through depots either in Edinburgh
or in Carlisle, the latter being less than forty miles from the Scottish
border and being used also for deliveries in Cumberland. Under the
zoning scheme for self-raising flour they were excluded from
Cumberland, but admitted to Scotland; and they therefore requested
permission (*a*) to deliver direct to customers in the S.E. Scotland
border counties (*b*) to use their Carlisle depot for deliveries in Gallo-
way. But these requests had to be refused as contrary to the Sector
Scheme, with the result that all the firm's Scottish deliveries had to

Y

pass through their Edinburgh depot—the negation of transport economy. The solution of such problems as these was found in removing 'zoned' goods from the Sector Scheme altogether, as being preferable to the grant of innumerable individual licences that might have weakened zoning as a whole.

Self-raising-flour zoning provided a good instance of another problem, that of equality of treatment between wholesalers and manufacturers. Where exporting zone ('A') and importing zone ('B') were adjacent, a manufacturer in A was free to trade in both; but a wholesaler in the border area of B, who had been accustomed to buy in A for re-export to retailers there, found himself excluded from this trade. The wholesalers seized on this anomaly to protest; but as no one knew to what extent the real hardship would exist, the Ministry was able to escape for the moment with a temporary concession to the wholesalers in one particular 'border' town—Sheffield. The wholesalers thereupon asked that this concession be extended to all 'zoned' commodities, and the Ministry agreed that, in general, wholesalers might re-export 'permitted' goods back into the zone of origin within forty miles of their premises. It further undertook to consider favourably the grant of licences to enable wholesalers to procure and re-export goods not allowed to be sold in their own zone. (An example may make this concession clearer. Zone A produces commodities X and Y. X may be sold both in A and in adjacent zone B; Y is confined to A. A wholesaler in B might re-export X to A (within forty miles) without licence, but must be licensed if he wanted to import and re-export Y.) Another complication of more general importance was provided by the Co-operative Wholesale Society. It was not possible to bring the C.W.S. into zoning schemes, unless the identity of their goods was submerged by pooling; not because of their own objections, but because retailers might reasonably object to building up goodwill for a product that they would not be able to sell after the war. The Ministry had to be content to satisfy itself, so far as it could, that Co-operative goods were handled with reasonable transport economy.

Zoning was, of course, necessarily carried out on the assumption that demand for a food within any zone would not change as the result of limiting choice of brands. In fact, however, this did not always happen, with embarrassing results particularly where points rationed foods were concerned. Sometimes, indeed, zoning was blamed for symptoms—such as the chronic unsatisfied demand for treacle in East Anglia—that might possibly have been put right by a less rigid system of allocation (even within a zoning scheme), or even by an upward movement of points values over the whole country. More troublesome, however, than local shortages, which could always be more or less convincingly explained away, were local surpluses, owing to the unpopularity of a particular product. Thus a shortage in London of cereal breakfast foods was balanced by a surplus in Eastern I Food Division, which was restricted by zoning to one not very popular brand of corn flakes. In Scotland one of two brands allowed was unable to sell the whole of its production. Wartime rigidities of factory space and labour, apart from zoning, rendered impossible the commonsense solution of a transfer of production from one firm to another. Instead, resort was had to two devices—extending by licence the area of distribution of a particular firm; or 'dumping' the surplus on N.A.A.F.I. or similar organisations. Such expedients were the only alternative to an intolerable pooling and standardising of every small semi-luxury.

The zoning scheme for beer deliveries is worthy of more than passing mention, not only for its intrinsic interest as a technical achievement, but because it illustrates very clearly the mixed motives underlying zoning policy. What made beer attractive as an object of zoning was its sheer bulk (five million tons or so a year) and the enormous problem of returned empties. It was these qualities, of course, that had made brewing a very localised industry with a very short haul—estimated by the Brewers' Society at an average of fifteen miles. The tied-house system, however, meant that there was a large amount of local cross-haulage; and the voluntary zoning scheme worked out by the trade and the Ministry during 1943, therefore, proposed to divide England and Wales into no less than seventy-six zones,[1] within each of which, by exchange of deliveries, cross haulage was eliminated, while movement across zone boundaries was reduced to a minimum. Thus A's beer might be on sale in some of B's houses, and *vice versa*; a scrapping of the tied-house system which sometimes led to complications where A's beer was different in gravity from B's, but on the whole seems to have been achieved without causing the customer any great uneasiness. Considerable economies were thus obtained in the less wasteful section of the brewing industry.

There remained what the Ministry called National and Category II brewers. The former were those—Bass, Guinness and Worthington—whose beers were called for by name all over the Kingdom. The latter were the scarcely less famous firms like Truman, Allsopp, and Marston of Burton, Watney and Whitbread of London, and Younger of Edinburgh—whose specialities, particularly bottled beer, had equally nation-wide distribution[2] and were in at least one case

---

[1] Twelve for Scotland, where the concentration of brewing in Edinburgh offered relatively little scope for economy.

[2] One of the more picturesque examples of long haulage by rail that came to light in 1941 was the transport of Whitbread's Stout in tank wagons from London to Glasgow; the return load consisting of Loch Katrine water for the breaking down of over-proof whisky. The Ministry of War Transport stopped the loading of the water, but the Ministry of Food was able to show that there was no alternative source of stout for the Clydesider.

linked with a network of bottling plants. These brewers accounted for fifteen per cent. or less of total production, but their total ton-mileage—most of it by rail—was about one-half of the whole in 1941. No one, it seems, would face so drastic a step as to deny these beers to any part of the country; some small restrictions were indeed placed on Category II brewers, but the only major attempt at economy was by securing better loading of rail wagons—a reform similar to those which, for biscuits and confectionery, had been dismissed as insufficient.

The picture of the economies achieved in beer transport between 1941 and 1943, as assessed by the Ministry on information supplied by the Brewers' Society, was thus a peculiar one. Though bulk barrelage had increased by nearly six per cent., the amount going by road had remained practically stationary; fuel consumption (and hence the average length of haul) had gone down by nearly twenty-two per cent. But the average length of haul by rail actually increased by ten per cent.; and when to this was added the increase in barrelage, the road economies were more than wiped out. So far from there being a saving of 40 million ton-miles, as had been estimated by the Ministry, there was an increase of over 10 millions between 1941 and 1943. These awkward facts are not, of course, a criticism of the zoning technique, nor ought one to infer that the savings on local beer transport were not worth while. But they do underline the severe limitations within which the Transport Division had to work.

Equally illuminating is the case of ice cream, the manufacture of which was banned for a long period, on the confessed ground of saving transport. Ice cream accounted for a small tonnage compared with 'national' beers; it travelled by passenger train, and it is probably safe to say that no extra train was ever run on its account. Admittedly its containers were heavy and awkward to handle, particularly for women porters. Nevertheless, one cannot avoid the conclusion that its drastic treatment was due, in part at any rate, to non-technical reasons—to first, its being an evident luxury at a time when austerity was fashionable, and second to the prominent labelling and easy identification of its containers. In short, it was a traffic that attracted notice.

IV

In considering the amount of transport economies actually achieved for food it must be borne in mind that, to many concerned, the appearance of economy was an end in itself; no less, indeed perhaps more, important than the reality. Only a handful of experts, it seems, saw the problem steadily and clearly as an essential means of preventing a complete breakdown on the railways in winter. Every traffic embargo imposed by the railways, it must be remembered, is a symptom of excess in demand over supply; and railway embargoes were chronic throughout the war, and indeed for some time after it. It is clear that economies could have been pushed further without major hardship to the consumer.

To these general considerations must be added the technical point that the assessment of economies in numerical terms is a task of almost insuperable difficulty. The Ministry of Food frankly, and indeed publicly, admitted that its estimates for different commodities were not strictly comparable; and the figure of 300 million ton-miles per annum for the total rate of economy when all the schemes were in operation was little more than an informed guess.[1] Moreover, one ton-mile is not really equal to another, where such a variety of goods and means of transport are concerned. One cannot compare the savings on beer, wholly in terms of road transport, with those, estimated as roughly similar in ton-miles, resulting from the fish zoning scheme, which largely eliminated long-distance fish trains and therefore eased the pressure on junctions and marshalling yards. Naturally enough, the most spectacular savings were on those semi-luxuries whose pre-war price—as with biscuits—was able to stand heavy delivery costs; least with necessities whose bulk alone allowed them to make a substantial contribution through relatively slight economies. The savings per ton on bulk flour were small; those on biscuits and confectionery enormous—some 200 miles per ton for the former. (Hence—apart from consumer objections—it does not appear that vast economies could be made in food transport under peace-time conditions.)

When all has been said, however, the savings were substantial and important; they cannot be justly measured merely as a proportion of the total ton-miles moved, even supposing that were possible. For the strain on transport resources was such that any economy might be decisive at the margin of breakdown; just as the relatively small tonnage carried by coaster gave effective relief to the railways. The contribution of food control to transport economy must be judged less in terms of the ton-miles saved by specific zoning schemes than by the ample evidence of a continual striving to move food in the most efficient way. Such devices as the planned movement, from 1941–42 onwards, of one-third to one-half of the Scottish seed potato crop by coaster, instead of rail; the insistence that full wagon loads only be moved; the elaborate and detailed arrangements for handling the transport of the vastly increased supplies of home-grown grain to the mills, the introduction of nominated loading days for Cornish

---

[1] These estimates were published at a Press Conference on 11th January 1944.

vegetables, are examples of innumerable efforts, big and small, arousing little controversy or even attention, and sometimes meaning financial sacrifice for the trader.[1] In no field of the Ministry's activities were technical expertise, skill in negotiation, and public spirit, more continually evident.

---

[1] For the Ministry of Transport had not found it possible to equalise rates as between rail and coaster; the former were pegged after 1940, while the latter were much enhanced by war risk insurance. In the case of Scottish seed potatoes, the Treasury did indeed authorise the payment of compensation to growers; but others—such as Edinburgh maltsters obliged to ship coastwise to London—had to bear the extra cost themselves.

CHAPTER XXVII

International Wheat Negotiations, 1939-45

I

RUNNING as a continual undercurrent to the Ministry of Food's
international activities, whether in the field of procurement or
in the wider context of inter-Allied collaboration, was the
world wheat problem. Wheat was like other foods in that, over-
plentiful before the war, even more so after the fall of France, it
eventually became acutely scarce. It was, however, the last food to
do so, and until the very end of the war there was room for doubt
whether a genuine world shortage would ever materialise, and no
likelihood that a shortage would be lasting. The pattern of world
wheat trade, unlike that for sugar or for non-foods like tin and
rubber, was never broken by the cleavage of the world into hostile
camps, which perforce put existing international controls for these
commodities into cold storage. Of the four wheat producers that really
count in world trade—the United States, Canada, Argentina, and
Australia—three were Allies, while the United Kingdom was the
largest wheat consumer.

From the point of view of food supplies and prices, the wheat
problem was omnipresent; from that of the economic and political
aspects of the Grand Alliance, it was scarcely less so. All discussions
of post-war reconstruction, all attempts to put the economic state of
the world on a more stable basis, had sooner rather than later to
reckon with it. It could not be treated as a technical problem to be
left to experts; on the other hand, as events were to demonstrate
afresh, want of expert knowledge could not but lead to misunderstanding or frustration. Indeed, the handling of wheat negotiations
during the war affords an object-lesson in the qualities that a determination to introduce an internationally managed economy will
require of the managers.

It was fitting that those engaged in a second world war should find
themselves grappling with a problem that had been conjured up by
the first. It was then that the 'big four' producers had enormously
increased their acreage under wheat; afterwards, as wheat production in Europe slowly recovered from war, the world market for
wheat failed to keep pace with the permanently increased output.
World consumption of wheat increased but slightly; the world wheat

yield per acre remained almost stable; but wheat acreage remained obstinately in excess of what was needed to satisfy demand. From 1927 onwards surpluses began to accumulate; in 1930–31 wheat prices collapsed; the world slump was followed by a whole series of trade restrictions which diminished world trade in wheat still further, and which by encouraging production in the importing countries threatened to perpetuate the world wheat crisis.[1]

The International Wheat Agreement of 1933 was a first and rather half-hearted attempt to solve the problem by mutual action. The signatory exporting countries each accepted for the next two years an export quota, fixed in millions of bushels; the big four undertook to reduce acreage by fifteen per cent. The importing countries, including the United Kingdom, undertook not to increase their wheat production, to encourage wheat consumption, and to remove import duties on wheat when the world price should have recovered. The Agreement, made for only two years, did not survive that long; for Argentina, pleading that Canada had not fulfilled her promise to reduce acreage, exceeded her quota for 1933–34. All that remained of it was a representative 'Wheat Advisory Committee', with an office in London.

For a time, bad crops in the United States, Canada, and Argentina, combined to mitigate the effect of the collapse and reduce the surpluses while giving the opponents of restriction, particularly in Canada, an opportunity to bury their heads in the sand. (The Mackenzie King Government was returned on an anti-restriction ticket.) The world crop of 1938, however, was a record for all time, and in January 1939 preparatory negotiations were set in train for a new agreement. As drafted, it differed from the old in two important particulars; first, a proposal to fix a 'basic minimum price' for wheat below which export would not be allowed, together with a 'basic optimum' price, above which export quotas would be increased;[2] secondly, an undertaking by the 'big four' to maintain minimum, and not to exceed maximum stocks, or in other words to maintain the 'ever-normal granary' sponsored by Mr. Henry Wallace, then United States Secretary of Agriculture. The Wheat Advisory Committee was to be converted into an 'International Wheat Council', with extended powers.

These draft proposals seem to have been regarded by British

---

[1] Hevesy, P. de, *World Wheat Planning* (1940), Chapter I. It is not proposed to discuss here the vexed question of the relations between the world wheat slump and the general economic depression after 1929; but the evidence assembled by Hevesy seems to demonstrate the peculiar maladjustment of the wheat market beyond all doubt.

[2] These prices were calculated by an arbitrary formula, the justification for which is anything but clear. They were to be 75 per cent. and 100 per cent. respectively of the product of the Board of Trade monthly index of wholesale prices and 35s. 6d., i.e. the average United Kingdom market price for 1909–14.

officials with indifference, though the Ministry of Agriculture was opposed to any commitment that might limit the United Kingdom wheat acreage. The effect of the price and quota provisions on the working of the international grain trade does not appear to have been considered; nor had the Board of Trade, the Department principally concerned, formulated any views on what the maximum and minimum stock figures that would constitute the 'ever-normal granary' ought to be.[1] Yet technicalities like these would determine, not indeed whether an agreement would be reached, but whether it would achieve its purpose of adjusting supply and demand. If, for instance, the minimum stocks were fixed too high, an agreement might do no more than perpetuate surplus conditions. If price fixing would destroy the organised grain markets, an agreement would be dearly bought; certainly one would need to be very sure of success in order to pay such a price. In short, when war broke out the United Kingdom had no thought-out policy for dealing with the world wheat crisis, and hence ran the risk of having a policy thrust upon it.

In September 1939 an attempt was made, under the ægis of the Wheat Advisory Committee, to apportion export quotas between the big four; but this broke down in face of Canadian opposition. The Committee itself was put on a 'care and maintenance' basis, and its Secretary[2] joined the Ministry of Food. With the fall of France, the wheat surplus became one among many; the blockade of Europe and the shortage of shipping combined to pile up enormous surpluses, more especially of tropical products. To the War Cabinet Committees set up to deal with this problem,[3] the prime necessity was to enlist the co-operation of the United States, which was itself taking vigorous action to deal with surpluses in the New World. When the blockade was lifted, as it would be some day, some of these surpluses would be needed for European relief, and planning would be necessary to secure that supplies were readily available. Advance provision for relief might truly make a virtue of necessity. Though the problem was in essence one, the methods of dealing with separate commodities might well be different; while purely *ad hoc* measures were to be avoided, it was felt in London that use might be made of such bodies as the Wheat Advisory Committee and the International Sugar Council.

Perhaps owing to the imminent Presidential election, the State Department, to whom these views were put in September 1940, was

---

[1] It is fair to add that officials were overburdened in the early months of 1939. They were, for instance, heavily engaged with the sugar restriction scheme (Chapter II).

[2] Mr. Andrew Cairns, formerly statistician to the Canadian Wheat Pools, and the chief architect of the new draft agreement.

[3] The Ministerial and Official Sub-Committees on Export Surpluses. Only the latter met at all regularly.

inclined to be wary of any general approach to the problem. The suggestion that the Wheat Advisory Committee should be revived evoked more response, and naturally won support in the United States Department of Agriculture, which suggested that a meeting of the major countries concerned might be held in Washington. Soundings in Ottawa were less promising. Although the Ministry of Food had been obliged by shortage of ships to buy abnormally heavily in Canada, the Canadian wheat surplus (thanks to an excellent crop in 1940) was still growing. Even so, it was not until March 1941 that the Canadians were persuaded to agree to a meeting being held. Though formal invitations were to issue from the United States, the original initiative had come from the United Kingdom.

II

In the drafting of instructions for the British delegation, discussion again centred on how far, if at all, the United Kingdom should undertake to reduce its wheat acreage after the war. The Ministry of Agriculture now reinforced its former objections by the technical argument that the 'healthy and well-balanced agriculture', to the maintenance of which the Government was publicly committed, would demand a higher wheat acreage than before the war; and it took the point to the Lord President's Committee. Only after the Embassy in Washington had been expressly consulted, and had advised that the Americans would not be satisfied by a vague undertaking not to expand wheat acreage beyond what was technically necessary, were the instructions varied to allow an undertaking that the pre-war acreage would not be exceeded.

This issue, though it had some domestic importance, was insignificant[1] compared with the main problems any wheat agreement would have to solve. It was indeed obvious that export quotas combined with maximum and minimum prices would be unworkable so long as the shipping shortage persisted. But no doubts were raised about their applicability in peace-time; the price formula aroused no murmur; no opinion was expressed about the limits within which the stocks in the 'ever-normal granary' should fluctuate. On all these points in the 1939 draft, the United Kingdom delegate was given a blank cheque; he was to agree to police a scheme which in all its most important features would be devised by the big four and the secretariat of the Wheat Advisory Committee.

The initial course of the Washington Wheat Meeting, which at length opened on 10th July 1941, was thus almost a foregone conclu-

---

[1] One of the arguments used against any reduction in the British wheat acreage was that it was insignificant in relation to the world acreage.

sion.[1] By the first week in August it had prepared a draft agreement for consideration by Governments. This was very largely based on the 1939 draft, but modified and tightened up in a way wholly favourable to the producing countries. Not only was the minimum price far higher,[2] but the vague obligation on all signatories to concert measures against a country that should exceed its export quota was replaced by a clause that would place upon importing countries the onus of seeing that quotas were not in fact exceeded; the agreement would thus be preventive instead of merely punitive. To the regulatory provisions were added a proposal for a special 'relief pool' of wheat, to be administered by an 'International Wheat Union'; and a preamble condemning restrictionism and proclaiming a common policy designed *inter alia* to secure world consumers an 'abundance of high-quality, low cost wheat'.

The explosive reaction that these proposals aroused in Whitehall must have bewildered the United Kingdom delegation. Mr. Keynes described the draft terms as a 'fantastic piece of chicanery'; the Minister of Agriculture found in them good reason for pressing his technical objection to acreage restriction, and asked where was the *quid pro quo*; all agreed that the price proposals were unreasonably high, calculated as they were to mean a shilling quartern loaf once the Treasury subsidy were removed. The objections of the Cereals Division of the Ministry of Food were more fundamental; the price and quota provisions, it said, would make it impossible for the United Kingdom to revert to private importation of grain during the life of the Agreement. If, as was proposed, the Agreement were to last five years, this would probably extinguish the grain trade for good. Hence the article providing for the regulation of export quotas by reference to a freely determined United Kingdom import price could not operate, since there would be no such price. Moreover, the Division questioned whether acreage limitation in this country could be enforced if the c.i.f. price of wheat rose, as it would under the Agreement, to 55s. 6d. a quarter.

These criticisms went to the root, not merely of the specific proposals now under debate, but of the principles that had been hawked around Whitehall at intervals during two years without arousing suspicion or protest. The price and quota provisions of the 1939 agreement had been scarcely less drastic than these in their implications for private trade in grain and the working of the futures market.

---

[1] The United Kingdom delegate was elected Chairman, and took scarcely any active part in the discussions. On the all-important sub-committee on prices, the United Kingdom was not represented.

[2] The 1939 'basic optimum' price was first recalculated in relation to the 1922–39 United Kingdom average landed price (i.e. to 38s. 6d. instead of 35s. 6d. per quarter); the whole of the figure thus obtained, instead of three-quarters of it, was then taken as a minimum.

What was in question was not the livelihood of a few speculators, but the existence of a sensitive and effective mechanism that not only procured supplies at the lowest possible cost, but contributed to invisible exports both directly and indirectly through the shipping and insurance business that went with it. This was now threatened, not as a result of a high-level decision taken after due deliberation, but through sheer inadvertence. Worse, the United Kingdom was more than half committed to an agreement likely to have such far-reaching effects at a meeting of its own seeking.

Far though the Cereals Division went in criticism of the proposals, it is possible to go farther. If acreage restriction would be difficult in this country with wheat at 55s. 6d., how much more so would it be in the big producer countries? Would not the Agreement perpetuate the surplus instead of curing it, and would it not then eventually destroy itself? If so, there could be even less justification for putting the world wheat market in jeopardy. It was to be left to a non-official expert to elaborate these points, a year later;[1] but they reinforce the policy that was now urged by the Ministry of Food and the Treasury. The United Kingdom, while giving a welcome to the general objectives of the conference, should reject the price proposals, should agree in general terms to police export quotas from signatory countries only, and should point out the difficulties in imposing acreage restriction and other provisions on the European importing countries. It should agree to contribute to the Relief Pool, while discouraging any separate organisation to distribute it. Implicit in this attitude would be a proviso for the continuation of bulk imports of wheat for at least two years after the end of the war.[2]

These views appeared to gain some sympathy from officials of the United States Department of Agriculture with whom they were discussed informally in London. When, however, the Washington discussions began again at the end of October, the British delegation, now for the first time competently briefed, was pressed very strongly to agree to a minimum export price. The United States in particular was said to be taking an emotional attitude that was quite irrelevant to the merits of the case. 'There is much embittered feeling'—the delegation reported—'that America makes bold and generous gestures on great scale, e.g. Lend/Lease, while in our negotiations we haggle'. A new and complicated, but little more acceptable, price formula was

---

[1] Davis, Joseph S., 'New International Wheat Agreements'. *Wheat Studies* of the Food Research Institute, Stanford University, November 1942. This is incomparably the best study generally available.

[2] An attempt to blame Mr. Cairns, who had been chairman of the official group drafting the United Kingdom delegate's original instructions, was both unworthy and baseless. He was indeed the author of the 1939 draft, and willing to go to great lengths for the sake of some sort of agreement. But he made no secret of his views, and it was not his fault if his colleagues (who included two academic economists) were not sufficiently wide awake.

put forward by the importing countries, and it looked as though the only alternative to deadlock was a major concession by the United Kingdom.

The extension of the war, however, suggested a way to escape this dilemma. Surely neither Britain nor the United States could commit themselves to such far-reaching proposals without consulting their Russian ally? This view, with its implications that the Conference should adjourn after reporting progress, was accepted by the State Department. The Americans felt, however, that some sort of minimum price should be agreed on for the period immediately following hostilities; and suggested that this interim price should be that paid by the Ministry of Food for the last bulk purchase from Canada before hostilities ended. The Ministry of Food demurred to this; now that the Canadians were supplying Great Britain under the Billion Dollar Gift there could be no certainty that the price of future contracts would not be nominally enhanced.[1] Other Departments, however, clutched at the opportunity, and the Ambassador in Washington, in particular, pointed out that it would be unwise to indulge in further argument: 'You have been conceded an absolute veto on all substantial points'. If this had been true in fact as well as in form, there would be little to complain of. But, as the Board of Trade admitted in recommending Government acceptance of the Memorandum of Agreement, the United Kingdom should be morally bound to support the terms of the Draft Convention at the full-scale Wheat Conference that would be summoned in due course, 'unless new circumstances affecting the issues develop'.[2]

The Memorandum of Agreement finally reached provided for the immediate setting-up of an International Wheat Council, to have its seat for the time being in Washington. It was to be responsible for administering the Relief Pool of 100 million bushels. Production control by the four exporters was to operate at once. Directly the war ended, the export quotas and an interim minimum price were to come into force, the latter to be determined by unanimous agreement of the Council or, failing agreement, to be the latest price at which the United Kingdom should have bought Canadian wheat in bulk. At the very first meeting of the Council, in August 1942, it became clear that the United States would press for an early price decision. During the autumn, the British and Canadians had to resist pressure for the disclosure of the latest contract price to the Council Executive Committee. At the Council meeting in January 1943 the British members successfully blocked a decision, though at the expense of

---

[1] A fear echoed by the Canadian delegation itself, presumably concerned lest the task of acreage restriction became impossibly difficult.

[2] The Lord President's Committee gave assent on 30th April; the Chancellor of the Exchequer expressed his dissent with the Board of Trade view that the arrangements were of positive advantage to the United Kingdom.

some good will; the Americans once again complained of Britain's non-co-operative attitude. It seemed impossible that a price discussion should be avoided at the next meeting in August, but in the event it was postponed by American request to October, and then again to January 1944.

III

By that time the world wheat situation had been changed, in prospect at any rate, by the record production of hogs in the United States, and a large increase in the use of wheat for fuel in Argentina and industrial alcohol in the United States. Already, in May 1943, the British delegation at the Hot Springs Conference[1] had secured the adoption of a resolution suggesting that a world shortage of wheat was likely if the United Nations did not go slow on the rebuilding of flocks and herds in liberated Europe, and this notwithstanding a prospective carry-over into 1943–44 of 1,600 million bushels, a record for the big four. Transport difficulties in North America were certainly hindering the free movement of wheat so much as to produce all the symptoms of real shortage; the United States was importing Canadian wheat in large quantities for animal feeding, but even so felt constrained to come forward to the August 1943 Wheat Council with the announcement that it was increasing its 'target acreage' from 54 to 68 millions. This would, by shifting the acres of cultivation, relieve transport difficulties, but it would reduce yield per acre and increase average cost of production. Under-Secretary of Agriculture Appleby was thus enabled to take the line that the long-term trend in wheat prices would be upward, but that there was no likelihood of a world wheat shortage.

This view was endorsed by the Wheat Council at its meeting in October 1944; but it aroused strong opposition in the Ministry of Food, which by this time was convinced that shortage was all too likely. London estimated that while the 1944 carry-over might still exceed 1,000 million bushels, there was a distinct possibility that unless yields continued to exceed the average, demands for relief and industrial purposes might be such as to bring it down in 1945 to 300 million bushels, and in 1946 lower still. The Ministry pressed for an increase in acreage in the producing countries, and took particular exception to a letter addressed on behalf of the Council to the Chairman of the newly formed UNRRA, conveying the impression that the wheat prospects were satisfactory. It argued that the Council could have no knowledge of relief requirements, that wheat for relief

---

[1] See Chapter XXVIII.

could not be discussed apart from other foods, and that the proper place to clear these matters was the Combined Food Board. While these arguments had point, it remained true that the Wheat Council had been given specific responsibility for relief wheat; and the sceptic might wonder whether they would have been so strongly urged had the Wheat Council not been at statistical variance with the Ministry of Food.[1]

The Ministry's apprehensions certainly weakened its ability to argue against fixing the post-war price as soon as possible. For if wheat at two dollars was a probability for 1945, there might be tactical advantage—at any rate so the Treasury thought—in fixing a maximum price even as high as $1.25, the nominal figure that the Canadians had declared when they closed the Winnipeg market in September 1943. Informal soundings, however, on the chances of getting agreement to a price range somewhat lower than this came up against a difficulty in the Canadian exports of wheat to the United States.

Since the closure of the Winnipeg market in 1943 the Canadian Wheat Board had pegged the price for these exports at a fixed differential below the price at Chicago, which was still in effect uncontrolled. As early as March 1944 they were fetching $1·45 Canadian. It was clear that the Canadians would not agree to a ceiling price lower than this, but even so, the Ministry of Food was at length persuaded that an attempt to prevent it from going higher by using the machinery of the Wheat Agreement could do no harm and might do good.

However, at the Council's meeting in April 1944 the Canadians asked for a maximum price equal to the United States domestic ceiling price, or about $1.90; after further haggling it was agreed to fix a minimum of $1 and a maximum of $1.50 to remain until 1947 or two years after the end of European hostilities, whichever was the later. Canadian-United States trade was to be excluded from these provisions—an exception to which the Ministry of Food agreed only reluctantly, under pressure from other Departments.

This agreement never came into force, for its conclusion was held up for so long by a technical hitch about the proper price equivalents for Australian wheat that the exporting countries all had second thoughts. At the Council meeting on 31st August–1st September 1945 it was agreed to drop the whole question of maximum and minimum prices for the time being, and merely to pass a resolution urging producing countries to keep their export prices low. At the same time it was agreed to begin preparations for an international conference which, perhaps in 1947, might undertake a complete revision of the existing Draft Convention.

---

[1] See Chapter XIX.

Any temporary benefit the United Kingdom might stand to gain from the prescription of a maximum price in time of acute but essentially transient scarcity was, the Ministry of Food rightly judged, unimportant compared with the damage resulting from adherence to an unreasonably high long-term minimum. But the tactics of price negotiations were only one part, and that the least important, of the problems posed by the original Draft Agreement. It remained true in 1945, as in 1939, that the British Government was without an international wheat policy. The Ministry of Food's trade experts had devastated the original proposals; but its General Department had never sat down to consider the problem as a whole, and what the provisions of a workable scheme should be. Serious thought on the subject anywhere seems to have been confined to unofficial experts without the advantage of access to Government records.[1]

The proceedings of the International Wheat Council had been singularly barren, but they served at least to bring out the central dilemma of the world wheat problem. Short of means being found to stimulate consumption enormously, the surplus created by the war of 1914–18, sustained during the twenty years' truce, and likely to be exacerbated in the long run by the Second World War, could only be got rid of by a reduction in acreage.[2] But this could only be secured, if at all, by a reduction in price to which producing countries were unwilling to agree, but which in any case was indispensable if consumption was to increase. The criticism that the Draft Agreement was restrictionist must thus be qualified by saying that it none the less seemed likely to perpetuate a surplus. Again, it was urged that a minimum carry-over of about 300 million bushels was unnecessarily high and burdensome, and that export quotas would tend to stereotype the existing balance of production.[3]

It was these and similar questions of principle that urgently needed attention by all Governments; and the United Kingdom's vital interests demanded that she should be in the forefront of their investigation.

---

[1] See citations earlier in this chapter.

[2] Merely regulatory devices such as buffer stock schemes would of course be useless to deal with chronic surplus. It must be re-emphasised that between the wars, supply had only balanced demand in years of general crop failure.

[3] See Davis, *op. cit.* The separate minima were far from being scientifically determined, as a study of the negotiations shows. But even had they been, any agreement with rigid export quotas, which prevent the offsetting of stock deficiencies in one country by stock surpluses in another, cannot but have the effect of inflating the total minimum carry-over required. The agreement proposed, in short, not an ever-normal granary for the world, but four separate ever-normal granaries. Hevesy's scheme for negotiable quota certificates is one proposal for getting over this difficulty (*op. cit.* Chapter VI).

CHAPTER XXVIII

The Hot Springs Conference; a World Food Organisation

I

AT the beginning of 1943 President Roosevelt suddenly, and without warning, proposed that an inter-Allied conference of experts and technicians be called forthwith to discuss post-war food problems. The President appears to have been prompted by the thought that food would be a suitable subject for initiating United Nations' collaboration, rather than by any consideration of food problems as being especially urgent. In Whitehall the suggestion was received with surprise and mixed feelings. Concern lest the Conference trespass on more general economic questions that the United Kingdom was not yet ready to discuss; scepticism about the usefulness of reopening questions already dealt with by the League of Nations Mixed Committee on Nutrition, caused some Departments to treat the Conference with reserve.

But the Ministry of Food, increasingly preoccupied as it had become with prospective as well as present scarcities in world food supplies, was quick to see the opportunity a conference would offer of warning the Allies that an armistice might bring with it, not instant plenty, but still greater stringency, and that the system of allocation through the Combined Food Board, or something like it, must continue if a runaway commodity boom followed by a disastrous slump were not to occur. The United Kingdom, depleted as it would be both of shipping and foreign exchange, might find its own supplies in jeopardy and others might be still worse off. The British should try, the Ministry urged, to get the Conference not merely to accept this prospect of scarcity but to resolve on a world-wide drive for increased food production.[1]

The tactical implications of this were tricky. Unless carefully handled, the Conference might do little more than advertise a fundamental cleavage between producers in exporting countries and those in importing countries. To insist over-much on scarcity would be to encourage rapacity in exporting countries, who would in any case have to be given a *quid pro quo* for increasing production, in the form

---

[1] Chapter XIX.

of some sort of insurance against future slump; from the United Kingdom point of view the course of the international wheat negotiations[1] was an evil omen. Moreover, general acceptance of the British view might recoil on the heads of its proponents in the form of a request to reduce rations still further in order to prevent starvation in Europe.

Besides these short-run considerations, questions of long-term policy would arise. It seemed likely that delegates to this, the first of a series of full-dress Allied Conferences, might wish to leave their mark on history in the form of a new international organisation; yet the case for such an organisation was debatable.

Nevertheless, Whitehall generally agreed that it would be unwise to adopt a merely negative attitude towards any such proposal, lest the vacuum be filled by a more or less disguised conspiracy of producers. Numerous forms of restriction scheme had long been hawked abroad and their projectors' voices would undoubtedly be heard behind, if not before, the scenes at the Conference. It was felt, therefore, that the United Kingdom delegation ought rather to take the lead in proposing that a new organisation be set up; but should endeavour to secure that it be endowed with no executive powers, and indeed that no attempt be made by the Conference itself to draft a constitution. Rather should some continuing committee be left with the task of working out plans for bringing it into being.

To what purpose should a new body be dedicated, apart from any short-term duties which might be put upon it? An answer was to be found in the clamant need to improve nutrition throughout the world at large. Research and the pooling of information might do much to promote the general adoption of national policies designed to improve nutrition. The British might emphasise the extent to which nutrition standards had been maintained, and perhaps even enhanced, under war-time conditions; might point to the proposals for family allowances, to their experience and intentions in the Colonial Empire. While the delegation could not but draw attention to the wider economic and social implications of a policy of improved world nutrition, and might even air, in a manner deliberately tentative, the proposals for the international regulation of primary products that had been worked out in London, it should insist that detailed discussion on such questions was beyond the scope of a food conference.

Instructions in this sense were hammered out by the Departments during March and April, and approved by the War Cabinet on 22nd April, with but one amendment; the delegates were not to take the initiative in proposing the continuance of rationing after the war. If, however, the United States delegates expressed willingness to do so for the sake of post-war relief, the British might respond that they

---

[1] Chapter XXVII.

would 'not fall behind other countries in our willingness to apply in common with others, and having regard to the condition of our island, some measure of control over home consumption while the stringency lasts'.

The Conference had been postponed from 27th April till 18th May, both the Russians and the British having protested that the earlier date was too soon. Even so, there was barely time for the drafting of adequate instructions to the delegation; and the accompanying documents bore marks of the extreme haste with which they had been prepared. The delegation was soundly briefed on principles and tactics; but its policies had not invariably a firm statistical foundation. To take only the most conspicuous example, the assertion that the dominant problem in the first phase following the end of the war would be that of providing sufficient energy foods to relieve hunger, and that it would be rash to switch over to livestock production immediately was distinctly debatable,[1] based as it was on necessarily imperfect knowledge of the requirements of liberated Europe on the one hand, and a somewhat empirical estimate of future production on the other. Only experience could show whether such an opinion was justified. Symptomatic, again, of the haste of the preparations was the late stage at which the British Food Mission was brought into full consultation.[2]

If the British delegation was somewhat handicapped by lack of time, others were even less favoured; for it at least had the advantage of preliminary discussions with the State Department and a preview of the agenda and 'working outline'. Small wonder that the Conference opened in an atmosphere of 'absolute bewilderment' made worse by an indifferent public and a hostile press. The venue, Hot Springs, Virginia—a fashionable holiday resort—in itself invited ridicule; the press was indignant at its exclusion from meetings; Congress was suspicious lest the Administration be entrapped into far-reaching commitments. The British delegation, led by the Minister of State, set itself to rescue the Conference from disaster. The press was won over by a series of conferences in which Mr. Law and his colleagues made it clear that Great Britain was anxious that the Conference should succeed. This lead proved effective; the Conference settle down to work with amity and enthusiasm and broke up in an atmosphere of real good will. Yet when it assembled there had been every reason to fear, as the Minister of State reported to his colleagues, that it might 'dissolve in a welkin-shattering howl of derision'.

---

[1] This is no less the case because a crisis in world grain supplies did actually occur in 1946–47.

[2] e.g., as late as 5th May Mr. Brand was not informed of the 'International Food Office' scheme, except at second hand; and it was originally planned that the British Food Mission representative should be an 'Adviser' instead of a full delegate.

II

The conclusions of the Conference took the form of thirty Resolutions[1] normally consisting of a preamble followed by a recommendation. They may be classified under three heads; first, general recommendations of more or less universal application; second, interim recommendations covering the period of emergency; and third, recommendations for machinery for carrying on the Conference's work. The last was put first by the Conference, which not merely recommended that a permanent organisation for food and agriculture be set up, but resolved that an 'Interim Commission' be set up in Washington, not later than 15th July, to formulate a specific plan for the permanent organisation, together with any other proposals necessary to give effect to the Conference resolutions. Governments were exhorted to undertake the improvement of their peoples' diet and food resources, particularly of the so-called 'vulnerable groups' within the population. They should combat, by research and propaganda, malnutrition and deficiency diseases, setting up 'national nutrition organisations', and making use of existing bodies for this purpose; they should exchange information and provide mutual help directly or through the proposed internal organisation. The basis for all this work should be dietary standards scientifically ascertained, but the practical possibilities of immediate improvement should also be taken into account.

The Resolutions went on to lay down principles that should govern production and distribution of foodstuffs, if 'an economy of abundance' were to be achieved. Each country should grow that for which it was best fitted, but single-crop production should in general be avoided, and due regard be had to keeping the land in good heart. Production of protective foods should be encouraged where appropriate. Stress was laid on the importance of credit facilities, producers' and consumers' co-operation, proper systems of land tenure, and the prevention of soil erosion and water losses. Governments should survey the possibilities of increasing food production through new land settlement; migration, where necessary, should be assisted by international action. Agricultural over-population might be relieved by industrial development, particularly in the form of food-processing plant and the manufacture of agricultural machinery and fertilisers. The Conference urged specific measures, such as family allowances, as an indirect means of ensuring adequate distribution. Improvement in grading standards and marketing facilities, the widespread use of

---

[1] Published in Cmd.6451. There were actually thirty-three Resolutions including the General Declaration and formal Votes of Thanks.

modern methods of food preservation and transport, the minimising of marketing costs, and the protection of the consumer against malpractice and fraud, were all recommended as subjects for national action and international inquiry.

These measures must be complemented by others more specifically international; and here the Conference was not to be deterred by its 'expert' status from making political pronouncements. 'Freedom from want cannot be achieved without freedom from fear'; the uneconomic use of resources was due to war and the fear of war. International security was a pre-requisite of world prosperity, which must be assured, since 'the first cause of hunger and malnutrition is poverty'. Tariff barriers, exchange instability, and other hindrances to international trade were condemned. But since 'excessive' short-term price changes not only hindered the 'orderly' production and distribution of foodstuffs directly, but also indirectly by aggravating general economic instability, the possibility of commodity regulation, with proper safeguards for the consumer, was worthy of urgent study; so were special measures to help countries whose food supplies were especially inadequate, whether as the result of catastrophe or not.

A history of war-time food control is not the place to analyse the detailed phrasing and implications of each of these Resolutions, and it seems at least doubtful whether, even in the long run, such analysis would be profitable, except for those seeking sanction or condemnation for a particular project, or loopholes for escape from the wider implications of the Conference. These were unambiguous enough; the delegates of forty-four nations had publicly gone on record against restrictive policies and economic nationalism—a hopeful gesture, even allowing for the inevitable mental reservations. Of more immediate practical importance were the recommendations for the interim period before peace was established. The Conference accepted the British view that the general shortage of food called for a production drive on the one hand, and a continuation of international schemes for the allocation of food and shipping on the other. Indeed, it went further, calling upon countries to increase wherever possible the acreage under crops for direct human consumption, 'and even to hold back the rebuilding of depleted livestock herds—essential though this rebuilding will ultimately be—as well as the production of other crops which compete for acreage with essential foods'. This course of action, it implied, should also be followed by liberated Europe.

There could be no better instance of the ascendancy of the British delegation over the Conference. For these short-term resolutions were not of a piece with the rest; they asserted not principles, but a specific policy whose validity depended on a particular statistical premise, namely that there was likely to be a shortage of bread grains after the armistice unless remedial action were taken, and for this the *ipse dixit* of the Ministry of Food was scarcely sufficient evidence.[1] It was indeed possible to forecast, within certain limits, the likely production of the big four wheat exporters; possible also to discern that the growing hog population of the United States might trench severely upon North American wheat stocks. But neither the extent of these inroads, nor the net requirements of a Europe whose date of liberation was uncertain, could at this stage be assessed with any pretence at accuracy. A shortage of some foodstuffs—livestock products, perhaps oils and fats—was a virtual certainty; a shortage of cereals was at most a contingency that might have to be faced.

III

But for the importance the Ministry of Food attached to these short-term measures against shortage, the United Kingdom's acceptance of the whole body of resolutions might have been tardier and more hedged about with reservations.[2] Even so, it was qualified by the cautious, if self-evident proviso that the resolutions could only be obligatory on a country so far as they were applicable to conditions there. This caution reflected the division of counsels that had marked Whitehall's initial approach to the Conference itself, and that, despite the success of the British delegation, still persisted among Departments.

Within the Ministry of Food itself there were some who would have liked to go a long way with what London called the 'wild men' or the 'ginger group'—mainly of nutrition experts turned social and economic reformer—in Washington who would have endowed the permanent organisation for food and agriculture with wide executive powers in the field of commodity control, and the opportunity to exercise continual pressure on Governments in the interests of better nutrition. Prevailing Ministry opinion, however, while insisting that the organisation be limited to what it could reasonably hope to perform in the way of research and advisory functions—themselves undertakings of great magnitude—held that the British representative should take an active, forward-looking rôle on the Interim Commission, which duly began its work on 15th July 1943. The Ministry felt that to take too rigid an attitude in the course of drafting the

---

[1] There is no evidence that wider considerations, e.g., apprehension about the future political state of Europe, played any part in forming the British attitude. The insistence on the likely shortage of bread grains is traceable to the informed guessing of one or two individuals in the Ministry of Food.

[2] In commending the Resolutions to the War Cabinet, the Foreign Secretary laid special emphasis on the importance to the United Kingdom of these short term Articles.

Constitution of F.A.O.[1] would lose Britain much goodwill as well as fail to achieve its object.

The British representative on the Interim Commission consistently fulfilled his instructions in a liberal spirit, steering skilfully between the rash enthusiasms of the 'wild men' and the recurrent tendency of London to raise a hue and cry after the implications of some drafting point in the Constitution. At one point in the long and tedious negotiations, in March 1944, he personally came to London and successfully persuaded his colleagues to recommend that Ministers accept without amendment the Constitution and Declaration that the Interim Commission had prepared. Some provisions in the Constitution, particularly those relating to international investment and commodity arrangements, might be held to justify the future Organisation's officials in shifting its emphasis from advisory to executive functions without getting a fresh mandate from member Governments, or to take on work that might be better done by another international body yet to be set up. London was bound to admit, with whatever reluctance, that it was impossible to write a Constitution that was wholly watertight against aberrations of this sort.[2] In any event, since no other Government showed signs of alarm (or even, once the first enthusiasm generated by Hot Springs had died down, of any great interest) the United Kingdom could not well bring upon itself the odium of being the sole objector. So too it was decided to accept the Draft Declaration even though it meant jettisoning the reservations that had attached to the original acceptance of the Hot Springs Resolutions. The War Cabinet in assenting to the draft documents on 16th March 1944 naturally reserved the right to raise amendments if other countries did the same.

For a time in April and May it looked as if further long debates were possible in Washington, more particularly when a United States Congressional Committee to whom the State Department submitted the draft Constitution thought fit to propose a complete re-wording of it. Moreover, Governments had been unexpectedly slow in signifying their readiness to proceed with formal approval of the documents. In the end, however, the critics were persuaded to accept only minor drafting amendments; toward the end of June the final form of the Constitution and Declaration were at length unanimously agreed on by the full membership of the Interim Commission; in August they were transmitted to Governments for approval and published. The organisation, it had been agreed, was to be brought into being

---

[1] The title 'Food and Agriculture Organisation of the United Nations' was chosen at a late stage in the Interim Commission's discussions precisely because it could be abbreviated as F.A.O. (cf. I.L.O.) instead of the more clumsy P.O.F.A.

[2] The actual technical and legal details of the drafting were greatly helped by the advice of numerous experts of international standing, and more particularly by Mr. Alexander Loveday, of the League of Nations, and Mr. C. Wilfred Jenks of I.L.O.

when twenty nations had signified their assent. But this process again took time; the British War Cabinet itself did not approve the documents until the last day of November, and it was not till mid-April 1945 that the requisite quota of adherences was obtained. The all-important approval of the United States Congress was delayed still further, till July.

Meantime the Interim Commission, or rather the tiny group of members who remained active after the Commission had approved the Constitution, had been getting together material for the inaugural conference of F.A.O., which it was planned to hold in the autumn. The crusading spirit of woolly idealism, which the United Kingdom representative had done so much to hold in check, became active again when in the spring of 1945, the Commission was deprived of his guidance.[1] An inflated and congested agenda was proposed for the Conference, which, if the enthusiasts had had their way, would have ranged far beyond its primary task of bringing the Organisation into being, and the discussion of technical problems of food and agriculture, into wider questions of economic policy. Once again it fell to the British to undertake the task of deflation, with the support of the State Department; and after some further discussions revised proposals were reached which in substance conceded London's points. After more than two years and many vicissitudes, the work of the Interim Commission was drawing to a close, and all was ready for the birth of the first of the specialised institutions of the United Nations. Writing in August 1945, the British representative on the Interim Commission summed up its prospects thus:

> 'There is every reason why the F.A.O. should be a success. It has a well-defined field of activity and a useful function to perform which should be of direct benefit to many governments and of indirect benefit to large numbers of people. It should, therefore, command a wide measure of popular support. But an international organisation of the second rank, such as the F.A.O. will be, is most vulnerable unless it receives the right kind of support from the Governments and obtains the right people to run it. It is in constant danger either of becoming the prey of axe-grinders, special interests or cranks, or of petering out through lack of official interest and public support.'

These dangers, he thought, might best be averted by appointing first-class men to the leading posts and, so far as the British Government was concerned, by judicious encouragement.

> 'Often, in the past, the attitude of departments of His Majesty's Government to international bodies has been to regard them as rather a bore; to concentrate on the "technical" aspects of their work; and to restrict and even to discourage initiative on their part or any extension

---

[1] The aircraft in which Mr. E. Twentyman, who had been the United Kingdom representative on the Interim Commission from the beginning, and other British officials were returning to the United States, was lost without trace in March 1945. It was not until 1st June that a successor was appointed.

of their activities. It is true enough that international bodies are fertile soil for the tares of irresponsible resolutions and impracticable and extravagant schemes, but they also depend for their vitality upon positive and even enthusiastic support . . . we should, I think, be careful that, if for some compelling reason, we have to pour cold water upon their plans and projects, we do not extinguish the life of the organism.'

It was more than difficult, though not unexpectedly so, to recruit for F.A.O. a staff that should command the support for which the British representative was pleading. The personal qualities that would be required were not readily to be found in combination with unquestioned authority in the organisation's sphere of activity. It was not merely that many of the best men could ill be spared from their present employments, or that others, for whatever reason, might not be *persona grata* with a member Government; though it is true that the definite views and outspoken opinions of some of the most eminent experts were a stumbling-block to their appointment.

The problem went beyond the reluctance of Governments or other national institutions to give up their best men, or the dislike of officials for independent criticism. There was, in fact, a world shortage of persons with the kind of knowledge and the sort of approach that F.A.O. would require. Particularly was this true of the economic field in which, perhaps, its main work would lie. The extent to which, for instance, a scholarly appreciation of the world wheat problem was lacking to the international conferences that were trying to settle it is almost beyond belief. It is the sober truth that more wisdom is to be found in a single contribution from the Stanford Food Research Institute than in the whole verbatim proceedings of the Washington Wheat Meeting.[1] One of the tasks to be faced was the ending of a situation in which sustained study of the economic problems of food was virtually confined to a single academic institution. No doubt the very existence of F.A.O. would do much, in the course of time, to remedy this deficiency. But for the present the shortage of food experts was as great as that of food itself, and likely to last longer. All the less reason, then, to hold out to the peoples of the world the prospect that the very foundation of F.A.O. was a great step towards the millennium. Its most valuable service might rather prove to be the demonstration of the gap between present aspirations and present knowledge.

---

[1] Cf. Chapter XXVII and the authorities cited therein.

CHAPTER XXIX

The Aftermath

I

THE period covered by the present study ends with military victory and the break-up of the war-time coalition Government; it deals with the growth and maturity, but not with the senescence, of food control. The steady, if slow, movement towards de-control that was expected when, in 1943 and 1944, the Ministry of Food was working out reconstruction plans, did not set in at once in 1945. On the contrary, the world food shortage[1] became worse; just as the lowest point in sugar supplies after the first Great War was reached as late as January 1920, so in 1946 the British Government was constrained to do what it had avoided throughout the worst of the U-boat attacks—ration, however mildly, bread and flour. For a short time in the spring of 1947 it had to restrict potato supplies also by a quasi-rationing scheme. Not till 1950 was there any substantial easement of restrictions other than those on food transport.

Of all the differences between food control in the two world wars, this one of sheer duration is the most striking. The first Ministry of Food was not established till December 1916, after well over two years of war; rationing did not begin till a year later, and for only two foods, sugar and butter, did it continue beyond the end of 1919.[2] The control machine, in its complete and comprehensive form, did not on the first occasion have to pass the stringent test of time; it began to be dismantled almost as soon as it was complete, and while normal trading conditions were something more than a remote memory.

Nevertheless the end of hostilities in 1945 was a definite landmark in the history of British food control, for all that it seemed to bring little with it but changes for the worse in ration levels. It marked the end—already for some time in sight—of the period of expansion, not only of actual controls, but of ideas and ambitions about food policy. One might say, in no derogatory sense, that the controllers had passed from the offensive to the defensive phase of activity. Many of the moving spirits of the Ministry of Food had either already departed,

---

[1] *The World Food Shortage.* Cmd. 6785 (1946).

[2] Beveridge, *op. cit.* pp. 224–25 (Table VII). Margarine was de-rationed in February 1919.

or were ready to depart, when peace came; and the remaining years of control were to have the unmistakable quality of an aftermath. They would bring their own peculiar problems; but these would be dealt with by the existing momentum of the control machine.

The change of atmosphere was aptly, if perhaps not altogether consciously, signified in the post-war reorganisation of the Ministry that took effect at the beginning of 1947. Its details do not concern this volume; but one major alteration calls for discussion. The General Department, set up in 1940 largely at the instance of Lord Woolton himself,[1] was dissolved and its functions dispersed. Only the Statistics and Intelligence, and the Scientific Adviser's, Divisions retained their previous form.

The General Department had been much more than a piece of administrative machinery; it was a symbol of the intellectual unity of food control. Its purpose had been to formulate a broad policy of food welfare, based on expert advice, and kept as a single whole under continual review. That policy might be said to have two distinct aspects. In the first place, it strove to relate import, home production, and rationing programmes to objective standards of need; that is to say, it set up a clearly defined end that food control should seek. In the second place, it aimed at securing the greatest possible rationality in the means used; to substitute foresight for improvisation, to keep one control in line with another, to avoid the contradictions that might arise from piecemeal or independent action.

The Department had been an attempt to supply what had been a notable omission in the pre-war plans, and a recognition that good administration, at any rate in war-time, must comprise something more than the competent and honest application of rule-of-thumb methods. Its foundation had acknowledged, and sought to discount so far as possible, the element of good fortune that had helped to stave off disaster during the first two winters of war. How then, when the Ministry was not yet out of the wood, could a central planning machine of this type be regarded as dispensable?

The Ministry's own feelings on its experiment can be stated very briefly. Roughly speaking, the first aspect of the Department's work was accepted as useful and necessary; the second aspect was dismissed as a luxury. That judgement corresponds broadly to saying that scientific advice was useful to administrators, but economic advice was not, either because it was impracticably remote, or because untrained common sense was held to be sufficient to solve the Ministry's general, as distinct from its technical, problems. Both opinions were based on experience, and not merely on prejudice; both are worth brief investigation.

---

[1] Chapters IV and XVII. The reader is reminded that the General Department did not come into fully effective operation until the middle of 1941.

II

Inasmuch as food policy was, from 1940 onwards, increasingly referred to scientific criteria as the supply situation became increasingly stringent, the value of scientific advice can reasonably be assessed in terms of the results on the national diet, in so far as they can be measured either directly, or indirectly in terms of health. On this subject there has accumulated a considerable literature, both official and unofficial. To review this in detail would itself demand a substantial monograph and might even so be deemed premature.[1] But the formidable bulk of the evidence largely arises from the haphazard form its collection has taken, and it is possible to state the essentials of the problem—which is largely one of measurement— quite briefly.

Except for the clinical type of inquiry, which attempts to assess the nutritional state of individuals by direct tests of certain indices of physical condition—for instance, the haemoglobin level of the blood —all measurements of this sort proceed by computing, either from supply estimates or surveys of consumption habits, the amount of food available to individuals, groups, or the whole population, and comparing the results so obtained with an estimate of requirements. This procedure has certain inherent limitations. First, that the food requirements of any group of human beings cannot be ascertained within narrow limits because of the difficulty—except perhaps for chattel-slaves, prisoners, and volunteer 'guinea-pigs'—of controlling or estimating the degree of their physical activity. This means, for instance, that an estimate of the food requirements of a whole national population has to depend on rough assumptions about the proportion of 'active,' 'moderately active', and 'sedentary' persons in it. (These rough assumptions may of course be concealed by a single assumption, e.g., that no serious error will arise if *all* adults are taken to be 'moderately active'.) Secondly, that the evaluation of a national food supply in terms of nutrients cannot be more accurate than the supply figures themselves, whose shortcomings are particularly marked for home produced foods, will allow. Thirdly, that the most sensitive index of food control is not the diet of the average consumer, but that of those least favoured either by social circumstances or because of the inequities of even the best-devised control machinery.

---

[1] The latest review by an authoritative committee specifically describes itself as an 'interim report', the preparation of which is justified on the grounds that even the present imperfect knowledge is well worth having. It is not proposed to repeat here the long list of authorities therein quoted. *British Medical Association: Report of the Committee on Nutrition*, March 1950. For a more general discussion of health problems, including their relation to food, reference should be made to R. M. Titmuss, *Problems of Social Policy* (*op. cit.*) Chapter XXV.

These principles have all too often been overlaid by a mass of statistical detail—most notably in the series of inquiries into food consumption levels in the United States, Canada, and the United Kingdom, undertaken during 1943, 1944, and 1945.[1] In these, as well as in a great many of the calculations of average food consumption in the Ministry of Food Wartime Food Survey, there has been a tendency to draw comparisons that are not only more minute than the basic evidence warrants, but that would not be significant, from the point of view of consumption, even if they could be calculated with the degree of accuracy to which they pretend.

In point of fact, the wartime changes in the United Kingdom diet that are both important in themselves and established beyond doubt are few and simple. There was, on the average, no significant change in total calories (after the initial drop when rationing started in 1940); there was a sharp fall in animal protein (1941),[2] followed by a recovery after the arrival of Lend/Lease supplies; total protein supplies rose slightly. There were dramatically sharp rises, after 1942, in the supplies of minerals, particularly calcium and iron, and vitamins of the B group (aneurin, riboflavin, and nicotinic acid); calculated rises in vitamin A and ascorbic acid (vitamin C) should perhaps be regarded with greater caution on account of the uncertainties of vegetable supply statistics. Generally speaking, and on an average, that is to say, the diet theoretically available to the British civilian was not only maintained but actually improved during the war.

But what of the deviations from the average, particularly those downwards? Before the war, dietary surveys had adduced evidence that poverty and underfeeding went hand in hand. It is evident that rationing on the one hand, and the existence of full employment on the other, must have tended to reduce inequalities of distribution that resulted from unequal purchasing power; though neither of these converging forces was fully in operation during the first two years of war. Milk, the consumption of which was notoriously uneven before the war, provides the sharpest example of war-time change. In some industrial areas, particularly those afflicted with chronic unemployment before the war, milk consumption per head in 1943 was three times what it had been in 1935; in some 'residential' areas it had fallen. These changes reflect the introduction of the National Milk Scheme and the restriction of supplies to 'non-priority' adults. (They also reflect—and this is sometimes forgotten—the disappearance of cheap condensed skim milk, from the Continent.)

---

[1] A Note on these Inquiries will be found in Appendix B.

[2] This coincided with a low point in calorie supplies as calculated, and it is sometimes claimed that these fell to or below the margin of safety. It seems likely, however, that the want of variety in the diet during the winter of 1941, and the inequalities of distribution that still persisted then were more important. In any event, the supply of calories was unrationed at that time.

But, of course, disparities were bound to remain. Certain foods, notably fish, poultry and game, rabbits, and eggs, eluded control partly or wholly; meals 'out' were not evenly distributed throughout the population. (Had they been, their contribution to its feeding would have been negligible.) Some allowances, for instance those of cheese, dried egg, and vitamin supplements, appear not to have been fully taken up by the poor; the better-off continued to enjoy such advantages as domestic help and better cooking facilities. No effective attempt, however, to measure differences of food consumption arising from different incomes has yet been made.[1]

Regional differences in eating habits also persisted under control. For instance, the consumption of fresh vegetables in Scotland remained obstinately and, to the experts, undesirably low and some effort was made to stimulate it by publicity. On the other hand, Scottish consumption of fats and sugar in the form of cakes remained —under the datum system of allocating these ingredients—quite markedly higher than that in other parts of the country; and there were regional differences of a similar kind for 'manufactured meats' —sausages, pies, etc. The amount of the B-vitamins (aneurin, riboflavin, and nicotinic acid) available to Scots may have been lower both by reason of a greater admixture of imported white flour in bread, and the more widespread use of raising agents other than yeast.

How significant these variations may be it is scarcely possible to say. On the other hand it does seem fairly safe to say that the most dramatic improvement in the quality of the diet, that due to the reluctant increase in the extraction rate of flour and its fortification with chalk, must have been almost universal in its effect; and the same applies to the fortification of margarine with vitamins A and D. The incidence of other changes, whether through deliberate action, as with the Welfare Foods Scheme, or where a change in consumer habits was called for, must necessarily be unequal, though not always undesirably so.

---

[1] The B.M.A. Report (*op. cit.* paragraphs 109–115; Tables XII–XIV) and R. M. Titmuss (*op. cit.* p. 523, footnote 1) cite figures from the Ministry of Food's War-Time Survey to show that both in 1941 and 1943 consumption per head, even of rationed foods, increased with increasing expenditure per head on food.

A detailed analysis of the individual families included in the survey shows, however, that expenditure on food was not simply correlated with income. In particular, a low average expenditure, as recorded in the survey, could be explained either by the presence of young children, whose requirements were less than the ration allowances, or by the fact that the family in question took a high proportion of its meals away from home, and these were not recorded in the survey.

It is, therefore, not to the point to argue (B.M.A. report, paragraph 113) that twenty per cent. of the families studied were receiving less than ninety-five per cent. of average calorie requirements. (In any case this statement is not in accordance with Table XIV of the report, which shows forty per cent. of families whose calorie intakes averaged less than ninety-six per cent. of average requirements in 1941, and an almost identical proportion for 1943. One may further question whether a discrepancy of this order of magnitude falls without the margin of error.)

The writer understands that the Ministry of Food is working on this problem at present (1951).

Can one assess the influence of food supplies indirectly, in terms of public health? That the health of the people was in general well maintained during the war seems beyond doubt; such indices as maternal and infant mortality set up new low records that go far beyond a mere projection of the pre-war trend, and this in spite of setbacks in the first two years of war. One needs to be wary, however, in collating these initial setbacks and later improvement with contemporary movements in the level of food supplies. There were too many other adverse factors at work, particularly in the second winter of war, for food deficiencies to be singled out as a decisive, or even important influence on health. Conversely it becomes difficult to adduce the Welfare Foods Scheme as definitely bringing about the low rates of maternal and infant mortality, when one recalls that as late as 1944 only fifty-seven per cent. of orange juice, and only thirty per cent. of cod-liver oil, entitlement, was taken up.[1] In short, while the state of public health was certainly not consistent with a generally inadequate standard of feeding, definite examples of improvement attributable solely or mainly to dietary causes are not easy to find.

It is possible that as time passes, more positive evidence on these matters may come to light, whether through the progress of scientific inquiry or the working-out of long term trends that war-time measures may have set in motion. But even were the eventual verdict on the national diet during the war years to be less favourable than at present seems likely; even if one takes into account its manifest decline in variety and flavour, emphasised by the national want of culinary resource: it would still be a noteworthy performance to maintain so high a standard of feeding on imports that, in the worst years of the war, were running at about half the pre-war level.[2] As in the first World War, such an accomplishment would have been impossible without continual recourse to scientific advice.

III

Food scientists had succeeded, therefore, in furnishing obvious proof of their utility to the practical administrator. But in the summer of 1940 the contribution of scientific advice, narrowly defined, had been seen as forming part of a larger body of useful knowledge that

---

[1] Little is known about the distribution of these vitamin supplements among the population. It is possible, for instance, that the low cod-liver oil figures are partly explicable by a lower dose being given, especially to the youngest infants, than that prescribed by the Ministry, in which case the therapeutic value might still be considerable. Alternatively, older children among those entitled to the supplements, i.e., those most likely to get their vitamin requirements from other sources, may have been going without. Moreover, Ministry propaganda in favour of welfare foods may have been partly responsible for increased use of proprietary versions of the same vitamins. More investigation is needed before any certain conclusion can be reached on this subject.

[2] See Table II, p. 392.

might be drawn from the social sciences and applied to the problems of food control generally. The General Department had embodied a broad vision of a new and better way to deal with the problems of a new world; the same vision that was expressed, for instance, in the proceedings of the Hot Springs Conference. Within two years of the end of hostilities, that vision had faded; and its embodiment was to be weighed and found wanting. The fact can partly be explained on personal grounds; there arose a Pharaoh who knew not Joseph. But only partly; there must surely have been some weakness about the organisation to account for the change.

The General Department, it must be remembered,[1] was at once a complete novelty—for nothing of the kind seems to have been attempted under Lord Rhondda—and a late-comer in the organisation. Hence it was bound to become as much an apologist of existing policies as an initiator and co-ordinator of new ones. Its expository functions were performed with great skill, as witnessed by the impressive showing of Ministry representatives at, for instance, the Hot Springs Conference. The briefing of the Minister and his senior advisers for interdepartmental and international discussions was almost invariably efficient, pointed, and lucid. The very task of exposition assisted, over a period of time, in hammering policy itself into greater coherence; the self-awareness of the Ministry's later years was an asset, even though on occasion the pointer of the lecturer would be transmuted, almost imperceptibly, into the wand of the propagandist, or the useful reference to scientific principles degenerate into pretentiousness.[2]

Except in the field of nutrition, however, the impact of the General Department on the actual functioning of the food control machine never seems to have been as effective as the talents enrolled in it or the sheer scale of its activities might lead one to expect. The liaison between general staff and field officers was apt to be intermittent and haphazard, instead of continuous and firm. One has only to look at the history of points rationing, at the proposals for meals rationing and bread rationing in 1943, or even at the controversy over minimum stock levels, to see the persistence of the same weakness that had been evident in the handling of reserve sugar stocks before the war.[3]

This weakness is not easy to describe; it might best, perhaps, be set down as a kind of defective vision for the middle distances. Good at perceiving the ultimate ends of policy, the General Department often

---

[1] See Chapters IV and XVII. The term 'General Department' is used here in a narrower connotation than it actually bore in the Ministry, inasmuch as, particularly in the fields of imports and statistics, the Department actually undertook quasi-executive functions.

[2] As, for example, when a special survey was made of queues for cake: a proposal which one establishment officer described, without effect, as 'belonging to the pages of Edward Lear'.

[3] See Chapter II.

failed to grasp the wider implications of a particular decision, or to set it in its right proportions in terms of the whole task ahead. The individual administrator, intent on his own especial corner of the picture, might be forgiven if he pressed a particular point beyond reason. But a similar aberration on the part of a planner was more serious when it resulted in months of controversy over some slight paper deficiency in feeding-stuffs supplies, or in the lengthy elaboration of some detail of nutritional betterment that was turned down on sight by the Minister.

Ministry critics of the General Department were apt to refer to it as academic. The epithet was probably not carefully chosen; but one can readily see why it should have been used. So many of the Department's activities and discussions have the appearance of being undertaken for their own sake, as contributions to knowledge rather than to the practical purposes of food in wartime. So often were all facts regarded as free and equal, instead of being ruthlessly graded in degrees of usefulness; so seldom was the law of diminishing returns applied to the collection of numerical data, or the minuteness of calculations restrained by the likelihood of substantial margins of error.

This tendency to over-elaboration was reflected in a hasty and almost certainly excessive recruitment of research staff. Establishment officers during the war fought vainly against this overgrowth, for it could always be represented that each individual addition was essential to a project that higher authority had approved, and the traditional pre-war staffing criteria afforded little assistance in dealing with non-administrative problems. By these criteria, indeed, the General Department could scarcely be said to be overstaffed, for the ratio of junior to senior staff was lower than in the rest of the Ministry. As time went on, however, the Department's critics gained influence, and in the end it was swept away.

One ought not to conclude that the foundation of the General Department was a mistake in the first place; any more than one should forget that its abolition may be set down not merely to its imperfections, but also to the persistence, thanks partly to those imperfections, of the very habits of thought it had been set up to exorcise. It is by no means clear that, even at so late a date, its admitted faults could not have been put right by judicious pruning, skilful weeding, and a short way with ornament. It must be remembered that the Department started off with a heavy handicap. The 'practical men' were in possession of the field; they had weathered many difficult months without feeling the need, many of them, for a more general approach to food policy; and they were ready to be impressed more by the seeming unpracticality of the academic or quasi-academic persons who formed the greater part of the Department's staff than by their intellectual gifts. The only way the latter could, and to some extent did, overcome this disadvantage was by establishing their mastery of practice as well as theory. But this—except for those who served an apprenticeship in a trading or administrative division—was by no means easy. Busy trade directors had neither the time nor the inclination to instruct a series of inquirers in the technicalities of this or that control, and were apt to be impatient of *questionnaires* and cynical about statistics. The imperfect sympathy between theorists and practical men was recurrent, if not persistent. It was at once a cause and a consequence of the remoteness and immersion in unimportant detail of which critics complained.

The experts in nutrition or food technology cannot be completely exonerated from this reproach; nevertheless they did make a decisive mark on food policy. The economists, using the word in its broadest sense,[1] must by contrast be judged to be only patchily effective. If personal factors be discounted, this may be explained by the pre-war and indeed present dearth of organised knowledge, as distinct from practical experience, of the working of the food trades. The application of scholarship even to such a capital problem as that of the world wheat surplus was a rarity; and it was the qualities of the scholar, as distinct from the pedant, that were needed to raise food control from being a series of expedients to something more. It was not enough for brilliant dons to vie with their 'permanent' colleagues in putting over the Departmental view with Ministers, or even in the devising of ingenious schemes. Still less was it right that they should be left busily compiling factual memoranda that might never be used.

Both these courses, as it seems, were largely unconscious ways of escape from the task that the General Department had been called into existence to perform, a contribution to the Ministry's work that can be described as academic only in a favourable sense. To the problems of economic control there needed to be brought a sufficient detachment to offset the danger of the purely short-term, 'practical' view, and a sufficient knowledge to ward off the dilettantism that lies in wait for the most versatile of professional administrators. The sources from which this history is compiled are rich in material that, critically examined, reveals want, not of intelligence, public spirit, common sense, or practical knowledge, but of mastery over first principles;[2] knowledge of how a particular piece of control machinery

---

[1] 'Mr. Runciman and Lord Rhondda were both economists, that is to say, they considered the remoter as well as the immediate consequences of their own and other people's actions; they were both of the tiresome sect which keeps on asking what happens to exports if one shuts out imports'. Beveridge, *op. cit.*, p. 341.

'Economists are gradually displacing lawyers as the blunted instruments of State policy. . . '. Coller, *op. cit.*, p. 310.

[2] For a demonstration of the kind of deficiency referred to here, see the penetrating analysis of the Report of the Lucas Committee on Agricultural Marketing, by P. T. Bauer; *Economica*, New Series Vol. 15, No. 58, p. 132 (May 1948).

operated was not always matched by deeper understanding of its function. The General Department was only successful to a limited extent in remedying deficiencies of this sort.

These conclusions may, at first sight, seem derogatory of a remarkable administrative accomplishment. But they touch, it must be emphasised, but one facet, though an important facet, of the work of food control. Moreover, they are not really very surprising. Economic planning on the scale and over the length of time that the Ministry of Food practised it is still a novelty to British administration; and it would be odd if a country that prides itself on its empirical approach to problems of Government should almost overnight be found to master completely a different, more systematic way of doing things. It is perhaps more remarkable that, within the first year of war, steps should be taken towards providing the machinery of forethought, than that there should be occasions where that machinery failed, or should not be invited, to function. And these occasions justify its existence no less than those, for instance, in the field of price policy, where its contribution was substantial and effective.

*   *   *

The present volume might well have been entitled 'The Expansion of Food Policy'. That theme, or perhaps one should say succession of themes, must not be allowed to obscure another, less spectacular but scarcely less important in the whole work of the Ministry of Food: the continuous adaptation of both old and new control machinery to the fortunes of war and to the inexorable fact of economic change. On the one hand, the procurement, shipment, and distribution work of the commodity divisions had to adjust itself to changing conditions; on the other, the rationing mechanism, originally devised for four or five foods, had to include twice that number without falling down under its own weight, over-burdening the trade, or the resources of man-power and paper, losing face with the consumer, or failing in its object of conserving and equitably distributing supplies. An analysis of the more important of these administrative problems of control will be attempted in the second part of this history.

APPENDICES

APPENDIX A

Sir William Beveridge's Memorandum
of October 1936
on 'Wider Aspects of Food Control'

THE terms of reference to the Rationing Sub-Committee, as explained by the Minister for Co-ordination of Defence in answer to a Parliamentary Question (27th May 1936) and as interpreted in the foregoing Report, are narrow. Standing by itself, the scheme outlined by the Sub-Committee is nothing more than a scheme for prevention of queues at the shops of retailers, by ensuring that people can buy only at one place and get their fair share of whatever food is available in a locality.

Acceptance of this scheme will not mean that anything will have been done to secure that supplies sufficient to meet the rations of his registered customers reach the shop of the retailer. Rationing, in the narrow sense, is useless (perhaps even harmful) except as a supplement to other operations of greater importance and difficulty, though hardly more costly to carry out.

The substantial requirements for dealing with food in a future war are:—
1. A decision to appoint a Food Controller with full powers as from the first day of war.
2. A feeding policy, thought out in advance, for adequate total supply in the country at all stages of a possibly protracted war.
3. A control plan, prepared in advance, in regard to each essential food —for taking over supply, regulating prices, and directing distribution.
4. 'Outbreak plans' for the probable initial emergency resulting from air attack.

1. A FOOD CONTROLLER WITH FULL POWERS AS FROM THE FIRST DAY OF WAR

As is indicated in the Report of the Rationing Sub-Committee, it is not likely that the condition in which rationing is appropriate—of general shortage in the country of an essential food—will arise in the early months of war. But some problems in regard to food will arise at the outbreak of war, as they did in the 1914 war, *e.g.*, the need for victualling the enlarged fighting forces, shortage anticipated or actual of some particular food (next time it is likely to be bacon rather than sugar), uncertainties leading to hoarding, speculation and soaring prices. And there will be two new outbreak problems—those of providing for people in districts subject to intensive air attack and of adjusting distribution to a diversion of imported supplies from the usual ports. It is essential that there should be a Food Controller in the saddle with a policy thought out in advance as from the first day of emergency, to deal with all these problems together. Otherwise they will be dealt with piecemeal, as they arise, by the different parties directly interested, and the seeds of future trouble will be sown. The dis-co-ordination which in the last war led to the imported meat supply of the civilian population being controlled in the interests of the fighting forces by the Board of Trade, and to the setting up of independent Sugar and Wheat Commissions never fully absorbed in the Ministry of Food, was a weakness which should not be repeated. The food problem for the whole population, military and civilian, must be looked at as a whole, from the first day of war. Whatever steps are necessary to ensure this, should be taken now.

2. A FEEDING POLICY, THOUGHT OUT IN ADVANCE, FOR ADEQUATE TOTAL SUPPLY IN THE COUNTRY AT ALL STAGES OF A POSSIBLY PROTRACTED WAR

Consideration of the building up of a reserve stock of food in peace is part of this policy. But the purpose of having such a stock is often mis-conceived by its advocates. It is unnecessary to anticipate a cessation of all or most of our imports of food with the outbreak of war. If the enemy were able to establish such superiority in the air or on the sea as to deny us for any appreciable time the use, not only of some ports, but of most or all of our ports, the war would be over, for reasons other than starvation. Fear of this can, I hope, be dismissed as chimerical. The object of having reserve stocks is not to avoid starvation in the first year of war, but to give us time to develop home production, perhaps in a protracted war, as attrition and diversion of shipping, or desire to economise defensive effort, brings a gradual decline of imports. We ought to plan for a long war as well as for a short one. Our present anticipations that any future war will necessarily be short can hardly be more confident than those that ruled in 1914 and may be as badly mistaken. I am not able to judge whether the scientists who talk to me of the possibility of so increasing production under emergency conditions as to be nearly independent of oversea supplies for some foods now largely imported are talking practical sense or impractical theory. But they may be talking sense. If they are, there may be reasons for taking preparatory steps in peace quite different in character from the slight stimulation of home production at the cost of imports. Previous preparation for becoming as nearly as possible independent in a long war is probably more important than becoming slightly less dependent on imported food in peace.

Feeding policy, again, involves decisions as to national dietary in war. Are we to live more on cereals or potatoes and less on meat? Shall we aim at maintaining our herds or not, at full fatted cattle or at something else, at killing off pigs or poultry or increasing them? (On such topics as the last, it is desirable for H.M. Government to speak with one voice, not as in the last war with two or three voices.) What rations of meat, butter or margarine, sugar, tea, etc., shall we aim at? (Here the Royal Society experts should be brought into previous consultation so that they do not criticise and cause confusion of public opinion later.) Are we to adopt once more, as a fundamental policy, avoidance of rationing of bread, and are we to be prepared again to keep its price down by a subsidy? (We may decide on a general policy of price subsidies for essential food as a means to stabilising prices and wages.) How far and at what period of the war shall we carry the policy of increasing cereals for human consumption at the expense of feeding-stuffs for animals and beer, by lengthening the extraction of flour and by diluting wheat with barley or other cereals? (We are practically certain to adopt this policy to some extent for it is the simplest way of increasing our reserve stocks of food at once. But adequate preparation for this policy involves devising beforehand from past experience or new experiments a set of clear instructions to bakers as to how to make proper use of unfamiliar flour and how to avoid 'rope' and other unpleasant incidents of the spring of 1917.)

3. A CONTROL PLAN PREPARED IN ADVANCE IN REGARD TO EACH ESSENTIAL FOOD—FOR TAKING OVER SUPPLY, REGULATING PRICES, DIRECTING DISTRIBUTION

In regard to all foods many of the same problems will arise—of the terms on which stocks or businesses shall be taken over, of the degree to which existing channels of trade shall be observed, of whether prices shall be fixed at various stages or only margins, of how margins shall be related to turnover, of whether a uniform retail price shall be aimed at throughout the country or a price varying with costs of transport and other expenses. But each food must be treated individually, as the circumstances are different in respect of source of supply and existing trade organisation methods of distribution, local varieties of consumption and the probability or the reverse of rationing. The technique of the various controls was fully worked out in the last war and is described briefly in my book on *British Food Control* and in more detail for some of the more difficult and important foods by Mr. E. M. H. Lloyd in *Experiments in State Control*.

The taking over of imports is relatively simple—requisitioning of supplies at sea or contracted for, bargains with producers for further supplies, constitution of an import board for allocating supplies to wholesalers, manufacturers and others under Government instructions. Complications enter at the later stages of control and in relation to home produce.

The problem of control will be affected by the development since the war of agricultural schemes and the setting up of such bodies as the Wheat Commission, Sugar Commission, and the various marketing boards (for potatoes, pigs, milk, etc.). In itself, that is an advantage—as affording a nucleus of organisation. But it makes even more necessary the immediate establishment of a Food Controller, to whom responsibility for all those bodies will presumably be transferred. The proper co-ordination in war of the functions of the Agricultural Departments concerned with home production and the Food Controller will be important and should be agreed in advance.

The following notes mention a few salient points in regard to each principal food, as suggested by experience in the last war.

Wheat and other Cereals. The corner-stone of cereal control in the last war was the taking over of the flour mills so that they could be run on Government account under continuous instruction from the Wheat Commission. Imports of wheat were controlled through shipping. All home-grown wheat had to be delivered to the mills, who paid the price fixed by the Food Controller, and ground flour according to his instructions. The flour mills in the last war were taken over under an elaborate bargain, exhaustively discussed with the parties interested. The nature of the bargain to be made in a future war will depend upon the general economic policy of the Government in regard to war profits and the remuneration of war services of every kind.

In the last war the Ministry of Food had under consideration also the taking over of bakeries, and the concentration of baking in a limited number of more efficient establishments. This scheme was never carried out, but might become desirable in certain conditions.

Other sides of cereal control are regulation of brewing and prevention of wrongful use of cereals on the farm and elsewhere.

Sugar. Imports were taken over by the Government in August 1915 and a Sugar Commission was established. In a future war, there will also be home supplies. The control of these, probably by taking over the factories, should be relatively simple. There is a considerable use of sugar in manufacturing (biscuits, jam, sweetmeats, cakes) and regulations governing such use have to be framed.

Meat. This presents some of the hardest problems of all, both through the variety of articles covered (beef, mutton, pork, bacon and hams, offal, poultry, rabbits, canned and preserved meats) and through the importance and difficulty of controlling the home supply. Matters requiring consideration will be control of refrigerated tonnage, the taking over of cold stores and of wholesale markets like Smithfield, regulation of slaughtering, grading and pricing of cattle and sheep, and, in the event of rationing, arrangements for distribution to each butcher his proper share of home and imported supplies of various qualities and the making of schedules of retail prices for varying cuts. In regard alike to butcher's meat and to bacon there are considerable local variations of cut and of taste.

Dairy Products. Milk in the last war was never fully controlled; its price, though fixed, was usually high enough to encourage production and discourage consumption. The desirability of national or municipal buying supplies of milk for possibly subsidised distribution in urban districts needs consideration. The production of margarine in substitution for butter was organised on a large scale; involving control of oil seeds, crushing mills, and ultimately of feeding-stuffs and soap. Both butter and cheese were controlled in complicated ways. But cheese, whose consumption varies locally, was never rationed; like bacon, it is of special importance in mining areas.

Potatoes afford a great opportunity of increasing the supply, marred by extreme uncertainty as to the yield, and difficulty of turning a surplus into non-perishable form. The Ministry of Food, faced by a glut of potatoes as the result of its guaranteed price and a high yield per acre in 1918, had schemes and machinery for making potato flour on a large scale. I do not know how these schemes would have worked or what progress, if any, has been made in the utilisation of potatoes since 1918.

4. PLANS FOR INITIAL EMERGENCY RESULTING FROM AIR ATTACK

In one vital respect a future war will be different from any of which we have experienced. We shall be subject to attack on British soil from the air; our civilian population may be exposed to risk indiscriminately with the fighting forces. How far our prospective enemy will go in ruthlessness at various stages of the war it is impossible to say. But clearly we must not count on any restraint whatever. He may begin by giving legal colour to his actions by declaring that all ports, as channels of munition supply, are subject to bombardment. But all our large ports are centres of crowded population; and if bombarding ports does not serve to break our resistance, he will include all factories—for they may make munitions—in his declaration. We shall not be attacked by anyone, unless he thinks that he can beat us and means to do so by every means in his power.

For the purpose of discussion, I assume that a substantial portion of Britain will prove to be defensible against air attack—in the sense that raids, though they may not be prevented altogether, can be made so expensive to the raiders that frequent and sustained attack will not be attempted; on any other assumption we cannot survive a future war. I assume on the other hand (as the worst condition consistent with our ultimate success in the war) that a substantial part of Britain, including London, proves to be indefensible, to the extent that we cannot (a) trust to the ports in that region as important channels of supply or (b) expect the civilian population to remain there, subject to recurring risk of explosions, fires and gas.

This anticipation is likely to be realised, if at all, at the very beginning of war, and calls for outbreak action in two directions.

First, the putting of London (and other eastern or southern ports) out of action will disorganise the food storage and distribution system of the whole country, that is to say of districts which are not themselves under air attack. It may be possible for all our ships to be diverted to other ports and even for the other ports to pass the traffic through[1]; but it is of no use passing traffic through a port without instructions making sure that it will go where it is needed. The port authorities will have to get their instructions on that from the Food Controller. The problem of internal distribution is vital and, so far as food is concerned, should be treated, not as a port or transport problem, but as a feeding problem.

As some of the principal traders have been consulted already on the question of stocks in the London area, they should be consulted further as

---

[1] On general grounds, I feel pretty sure that the opinions of the various port authorities, as recorded in the report of the . . . [Committee on the Distribution of Imports] . . . are unduly optimistic about this.

to what steps they could and would take—knowing the demand to be met in each locality—to meet the demand if all or a given proportion of supplies came in elsewhere.

Second, the evacuation of London needs to be thought out in terms, not of transport only, but of reception, housing (by compulsory billeting if necessary) and feeding—probably on a free communal basis at first. Adequate emergency stocks of food in a transportable form will be as necessary as gas masks. No doubt those who are concerned with evacuation are making plans about food as well. But if on the outbreak of war the evacuation authorities start dealing with food, without reference to any general authority concerned with food, chaos will follow. In regard to evacuation, feeding is a small part of the whole problem. But there must be a Food Controller at once to deal with it.

It may be added that evacuation of London needs to be thought out also in terms of the break-up of economic organisation that is involved and of taking steps in peace to make evacuation less difficult and disastrous in war. Judging by events this is not being thought of seriously as yet by anybody; it raises difficult political and economic issues going beyond the question of food.

Two special air attack problems, which do concern the food supply, are worth mentioning.

One relates to cold storage. The fact reported by the [. . .] Committee that practically the whole production of ammonia for cold stores is concentrated in one or two spots is a serious danger. The position should be rectified at once by transfer or establishing new factories. Ammonia is as important as filling shells.

The other relates to bacon, supplied at the present time as to nearly(?) sixty per cent. of the total consumption from Denmark. The Danish supply may be cut off completely and at once by a war with Germany, and acute general shortage of bacon will ensue. This will hardly by itself make a case for immediate rationing (though bacon was rationed with other meat in the last war) but it will call for emergency action—probably the taking over of the whole supply and the bacon factories, and preferential distribution of bacon to mining areas where it is of special importance as a sustaining food that can be taken underground. Here again the Food Controller is wanted at once.

This outbreak problem is not dealt with at all in the report of the Sub-Committee because it is so much less a problem of food than of the general conduct of war. As rationing is embedded in the larger problem of food control, so food control is embedded in larger problems of civilian mobilisation and defence. This has been illustrated above, in reference to national registration and to the possible evacuation of London. But it has wider implications. The circumstances of a future war are likely to emphasise the lesson of the last that war is now 'of nations and not of armies' and that for success a sufficient proportion of the national effort must be put in maintaining the health and *morale* of the civilian population. The circumstances of a future war will emphasise this lesson, by blurring distinctions between the civilian population and the fighting forces. The men, women, and children of London will be exposed to destruction. Failing a rapid defeat of the attackers, those whose work is not required in London must have help to leave it; those who are required to stay there—e.g. for work in the docks—can hardly be expected to do so, except as war service. The precedent of the Liverpool Dockers Battalion in the last war may deserve general adoption. How far do we propose to go in a future war in enforcing on all the obligations of national service, under discipline, irrespective of reward, and what policy do we contemplate for wages, salaries, profits and the taking over of businesses? We cannot have one Department taking one line on such matters, and others taking a different line; manifest justice to all will be a condition of unwavering popular support for stringent measures of control.

To think out in advance *and as a whole*, the civilian side of the next war is as important as to design measures of military attack and defence.

APPENDIX B

Note on the Consumption Levels Inquiries
of 1943, 1944 and 1945

THE series of inquiries into consumption levels in the United States, Canada, and the United Kingdom, undertaken during 1943, 1944 and 1945, had their origin in the crisis of 1943 over Lend/Lease shipments of meat and cheese.[1] At that time the British Food Mission had been confronted with American calculations purporting to show that total food consumption in the United Kingdom was little worse, and in some respects better, than that in the United States. The British therefore suggested, and it was eventually agreed, that officials of the United States, United Kingdom, and Canada should attempt to work out a common statistical basis on which consumption levels could be compared. If this could be achieved, it would provide a yardstick for the allocation of scarce foodstuffs between these countries. Informal discussions in Washington during the Hot Springs Conference were followed, later in 1943, by joint investigations in London and Ottawa; a published version of the findings, complete except for certain figures withheld for security reasons, appeared in all three countries early in 1944; and further issues, in which the figures were brought up to date, were published for 1944 and 1945.[2]

The initial inquiry more particularly was influenced by the practical purpose that lay behind it. The end—agreement—was more important than the means; unanimity was imperative, even though it necessitated using inadequate and hastily assembled data and methods of doubtful validity. Circumstances that militated against a rigorous analysis yet dictated that the conclusions should be supported with a full panoply of statistics, tables, and charts. Nevertheless, the inquiry did represent a serious contribution to a genuine problem; by the same token, its conceptual weaknesses cannot wholly be explained away by the accidents of circumstance.

Strictly speaking, what the inquiry sought to assess was not consumption levels, but the total supplies 'moving into consumption' in each of the three countries. Estimates of these total supplies were evaluated in terms of nutrients, by a series of intricate and painstaking calculations, which took into account such factors as the varying composition of butchers' meat from country to country, or the varying amounts of protein in different types of wheat. The results were then compared with an assessment of requirements, based on the 'recommended dietary allowances' of the Food

---

[1] See Chapter XIX.

[2] *Food Consumption Levels in the United States, Canada and the United Kingdom:* the first, second and third reports of a committee set up by the Combined Food Board. The first report was printed simultaneously in all three countries (April 1944), the second and third in the United States only (December 1944, February 1946).

and Nutrition Board of the National Research Council of the United States. Both the estimates of supplies and those of requirements, were hedged about, in the text of the report, by every sort of cautious qualification. Yet, on turning from the text to the tables, one finds such statements as the following:

Supplies per head per day

Calories (U.K.)	Pre-war	2,984
	1940	2,772
	1941	2,795
	1942	2,864
	1943	2,827

The notation of these figures, to the nearest calorie, would on the face of it imply that the average supply per head could be calculated to within less than four ten-thousandths of the daily requirement. Yet in a note to the very same table it was admitted that a change in the conversion factors used in evaluating certain foods could make a difference of over 100 calories a day in the final results.

This fictitious appearance of accuracy arises from a convention that is apt to mislead; namely, the presentation of the result of a calculation in terms of its arithmetical correctness without regard either to the data from which it is derived or its own significance.[1]

It seems clear, for instance, that this and similar calculations of calories tend to be more fine drawn just because the unit itself, in relation to the daily requirement, happens to be very small. (Figures for protein and iron, by contrast, appear to be computed more roughly.) It also seems proper to infer that on this occasion the difficulty of estimating the error in the basic material led to a more or less tacit decision to leave it out of calculation altogether.

To assess the error at zero is no less arbitrary, and is surely less plausible than the assumption of a small percentage error would be.[2] In default of such help from those responsible for compiling the supply statistics, let it be supposed, for the sake of illustration, that the weighted average error in those affecting the computation of total calorie supplies is of the order of three per cent. That would imply that the smallest significant change in average calorie supplies per head per day is 100 (i.e. $3\frac{1}{3}$ per cent. of 3,000). In the present state of knowledge, a change of this order seems also to be the smallest that need be taken into account in discussing requirements.

---

[1] 'There is no more common error than to assume that, because prolonged and accurate mathematical calculations have been made, the application of the result to some fact of nature is absolutely certain'. Whitehead, A. N., *Introduction to Mathematics*, p. 27.

[2] In the 1944 Consumption Levels Inquiry a table (Table 3, p. 27) grading the supply statistics by letters (A, B, C, etc.) was inserted. The British Medical Association report of 1950 states (paragraph 68):
'For the United Kingdom, the calculations of the amounts of nutrients in the food supplies, although subject to a series of errors in the primary estimates as well as in subsequent allowances for wastage, are substantially accurate'.
In each case, the authors appear to be aware of the problem, but do not recognise that its solution is, logically speaking, a prerequisite of using the figures at all; or to put it another way, that any conclusion expressed in numerical terms implies an estimate of the error in the premises.

In effect, therefore, one can only conclude from the figures quoted above that from 1940 onwards the energy-value of the national diet remained to all intents and purpose constant. Since bread and potatoes—the chief sources of calories—remained unrationed throughout the war, and the supply of calories was therefore determined by the effective demand, this is a conclusion that might be expected.[1]

Estimates of calorie supplies, moreover, were tolerably reliable because those foods covering the greater part of the calorie supply were at one stage or another in Ministry control. For nutrients like Vitamin A that were largely derived from unrationed sources the possibility of error is obviously greater. Thus in estimating the annual supply of 'leafy, green and yellow vegetables', which accounted for about half the Vitamin A available, the inquiry could do no more than assume that three-quarters of the estimated harvest 'moved into consumption' irrespective of the size of the crop. Yet experience with potatoes went to show that the greater the supply, the greater the wastage.[2]

This note does not seek to deny all value to the Consumption Levels Inquiries. On the contrary, it is clear that much of the information they gathered together, not only on broad consumption trends in the three countries, but also on the consumption of particular foods, was both useful and illuminating. Moreover, they did effectively dispose of the claim that the British were, on the average, as well off as North Americans for food. Where too much was claimed for them was in asserting that they could be relied on for minute comparisons, and that these comparisons when made would be of either scientific or practical significance. It is, on the contrary, fortunately true that close measurement of national food consumption is unnecessary as well as impossible. 'Operational research', of which the Consumption Level Inquiries and the Ministry of Food National Food Survey are examples, might sometimes be more expeditiously conducted if it were kept in mind that limitations on accurate knowledge, freely admitted, do not preclude and may even assist effective action.

---

[1] It was for this reason that the League of Nations publication, *Food Rationing and Supply, 1943-44*, dismissed any attempt to estimate the number of calories consumed in the United Kingdom as 'without direct interest' (p. 55).

[2] These observations apply to the first report in the series. In the third, the estimates of vegetable consumption were sharply pruned; but attention was not drawn to the alteration. A full account of potato problems will be given in Volume II.

TABLES

TABLE I

Civilian Supplies of the Principal Foods

(a) Pre-war (b) 1944

	Pre-war	1944
	(*lb. per head per annum*)	
Dairy Products (excluding Butter) (Total as Milk Solids)	38·3	49·0
Meat (including canned meat, bacon and ham) (as edible weight)	109·6	96·1
Fish, Poultry and Game (edible weight)	32·8	23·5
Eggs and Egg Products (fresh egg equivalent) ..	24·0	23·2
Oils and Fats (visible) (fat content)	45·3	39·0
Sugar and Syrups (sugar content)	109·9	75·7
Potatoes	176·0	274·6
Pulses and Nuts	9·6	6·8
Fruit (including tomatoes) (fresh equivalent) ..	141·4	93·6
Vegetables	107·5	124·8
Grain Products	210·1	252·8
Tea, Coffee and Cocoa	14·7	12·8

Ministry of Food:

Statistics and Intelligence Division

September 1949

Note: The figures refer to all food provided for civilian consumption, i.e. not merely the domestic ration but also manufactured foods and food consumed in restaurants, eaten by Servicemen on leave, and so forth. The average figure calculated by dividing this total by the civilian population does not, moreover, represent the amount actually eaten; losses occur both in the course of distribution and in the household.

TABLE II

Imports of Food and Animal Feeding-stuffs into the United Kingdom

(Excluding Imports of Unrefined Whale Oil from British Whale Fisheries)

Thousand tons

Commodity	1934–38 Annual Average	1940	1941	1942	1943	1944	1945
Wheat	5,031	5,754	5,393	3,487	3,256	2,824	3,552
Wheatmeal and Flour	420	577	708	374	718	791	543
Rice, Other Grains and Pulses	1,403	1,077	514	163	257	137	340
Maize and Maize Meal	3,395	2,192	702	135	66	118	510
Oilcake	595	417	204	55	—	68	190
Other Animal Feeding-stuffs	1,147	648	120	19	12	30	10
Meat (a)	1,096	1,128	1,073	1,047	1,051	1,182	832
Bacon and Ham	387	241	281	362	387	408	244
Canned Meat	63	122	226	249	246	206	97
Oilseeds and Nuts	1,522	1,630	1,506	1,361	1,621	1,468	1,055
Oils and Fats (excluding Whale Oil unrefined)	395	366	439	539	542	507	304
Whale Oil unrefined	88	82	31	42	14	—	39
Sugar	2,168	1,526	1,652	768	1,425	1,155	1,066
Dairy Produce:							
Butter	480	264	218	134	152	153	190
Cheese	142	156	203	315	207	252	191
Processed Milk	104	87	167	261	223	177	96
Eggs in shell	159	99	59	23	15	23	48
Other Dairy Produce	50	42	48	65	74	80	37
Dried Fruit	175	128	210	198	181	253	155
Fresh Fruit (including edible Nuts)	1,502	839	115	131	58	213	398
Canned and Preserved Fruit, Pulp and Juice	257	202	112	114	72	125	87
Vegetables (including preserved)	705	392	105	67	23	58	79
Tea, Coffee, Cocoa	346	370	371	344	422	381	321
Other Foods	861	847	609	584	591	546	591
	22,491	19,186	15,066	10,837	11,613	11,155	10,975

(a) Including carcase weight equivalent of imported fat cattle.

Source: Annual Statements of Trade (Board of Trade)

TABLE III

Estimated Production of Principal Crops in the United Kingdom[1]

Thousand Tons

	Wheat	Barley	Oats	Potatoes	Sugar Beet	Vegetables
1936–38 average	1,651	765	1,940	4,873	2,741	2,371
1939	1,645	892	2,003	5,218	3,529	2,403
1940	1,641	1,104	2,892	6,405	3,176	2,617
1941	2,018	1,144	3,247	8,004	3,226	2,884
1942	2,567	1,446	3,553	9,393	3,923	3,693
1943	3,447	1,645	3,064	9,822	3,760	3,144
1944	3,138	1,752	2,953	9,096	3,267	3,423
1945	2,176	2,108	3,245	9,791	3,886	3,240

[1] Excluding holdings of one acre or less in Great Britain, and of one-quarter of an acre or less in Northern Ireland.

Source: Ministry of Agriculture and Fisheries

TABLE IV

Numbers of Livestock in the United Kingdom[1]

Millions

Mid-year	Cattle			Sheep and lambs	Pigs	Poultry[2]
	Cows in milk and calf	Other cattle	Total cattle			
1939	3·3	5·6	8·9	26·9	4·4	74·4
1940	3·3	5·8	9·1	26·3	4·1	71·2
1941	3·4	5·5	8·9	22·3	2·6	62·1
1942	3·4	5·7	9·1	21·5	2·1	57·8
1943	3·6	5·7	9·3	20·4	1·8	50·7
1944	3·6	5·9	9·5	20·1	1·9	55·1
1945	3·5	6·1	9·6	20·2	2·2	62·1

[1] Exceptions as for Table III.
[2] i.e. fowls, ducks, geese and turkeys.

Source: Ministry of Agriculture and Fisheries

TABLE V

*Total Supplies of Certain Foods in the United Kingdom,
showing Percentage Home-produced and Imported* (a)

Commodity	Pre-war Average			1944		
	Total Supplies 'ooo Tons	% Home Produced	% Imported	Total Supplies 'ooo Tons	% Home Produced	% Imported
Wheat and Flour (as wheat equivalent)	6,361	12	88	6,414	39	61
Oils and Fats (crude oil equivalent)	1,133	16	84	1,184	5	95
Sugar (refined value)	2,415	16	84	1,466	27	73
Meat (including canned, product weight)	2,166	49	51	2,128	36	64
Bacon and Ham	583	34	66	511	20	80
Fish (including canned fish)	1,209	85	15	614	54	46
Butter	526	9	91	171	10	90
Cheese	186	24	76	270	7	93
Condensed Milk	292	70	30	204	54	46
Dried Milk	36	59	41	106	22	78
Shell Eggs	450	65	35	204	89	11
Egg Products (dried egg equivalent)	12	—	100	80	—	100
Dried Fruit	175	—	100	253	—	100
Citrus Fruit	655	—	100	183	—	100
Milk for human consumption as liquid	4,609	100	—	6,238	100	—
Potatoes for human consumption	3,308	94	6	6,159	100	—

(a) Imports include quantities for re-export.
Home production of livestock products includes that by 'self-suppliers'.
The figures for wheat and flour relate only to supplies intended for human food: those for home production are therefore based on flour millers' receipts of home-grown wheat.

Source: Ministry of Food

TABLE VI

Main Sources of Imports of Principal Groups of Food and Feeding-stuffs (a) *1934-38* (b) *1944*

Commodity Group	1934-38		1944	
	Imports '000 Tons	Main sources, i.e. those supplying 10% or more of group total	Imports '000 Tons	Main sources, i.e. those supplying 10% or more of group total
Wheat and Flour	5,451	Canada 39%; Australia 24%; Argentina 15%	3,615	Canada 83%; Argentina 12%
Rice, other grains and pulses	1,403	Canada 20%; Continental Europe (excluding Soviet Union) 18%, Iraq and Iran 12%; Soviet Union 12%; U.S.A. and South America 17%	137	U.S.A. 58%; Argentina and Brazil 31%
Animal feeding-stuffs (including maize and maize meal)	5,137	Argentina 57%; British India and Burma 11%	216	Argentina 72%; Iceland 14%; U.S.A. 10%
Meat (including canned meat and bacon and ham)	1,546	Argentina 31%; Australia and New Zealand 31%; Denmark 12%	1,796	Argentina 32%; U.S.A. 24%; Canada 20%; Australia and New Zealand 16%
Oilseeds and nuts, vegetable oils and animal fats	1,917	Egypt and Sudan 22%; British India and Burma and Ceylon 19%; British West Africa 16%; Argentina and Brazil 11%	1,975	British West Africa 36%; British India, Burma and Ceylon 19%; Argentina 16%; French West and Equatorial Africa 11%
Whale oil, unrefined (excluding whale oil from British fisheries)	88	Netherlands 47%; Whale Fisheries (Foreign) 30%; Norway 17%	—	—
Sugar	2,168	Cuba and Dominican Republic 37%; Australia 15%; Mauritius 11%; British West Indies and British Guiana 11%	1,155	Cuba and Dominican Republic 77%; Union of South Africa, Mauritius, British West Indies and British Guiana 16%
Dairy Produce	935	Continental Europe including Soviet Union 46%; Australia and New Zealand 37%	685	United States of America and Canada 59%; Australia and New Zealand 34%
Fruit and vegetables (including tinned and preserved)	2,639	Europe (including Eire, Channel Islands and Soviet Union) and Canary Islands 41%; British West Indies, Palestine and Brazil 20%; U.S.A. 12%	649	U.S.A. 28%; Europe (including Channel Islands, Eire and Soviet Union) and Canary Islands 27%; Union of South Africa 13%; Palestine, Turkey and Iraq 14%; Australia and Canada 11%

Source: Ministry of Food

TABLE VII

Lend/Lease Arrivals of Food in the United Kingdom

Thousand tons

	1941	1942	1943*	1944	1945
1st Quarter	—	405	287	276	289
2nd Quarter	27	281	475	406	319
3rd Quarter	382	403	531	286	101
4th Quarter	664	338	412	312	—
Total	1,073	1,427	1,705	1,280	709
Total as percentage of total arrivals	7·3	13·7	14·6	11·7	6·6

* Year of fifty-three weeks.

Note: In addition to the above Lend-Lease arrivals originating in U.S.A. there were also the following Lend-Lease arrivals from other countries:

1942:   154 thousand tons—mainly sugar from the Caribbean
1943: 1,131 thousand tons—mainly sugar from the Caribbean
1944:   83 thousand tons—mainly sugar from the Caribbean

Source: Ministry of Food

TABLE VIII

*Losses at Sea of Food and Feeding-stuffs Destined
for the United Kingdom (a)*

	January-March	April-June	July-September	October-December	Annual Total
	Thousand tons (net weight)				
1939	—	—	—	142(b)	142(b)
1940	94	86	292	256	728
1941	254	288	138	107	787
1942	127	72	136	186	521
1943	209	117	26	19	371
1944	11	4	7	18	40
1945	12	—	—	—	12
	Expressed as percentage of imports (c) plus losses				
1939	—	—	—	2·5(b)	2·5(b)
1940	1·7	1·5	6·5	7·4	3·7
1941	7·6	6·9	3·2	3·0	5·1
1942	4·1	2·1	5·2	9·1	4·7
1943	9·3	3·4	0·8	0·6	3·1
1944	0·4	0·1	0·2	0·7	0·4
1945	0·5	—	—	—	0·1

(a) Classified by date of occurrence.
(b) Four months, September-December.
(c) Excluding unrefined whale oil and identifiable imports from Eire.

Source: Ministry of Food

TABLE IX

Tonnage of Foods and Feeding-stuffs Lost or Damaged by Air Attack

Period	Thousand tons
Up to end August 1940 ..	16
September–December 1940	159
January–March 1941 ..	37
April–June 1941	63
July–December 1941 ..	9
Year 1942	9
Year 1943	10
Year 1944	6
TOTAL[1] ..	309

[1] About one-third of this total was salvaged for food or animal feeding. See Chapter XI.

Source: Ministry of Food

TABLE X

*Stocks of Food and Feeding-stuffs in the United Kingdom
under control of the Ministry of Food (a)*

Thousand tons

	End March	End June	End September	End December
1940	2,815	3,738	4,077	3,875
1941	3,469	4,244	4,890	5,298
1942	5,183	5,479	5,012	4,595
1943	4,424	5,347	5,927	6,668
1944	6,222	6,302	6,496	6,221
1945	5,363	5,440	5,266	4,820

(a) Including stocks held against relief commitments.

Source: Ministry of Food

TABLE XI

Insured Persons in Food Trades (a) (Estimated)

Thousands

	July 1939(b)	July 1940(b)	July 1941	July 1942	July 1943	July 1944	July 1945
Manufacture of Bread, Biscuits, Cakes, etc.	199	184	167	156	138	134	137
Grain Milling	36	33	32	32	31	31	31
Manufacture of Cocoa, Chocolate and Sugar Confectionery	90	79	60	46	34	33	35
Other food manufacturing industries	151	149	142	139	126	121	122
TOTAL	476	445	401	373	329	319	325

(a) Not including Food Distribution.
(b) Women aged 60–64 ceased to be insured in 1940 and non-manual workers earning £250–£420 a year became insured that year. For the purpose of this table all the figures from 1939 and 1940 have been adjusted to take account of these two changes and they are therefore comparable with those for later years.

Source: Ministry of Labour and National Service.

TABLE XII

Net Annual Cost of Food Subsidies 1939–1945 borne by the Ministry of Food

£ million

	1939–40	1940–41	1941–42	1942–43	1943–44	1944–45
Flour, Bread, Oatmeal, etc. ..	10·2	31·8	38·1	34·0	52·2	44·1
Meat	5·5	18·5	19·6	20·5	16·2	17·5
Bacon	0·7	6·5	—	2·1	1·7	0·7
Potatoes	—	0·2	14·4	23·5	16·3	13·2
Eggs and Egg Products	—	−0·5	7·2	14·0	13·9	14·8
Sugar	−4·2	—	3·4	16·3	10·2	15·2
Milk	2·6	3·6	3·2	10·8	11·5	17·3
Milk Schemes	—	7·8	14·4	17·6	20·6	20·3
Milk Products	−0·6	−2·1	−0·3	4·8	9·1	8·3
Net cost of subsidies on other commodities	−1·0	−2·7	−4·3	−1·0	0·1	10·9
TOTAL	13·2	63·1	95·7	142·6	151·8	162·3
Administrative and Publicity Costs and an Allowance for expenditure incurred by other Departments on behalf of the Ministry of Food included in the above total ..	2·6	8·0	10·0	12·4	14·1	14·1

During the war, the Ministry of War Transport bore the excess cost of carrying imports to the United Kingdom arising out of stabilisation of freight rates at a level insufficient to cover the full cost of war risk insurance. Owing to the complications arising from the movement of ships from one service to another and other causes, it is not possible to state these amounts precisely; the loss on food imports is estimated at £5 million in 1943–44. In addition since 1943–44 other Departments have borne the cost of subsidies on fertilisers for farms and of the acreage payments on wheat, rye and potatoes. The acreage payments are not, however, true subsidies since they are taken into account in fixing the prices of these foodstuffs.

Source: Ministry of Food

TABLE XIII

Catering Establishments and Meals Served

	May 1941	Jan. 1942	July 1943	Dec. 1944	Aug. 1945	Jan.-Feb. 1946
Number of catering establishments (thousand)	111·0	114·1	137·5	147·2	149·5	143·2
Number of meals served weekly (millions)	79·0	144·0	170·5	170·5	181·7	157·1

Source: Ministry of Food

TABLE XIV

Estimated Food Consumption by Non-Residents in Catering Establishments as Percentage of Total Civilian Consumption[1]

(*December 1944*)

Type of Catering Establishment	Sugar %	Meat %	Bacon %	Fats %	Tea %	Preserves %	Cheese %
Voluntary Service Canteens ..	0·56	0·12	0·16	0·55	0·81	0·57	0·48
Canteens serving fire, police and civil defence personnel ..	0·24	0·16	0·17	0·22	0·38	0·28	0·20
School Canteens and Feeding Centres	0·62	1·99	0·31	0·73	0·06	1·06	0·28
War-time Nurseries	0·07	0·07	0·04	0·07	0·02	0·10	0·03
Public and private day schools	0·04	0·11	0·01	0·07	0·01	0·06	0·02
Industrial 'A' Canteens ..	1·34	1·41	0·50	1·10	1·49	1·22	0·82
Industrial 'B' Canteens ..	2·06	1·96	1·04	2·35	3·07	2·74	2·10
Youth service centres and clubs	0·04	..	—	0·05	0·07	0·08	0·05
Workers' recreational clubs, staff dining-rooms, luncheon clubs regularly serving meals ..	0·36	0·33	0·23	0·40	0·58	0·51	0·41
British Restaurants	0·24	0·76	0·19	0·34	0·12	0·47	0·13
'Exclusive' Restaurants and all Hotels and Residential Establishments	0·30	0·34	0·28	0·38	0·39	0·37	0·25
Other Restaurants, Cafés, etc.	1·72	1·48	0·70	2·12	2·53	2·47	1·69
All other Catering Establishments	0·38	0·18	0·12	0·37	0·52	0·26	0·43
TOTAL	7·97	8·91	3·75	8·75	10·05	10·19	6·89

.. Less than 0·005 per cent.

[1] The last four categories in the above table make up the total of Catering Establishments open to the general public.

Source: Ministry of Food

TABLE XV

Effect of Subsidies on Retail Prices at 1st May 1945

	Unit	Current retail price (as used in cost-of-living index)	Estimated retail price if the amount of the subsidy were to be provided by an increase of price
		s. d.	s. d.
Bread	4 lb.	9	1 1
Flour	6 lb.	1 3	1 9¼
Oatmeal	1 lb.	3½	5
Meat (home killed) ..	1 lb.	1 0¾	1 4½
Bacon	1 lb.	1 10½	1 11
Potatoes	7 lb.	7	10¾
Eggs (large)	doz.	2 0	3 6¼
Eggs (small)	doz.	1 9	3 3¼
Sugar (domestic)	1 lb.	4	6
Milk	1 quart	9	10
Cheese	1 lb.	1 1	1 4
Tea	1 lb.	2 10	3 0

FIGURE I

Percentage Changes in the Cost of Living Index in Two World Wars

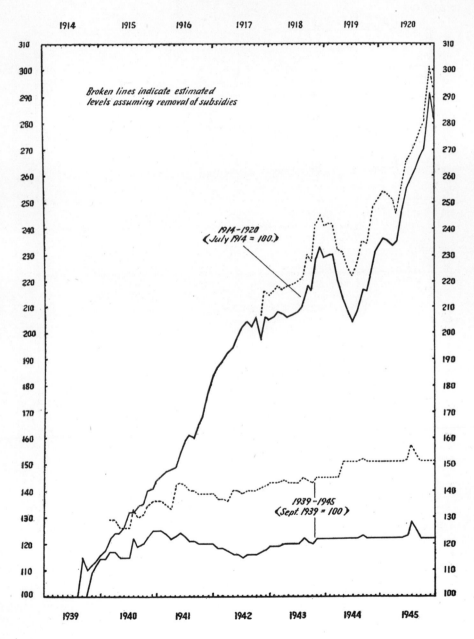

FIGURE II

Ration Changes, 1940–1945: Weekly Rations per R.B.'s 1, 2, and 4[1]

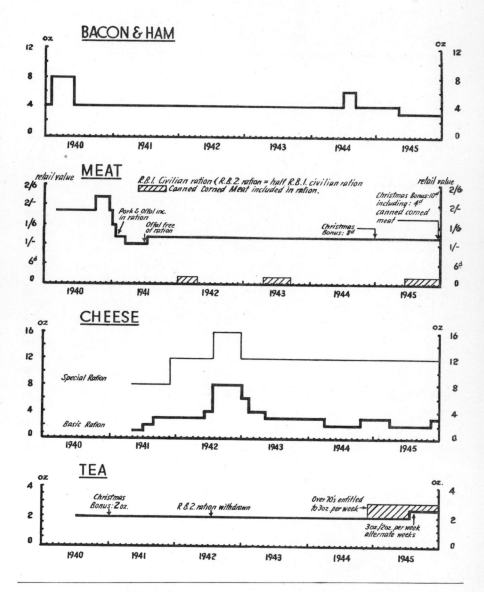

---

[1] R.B.1: Adult Ration Book.

  R.B.2: Child's Ration Book (under 6 years until mid-1942, under 5 years thereafter).

  R.B.4: Junior Ration Book (5–16 years, 1943–44, 5–18 years thereafter).

FIGURE II—*contd.*

SUGAR

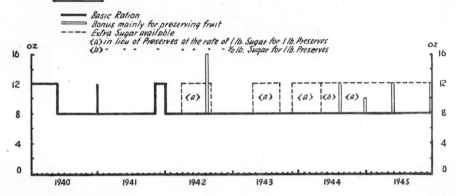

PRESERVES

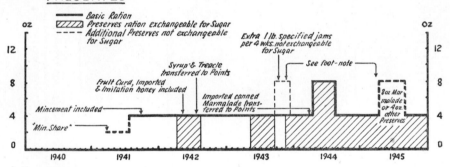

FATS

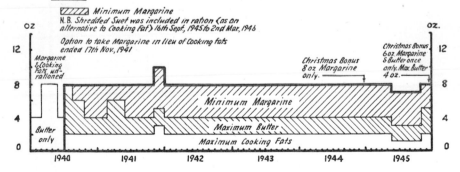

N.B. *Additional 1 lb. Preserves obtainable in exchange for 1 lb. Sugar from 14th November, 1943 to 29th April, 1944, and 2 lb. Preserves in lieu of 1 lb. Sugar from 30th April, to 19th August, 1944. 20th August, 1944 to 31st March, 1945 1 lb. Preserves in lieu of 1 lb. Sugar. 1st April, 1945 Preserves option ended*

FIGURE III

Staff of the Ministry of Food, 1939–1945

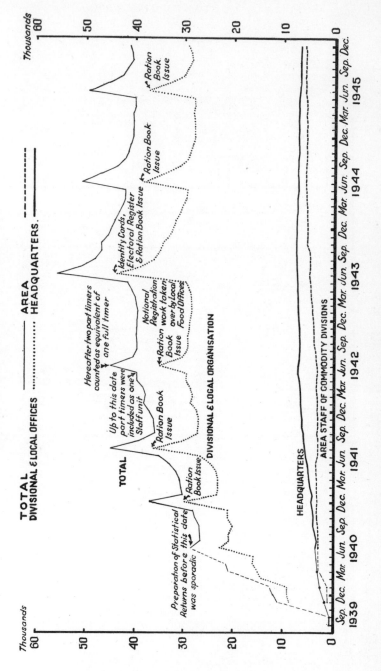

Index

INDEX

(A number in brackets indicates a footnote reference, where it is the only reference on that page)